AUTOBIOGRAPHY OF PROTEST IN HAWAI'I

AUTOBIOGRAPHY OF PROTEST IN HAWAI'I

Robert H. Mast and Anne B. Mast

UNIVERSITY OF HAWAI'I PRESS, HONOLULU

© 1996 University of Hawai'i Press
All rights reserved
Printed in the United States of America
96 97 98 99 00 01   5 4 3 2 1

Library of Congress Cataloging-in-Publication Data
Mast, Robert H., 1928–
Autobiography of protest in Hawai'i / Robert H. Mast and Anne B.
Mast.
p.   cm.
Includes index.
ISBN 0–8248–1784–2 (paper : alk. paper)
1. Social reformers—Hawaii—Biography. 2. Political activists—
Hawaii—Biography. 3. Working class—Hawaii. 4. Quality of life—
Hawaii. 5. Hawaii—Social conditions. 6. Hawaii—Economic
conditions. 7. Hawaii—Politics and government. I. Mast, Anne B.
II. Title.
HV98.H3M37   1996
303.48'4'092—dc20   96–31153
[B]   CIP

University of Hawai'i Press books are printed on acid-free
paper and meet the guidelines for permanence and durability
of the Council on Library Resources

Designed by Ken Miyamoto

Contents

Introduction   1

1 HAWAI'I TODAY   9
Gary Gill   16   /   Brahim Aoudé   28   /   Wayson Chow   42   /
Ed Rampell   50

2 LAND AND ENVIRONMENT   56
Gigi Cocquio   61   /   John Kelly   75   /
Guy Nakamoto   91   /   Marion Kelly   102   /
George Cooper   110

3 HUMAN RIGHTS AND FREE SPEECH   118
Oliver Lee   124   /   Setsu Okubo   139   /   Tracy Takano   144   /
Bill Hoshijo   152

4 STANDARD OF LIVING: HOUSING, HEALTH, WELFARE   159
Rick Rothschiller   166   /   Mary Choy   179   /
Christine Brown   185   /   Will Butler   192   /   Jim Brewer   209   /
Rachel Saiki   221

5 WOMEN'S STRUGGLES   228
Meda Chesney-Lind   235   /   Lucy Witeck   245   /
Ho'oipo DeCambra   254   /   Frances Viglielmo   263   /
Susan Hippensteele   276

6 ORGANIZED LABOR   283
Bill Puette   290   /   Ah Quon McElrath   305   /
Tommy Trask   318   /   Liana Petranek   326   /   John Witeck   337

7 SOVEREIGNTY   353
Kekuni Blaisdell   363   /   Lynette Cruz   374   /
Mililani Trask   389   /   Davianna McGregor   399   /
Hayden Burgess (Poka Laenui)   407   /   Kuʻumeaaloha Gomes   419

8 CONCLUSIONS   429

Index   437

Introduction

We are beginning this introduction in Honolulu, just as the Republican Party's "Contract with America" has passed its one-hundredth day of implementation—with the complicity of the Democratic Party—in the 104th Congress of the United States. The "Contract" is a pivotal event for the peoples of Hawai'i, the United States, and the world because it dramatizes the current crisis in free enterprise. It illuminates a design by the class that rules to add to its affluence and strengthen its power at the expense of the poor and powerless. The "Contract" also has become a call-to-arms to all those in the United States and elsewhere who are struggling to survive or to find a better way of life.

We write this as sugar production is ending on the island of O'ahu and the first modern shotgun holdup takes place in a Honolulu convenience store. The radioactive waste carrier *Pacific Pintail* passes Hawai'i enroute from France to Japan. Imelda Marcos and her son Bongbong engage in Filipino electoral politics. Nerve gas immobilizes Japanese subway stations. The United States braces for more Oklahoma City-type explosions, while the stock market and poverty rates rise in tandem.

We write while over 20 percent of the world's population (about 1,300,000,000 people) live in absolute poverty, 820,000,000 workers are unemployed or grossly underemployed, and 1,500,000,000 people have no access to the most basic health care. In the United States about 10,000,000 workers are unemployed, 80,000,000 persons live below the poverty line, 8,000,000 are homeless, and 1,500,000 persons are behind bars—with 3,000 on death row. Family income has been declining for twenty years. The hard-won gains of minorities are eroding, the power of organized labor is waning, crime and violence are at epidemic levels, and people are confused and angry. Yet the establishment has no improvement plan except through the mechanisms of the free market. These must be very bad times!

1

"No," say the pundits of free enterprise, "these are good times": no depression, no serious recession, low inflation rate, an "acceptable" unemployment rate, high worker productivity, high corporate profitability. The times are very good for the rich, very bad for the poor, and getting worse for the middle class.

It is interesting how one large class of people—the workers, the majority—can go down so far and so fast while another small class— the owners—can do so well. Perhaps it is really not too hard to understand. A new world reality, engineered by the rich, has been developing for years and now is in full swing. It is distinguished by a world-level multinational economy and greater private central control of finance. The new reality features a near-total dismissal of collectivist ideology and the de-emphasis of public sector activities. Meanwhile, a rapidly evolving electronic mode of production dramatically reduces the need for productive labor power. The result is a shocking deterioration in the quality of life of the masses, coming partly from formal policy and partly from benign neglect.

But there is also good news! We observe another unfolding process: thousands upon thousands of people throughout the world are getting fed up with the way the new reality is unfolding. Let us call this the left-progressive sector. They do not like what they see around them in their everyday lives. They cannot stomach the foreboding future predicted by current trends. In virtually every country and every community, left-progressive people are protesting and mobilizing. They draw upon the experience of earlier generations of radical reformers and revolutionaries to help shape a new liberation movement. But it is an extremely difficult job today because past reform models were built when demographic, economic, and political conditions were quite different. Thus there is more caution in the search for solutions.

Hawai'i, the case study in this book, is not exempt from all the processes that so conclusively interact today and shape the direction of our world. We see Hawai'i as a rare and singular place, caught in the colonial substream of several hundred years of capitalist development and exploitation. Having emerged out of an agricultural economy, Hawai'i is a full-scale service society today. Modern Hawai'i, shaped for nearly two hundred years by various forms of economic and cultural imperialism, continues to be impacted by investment and political decisions by elites who are thousands of miles from her shores. The result is a unique microcosm of all that contemporary capitalism represents.

This book of oral histories approaches Hawai'i through the experiences and views of its activists—its protesters—who have devoted much of their lives to analyzing their world and struggling to make it better. The activists tell about their lives and what shaped their politics and philosophy over the years. Together, the stories are a history of social movements in Hawai'i and the United States that, over the last fifty years, have arisen to fight injustice and build a better life. Most of the speakers in this book are still activists; they still care about justice, equality, and freedom; they still analyze Hawai'i and the world. They help the reader think through some of the ponderous issues of the day and, hopefully, inspire others to join them in the difficult task of building the urgently needed new movements for today.

The speakers in this book represent a cross-section of Hawai'i's residents. Over half were born in Hawai'i, one third elsewhere in the United States, and about 10 percent in a foreign country—a close approximation of the actual state statistics. Caucasians in our sample comprise about 4 in 10 of the total, Asians 3 in 10, and those with Kanaka Maoli (Native Hawaiian) blood also 3 in 10. The speakers range in age from their thirties to their eighties, with a median age of about forty-four and a reasonable gender balance. Nearly 70 percent of the speakers had all or part of their education in the continental United States, many at the height of the civil rights and antiwar movements. Among the occupations represented are politician, professor, attorney, writer, labor leader, secretary, educator, waiter, physician, community organizer, flight attendant, social worker, writer, and farmer.

Most of our speakers are complex political people who are hard to classify into a neat set of book chapters. After several false starts, we organized the speakers according to their identification with major social movements: land and environment; human rights and free speech; standard of living: housing, health, and welfare; women's struggles; organized labor; and sovereignty. With the exception of sovereignty activists whose specific goal is to improve the condition of the Kanaka Maoli, we "forced" speakers into one of these movement categories. Yet this is not fully satisfactory, as some were active in many movements over the years. Such is the nature of dedicated left-progressive activists. In any event, the scheme to classify by movement provided the opportunity to write introductory essays in an attempt to fill in a few gaps left by the speakers and allow us to express our own views on subjects of importance to Hawai'i and to other parts of the world.

Readers of this book may wish to know something about our background and why we undertook this project. We are academic educators in sociology. Over our years of teaching and research we have watched as the limited intellectual objectivity that existed in the United States descended further into opportunistic service to the new conservative and right-wing establishment. The people and movements in the left-progressive sector today are given little attention by professors, textbook writers, and media intellectuals. Therefore, our major motivation was to provide a document for left-progressive activists to express their experiences and ideas. For decades now, that body of citizens has been denigrated, isolated, and manhandled. Readers today, especially youth, have limited access to the rich left-progressive tradition that might be drawn upon (but not necessarily copied) by those who wish to once again start building movements to cope with life in the twenty-first century.

We also are activists in the left-progressive tradition, meaning a dedication to the principle of relative material equality and full human and civil rights for all people. Some might call this an endorsement of the socialist vision, and we would be comfortable with that. Like many of the speakers in this book, we have been involved in antipoverty, civil rights, anti-imperialism, and pro-feminist movements over a span of years. We learned from these involvements that it is absolutely necessary to pay attention to the economic factors associated with poverty, race, war, and gender. Because economic factors get quickly to the nitty-gritty of our social system, sometimes we have been less than popular in both movement and establishment circles. Nevertheless, economics—the "dismal science"—is the heart of it all, and economy is the motor of change.

This book is one of a series of oral histories of activists we are compiling in places we know well: Detroit, Hawai'i, Pittsburgh, and Atlanta. Though different in many aspects, these four sites are multiracial areas whose major means of production is being deindustrialized or downsized. We find it amusing that tourism—the great balm—is being promoted as an antidote in each place. To date we have interviewed over two hundred people, all with a known activist track record, all still inspired and deeply involved, and all still analyzing. Their collective contribution to improving the human condition is inspiring. We have learned a great deal about our country, our world, and the condition of the left from these interviews.

To meet our speakers we often visit locations that most middle-class Caucasians avoid. Nothing has shaped our thinking more than this fieldwork. We see the social deterioration and infrastructural decay that is setting in. More important, we see the great potential for a new political force of working-class people, displaced from productive jobs by the relentless thrust of technology and investment decisions, and abandoned by social policy.

Why a book on Hawai'i? We visited the Islands three times and lived there a total of fifteen months. In academic year 1981–1982 we both taught sociology in Honolulu institutions. For a brief time we were enticed by the beauty and ambience of the Islands, much like tourists. But then we began to learn about the other side of Hawai'i that the tour promoters, with entrepreneurial cunning, render unseen and unknown to the casual traveler.

A lot of basic information came from excellent studies by academic and activist scholars, many published by the University of Hawai'i Press. We learned of the sordid exploitive history of land and agricultural labor by westerners. We learned about and witnessed the transition of the labor force into service occupations, mostly with low wages. We found out about the ecological sensitivity of the Islands that was being terribly imbalanced by pollutants and imprudent land use by the tourist industry and landholders. Our understanding was greatly heightened at the forums of the Hawai'i Union of Socialists, an eclectic group with a lot of aloha. Their Modern Times Bookstore, where we both volunteered our services, was an engaging center for intellectual discourse and social conviviality. When we finally met Kanaka Maoli activists, our education became fully rounded. They taught us a wrenching history of exploitation, land theft, and genocide of the indigenous peoples. Here was another example of a native people oppressed by a self-indulgent foreign power, yielding yet another case of extreme deprivation today, with little contrition or recompense by the powers-that-be. Our long-standing support for minority rights and oppressed peoples' struggles was now extended into the Pacific Islands.

Ten years later, in early 1993, we visited Hawai'i on a six-week working vacation to review the damage done by the free market during the Reagan-Bush years. At that time we also embarked on the oral history project that resulted in this book. We invited our speakers to tell of the events in their past that shaped a will to take action. We wanted to know what insights were gained that might be applicable today.

Two years later, from January through April 1995, we returned to complete the project. By then, the right-wing revolution in the United States was in full swing. We wondered what the consequences were in Hawai'i, where most events that occur on the continental United States don't fully impact until some time later. We found that the new conservatism had taken firm hold. Many people in Hawai'i were shaken and confused by the dramatic turn of events. We completed a few more interviews to fill in gaps. We observed, read, and talked a great deal. The most important experience this time was our participation in the forums, educationals, vigils, and demonstrations of the sovereignty movement. We needed this exposure to understand better the condition of the Kanaka Maoli and the objectives of the movement.

We tried to democratize the project by submitting all interview transcripts to our speakers so they could correct errors and provide updates. The many changes they made added to the accuracy of the book, but created a seemingly endless editing job for us.

Finally, we offer a few technical comments. The statements by our speakers that follow have gone through a great deal of editing by us and most of our speakers. At the suggestion of a reviewer, but at the great risk and possible insult of error, we made our best guess at the speakers' ages. We think they represent a good cross-section of activists from O'ahu. A limitation of the sample is that residents of the neighbor islands were not included. This dissatisfies us because a great deal of the sovereignty movement's energy comes from those more rural and traditional Kanaka Maoli. In our writing we will refer to the indigenous people of Hawai'i and their descendants as Kanaka Maoli. The forty-eight contiguous states plus Alaska will be called the United States, not the mainland. Both of these designations are to honor the preferences of some of our friends in the sovereignty movement.

Acknowledgments

Many people helped us bring this book off. One of our greatest debts is to the sovereignty activists who took us under their wings and patiently led us through a maze of history, politics, and culture. We particularly want to acknowledge Kekuni Blaisdell, convener of the Pro-Kanaka Maoli Sovereignty Working Group (formerly Pro-Hawaiian Sovereignty Working Group), and Lynette Cruz, who wears many hats and is one of the best organizers we've known. They and their fellow activists with Kanaka Maoli blood truly represented the spirit of aloha. Brahim Aoudé of the Ethnic Studies Program, University of Hawai'i, gave inestimable help throughout the project. We thank the People's Fund for providing a grant to transcribe most of our interview tapes. The People's Fund provides grants to progressive grassroots social change activities in Hawai'i and the Pacific region. Cara Kimura, from her base in Honolulu, did a marvelous job of transcribing. We want to thank the faculty and staff at the Department of Sociology, University of Hawai'i, Mānoa, particularly professors Kiyoshi Ikeda, Gene Kassebaum, Eldon Wegner, and Michael Weinstein, for providing hospitality and amenities to conduct this project. The department secretaries Jessie and Jan were, as usual, extremely helpful. We enjoyed the intellectual and social companionship of Shi-jen He, Franz Breswimmer, and Stephen Philion—graduate students in the Department of Sociology. Technical computer assistance given by Zhifeng Cai and Harry Partica made our word processing lives considerably easier. George Simson, director of the Center for Biographical Research, University of Hawai'i, provided a lively forum for our work to be presented. Our friends of long standing—Brahim Aoudé and Liana Petranek—provided guidance and warm hospitality. We also want to acknowledge the aloha of Doug Birge, Mary Choy, Lynette Cruz and her husband James Nakapa'ahu, Jim Kaufman, Marion and John Kelly, Ed Rampell, and Frances and Val Viglielmo. They all helped make our stays in Hawai'i both pleasant and intellectually productive.

1

HAWAI'I TODAY

Just five hours away by plane from California, Hawai'i is a thousand light years away in fantasy. Mostly a state of mind, Hawai'i is the image of escape from the rawness and violence of daily American life. Hawai'i—the word, the vision, the sound in the mind—is the fragrance and feel of soft kindness. . . . To Hawaiians, daily life is neither soft nor kind. In fact, the political, economic, and cultural reality for most Hawaiians is hard, ugly, and cruel.

In Hawai'i, the destruction of our land, the prostitution of our culture is planned and executed by multi-national corporations (both foreign-based and Hawai'i-based), by huge landowners (like the missionary-descended Castle and Cooke—of Dole Pineapple fame—and others) and by collaborationist state and county governments.

Thus wrote Haunani-Kay Trask in her book, *From a Native Daughter* (Common Courage Press, 1993). Trask is a leader in the sovereignty movement. (See chapter 7 for more about this movement.)

Most Americans are doubtlessly shocked at this characterization of their tourist paradise, shocked that Dr. Trask, a Kanaka Maoli woman, would see their tourist dollars and the Japanese yen as a degradation. These same tourists mostly have only vague approximations of Hawai'i's actual geographical location in the Pacific, and few are aware of the presence of the nearly ten thousand islands spread over an ocean that covers one-third of the globe. Nor would they ever conceive of the racist and imperialist history in which a handful of missionary progeny and American marines simply "annexed" the Hawaiian islands to the United States of America near the end of the nineteenth century.

Perhaps they would be less surprised at this history if they recall the millions of Native Americans on the U.S. continent who became the "forerunner victims" of this colonial venture in the Pacific. America's world hegemony today is, in fact, the result of a long ascent to power and long years of colonization at the sacrifice of indigenous peoples. Trask says further, "until recently, neither Americans nor Hawaiians have understood this colonial status because America's ideology has represented itself as the main force of anti-colonialism around the world" (Peter Manicas, ed., *Social Process in Hawai'i: A Reader* [New York: McGraw Hill, 1993], 1).

Hawai'i lost control of its economy long before it attained statehood in 1959, and long before it became a territory in 1900—in fact, even before the missionaries instituted their Calvinist autocracy in the 1820s. University of Hawai'i anthropologist Marion Kelly explains that traders from foreign countries began stopping on their way to and from China as early as the 1780s. Carrying cargoes of furs purchased at prices that exploited Native Americans of the northwest and bound for the orient, these early merchant seamen offered nails as a shabby exchange for food and water. Later, Hawai'i's priceless stands of sandalwood were totally depleted in exchange for various low-value objects. (Marion Kelly, "Foreign Investment in Hawai'i," *Social Process in Hawai'i* 35 [1],15–39).

Hawai'i's economy today results from Hawai'i's economy yesterday. Subsistence farming and fishing dominated the economy in the pre-missionary days, followed by agriculture, which became the leading source of revenues until the recent past. When the historic land division known as the Great Mahele took place in the mid-nineteenth century, Caucasians and some Hawaiians were permitted to own land outright, or in "fee simple." Island missionaries, along with other profiteers from the Western gold rush, traders rich from whaling and product extraction from the Pacific, began to gamble in Hawaiian real estate. Sugarcane grew wild in the Islands, and by 1866 there were thirty-two thriving plantations.

With sugar prices beginning to rise, growers were forced to look for a new labor supply to increase production. The population of Native Hawaiians had been steadily declining from diseases, and perhaps a mind-collapsing ennui from white man's religious and cultural imperialism. They could supply only a fraction of the accelerating need for labor. Importation of contract labor began with the Chinese, who, after working out their time, settled in towns. The large numbers of Japanese, Korean, Portuguese, and Filipinos who followed set the pattern of immigration that produced the rich patina of multiculturalism for which Hawai'i is so famous today.

In 1875, the historic Reciprocity Treaty with the United States allowed sugar growers to ship their product *duty-free,* a favored-status category that forever set the tone for the special commercial relationship with America. Some of the wealthiest and most influential of this new group of large-scale growers were men from California who made fantastic fortunes on the growing and refining of sugar. These sugar interests were able to control the policies of Washington and those of the Hawaiian Legislature. Sugar's power extended to the inner chambers of the Kanaka Maoli monarchy. Over time, this commercial cabal established a link still somewhat extant between the West Coast of the United States and the Islands.

In the winter of 1995 we witnessed the closing of the last sugar planation on O'ahu in the town of Waipahu. This is expected to affect all of the ancillary services to the people who live close by, such as stores and restaurants. Pineapple plantations are also moving to areas of much more exploitable labor, such as the Philippines. It appears to be the end of an era of large-scale agriculture, and the passing on of profit making to big tourism and the land to continued military use. The military establishment occupies a significantly large proportion of the land area.

The expanding population base swelled by the military and continuous immigration has given rise to new "mall cities," which have few U.S.-type central-city specialized services, high-speed transport systems, parks, or cultural facilities. Towns such as Pearl City merely extend the vulgar, small-shop consumerism beyond Waikīkī to the former suburbs of Honolulu. Every fast-food kiosk from the continental United States is replicated here, complete with mountains of plastic litter.

Environmentally, Hawai'i is a disaster waiting to happen. Land developers and highway developers have already succeeded, in spite of the people's angry protests, to whittle away characteristic points of topography and superb views. They have diverted water for exclusive use in the greening of luxury membership golf courses. Diamond Head has not yet been cut flat for sea-view condos, perhaps saved by its pictorial significance in tour brochures. Highway developers have strung an obtrusive base of concrete along the green crenellation of the Ko'olau mountain range, the stunning backdrop of the cities of Kāne'ohe and Kailua. Activists on the North Shore are fighting for the life of these world-renowned beaches. The military has stored vast amounts of nuclear materials and weaponry underground in Hawai'i, the stuff of nightmares. Many groups have expressed their concern about this, including Science in the Public Interest and Physicians for Social Responsibility.

It is impossible not to be aware of the military in Hawai'i, if only from the projectile bursts of the military jet engines overhead. The growing militarization of the entire Pacific region is comprehensively described in the recent book *Tu Galala,* edited by David Robie and published in Australia. The title is translated as "Sovereignty, Freedom, and Self-determination," and the book examines the entire region in a wider Asia-Pacific context. Nowhere is today's expanding-rich, expanding-poor dichotomy more obvious and problematic. The Pacific Rim nations are rich: the United States, Japan, Australia, Taiwan. Thousands of islands in the middle are poor, with millions of people, and they are almost all present or former colonies of Europe and America.

These semi-impoverished islands still remain open game for modern predator nations. An example occurred in 1975 when the militarized capitalist nation of Indonesia sent troops to attack East Timor in the western Pacific. Reminiscent of the Hawaiian takeover in arrogance and speed, it simply declared that this small, former Portuguese colony is now its twenty-seventh province.

In terms of foreign born, Hawai'i ranks third among the states in numbers of these new residents, following only California and New York, both of which have enormous populations. The United States has a total of almost 20 million foreign born, double the number in 1960. The 1990 census shows that Asian peoples of all generations are a dominant population sector in Hawai'i, with Japanese, Chinese, Filipinos, and Koreans accounting for 37 percent of the population. Combining this Asian two-fifths of the population with the Kanaka Maoli's one-fifth, the Caucasian in Hawai'i is in the singular position of a minority, a position that will become more common in the future world system.

As American tourists of the middle class begin to drop off from loss of jobs and loss of discretionary spending power, other world groups fill the gaps. The rising cities of Asia, primarily those of Japan, provide highly sought-after tourist consumer groups. Prices in Hawai'i are low to the average Japanese consumer. The over 6 million tourists who visit Hawai'i every year outnumber the resident population by six to one. This renders the "real" nature of Hawaiian multiethnic culture, much less the authentic Kanaka Maoli culture, only a vague guess. The Disney World of tourism cannot be used to characterize the real Hawai'i.

One of our speakers, Gary Gill, when first elected chairman of the Honolulu City Council in 1992, suggested that the tax burden should be shifted away from individual homeowners to the tourist. "If you look at the demographics of the past twenty years, local people are getting poorer in relation to the cost of living. Our tourist-based economy is, in fact, increasing poverty in Hawai'i" (*Honolulu Advertiser*, Dec. 20, 1992). In addition to this impoverishment, the daily newspaper notes that the number of business and personal bankruptcies have grown by more than one-third in the past several years.

Art and artists working in Hawai'i make a statement about the culture and politics of the Islands. Stretching the definition of activism, they might be included among those who protest. Working in some isolation from others, their contribution is more difficult to identify as political, although we are certain this kind of art could have been located. That it was not makes us a bit uneasy. Several times a year, Kanaka Maoli artists exhibit their work at arts and crafts fairs, where the use of older, traditional forms and materials, such as tapa cloth and palm leaves, produce aesthetically pleasing and useful articles of clothing. These cultural expressions give some insight into the ancient Kanaka Maoli way of life. Perhaps unlocated photography could have shown the spirit of protest and activism. One "mainland" artist, Janet Easley, became part of our consciousness through her support of the sovereignty movement. She became inspired by the flora, the stunning topography, and elements of Native Hawaiian culture, from which she produced brilliantly colored collages of life and symbols of the Islands. Expressing the outcry of the Kanaka Maoli for the beauty of their ancient lands, she seems to capture the life and archetypes as well as the ominous omnipresence of the military.

As urban sociologists, we have found the relatively recent rise in violent crime among teenagers and young men in their early twenties to be somewhat expectable. The death of the sugar industry has spelled higher unemployment, especially on the "Big Island" of Hawai'i. It is logical and to be expected among those who have no future and are committing suicide in ever greater numbers that these youth might feel some of the "black rage" of violent crime. This rage was suggested by defense lawyers in the continental United States as an important contributing factor for random murders in public places, such as the Long Island Railroad incident. The unemployed young people of Hawai'i would have to feel some rage when they daily witness the engorged excesses among tourists on the Big Island and in Waikīkī: stretch limousines, commercial luau (feasts), penthouse suites, open street prostitution. Impoverished youth from all resident ethnic groups would be affected. Surely some Kanaka Maoli youth must feel rage when their long-suffering grandparents wait decades for their homesteads and then die before they are ever apportioned their small share. Youth—who have the greatest optimism and idealism, whose energy is at its penultimate—must feel dashed to the ground when opportunities fail and life's chances seem cruelly quashed. For youth denied full access to the "American dream," it would be normal to feel rage. The other side of anger is depression or even suicide. Clinical depression is virtually an epidemic in these times, for adults and youth alike.

Just a word on ethnicity is appropriate here. The most dynamic expression of ethnic identity is the Kanaka Maoli sovereignty movement. That movement drives a motion that boldly proclaims: "I am Kanaka Maoli, and I want my stolen land returned. Whatever consequences derive from that, I will accept." Other ethnic or national-origin groups in Hawai'i are more recent arrivistes, but they preserve to some extent their origins—by speaking Japanese, for example. Other institutions are firmly supported, such as church and religion, which also uphold the ancestral national traditions. Church of the Crossroads near the University of Hawai'i (UH) Mānoa campus offers a meeting of Eastern and Western religious traditions and philosophies. The Ethnic Studies Department of UH, a department that survived budget slicing because of support from the outside grassroots community, helps in the understanding and communication of these groups. It is hoped that peoples' actions can one day take root from these various organizational auspices.

The contributors to this section on life in Hawai'i today share the common fact that they tend to take the broad, analytical view, all of them seasoned by years of their own particular kind of activism. They also view the world from a perspective of political economy, rather than various micro-perspectives, such as individual or group psychology. Destruction of life-giving ecology and the importance of world-level economic forces serve to inform and broaden their views. They all feel the frustration of immediate dilemmas without immediate solutions. Interestingly, they represent a wide ethnic spectrum.

Gary Gill, a Caucasian who was born in Hawai'i and grew up as the son of a congressman, spent his early years as an activist in student peace issues and antinuclear bomb storage. Later as a hotel worker, his activism was expressed as a union organizer and shop steward. In summing up some of his thoughts on the economy, he offered this thought: "Sometimes I see Honolulu, or Hawai'i, as a Ping-Pong ball that's being batted back and forth across the Pacific tennis table between California and Tokyo."

Brahim Aoudé is an associate professor of ethnic studies at UH Mānoa. As a person born in Palestine, his young years were filled with the politics of land, as the Zionists lodged their claim on the land of Palestine. Aoudé has authored a penetrating analysis on a related subject in his recent book, *Lebanon: Dynamics of Conflict*. The Native Hawaiian movement, with its anticolonial drive, is an arresting comparison for Aoudé, both as scholar and activist. He has been involved in the very effective movements around tenants' rights and low-cost housing.

Wayson Chow, from an Asian background, grew up in 'Āina Haina when the adjacent neighborhood of Wailupe had restrictive covenants against Chinese-Americans and Japanese-Americans. Part of his activist energy was joined to that of the housing activist organization People Against Chinatown Evictions to legally enjoin the government from evicting longtime and often elderly tenants.

Ed Rampell is a freelance journalist and correspondent for *Pacific Islands Monthly,* a publication that examines the culture and colonial politics of the entire Pacific region. Originally from New York, Rampelle combines his urban background with years of residency in the Islands. The monthly has already published several of his articles describing the sovereignty movement.

Gary Gill

Past chairperson of the City Council of Honolulu, about thirty-five years old.

I was born in 1960 at Kaiser Hospital in the Ala Wai Yacht Harbor, which has now been knocked down and turned into a hotel. My father was born and raised in Hawai'i as well. My roots in Hawai'i go back into the last century when my grandfather arrived here in 1898 as an architect. My grandmother on my father's side was a journalist who wrote for both local papers and for the Bishop Museum.

My father, who was a politician, has been the most dominant force in my life. He went to law school at Berkeley, served in the army in World War II, came back to Hawai'i, and became a labor lawyer. He was very active in the building of the Democratic Party. At that time, the Republican Party, which represented the Big Five [businesses] and the mercantile interests in Hawai'i, dominated local politics and the economy. My father was one of the local Democratic insurgents that basically built a new political institution out of the changing demographics of the time. Asian Americans who were born and raised in Hawai'i had been excluded from the political scene. My father's career spanned the Territorial House, the U.S. Congress, and lieutenant governor of the state.

I was raised at a time when politics was just part of life: discussions at the dinner table and campaigns every two years. I was raised in a political family. There was a political analysis to virtually everything that went on in the world. I'm the youngest of six. And I think my father's attitude has always been one of allowing his children to go out and explore and come to their own conclusions. My mother was the one who raised the family, basically. She was a full-time mother, transferring values down to the children, and a very active, strong person in her own right.

I remember standing on a street corner downtown when I was five years old, with my brothers across the street, passing out flyers for my dad who was running for office. People came up, patted me on my head and said, "Thanks son, but your brother already gave me one of those." It's just something we all did, no coercion, everyone accepted it. When you grow up in that kind of environment, children in the family are part of the movement. We believed in the ideas that my father represented and it was exciting.

I think people would basically term my father as an independent and a liberal. He was against the war in Vietnam. He was head of the Office of Economic Opportunity in Honolulu when he came back from Congress. People would term him as the leader of the ideological left within the Democratic Party, a reform-minded person who always attempted to represent the interests of labor and the working people and struggle for social and economic justice. I think anyone who was raised in Hawai'i during the period that he was—the twenties, thirties, forties—who wasn't part of the aristocracy and who was intellectually honest, would tend to gravitate towards the progressive side. It was a time of great activity in the labor movement. There were obvious class distinctions at the time.

I would say I took my father's liberalism a step further, as it was defined in my generation. Born in 1960, I caught the tail end of the baby boom and the activism of the sixties. I was exposed at an early age to the music, culture, and politics that my older brothers were participating in, in the antiwar movement. My oldest brother was studentbody president of his high school and they were leading demonstrations against the dress code and trying to get ROTC [Reserve Officers Training Corps] out of the school and all kind of fun things like that. He also was a conscientious objector in the war. Although I was only eight or ten years old, these things had an impact on me.

By the time I got to high school, I was expecting all this great fun and it was actually a lot quieter. The students seemed a lot more passive, less inspired. The biggest issue on campus was pep rallies for the football team, which I just couldn't relate to. So that, in part, also radicalized me.

I think I was a basic believer in my father's way of making political change, up until his second loss at running for governor, in 1974. My father dropped out of politics at that point and began private practice as an attorney. And I basically dropped out of politics too, electoral politics, being disgruntled with it. It became apparent to me that that was not the way to change society. It was the Watergate era.

So I think the next dramatic influence in my life, which many radicals who were raised in Hawaii had, was a high school teacher named Setsu Okubo. Setsu taught at Roosevelt High School. She's still out there in the movement, painting all the banners and things. I was in the eleventh grade when I took her class in international affairs and Asian studies. In her first lecture she described an evil nation in the world that took over other nations, dominated their economies, controlled the people, caused poverty, and was a threat to democracy around the world. And then with her pointer she slammed the map on the wall and said, "And this country is the United States of America." That made a mark in my memory.

We read about the Long March and Maoism and contemporary politics and Communist China. We were exposed to the ideas of American imperialism and colonialism, and always from an economic perspective which was totally contrary to the stuff that you're fed in school. I became excited by that, because, for the first time, world politics started to make sense. There was a reason for wars, other than they just happen. And there was an economic reason and a political reason that could be understood.

At the same time, one of my brothers was very much engaged in the new left movement in the United States, and he basically recruited me and some of my friends into the radical, revolutionary political activism of the late seventies. I became involved in a nationwide network of political activists and radicals, attending conferences on the mainland, and being directly involved in many of the struggles that were taking place in Hawai'i.

I'm not ashamed of any of my past. I did nothing illegal. In American democracy, there was ample room for political thought. I still adhere to the values of the time. They were nonviolent, radical kinds of political organizations that believed that structural transformation was necessary in the United States, and that the system of market capitalism that still dominates our economy and our political life needed to be transformed by peaceful means.

One thing I gained from that was a nationwide perspective. The groups of people that I came to know in conferences or forums, off and on the mainland, were the best and brightest of the activists. You all political sectarianism aside, these were people who were ded their life to social change, who were driven not by any sense of personal aggrandizement or careerism, but dedication to the public and the realization that this society needed more than a band-aid; it needed structural change. That was exciting. They're great people, and they're still out there.

The structure of organization at the time was based on a sort of Bolshevik model which was unsuccessful and inappropriate in America. People came to realize that pretty quickly. Activists and social change people are still looking for a structure that will lead to a form of transition that can bridge the gap between the system we have today, with its inequities, and the future system. Nobody's yet put a finger on how we can organize ourselves to make that happen.

I'd simply say that poverty is structural in a capitalist system. That's how it works. The few who are lucky, or have the capital to begin with, or the personal skills to accumulate capital, continue to accumulate capital, to the detriment of the majority of people who are left on the economic fringes or made homeless. I don't need to give a big lecture about it. I read it in the newspaper every day. New statistics come out that show the gap between the rich and the poor is widening, and that is a natural by-product of our market system. I do believe the government is responsible for regulating that market system and assuring that the value generated by production is fairly distributed, and that the people are empowered to the greatest degree possible and not alienated from the means of production, to use those terms.

I've always had a practical bent. I'm not a great philosopher. I don't plow through volumes of collected works of this or that. I've always wanted to be in the front row and participate in the action. So, after my radicalism in high school, I got a summer job in what I termed the new plantation in Hawai'i's economy, the hotel industry. My job was at the lowest rung possible in the housekeeping department of Sheraton Waikiki. That summer job lasted about seven years. I was directly involved with the union as an elected shop steward, and a union activist and organizer. I'm proud to say that three years after I left the union and took a political job here at City Hall, when the union went out on the job, not a single one of my shop crossed that picket line. They were strong. I like to take a little bit of credit for laying the base for knowledge and empowerment that comes with workers being directly involved with their union and understanding the big picture.

My political perspective has always been inclined toward the working class and liberalism. My leaning toward practical activity induced me to get involved in the workplace. My political association had at the time stressed building grassroots bases within industrial concentrations of different industries around the country. You know, the industry that drives the Hawaiian economy is the hotel industry and that's the place to get involved and make a difference. I fully believed that the rest of my life would be spent organizing in the working class directly, as a way of making social change, as opposed to electoral politics and trying to take over or become directly involved with the government structures.

While I was at Sheraton, I served as the chief steward for the largest department in one of the largest hotels in Waikīkī. I represented over 350 employees, most of whom were working mothers or single women who clean the rooms. I participated with a group of other labor activists and we produced our own newsletter called *The Scoop*. We participated in campaigns for union elections. We helped get workers their back pay, prevented them from being fired, grieved their working conditions. We organized a system of communication within my shop so that the people felt that they were represented, that the union was a source of empowerment for them, that they had some say in their conditions of employment and the nature of their work, and that they were treated with dignity.

At the same time that I was doing the union work, I was directly involved in local struggles in the antinuclear movement. I was involved in a number of different political coalitions: Nuclear-free and Independent Pacific, Protect Kahoʻolawe ʻOhana, eviction issues, employment issues, other union support work. When President Reagan busted the PATCO union, I was directly involved in support of PATCO. I helped to organize the Students for Peace, and we did a number of demonstrations, mostly against nuclear bomb storage in Pearl Harbor. There were many things like that. I was really active in the community at the same time and most of that was coalition building. So, I think I picked up a number of practical skills and how to get along with people.

I guess the more I got involved with the union and with the community, over time I came to realize that to really make social change, it takes a lot of teamwork and it takes a broad approach. The analogy I would use is in writing a beautiful song and playing it on the piano—you can't do it with just one note. You need a broad range of notes and you need to strike them in harmony and in the proper cadence. And likewise, to make political change, you need to attack the inequities in society from a number of different angles at the same time.

There's only so long, I think, that you can be successful in organizing demonstration after demonstration, and I was pretty good at it. A group of us in the union were very good at organizing rallies and demonstrations. And I'd usually end up with the bullhorn and doing the speaking or leading of the chants. But there's only so much of that you can do before you feel that it's not really having a full impact, it's just being oppositional. Along with others, I came to the conclusion that not only did you need to organize in the working class, or organize oppositional struggles in the community, but you needed to make full use of the institutions that are available for social change in America today.

So that really led me back towards an analysis of how I could participate in making change through electoral politics. I knew how to run elections and how to be a candidate, probably better than many people in the movement for social change. I understood that the acceptable way of communicating political thought is through the electoral process. You can communicate through protest signs, and organize grassroots movements, and you can have a level of success in that, but there are many people in the community who do not relate to that sort of activism. You need to win them over as well. The greatest political activity that the majority will ever be involved in is punching a hole in the ballot every two years. That's their understood responsibility and it's part of American culture.

So how do you reach out to those people and get them involved in a political movement for social change? The fastest and most accepted way of doing that is running for office. Running for office has two basic elements. One is getting your ideas and philosophy across: the principle element. The second is actually getting elected and having power: the practical element. To the extent that the candidate is successful in merging the principle and the practical, he or she will be successful in bringing people into his or her political way of thought, and actually being able to implement change from electoral office. So that's been the focus of my activities now for the past seven years.

I put out newsletters to my community. I have a monthly newsletter that goes to the neighborhood boards and grassroots organizations. It basically updates people about what's going on at City Hall. I have a quarterly newsletter that goes out to the seven thousand people on my database. These are people who are directly involved in government, one way or the other. They've supported me in a campaign, or have been assisted by my office in a community problem, or are a member of a community association or neighborhood board. The quarterly newsletter deals in more detail with my political activities, the issues I'm pursuing, and the philosophical reasons for that. And then annually I send out a newsletter—to every household in my district with a registered voter—which covers a broad range of topics and usually has a survey. It has a personal message from me and an explanation of the votes I've taken and some of the projects I want to pursue for the given year.

The City and County [of Honolulu] form[s] one structure on this island. There are nine districts, each designed to be of equal population. I represent nearly 100,000 people. My district has 28,000 households with around 35,000 registered voters. About 26,000 people actually vote.

How radical are your newsletters?

My newsletters are not radical diatribes nor full of slogans or propaganda. They're straightforward English with practically based information. I don't think people are won over by slogans. My newsletters cover what I am doing as an elected official, and hopefully the reader will understand my reasons and be able to relate my philosophy to how it is practically applied. I don't view myself as some kind of minority or radical element. I don't have to hide my analysis or hide my ideology. I don't make any apologies for the way I feel.

Was it a tough election when you were first elected?

Yeah, it was very tough. I ran for City Council against an incumbent Republican. The district is dominantly Democrat. The incumbent was not disliked—he is a decent guy, pretty popular, and hadn't done anything to discredit himself. But it was primarily a Democratic district with Democratic traditions. And I think there was a sentiment for change in the electorate. I ran a very low budget, full-time, grassroots, door-to-door campaign and won a contested Democratic primary. Then I faced the incumbent Republican and squeezed through with just over a 1 percent margin. We worked our socks off. I have since won reelection once by a two-to-one margin.

The power of incumbency is always very strong. I've received a lot of media attention. My name recognition islandwide is above 90 percent because of the stands I've taken, like 'em or don't like 'em. I'm on TV and people know who I am. I think the average voter doesn't get involved directly in the intrigue or philosophy of politics. If you're on

TV and you're active and you're working hard, they like it. I don't think the majority of people anywhere have an ideological perspective. They have, maybe, a sense of style. Here in Hawai'i they like people who are independent and active, and honest, and hard-working. They'll accept your political philosophy, so long as you're honest about it and they think it's basically in the best interest of the public.

On the mainland, you might be given a label, like socialist.

Well, yeah . . . I am. People call me that, but it doesn't stick. People don't care. I mean, it's just another label. What's a liberal? The word doesn't mean very much. In my last election, my opponent, who was and still is the executive assistant to the mayor and ran against me with the mayor's machine, was openly criticizing me as a radical socialist, and putting it in writing, in full-page newspaper ads. Big deal. The mayor calls me a Communist at times. It doesn't bother me what label you stick on me. What I've stood for and what I'm fighting for is a matter of public record and people like it. And if you call that socialist, well, I guess they like socialism.

Would you break down what you're fighting for?

It's not easy to put it in a sound bite. If I have to boil it down, I guess there are a few philosophical foundations that I build my activities on. One is environmentalism: basically, the belief that the human society needs to live in balance with nature. That was very much a part of my philosophy in my growing up in Hawai'i; my understanding of the unique ecosystem that exists here. I spend a lot of my time hiking and camping, volunteering to build trails, doing things to preserve the native flora and fauna, and educating people on that.

I guess a second philosophy would be democratic empowerment of people at all levels: preventing the alienation of people from their labor, getting them involved in decision making, and making them involved in the institutions of their government. A lot of the focus of my newsletters is to empower neighborhood boards. I hold meetings that bring neighborhood board members together. I take them on a bus tour of the district so they can meet and communicate their common problems with each other.

The things I've stood for in the public eye have been sheltering the homeless, and supporting the disadvantaged, disabled, and underprivileged. I have the fundamental belief that government needs to be an equalizer, that we need to regulate the existing market so that it meets the needs of all of our people. The market takes care of a sector of our people who are in the upper economic categories. But the government needs to make sure that wealth, land, and power is distributed to everyone.

I don't think my perspective is radical at all; it's really mainstream. I don't want to give anyone the perspective that I'm out of the ordinary. I don't want to section myself out in the left wing or in the corner of political thought.

There are people in city government, on the council, who consider themselves to be very conservative. They're pro-business, at least in their rhetoric. But look at what our county government does. Every single action we take regulates this market. We control land use on this island. If you are a free marketeer, you would have to argue to disband the zoning code because we tell people how much value they can get out of their property. The city government regulates that fundamental American principle: the right of land ownership. We tell you where you can put a resort, where you can put a business, where you can put a home, how big your sign can be, how many parking spaces you can have. We regulate it, down to the last nail. So, you know, all I'm doing is putting a political philosophy into the everyday workings of regulating capital. Once in a while, a council member will argue that the city shouldn't be involved in building housing, we should let the free market do it. And I will argue with them, "Show me where in the world that works. If you're for free marketeering, you should quit your job because you violate your own principle every time you vote for a zoning ordinance."

I want to get away from the labels of radical and conservative. I think part of the problem with the progressive movement is it perceives itself as a movement of outsiders and limits itself because of that view. I view myself as an insider and have twenty thousand people who will vote for me as an insider, and I think I'm just as radical as anybody else.

If you take a step back and look at the progress that left-wing progressive activists have had, it's been profound. Look at the social structure in Hawai'i today, as opposed to when my dad was my age: radically different. Some of the outsiders got in and abused power, but look at this structure of our society: radically improved. You know, people don't get lynched any more in America.

They starve to death, though.

Well, okay—there's a higher form or the next level of exploitation—but it's not as heinous as it used to be. Maybe I stepped too far back to take a view of the big picture, but in this game that I'm in, I think you have to have a long-term view of your actions because change takes place in increments, slowly. If you expect to transform the ship of state at one haul in the dry dock, you know, it doesn't happen that fast. You have to get very practical about it.

Where do we, as a county, control the economy? We control it primarily in land use and development. We can control housing development. Who will benefit by housing development? We can assure that housing is developed as affordable for our local people, or we can ignore it and let the housing be built only for rich from somewhere else.

We control new resort development. If somebody wants to build a hotel here, my argument is, no, we don't want any more hotels here. We want to get away from our dependency on tourism, and yet capital wants to run to where the fast buck can be made, and the fastest bucks will be made in the tourist industry. Capital doesn't want to invest in manufacturing or small agriculture or communications technology or software development in Hawaiʻi. So we have to review fast-buck golf course developers and tourism resort developers, and we can tell them yes or no. And we have the authority and the power to direct our economy through land use.

Sometimes I see Honolulu, or Hawaiʻi, as a Ping-Pong ball that's being batted back and forth across the Pacific tennis table, between California and Tokyo. I don't think any country, any city, is fully in control of its economic destiny. We live in the age of global capitalism, where investment trends supercede or impose themselves upon any local interest in self-determination. To use a local surfing analogy, when you're out there surfing, you wait for the wave and you paddle to catch it and you ride the wave. Success is determined by whether or not you wipe out. If you wipe out, you lose. Maybe you had a good ride before you wiped out. But you don't generate the wave. The wave is being generated offshore. Wiping out is when you fall off the wave and get pounded on the reef. So we're here, surrounded by water, with all kind of waves coming in, waves of foreign investment and global capital, coming and going as the wind blows. We don't control the wind or the waves, but we can choose which waves we want to ride and we can build structures to catch the wind and harness it for our own energy.

A simple example of this is in golf course development. About four years ago the Japanese economy was booming, and one element of that was speculative golf course development. Golf course memberships were being traded like stocks and bonds in Japan. A conglomerate of businessmen—we call them *hui*s here—would name themselves a golf course company and sell shares or memberships in a resort golf course that hadn't even been built. Those shares trade hands, and the value changes, just like the stock market. Four years ago, we had nearly a hundred applications for golf course development on this island because that's where they could make a quick buck. The city threw a whole lot of bureaucracy at it. Ninety percent of those applicants are bankrupt. The big bubble burst in Japan. A lot of capital has been recalled to Japan. So we insulated ourselves effectively from that capital assault on our island. There are a number of golf courses that got through—that are still very controversial—but the lion's share of them didn't. That's a practical example of what we need to do as policy to protect ourselves from the waves of capital or monetary trends that attempt to wash over us.

The land use process in Hawai'i is very detailed. The state designates all land in the Island[s] into four different categories: conservation, agriculture, rural, and urban. Once the state designates land as urban, the county takes over and we will designate it as resort, residential, industrial, commercial, what have you. There's some control that the county has on agricultural land, but anything zoned "conservation" by the state is beyond county control.

There is developable land in central O'ahu in places which is now cane field. But before a developer can build on it, he has to get the state to designate it as urban. And once it's urban, he has to get the county to designate it as residential, and that process can take years. The developers will scream and moan that that's why development is so expensive. Taking developable land out of agriculture and building houses on it is a five- to seven-year process, and time is money, they say. There is some truth to that argument, but it is not true that if we were simply to abandon all land use controls and let developers build wherever they want that the by-product would be affordable housing.

We can grant exemption to that seven-year land use process and give a developer virtually immediate rights to develop the land if he's building affordable housing. He just has to build 60 percent of the units affordable to people who earn 120 percent of the local median income or below. They won't do it because they can't make a buck on that kind of housing. The market will not build affordable housing. Capitalism won't go where capitalism can't make money. They can't make money given the cost of land, development time, infrastructure, and labor, and still try to keep the final price to what our service-based economy will support.

We see a continual expansion of the role of government in health care, child care, human services, housing development. I don't want to negate market forces. Market forces exist. They exist in socialist states. The law of value exists. It is a law. The fundamental question is, Does that law of value—of supply and demand—control society or does society utilize that law to benefit its people?

What's in the future of Hawai'i? I think Hawai'i's economy has been mirroring that of Tokyo or Taiwan or Korea more than it's been mirroring the economy of Chicago or New York or Washington, D.C. We are a Pacific nation, we are a bridge. Well, either we're a Ping-Pong ball or we're a bridge. Our economy has been buffered from the economic collapse of the United States that has been taking place in the past decade or so. But we're certainly not immune to that. I think America has severe structural problems. If we don't deal with some of the structural problems, we won't get a grip on developing a productive economy. If we don't make a smooth transition from a military-based commandist economy to a civilian-based productive economy, then we'll be in big trouble.

On the longer-term view, I think I'm pretty optimistic about the United States economy because the workforce is highly skilled. Our educational infrastructure, although teetering, is still better than Third World nations. The natural resources that exist in the United States are phenomenal and accessible. Although some bridges are crumbling, at least we have bridges, as opposed to China, struggling to build a huge dam in the Yangtze River. So it will be easier to refashion the economy of the United States than it would be for the People's Republic of China.

But in the long-term future, I think, naturally and by necessity, the economy is going to have to be restructured to survive, to be more democratic. I don't think that there is the social basis for fascism in the United States. I think it's a possibility, but I think our people are more of a polyglot of cultures and political spectrums. American progressives and independents, and just the American psyche, would not support fascism.

Brahim Aoudé

An associate professor in the Ethnic Studies Program, University of Hawai'i, Mānoa; age forty-something.

I was born in Palestine and grew up in Lebanon. Political things were a central part of my life from early on. The land question for me was central because of the Zionist claim to the land of Palestine; the Palestinian Arabs en masse were kicked out when I was young. I grew up in Lebanon in the 1950s, the time when the entire colonial world was thrust into the fight against colonialism and later against imperialism. I became anticolonial and anti-imperialist because of my experiences.

When I was growing up in Lebanon, the entire area was undergoing an anticolonial, anti-imperialistic experience, including the Algerian revolution, the political revolution of Nasser in Egypt, along with other people like Nehru and Sukarno. So I developed an international view. Anticolonial struggles were central to my later experiences.

I grew up in Beirut in a fundamentally working-class, multiethnic, multireligious area. There were Lebanese, Palestinians, Armenians, Muslim Shiites, Muslim Sunnis, Catholics, Protestants, Eastern Orthodox. That experience, as I often reflect on it, has really given me a lot of understanding of multiethnic, multinational, multireligious coexistence, and how to relate to people of different backgrounds. It was fantastic, I think, for someone to grow up in such an environment, although we had a lot of hardships.

Another major experience was the civil war of 1958 in Lebanon, which came hard on the heels of the 1958 union between Egypt and Syria, the successful coup against the monarchy in Iraq, and the attempted coup in Jordan. The whole area was just boiling. And then Lebanon erupted in civil war. These events happened less than two years after the Suez War of 1956 when the British, French, and Israel invaded Egypt. So all these things had formed my political awareness from early on. I had commitments to anticolonialism and anti-imperialism at the age of thirteen with the confluence of all these experiences.

How did your family feel about these things?

When I was nine, I remember my mom saying, "Look what a hero Nasser of Egypt was. He was able to carry out the coup in 1952, get rid of the monarchy, and try to get political independence from the British." My dad also was concerned about what was happening in the Arab world and the Third World in terms of anti-imperialism [and] anticolonialism. He and his friends and visitors used to talk politics a lot. Especially during the 1958 Lebanese civil war, I got a lot of education by just listening in. Another important thing was the junior high school I went to. My professors of history, Arabic language, and math were nationalists; that is to say, anticolonial, anti-imperial. I also got exposed fairly early on—in the equivalent of eleventh or twelfth grade here—to all kinds of ideologies: Arab nationalist, socialist, Marxist, communist, whatever.

Did you have a label for yourself?

No. I just wanted liberation of Palestine, a better life for people in the Arab world, Arab unity, and so forth. There was a lot of fervor among the students. Most Americans don't have those kinds of experiences. It's something like the difference, say, between somebody from the ghetto and someone from a high suburban area. We were exposed to all kinds of ideologies. Like some students would say, "Oh, there's the Arab nationalist movement holding a meeting, let's go check it out." So we would go. The Arab Ba'ath Party would also have a meeting: "Let's go and see what's happening." Even then, I didn't like the organization of the Arab nationalist movement. My orientation was something more like democratic participation that crosses politics. I thought they did not give that kind of thing a very high priority. It was like you get orders from above, period. Or at least, that's what it seemed to me, rightly or wrongly. I wanted individuals to participate in the process. Another thing I didn't like was that the Arab nationalists were pro-Nasser at the time, and Nasser did not want any political parties. He wanted to dictate to the masses and the masses would follow.

I never joined the Ba'ath Party, but I was more inclined to them because it appeared to me that they were organizing people and having more individual participation. I began on my own just talking to friends and playmates. We used to go on long walks and talk about all kinds of stuff. But when things like the civil war happened, we started talking about politics. They wanted me to explain to them what's happening. I really didn't know what was happening, but apparently I knew a little bit more than they did.

The day before the civil war erupted in Lebanon a major Maronite (Christian) journalist got assassinated. The Maronites held the presidency in Lebanon, but he was against the pro-U.S. policies of the regime. So the regime basically assassinated this guy. The next day I was going to school with my neighbor and we had to transfer trams to get to school in the city center of Beirut. That was the first day of the civil war. All of a sudden, early in the morning, we heard a burst of machine-gun fire: "tat-tat-tat-tat!" We look and there's this taxi driver next to us, where his cab was parked. He was shot in the hip. It could have been me; it could have been my friend.

So after this, when I used to go with my friends, they wanted me to explain to them what's happening. I was forced to try and put things together so that it made sense to them. As I was talking to them, I was preparing, structuring, restructuring things in my mind. It forced me to get that kind of skill going. Some of us started having study circles on a weekly basis.

After I finished high school in 1961 I went to London, England, and studied in an aircraft mechanic school for three years. And there, on a more formal basis, I got more exposure to all kinds of ideologies that I already had an elementary understanding of. I read both in English and in Arabic.

I used to go for a few weeks back to Lebanon in the summers. The Arab students' movement in England was very strong and I connected with it from the first day. I was on the executive committee of the Arab Students' Movement in England, Wales, and Ireland for a year. We used to have study groups. We used to spend a lot of time in coffee shops and pubs and talk politics. Those were good days. My school had students from all over the world—Africa, India, Pakistan, England—so it was a good exposure. I could understand English spoken by different kinds of peoples, and that served me well later on.

Then I went back to Lebanon and worked within the Palestinian movement, in a sense, not joining the Palestine Liberation Organization or anything, but trying to see what could be done with the youth and so forth. I had shunted aside all nationalist ideologies like Arab nationalism. I went beyond them and began to think more internationally in terms of social justice, democracy, freedom, private participation of the population.

I worked as an aircraft mechanic at a company that did not have a trade union, so I and others were agitating for one. When a recession came in Lebanon a number of us were on the top list of people to be laid off. For a while I worked in other places in the Arab world, like Saudi Arabia.

And then in September 1968, I went to Canada for about a year, where I started a mechanical engineering degree part-time and worked full-time. I read a lot of books and had a good time. It would have taken me seven years to get a degree. My brother, who was studying at the University of Hawai'i, came to visit me in Canada and said, "Why don't you come to Hawai'i and work part-time and study full-time?" So I came to Hawai'i and began studying electronics at Honolulu Community College, where I eventually got an associate degree.

When I came to Hawai'i I really did not have any culture shock, and I felt right at home. I would write letters telling my folks that, and marvel at this kind of situation. A lot of things in the culture here, like warmth and generosity, are similar to Arab culture in the Middle East. In the household in which I grew up, all kinds of people would come to us and we would do all kinds of things for each other. So in Hawai'i, I just felt right at home. Because Arabic has a lot of vowels, I had no problem speaking names like Kapi'olani, Wai'anae, Mānoa, and all these. And a lot of people here helped me.

I met my wife Liana in 1971. We've been together since then. She was an important influence in my life. She was born and raised here and knew all kinds of people. She's an Island woman, very much attached to the land, down-to-earth, and yet artistic. So I got exposed to native Hawaiian culture. Liana is half Filipino and half German. Her stepfather was Native Hawaiian, so she was raised as Native Hawaiian and has those mannerisms. She didn't discover her Filipino roots until later on. So I got introduced also to Filipino culture.

When I went to Canada, the antiwar movement was still going on and the tail end of the civil rights movement. I listened to what happened in the 1968 Democratic National Convention. I listened to what President Johnson said and did. I got introduced to the counterculture.

What did you think of the counterculture?

I didn't care for it at all on the personal level. It was alien to me. However, I could understand the alienation of the youth to things that the United States had been doing. Coming from an anticolonial, anti-imperialist position already, I didn't have any time for the United States being in the Vietnam War. No way! I was against it all the way. Back home we used to hear about the Civil Rights Movement, so we knew that Blacks and Native Americans were oppressed. So our sympathies were with the minorities in the United States. We were aware of those things happening. So when I came over here, I didn't think that Americans were nutty people. There was a sense of alienation, and the counterculture was an expression of that.

I also got exposed to the literature of the anti-Vietnam War scene and the Civil Rights movement. I kind of integrated it into my understanding and my cosmology, if you will. I also started reading the Frankfurt School. I remember Erich Fromm. Liana was reading those things too. She had finished her masters degree when I still had one more semester to go for my B.A. Those experiences gave me another look at Marxism as an ideology.

Then I went to Cal State in Los Angeles to do my masters in business. I got a lot of exposure to politics there. Not so much L.A. politics, but Arab politics and American politics. I was juggling three or four things at the same time. I got introduced to all kinds of Chicanos and Blacks and white Americans, as well as Iranians. Cal State was fervent, at that time, in terms of peace kinds of issues. I had a great education there, in terms of understanding the American political scene, especially the American South and the working people's perspective. I tried at the same time to connect my Arab friends with my American friends. We would meet and talk about African Americans and Palestinian issues.

So I came back to Hawai'i and decided to do my Ph.D. in political science. Earlier I had been thinking that I might still go back to Lebanon and that business might be the way to get back into politics, not in the sense of getting elected, but in grassroots mass politics. First of all, I would figure out the scene, make some money, and then most probably leave business and just do politics full-time. But that couldn't work because of the Lebanese civil war which started in April 1975. I decided that I should do something else, and that was basically political science at the University of Hawai'i.

I finished my Ph.D. in August, 1980. My dissertation was on the

Lebanese civil war. I wanted to understand better what in the world had occurred there. Already I had the background to analyze what went wrong and what went right. Writing the dissertation was a great experience. I learned a lot from my reading and the interviews I did back home. I went back to collect material in Arabic which was not readily available in libraries here. It was a great experience.

Meanwhile, I started working at the ethnic studies program as a course lab leader. I got introduced in that way to ethnic events and politics here. I found that the ethnic studies program was like a pariah on campus. Everybody wanted to get rid of it. The ethnic studies program came out of the antiwar struggles and Civil Rights movement, both nationally and locally. The university administration and nearly everybody was against it. There was an ongoing fight to establish a permanent program.

Why did they not want it?

Because it was perceived as challenging the basic mainstream analysis of society and culture and politics. The slogan and chant of ethnic studies was and is, "Our history, our race, make ethnic studies permanent." After mobilizing and marching, on and off campus, we won permanence in 1977. We always had community support from people's struggles in Hawai'i like Waiāhole-Waikāne, Chinatown, Mō'ili'ili: people that ethnic studies, over time, had worked with. They came in to support ethnic studies permanence. We sat in at the administration building and we had a rally. We won permanence, so that was an important thing. Then, ethnic studies began to adapt to the new realities beyond the mid-'70s. It was becoming more of an academic program and moving along with the times, but still maintaining some of the ties to the past.

When I graduated in 1980 with my Ph.D., I started teaching here and there, like business economics and political science. In 1982 I started in ethnic studies as a lecturer.

I had been making observations in Hawai'i as far back as 1971, because I was not well aware of the scene. Of course, I had other things to worry about, like being a full-time student and working twenty to thirty hours a week. Liana was working for the airlines, so she helped me a lot. But I was observing what was going on, on all kinds of levels. At first, I was more interested in the ideas that were new for me. Then later on, I got more active on the political level.

One thing I was observing was the Native Hawaiian scene. I remember when the landing on Kaho'olawe occurred, and I was in Cal State L.A., Liana would send me newspaper clippings with the note, "Oh, there's hope." And I could very much identify with the landing on Kaho'olawe, because I remembered the Palestinian movement, and I remembered myself in high school, saying to people that the Palestinians are now dormant, or so it seems, but they're going to rise up. When Kaho'olawe happened, I said, "Hey, I've seen that one before. This is something that's going to grow because it's a land issue." Even if the masses of Native Hawaiians were not consciously anti-imperialist, Kaho'olawe was being bombed by the military. It didn't require much imagination to figure out that this is an antimilitary thing. A few people had landed "illegally" on the island being used for target practice by the military, and then got arrested. Then the Protect Kaho'olawe 'Ohana— *'ohana* meaning family—movement was formed, so it was an antimilitary thing in all its consequences. Liana was astute enough to see that this was an important thing with all kinds of repercussions.

I think Native Hawaiians would agree that the land question here marks the new phase of Native Hawaiian resistance. There had been some actions earlier on against evictions, like at Kalama Valley, spearheaded by Native Hawaiians, along with other eviction struggles. But they were not at the strategic level of importance of Kaho'olawe. They were not antimilitary, or Hawaiians confronting the state, whether it's the state government here or the machinery of the United States. *That* is a large, strategic thing. It wasn't very difficult for me to see that in terms of politics.

We have been struggling to keep ethnic studies permanent, and somewhat in the Native Hawaiian struggle. We do not want to be seen as chauvinistic, like joining and telling them what to do, but just giving them full support in terms of principle, which is self-determination for Native Hawaiians. We should not worry about what that might be; let them figure it out, but give them unconditional support. I think that is a principled position, since I am not Native Hawaiian myself.

We also have participated in the fights for low-income housing in Chinatown, especially in the 1980s, although it started around 1974. PACE—People Against Chinatown Evictions—started in 1975, although there were earlier formations. I was in Cal State, but I got to know people in PACE when I came home to visit. When I came back permanently, I connected with them and helped out somewhat. Most of my help was in the '80s and took the form of trying to organize and give material help to the people in the eviction fights. And not to tell them what to do, but to empower them so that they could fight for their own rights and organize themselves.

What kind of help was provided?

The main thing was providing whatever skills you might have. For instance, if they wanted lawyers to counter public defenders who think mainstream and have a different agenda than empowering the people, our lawyers would come in for free; lawyers like George Cooper, Bill Hoshijo, Wayson Chow, and Lowell So Chun Hoon. The government, especially the city, wanted a form of urban renewal in Chinatown. They would push the people out and "renew" the place by putting up highrises or doing renovations, or whatever the case might be, and then rent out the housing for more money. So where would the people go? PACE was fighting for the people to stay in Chinatown; fighting for the city or state to build low-income houses. From 1975, PACE has been successful in doing this. Before PACE, a lot of people got evicted from Chinatown.

PACE is still working in Chinatown on a number of problems in low-income apartment buildings. There are problems with management, like abuse of tenants, and all that kind of stuff. So the fight is still ongoing. The thing is to empower tenants to fight this kind of abuse. The tenants' association in one building, in conjunction with PACE, recently won eight of their nine demands, like cutting out management abuse and refunding illegally charged money. The only demand they did not win was getting rid of management. PACE was instrumental in helping out the tenants' association and empowering them to fight for their rights.

In our steering committee meetings we will talk about problems in specific apartment buildings: What's wrong with that building? What's happening? What do we need to do? In addition to working on individual problems, we try as much as possible to have a strategic thrust and get into the larger housing questions, like Chinatown as a whole. We discuss how to make alliances among buildings or how to proceed with the city and state. The thrust is to improve the lot of the low-income tenants and then go forward into the broader land and housing questions in Hawai'i.

We have had a housing crisis in Hawai'i for years which nobody can really solve. It is because of the land speculation that accompanies a tourist-oriented society. Tourism accounts for about $10.4 billion of the $31 billion gross state product in Hawai'i, so it's about one-third. I would put the number even higher. There's a commitment to building major projects—condominiums and office buildings—like in Kaka'ako and in the Aloha Tower area. These projects are for rich people. They already have increased the height limit in Chinatown and the downtown area to about 450 feet. There's also historic preservation stuff in which buildings are renovated and a lot of people make money.

One of the eviction fights we had in 1985 was Julie's Hotel on Maunakea Street, a single-room occupancy place. There were eighteen tenants involved in this fight: people from their forties to their eighties. The private company that did it was called Historic Properties—nice name. They wanted to evict those people and then jack up the price from . . . $105 to maybe $250 a room. Those people wouldn't be able to afford it, especially the old plantation workers who already had paid their dues for forty years or more. So now they are eighty-two. Where can they go? We entered this fight and forced the city to give the tenants first right to come back, after relocating them in Chinatown until the renovations were completed. The majority stayed and fought and won. For those who got back into Julie's Hotel, the rent was only raised $10, instead of $100 or $150. We did a number of actions. For instance, we went with the old people to the company's offices on Bishop Street and picketed and demonstrated. The media came and said, "Oh, these old people are going to be evicted." Now everybody knows that housing is a problem, so there was a lot of identification with the people who are going to be evicted. Another action the people did was to go straight to the mayor and talk with him.

With the aloha idea here, is it easier for local activists to be successful than on the mainland?

Without going around in circles, I don't think so because money talks. A lot of people are suffering from the housing problem. Only 54 percent of housing is owner-occupied, as opposed to 64 percent for the mainland. The median cost of a single-family home is around $365,000. No one from the working classes can make a down payment on a house. If you don't have the house already from thirty years back, that's it for most people.

The cost of rental housing on O'ahu is atrocious. There is around a 1 percent vacancy rate, which is nothing. Talk about supply and demand! A two-bedroom basic apartment in Makiki rents for about $900. Again, much of this is because of speculation and dependency on tourism.

Another major sector of the economy is the military, which contributes about $2.6 billion annually to the gross state product, so it's quite significant. So there is military, tourism, and agriculture, which is going downhill. They're trying to diversify agriculture to try to remedy the situation somewhat, but it's not that successful. There's a lot of construction, but that is basically related to tourism: hotels, freeways, office buildings, and so on.

Now, one of the things the state says is that people need to have better jobs in order to afford the homes and to relax zoning regulations to make the permit process easier. Suppose all these things were done. Suppose more land was released, permits relaxed, and home prices were reduced by, say, $100,000. You still have to pay $265,000. Low-income, moderate-income people can't afford it because household income is about $23,000, and you've got to pay taxes from this. Tourism brings primarily low-pay jobs. Few workers can afford a down payment on a house even if they work two jobs.

So the state is now saying, "Well, we have to have high technology industry, so let's try and build another sector of the economy, high tech." But high tech has a number of problems. One of the problems that already exists in Hawai'i is outside capital coming in, whether mainland capital from the 1950s and '60s or Japanese capital more recently. Tourism was led by outside capital, not Hawaiian capital, and led to this speculation in land and housing. This housing crisis has been developing over the past thirty-five or forty years. A lot of people are benefiting from tourism: haole professionals from the mainland, or local professionals, whether they're Japanese, Chinese, Hawaiian, Native Hawaiian, Filipino. But a lot more people are *not* benefiting. Native Hawaiians and Filipinos, by and large, have been on the receiving end because Filipinos have been hotel workers and so forth, and Native Hawaiians have been thrown out. Land and housing has a native component. They are low-income people. There's an intertwined class and ethnic relationship here. If the land-housing problem continues that way, then something has got to give.

So if they want to create a new high-technology electronics sector, they need foreign capital. If they get it, more of the same kind of development will be created, but now it will be electrified, so to speak. The other thing is that now there's a global capital problem. Japanese capital is not coming in as it did from 1986 to 1989, the years of fantastic foreign investment. And also, high technology is not going to become a major industry that would take the slack away from agriculture or tourism. In fact, even elite people in business and politics say that openly. There is intense global competition in high technology. In the United States alone, there are five, six sites at least that are competing with Hawai'i. So why would they want to come to Hawai'i? The only niche you might have here is research and development, and it's not going to be in the billions. There wouldn't be many high-paying jobs for Hawai'i's people. You cannot have an industry here to produce microchips—it's impossible. All these dreams about high technology being our future? No, it's not going to solve the problem; it's going to add to the problem. It would enhance tourism. People would come to conventions to talk about high technology. They would want a hotel and transportation, so you end up where you started.

So Hawai'i is basically locked into tourism, military, and agriculture, all of which are going down. In 1988 the combination of Japanese business, investment, and tourists constituted 45 percent of the gross state product. The figures are just mind-boggling. The Japanese tourists used to pick up the slack when the mainland markets dried up. Now Japan is in recession and the mainland market is depressed. Hawai'i is having a problem. The state budget is being cut and we're being cut at the University of Hawai'i. Hawai'i is now on the receiving end of this global economy. The local elite is committed to tourist development. Major sections of the population are on the receiving end. As a consequence, the housing crisis deepens. How this is going to be solved is a major problem for policy makers. On the basis of these events, political instability is going to increase in Hawai'i. Already the Native Hawaiians are fighting for their self-determination. Already problems in Hawai'i are being expressed in the political arena. But this is like kid's stuff now, compared to what will happen later on. One could see this coming some time ago.

How is all this affecting the quality of life?

Well, unemployment is low—about 3 percent—but this is an artificial figure for several reasons. Some workers go to the mainland if they can't find work here. That's a major safety valve. The second thing is that some people give up looking for work. And the third thing is the underground economy that doesn't show up in the gross state product. Along with tourism come things like drugs and prostitution. Visitors want to have a good time here. The government does not want prostitution to disappear because it's part of the tourist scene. They only want to contain it. If I said that to them they would say, "Oh, this is outrageous." But, you know, come on! There's an extensive cottage industry in drugs here. Everybody knows it. Bank of Hawaii people talk about it. Anybody who knows anything about Hawai'i politics talks about these matters.

There is increasing political action. You see the whole resurgence of the Native Hawaiian movement. Astute policy makers know that there is something happening and they must do something about it. They've tried to co-opt this movement in various ways since the late 1970s. But if they don't solve the problems, whatever co-optation happens is going to be only temporary. The movement will keep on coming up. I've seen this happen in the old country, you see. The movement can't be co-opted forever.

A few years back the state said that by the year 2000, if all goes well, they'll be able to solve 95 percent of the housing problems. That's if all goes well, but we know that plans don't go well. Even if their plan worked, there would be 5 percent left. Where would these people go? Housing and employment problems are going to remain. So because of that, more people are going to begin to fight for their rights, in their own interests. That means they're going to begin to question all kinds of things that they've been taking for granted for a long time.

The group Citizens for Rent Control collected twelve thousand signatures just in the space of about two months. That shows how much identification there is with the housing crisis. Sooner or later, the fight of people for housing and against homelessness will take a political shape beyond the demands of "Please, I'm going to come and testify in your committee, and please do something for housing." Politics is going to take a different form in the next five to ten years.

I speculate on the next people's movement. The problem to me, as a political scientist, is who's going to be leading this people's movement? Will they be misleaders who would co-opt it and send it down the garden path, or will they be people who are really committed and have a strategy that would see it to its conclusion? Those who are committed and have a strategy will be leaders coming out of today's movement. These people must have a strategy to win freedom and democracy and the rights of all groups to live in peace and harmony.

One problem at this point is that the Native Hawaiian movement and the housing movement are developing separately, so it seems, although there has been some cooperation between the Native Hawaiian and the environmental movements. What I would like to see happen is the integration of the movements around their commonalities in the

fight. Land and housing are Native Hawaiian issues, but also applicable
to others. However, this should not impinge upon Native Hawaiian
rights. The Native Hawaiians have not quite yet made the case that
their movement is also to the benefit of non-Native Hawaiians. This
would win them allies. Both the Native Hawaiian and housing movements are now separate, but more or less are moving in the same direction. They have the same target, so to speak. So they have to figure out
ways of cooperating and forming alliances and having the same thrust
so they can win.

Nothing is for certain. Leadership and an organized political body is
very important to guide this kind of thing. This political body is not
from outer space. It is made up of people arising out of the daily struggle for land and housing. It must have a strategy and organization that
allow this strategy to work. In terms of leadership there are some
encouraging signs, but leadership does not emerge automatically. It has
to go through the crucible of the struggle in order to be seasoned and
really committed to the people.

Many homeless people are Native Hawaiians. How can you fight for
Native Hawaiian rights for self-determination without solving the
immediate problem of the Native Hawaiian *makaʻāinana*—the com-
moner? They are working-class people who deserve to have their problems addressed right now. That makes the case that it is for the benefit
of all. The guys who are not Native Hawaiians are not going to win
their fight if they don't see that the Native Hawaiian issue is the basis
for it; it's actually the answer. This is the fight for survival now.

It's all very worrisome to the state. The state machinery knows that
they can't solve these problems while maintaining control. They are in a
predicament. Important things that have been taken for granted before
begin to be questioned. In the land and housing issue, the whole notion
of private property perhaps needs to be questioned. Who knows? In
Chinatown, we were told, "I am the owner of this building, and to hell
with you." In terms of Native Hawaiians, the whole notion of private
property is ludicrous. How did all this land become private property? It
was taken away from Native Hawaiians. People know and say that.
Why deny it?

I think that most organizations eventually will see that they have to
be based in the poorest sections of the working class, whether Native
Hawaiian or not. For Native Hawaiians, it makes sense because they
are about 18 percent of the state's population and most are poor working class. I think the term "working class" is very important. If you

don't base yourself in the working class, and you don't have the leadership of Native Hawaiians, then you don't have that anchor to the land. The same is true for the non-Native Hawaiian organizations. If they do not base themselves in that poorest, hardest-hit section of the working class, then they're not going to be able to do much.

In earlier periods in Hawai'i's history, before and after World War II, a lot of the fighters and organizers came out of the plantations. So we have, in fact, a tradition of working-class leadership. But those earlier times were different from now. Then, the whole system of capitalism was growing, developing, and extending itself globally. There's little room any more to maneuver it, globally or otherwise, because of high technology and the glut of commodities on the market. So we are in a contraction period across the board. That's why long-term trends will be going downhill.

Under crisis, don't capital elites move to the right when threatened by a movement of workers?

I don't think any place is exempt from historic trends and forces. But you know, these are the challenges for the people's movement. The more democratic that people's movement is, and the more its fighting strategy is skilled and intelligent, the more it can thwart this trend to the right, and build a genuine system of democracy, freedom, and rights for everyone. Everybody must be able to live in dignity, and have a job and education. If the system is oppressive and undemocratic, it has to be restructured.

And in order to restructure it, you have to have political power.

Wayson Chow

A local attorney in his forties, emphasizing personal injury, civil rights, and community organizing

I grew up in a lower middle class family that was not economically well off. One of the things that my mother constantly stressed was to do the right thing, at all costs. There were not the social pressures that Asian American families sometimes have. I grew up in the ʻĀina Haina area before it was noted as being relatively well off. There was a clear class and race distinction between us and those people who lived across the highway along the ocean, on Wailupe peninsula.

While growing up, I remember an incident where we were visiting a haole classmate who lived on Wailupe peninsula, right across from ʻĀina Haina School, a public elementary school. A haole neighbor came out and said, "What the hell are you boys doing here?"

We said, "We're just visiting our friend."

He said, "You have no business being here!"

We said, "We're just visiting."

So he gave us a bad time. The neighborhood then was affluent, primarily haole. For many years it was exclusively haole. Due to restrictive real estate covenants, the first Asian American family moved into Wailupe peninsula in the 1950s, and this is Hawaiʻi! The reason we kids were in that neighborhood, of course, was that it was right next to the beach where we often surfed. We would find ways to climb over the padlocked gate in order to reach the pier and launch our surf-boards.

When I attended the University of Hawai'i in the 1960s, the antiwar movement had a tremendous influence on developing my ideology. When the University decided to start an ethnic studies program, I became actively involved in planning and implementing a student-faculty evaluation. The Kalama Valley action and also the Oliver Lee sit-in at Bachman Hall occurred about then, and I was very supportive and joined both mass mobilizations.

When I decided to attend the University of Southern California Law Center in the early 1970s, I knew that the law should be a tool for social change. In the late 1960s and early 1970s, there were many progressive lawyers, and it was an exciting time to be a lawyer. I thought that this is the way that I could work for social change and, at the same time, put food on the table.

I graduated from law school in 1975, returned to Hawai'i, and went to work for legal aid as a community activist-lawyer. I eventually was fired because of my political views, due to my encouraging and supporting the rights of tenants to organize in Chinatown. In the mid-1970s and early '80s, Chinatown tenants were organizing and struggling for community control, self-determination, and to prevent the city and landowners from evicting them, as a part of the City's urban renewal actions. There were over half a dozen buildings in which people were given eviction notices.

The tenants banded together in an organization that subsequently became known as PACE, People Against Chinatown Eviction. PACE organized tenants in various buildings to demand decent housing, no relocation outside of the Chinatown area, affordable rents, and preservation of the residents' lifestyle in Chinatown. The attorneys were the legal arm that assisted the political struggle, assisting tenant leadership from the Chinatown area. Of our five court cases, two went up to the state supreme court. PACE and its supporters won all five court cases, and no one was ever evicted.

The Legal Aid Society of Hawai'i administrators said that the Legal Aid Society should determine which attorneys work on the Chinatown cases. The Chinatown tenants responded that "The Legal Aid Society supervisors are not with us one hundred percent. They don't come to our meetings and we can't count on them." The Legal Aid Society wanted to decide who works on the cases and to set all of the terms of representation. I was asked by the Legal Aid Society administrators,

"Why are you assisting tenants who insist on demonstrating inside and outside the court room? Are you fanning the flames of revolution? Which side are you on?"

I replied, "In this case, I'm with the tenants. In any large law firm, the clients decide who represents them. Why do you treat the poor and the elderly any differently?" I subsequently received a memo from my supervisor that stated that I was incompetent and that I could not frame a legal issue. So I sued legal aid for defamation. I eventually lost my lawsuit due to a technicality called a qualified supervisory privilege. A more positive outcome was that our legal team successfully represented every Chinatown tenant, stopped every single tenant eviction, and helped encourage the City to build over five hundred affordable apartments in Chinatown into which displaced residents would relocate directly. After my forced exit from legal aid, I collected unemployment, about $60 a week. My wife was still in school so we lived off savings and unemployment checks for over a year.

After the Hawai'i Supreme Court decisions overturned the Chinatown eviction orders, the city and the private landlords became more cooperative in working with PACE. The nature of PACE has changed from stopping evictions to tenant governance and the preservation of the quality of life in Chinatown, such as preventing Mayor Jeremy Harris from subverting a 1980 City Council Master Plan Amendment and over sixteen years of democratic participation by all concerned citizens by building a gymnasium and commercial space on the Smith-Beretania parking lot.

I'd like to see a more just society, where the have-nots have a greater say and have democratic control of their communities. It's outrageous that the mayor and others try to cram government projects upon command. Rents are so high in Hawai'i that people cannot have their fair share of the pie, and people cannot afford to own their own home, much less be forced to pay unreasonably high rents. Hawai'i once was an independent nation in which the Hawaiian queen was forcibly overthrown by U.S. Marines. The plantations next concentrated wealth and power in a very few hands. Today, the faces have changed but the real standard of living has drastically declined since the time I was a kid.

When I grew up in 'Āina Haina, a working class neighborhood, my father worked one and a half jobs to support our family of six. My mother stayed home to care for the family during our early elementary school years. There were times when we had no lunch money. There were times when we played on a baseball team, but could not afford to buy a baseball team uniform. So we grew up relatively poor. On the other hand, everybody else was in the same boat, struggling while moms were staying home taking care of the family, and dads went to work. Yet, our parents taught us to tell the truth, do your best at all times, work hard, and to fight against injustices and inequality. My mom would frequently remind me to "Never *ever* let any one walk all over you. You're just as good and smart as anyone else, including haoles."

It's difficult for us today to afford to buy a house in the neighborhood we grew up in, in which the homes are now at least forty to fifty years old. To buy that home today would cost over half a million dollars. We would need $100,000 for the down payment. We're talking about $120,000 a year income, which we do not have. We're not talking about preschool tuition. We're not talking tuition for private school, if your child attends private schools. We're not talking about saving for college or retirement. We are talking about the mortgage cost only, in the neighborhood I grew up in. Not many families in Hawai'i earn that much money, even with two people working. So you have an exodus of people out of Honolulu proper, away from the neighborhoods where they grew up, moving out as far as possible to Mililani, Ewa Plains, or to Makakilo. And still in these places, the median cost of a home is $350,000!

Children today remain longer in their parents' home because rents are so high. Families are doubling and tripling up. Both husband and wife are working, sometimes two and three jobs, often leaving the children at home alone because they can't afford after-school daycare. As a result, Hawai'i has more social problems, more juvenile delinquency, more intra-family conflict, more drinking, more drug use, and more family violence than in the past. An increasing number of Hawai'i residents are relocating to the continental United States. Hawai'i's cost of living is one of the highest in the nation, and the trend is that an increasing number of people are relocating to California, Oregon, Washington, Florida, and the Southwest.

I feel that my daughter will not be able to live and work here, unless she's highly skilled as a professional in business for herself, or as a professional proficient in information and technology management. If you work in the type of jobs that my parents held, you're going to constantly struggle just to survive. My father worked as a sheet metal worker. He grew up on the Big Island receiving just a fourth grade Japanese school education. My mother graduated from McKinley High

School and worked as a secretary. Within the next two to three decades, the better paying jobs, which are already very few, will disappear. Even in state government, the wages are slowly becoming less and less livable on. I feel that Hawai'i's future will become more and more bleak.

Real estate is down, tourism is erratic, and the construction industry is dying. State government is saying that because of the decrease in tax revenues they're cutting back in all areas, including the university. What area of the economy is going right? In the last decade, there was over-speculation in real estate, and tourism created a false sense of security that Hawai'i could cater to the rich and be recession proof. Hawai'i is going into a tailspin, like southern California did, and economic recovery is years away.

Due to the high cost of living in Hawai'i, you can't afford your monthly mortgage, your children's private school tuition, caring for your elderly parents, and saving for your retirement all at the same time. Even the professionals—bankers, doctors, and lawyers—have to make difficult economic choices. Although professionals still earn a decent income, what happens to people who don't have a college education, or don't have needed technical skills? What happens to those who only have a high school education, and have to work at McDonald's or Jack in the Box? The median rent in Hawai'i for a two-bedroom apartment averages a thousand dollars a month. The minimum wage in Hawai'i, at six, seven dollars an hour, for an employee of a fast-food place or in a hotel totals only about a thousand dollars a month!

Hawai'i may become only a location for wealthy retirees and businesspeople.

I think the trend is that way.

My forefathers, as Chinese immigrants, fled China and came to the United States because conditions were intolerable in China. Now people are starting to leave Hawai'i. It's a brain drain. The people with the most skills have options and can move. Other less-skilled residents who have family here want to stay because they don't know how to, or don't want to, live on the mainland. They don't know how to survive in a different environment.

I'll give you a personal example from my family. My brother graduated from college and moved from Hawai'i to Los Angeles because he had a better job offer as a computer programmer: one-third more salary than he was making here and excellent fringe benefits. He was laid off, so he returned home. He worked for a while for a large local medical services company before quitting. For over nine months he searched unsuccessfully for work.

Nobody's hiring. People in Hawai'i are either unemployed or under-employed. The wages are a lot lower, while the cost of living is much higher. But Hawai'i is a microcosm of what will happen, or is happen-ing, in many other areas. In a capitalist economy, multinational corpo-rations use massive layoffs, job insecurity, and weak unions to maximize profits. Economic problems are occurring throughout the United States, not only in Hawai'i.

In the Hawai'i legislature, Asian Americans and haoles are in posi-tions of power. But when you look at who really controls Hawai'i in terms of economic power, it's the major, multinational corporations along with a handful of large land-based Hawai'i estates. The real power of these multinational corporations has moved from Hawai'i to other areas where the decisions are made to lay off people and close plantations. Those decisions are made very easily, without concern for the people of Hawai'i who have sacrificed their blood, sweat, and tears for the ungrateful multinational corporations.

In Hawai'i, people have learned that you have to coexist. I think it stems from the plantation owners dividing the Filipinos and the Japa-nese and the Chinese into their separate camps as a divide-and-conquer strategy. The field workers realized that you have to join together in order to fight for better working conditions and joined the ILWU. Dis-crimination in Hawai'i is a lot more subtle than in other places. Posi-tions of power for Native Hawaiians, Samoans, Tongans, Fijians, Filipinos, and Afro-Americans are rare. In Hawai'i today, haoles and Asian Americans are in positions of power, and the rest are the have-nots. Most of Hawai'i's prime hotels and office buildings are owned by multinational corporations.

Do you think this might spark more political organizing?

I think it becomes more difficult to organize against a landlord that does not have their main office in Hawai'i. In the early Chinatown cases, it was real easy. We could visit the local landlord's home and picket on a Sunday morning, which can be very, very persuasive. When your landlord is a multinational corporation with headquarters in Cleveland, Ohio, how do you picket their headquarters? You can picket their Honolulu office, which may be on the twenty-fifth floor in a build-ing housing dozens of other businesses. But it isn't very effective.

Activists need to become increasingly skilled in gathering information and finding systematic pressure points in the technological age. For the last five years, as Hawai'i chapter president, I've been pushing for the National Lawyers Guild to organize nationally and internationally, using computers and modems to coordinate strategy and tactics. Unfortunately, the far right, the fascists, and the white supremacists have effectively coordinated their strategy and tactics with computers, deciding to meet on a certain day and time, in a certain place, and viciously attack and beat up nonwhites.

During the 1970s there were many activists who traveled statewide in support of community struggles and workplace struggles, flying from one community to the next. If bulldozers came, people would join together and link arms to form a human picket line. Now, you have to travel across the nation or even internationally to show solidarity, and it's very expensive from Hawai'i. We have to find better ways of organizing, using whatever limited resources we have.

When you organize locally and nationally, the multinationals move to foreign countries. So you have to encourage labor unions, organizing in other lesser developed nations, like the Philippines, Thailand, Korea, Taiwan, China, and Southeast Asia. The history of imperialism shows that multinationals will relocate to the area in which labor costs are the cheapest so that profits can be maximized. Labor organizers in the Marcos-led Philippines, South Korea, Singapore, Thailand, and Chile are often jailed and sometimes executed. Hawai'i lost the pineapple canning plants to the Philippines and Thailand. The multinationals just shut down and moved everything abroad. What can you do as a community labor activist when the multinationals flee abroad? The only thing they can't move is land.

We've got a tremendous task ahead of us and hard economic times are going to become even harder. There's no question about it in my mind. Both my wife and myself have advanced degrees. When my folks were growing up, the difference was that there were options for people who did not have the advantages of wealth or education. The reason my mom didn't go to college was because my grandparents couldn't afford it. She always dreamed of attending college, but at least there were good-paying jobs that allowed my parents to raise a family of six. In today's society, it's even more difficult.

If my ten-year-old daughter wanted to attend a private college, by the time she is eighteen her education would cost us $40,000 to $60,000 per year. How can you save $40,000 to $60,000 per year for four plus years, pay the mortgage, take care of your parents, and save for retirement? It's impossible, unless you're making megabucks. How much money do you need to live a middle-class lifestyle in Hawai'i? Then I remind myself, wait a minute, most people don't have your education and skills. Most people aren't as adaptable and flexible. So what does the future hold for the grassroots community of the poor and less-skilled working people in Hawai'i?

As for organizing in the future, we activists are hardworking, caring people willing to confront unscrupulous landlords and bureaucratic government officials who don't seem to care about the average citizen. Usually, several working-class mothers will rise to the occasion and say, "No! We will not put up with these oppressive conditions anymore. Let's organize together for a more democratic, more humane, and more just society—a society where material goods are distributed on the basis of human needs."

Ed Rampell

A forty-year-old freelance journalist and resident of the Waiʻanae area. In the photograph, Ed *(right)* interviews Archbishop Desmond Tutu.

I may be the only full-time, working journalist in Hawaiʻi that concentrates on reporting mainly on Pacific Island subjects and issues. I'm the *Pacific Islands Monthly* correspondent in Hawaiʻi. I also report for the Australian Broadcasting Corporation and its overseas shortwave service called Radio Australia. I freelance on sovereignty-related subjects and on travel, culture, and politics of the Pacific.

I also have freelanced with ABC's "20–20" and did an investigative program called "The Puzzle of Palau." There was a State Department campaign to keep it off the air. We proved that three boys who were convicted of assassinating the president of Palau—Haruo Remeliik— were framed-up political prisoners. Within two weeks of the program being broadcast in July 1987, the Supreme Court of Palau concluded that these boys should never have been charged with this crime and that this should serve as a lesson to this new developing nation as to how *not* to prosecute criminal cases in the future. Subsequently, the Australian Broadcasting Corporation and I collaborated on a ninety-minute, two-part documentary on Palau with Jeff Parrish, who is a top correspondent in Australia. We helped to prove who did assassinate the president of Palau. The tapes that Jeff Parrish did in Palau had Palauan prisoners state that the minister of state in Palau, John O. Ngiraked— who got into power after President Remeliik was killed—did a solicitation for homicide on the president. These tapes were made available to the U.S. Congress. The General Accounting Office investigated Palau. Charges were lodged against Mr. Ngiraked, he was found guilty, and he's not been released on appeal.

I also worked on an Australian Broadcasting Corporation TV segment for a program called "Foreign Correspondent." It was an exposé of the Hawaiian sovereignty movement. They talked about colonization. They didn't mince words. They presented interviews with such people as Bumpy Kanahele, Mililani Trask, grassroots Hawaiians, Americans descended from missionaries, and so forth. While the announcer talks about Hawaiians charting their own course, we see Hawaiians out at sea in an outrigger canoe. I was the local liaison in Hawai'i who worked closely with the crew. They did a great job.

I've written a lot on sovereignty. One of these stories was the November 1992 cover story in *Pacific Islands Monthly*. I did historical research on the coup of January 1893: an hour-by-hour description of what happened, culminating with the last statement that the Hawaiian nation is overthrown. Then I did a contemporary piece, interviewing a lot of the activists. I had a premonition that something big was going to take place at the time of the anniversary date of the overthrow. It turned out that it was the largest political demonstration in the history of Hawai'i.

There's a lot of revisionist history going on in terms of what actually happened in 1893. Being a journalist, I have been trained to report all viewpoints—what's traditionally called objective journalism. Hayden Burgess had been saying for a long time that the reason why the queen surrendered without a fight was because the Americans invaded with high-tech weapons of the day and superior forces. In my independent investigation, I found that the Hawaiian military and police force outnumbered the invading marines and haole businessmen. Also, the military of Hawai'i *did* have Gatling guns and artillery. So, there *was* the basis for a fight. In my piece I pointed out that it was a huge tactical error not to fight. In my interviews with Mililani Trask and Bumpy Kanahele, they both said that this was a mistake. We now know that the queen's tactic to force America to arbitrate did not work in terms of restoring an independent nation of Hawai'i. Hawai'i will never be liberated until the Hawaiians and their allies come to the appropriate conclusions about the events of 1893.

How did you come to Oceania?

When I was five years old, the first movie I ever saw was *South Pacific*. I grew up in New York City, which should be enough said about why anybody would come to the Pacific Islands. *(Laughter.)* I was a product of the New York left. I was a revolutionary. I tried to overthrow the system, but instead the system overthrew me. So, I decided to get the system out of my system.

When I graduated from Hunter College in 1976 with a major in cinema, I looked around and said, "Wow, where's the revolution? Looks like the Age of Aquarius is experiencing technical difficulties in ascending." I saw that people weren't going to make New York and America a better place in the immediate future; that it was going to get a lot worse. I decided to find my paradise somewhere else.

I got a job as a film distributor for New Line Cinema, my entrée to the petite bourgeoisie and ticket to big money. I quickly found out, working in business, that everything I had been saying as a student radical about capitalism was absolutely true. On my first payday I told the secretary I was going to lunch. Instead of that, I cashed my check, went to see my travel agent, and left for Tahiti on the longest lunchbreak known in human history. I had this fantasy about the South Pacific: there had to be something out there better than America. On my second day there, I decided to spend the rest of my life in the Pacific Islands. I always had this hunch that [people weren't] destined to be miserable, functional neurotics. In Tahiti people laughed a lot. Tahiti validated my sneaking suspicion that human happiness was possible on this earth.

Then I saw the other side of the coin: the besmirching and tainting of this paradise. Right away I started saying in French to Tahitians, "Push the French into the sea." I started speaking for independence. In 1977, Charlie Ching and Tahitian terrorists were accused of a series of bombings and political murders. Apparently, I was somehow linked with that. Possibly for this reason, and others, the French government wouldn't let me stay in Tahiti, so I moved on to American Samoa. That commenced an oceanic odyssey that has taken me to over 100 islands in Polynesia, Micronesia, Melanesia, and Indonesia. This has given me a real regional oceanic overview which very few reporters have. I became an expatriate covering social movements in the Pacific and traveling throughout the Pacific. I traveled to a lot of islands where English was the main language of the region. Often I was in places like Palau where there was state-sponsored terrorism against the left and I would be the only person who spoke correct English and would have the courage to tell the truth.

What have you concluded about the Pacific?

I learned that Pacific Islanders are just like all other ordinary human beings and they have lots of problems. With the possible exception of the Caribbean, it's the last region on earth to be still dominated by colonialism. There was a myth—the "Pacific way"—that these islands were different and so remote from the rest of the world that they could evolve in their own cooperative way between East and West. In some ways that's been given the lie. Through improved mass communications and transportation and the interpenetration of capital into the region, it's become more and more a part of the outside world. I think the rest of the world will greatly impact upon Oceania. We're in a period of great upheaval. Great social explosions have begun. We saw what happened in Tiananmen Square [China] in 1989, and then Eastern Europe. The peoples' power and pro-democracy movement will spread throughout Oceania as well.

If Stalinist Russia could allow the Baltic republics to become independent, then why can't it be conceptualized that democratic America's "Baltic republics" in Hawai'i and Micronesia can also become independent like they were for thousands of years before Captain Cook "honored" us with his presence here? I think that Hawai'i will become independent. Many other Pacific Island societies are nominally independent, but they are economically dependent. Perhaps they are neocolonies. But I think independence will be found in a loose confederacy of equals. I don't want Hawai'i to become the king of that. I think there will be big upheavals in Hawai'i and a lot of violence. Kiana Davenport has already written a novel called *Shark Dialogues* in which she predicts guerrilla warfare and armed struggle in Hawai'i. A revolution has gone on in Bougainville, a big island that's trying to split off from Papua New Guinea. There were the coups d'état in Fiji. There were two presidential deaths by mysterious gunshot wounds in Palau, and so on. We have all these problems in the Pacific. The Pacific should be stripped of the paradisiacal image of yore, and should be seen for what it is today: a group of underdeveloped developing nations [that] are still suffering from the yoke of a nineteenth-century type of colonialism.

Now, the history of all history is the history of class struggle. There's no reason why the Pacific is exempt from that. For present purposes, I'll define Oceania as Polynesia, Micronesia, and Melanesia, but not Australia. The dominant ethnic group in Oceania is Black people, or Melanesians. White people constitute the second largest ethnic group. I'm not sure if Polynesians or Asians are the third-largest ethnic group. The class issue is very important and very deep in the Pacific. In certain cases there is a tradition of elite privilege, coming from divine right and monarchy. This has led to great problems of democratization in places like Fiji. Tonga has a pro-democracy movement against a somewhat constitutional divine right monarchy.

In Hawai'i, the class issue is extremely important. We have to look at the overall sovereignty movement. Hawaiians are about 20 percent of the population if you include people with 1 percent Hawaiian heritage. What is the conception of the movement? Is it one of the minorities competing for pieces from an ever-shrinking pie; the crumbs from the system? Or is there another way to look at it? Should all the different groups get together and bake a new pie that will feed everybody? The overwhelming majority of people in Hawai'i—Hawaiian and non-Hawaiian—have common class interests. Just because one is white or Japanese does not mean that person has a deferment from high rents or exemption from high taxes.

The history of Hawai'i since the late 1880s bears out the fruit of the strategy of multiracial unity along class lines. Captain Wilcox was the great hero of the Hawaiians because he fought and had courage. He's the one who people should be looking up to. Indeed, just recently a statue of him was finally put up in downtown Honolulu. After his aborted red-shirt uprising in the late 1880s was suppressed by U.S. marines, he turned to the electoral arena. His Hawaiian Party united with a party of working-class whites. They won half or more of the seats in the legislature, which shows the power of multiracial, multiethnic unity. This gave the impetus to Queen Lili'uokalani to go ahead and promulgate the new constitution that would disempower the "haoleocracy" of the business interests and would re-empower the Hawaiians and the common people. It's interesting that a monarch had a more democratic program than the business interests that were backed by the great democracy, America.

We see it more clearly and it's more celebrated in the twentieth century when the labor unions stopped representing separate ethnic groups and became one big union. It should be added that the dirty little history and secret of Hawai'i was that the Communist Party played an enormous role in the social transformation of Hawai'i. The Communist Party probably had more success and influence in affecting people's daily lives than in any other state in the union. Proof of this is the John Wayne movie called *Big Jim McCain* in which Wayne comes out from Washington as a member of HUAC [House Un-American Activities Committee] to bust the "red ring."

The job is not finished. We have a new establishment now. The real question is, Will that job be finished? The Hawaiian sovereignty movement is the wild card in Hawai'i. It's the only movement now that won't play by the rules. Will the sovereignty movement work out unity in its own ranks? It's ridiculous to talk about unity with non-Hawaiian allies if they can't unite Hawaiian activists and the Hawaiian community per se.

In the context of the competitive arrogance of capitalism, the bourgeois individualism, the private-property mentality, some feel "it's *my* revolution and you can't play with it, it's *my* sovereignty and it belongs to me, it's *my* nation." I hope people can be able to put that aside for a new self, draw upon their higher angels, and see the *common* interest, instead of that which divides us. Whites and others in Hawai'i must be organized through a higher consciousness, not to be pro-sovereignty just because they're nice guys and have a social consciousness, but because it's in *their* interests; because the military owns 25 percent of O'ahu and *their* rents go up because of that. What does that military budget mean to *them?* How is that hurting *them?* Everything in the country is being cut back except the military. How does that affect *you?* How does that affect the Hawaiians? Where's the common ground? If there was some way to bring people together on common ground, while respecting the distinctiveness and rights of all oppressed minorities— particularly the Hawaiians—then we'll have the basis of an independent Hawai'i.

What we may be approaching is a co-opted, sold-out form of pseudo-sovereignty like the state-within-a-state model—an illegal entity within an illegal entity. We're in danger of a counterintelligence, [a] comprehensive, coordinated campaign and conspiracy to destroy Hawaiian sovereignty by dividing people.

Come now, brothers and sisters, we can do better, and we must do better. We *will* do better in aloha, by loving each other and identifying who the real enemy is instead of pointing fingers at one another. The Big Five is still alive and owns huge pieces of land. We must know our friends and know our enemy. We must come together as one, respecting our differences, while uniting around our common interests.

LAND AND ENVIRONMENT

The eyes of the casual tourist approaching the Honolulu International Airport are first drawn to the sea, the mountains, and the lush vegetation, for these parts of the landscape are dramatic and brilliant. Very quickly the eyes are brought to focus on man-made things like buildings, roads, wharfs, monuments, and playgrounds. For most of the 6 million tourists (150,000 on an average day) that come to Hawai'i each year, these man-made things remain the major focus during their brief stay. *And that is what the leaders of Hawai'i's most profitable industry—tourism—want and promote.* Tourists are momentarily awed by the natural splendor of Hawai'i in those few moments they are shuttled to some lookout or beach. But it would be rare indeed to come across a briefing by a tour guide that described how the land and other resources of Hawai'i were transformed from an earlier pristine splendor into a gaudy, rich/poor tourist haven. Similarly, you never come across a sign in Waikīkī that says, "The land upon which this hotel sits was stolen from the Kanaka Maoli."

The Hawaiian archipelago consists of 6,423 square miles (4,113,000 acres) on eight major and 124 minor islands. There are 750 miles of coastline. Current official statistics on land ownership show that about 38 percent is publicly owned (U.S., State, county), while private ownership is 62 percent. Statistics by land use indicate that 35 percent is forest land (1,419,000 acres), 26 percent is grazing land (923,000 acres), 10 percent is cropland (347,000 acres), 4 percent is urban/built-up land (157,000 acres), and 21 percent has miscellaneous use (852,000 acres). Nearly 50 percent of the land—1,956,000 acres—is zoned agricultural

(*The State of Hawaii Data Book: A Statistical Abstract, 1993–1994* [Honolulu, 1995]).

A quick look at these data should lead even the casual reader to the conclusion that Hawai'i should have food self-sufficiency in nearly every category of fruit, vegetable, and meat. And our speakers that follow in this chapter state that nearly every food that is needed could be produced in Hawai'i. The fact is, some 80 percent of food consumed in Hawai'i is imported from thousands of miles away. The milk one buys in the supermarket, where prices are easily 30 percent higher than on the continental United States, is bottled in Los Angeles. Even pineapples, the *one crop* you might think would be plentiful and cheap in Hawai'i, is now being imported from Florida. From the resident consumer's perspective, it makes no sense.

Certain universal principles underlie the subject matter of this chapter. First, the source of raw value and economic wherewithal is land (and waters). Next, the ownership and control of land (and waters) is the prerequisite to power. Finally, the prudent use of land (and waters) is essential to the quality of life of the people. These principles are well known by indigenous peoples and left-progressive activists throughout the world. The principles shape social awareness and political consciousness. In Hawai'i, land and environment provide the motor that drives social protest and activism.

Land ownership or control is decisive in determining the availability and distribution of food, housing, and other amenities, as well as cultural dignity. From the early history of the Islands to the present, land has been a magnetic force that has driven kings, chiefs, capitalists, and the common folk. As noted by George Cooper and Gavan Daws, "There never was a ruling group in the history of Hawai'i that did not base its power on land" (*Land and Power in Hawai'i* [University of Hawai'i Press, 1990], 446). In the last several hundred years, the expropriation of the Hawaiian peoples' land for military or market purposes has been a major scandal.

In 1848, during the reign of Kamehameha III, the Protestant missionaries orchestrated the Great Mahele (land division), which for the first time permitted private ownership of land, principally by the haole. In 1893, land control was instrumental in the overthrow of Queen Lili'uokalani by the haole, and it was the central reason for the 1898 annexation of Hawai'i by the United States. Land continued to be the crucial factor in 1959 when the people of Hawai'i were manipulated into statehood. And land is the cardinal reason for the development of the sovereignty movement. Its escalation began in the early 1970s when the Bishop Estate evicted pig farmers in Kalama Valley on Oʻahu in favor of residential development by Kaiser-Aetna.

The Hawaiian Islands have served the strategic interests of the United States for over one hundred years, while enriching U.S., British, and other haole capitalists through their investments in profitable export crops. Since the end of World War II they have been a paradise for foreign investors—principally American and Japanese—in luxury resorts, retirement housing, and a thriving tourist industry. The best of Hawaiʻi's land has been made into a commodity to be bought and sold by merchants and the rich. Rather than an undefiled beauty spot that nurtures its inhabitants, the land has become a tawdry illustration of commerce.

The land and waters of Hawaiʻi have become increasingly contaminated by misuse, overuse, and the various forms of trash and pollutants that distinguish the consumer society. The gist of these unwelcome trends was presented in a useful series called "Aloha ʻĀina" (meaning "love for the land") that appeared in several March 1994 issues of *The Honolulu Advertiser*. Nearly every caring person in Hawaiʻi deplores the direction in which things are going. More than eighty years ago, well-meaning and not-so-well-meaning officials and entrepreneurs began a "modernization" process that altered the natural ecology. The complex, multilevel forests in the upper lands experienced both commercial cutting and nutritional starvation. Natural streams were diverted into ditches and tunnels to serve the thirst of growing populated areas, sugar and pineapple plantations, resort hotels, and golf courses. Soil began to erode. Silt and mud settled into unnatural places and disturbed the natural balance. Former wetlands and native fishponds were filled. Cast-off agricultural chemicals, solvents, and fuels found their way into the natural water supply and eventually into the surrounding ocean. Beaches and reefs were altered by dredging and the construction of concrete walls. Both freshwater and saltwater fish are nearly gone. Aggressive "foreign" plants began to replace native plants. There were invasions of insects introduced by tourists, planes, and ships. Increasing amounts of industrial, consumer, and nuclear waste came from greater consumption by a burgeoning population and the latest "mature" military technology, with no safe techniques of disposal and storage. Litter, noise, and congestion abound in the built-up areas.

The above scenario reads like a modern industrialized, urbanized area anywhere but in a Pacific island paradise. We do not mean to be overly dramatic nor do we wish to appear as radical return-to-nature advocates. We know that population and technology changes cause some inevitable environmental problems for which few of us know the answers. But we became convinced, like thousands upon thousands of locals, that Hawai'i is on an ecological collision course if present trends continue. We are aware that ecological destruction from deforestation, soil erosion, and chemical pollution is a worldwide problem. We know also that, even with a militant environmental movement today, the natural ecology of planet Earth is in dire straits due to the unrestrained monetary appetite and growth obsession of free enterprise. With the right wing's ascendancy to power; with continuing deregulation, privatization, and to-the-end intercapitalist competition for markets; and with the escalating thrust of modern technology—all we can expect in the future is continued environmental degradation, unless the *people* protest and resist.

For many years, the Kanaka Maoli and left-progressive people in Hawai'i have resisted the expropriation of land for irrational use as well as the clear and present danger posed to the environment. In one way or another, nearly everyone in our interviews, both Kanaka Maoli and non-Kanaka Maoli, thought that the land-environment question was extremely salient in determining the quality of life and politics of Hawai'i. Some of our interviewees and many other locals are doing the research and analysis that is needed for us to understand the nature of the land-environment problem, and the grievous damage being done to health and well-being. Some fine groups like the Sierra Club Legal Defense Fund and Life of the Land and some hearty pro bono attorneys are doing yeoman work. The strong *movement* that is needed, we feel, is already rooted in activist Hawai'i, but it must develop further and more comprehensively in direct proportion to the gravity of the situation.

The speakers we have collected in this section are land-environment activists of the highest order. Individually, they apply their skills to the pertinent technical issues and organizational matters in the complex land-environment issue. Gigi Cocquio, rejecting the role of Catholic priest, learned how to be a farmer, conservationist, and youth organizer, and now leads the cutting-edge Hoa Aina O Makaha nuclear-free preserve in Wai'anae. John Kelly's talents in graphic arts and environmental instruction, joined by a dynamic organizing style and sense of struggle, have been put in service to the movement for decades. Guy Nakamoto represents the best in grassroots organizing through his work in the Waiāhole-Waikāne struggles, in such organizations as Life of the Land, and in such informal gathering places as McDonalds. Activist-scholar Marion Kelly—without bravado or pretension—applies her historical, anthropological talents efficiently to the needs of the movement. George Cooper *(Land and Power in Hawai'i)* quietly uses his legal training and strong sense of social commitment in the defense of activists, while applying his research proficiency to uncovering the "mysteries" of the political economy of land in Hawai'i.

These activists are only our sample of Hawai'i's land-environment cadres, but they illustrate the resolve and comprehensiveness of this most fundamental movement. When they join with the thousands of others who are dedicated to land and environment reform, they will become a powerful body and a force to be reckoned with. When the land-environment movement joins with the indigenous peoples' movement, a massive and unstoppable force may well be forged.

Gigi Cocquio

An environmentalist, farmer, teacher, and leader of Hoa Aina O Makaha in the Wai'anae area; in his late forties.

My daily work is with a lot of people, from children to adult. Our organization, Hoa Aina O Makaha, does community organizing. We try to look for different alternatives. We give people a chance to come together and talk to each other and exchange their experiences so we can learn from each other and we can have an impact here and also outside Hawai'i.

I come from a small farm village in Italy called Uggiate next to the city of Como, up in the north close to Switzerland. When I was eleven years old, I entered the seminary to become a priest. Well, I stayed in the seminary though they tried a few times to kick me out for some reason. I went through quite conservative training even though Vatican II happened at the time. Things really were not changing too fast; they're *still* not changing.

I was ordained in 1968 and joined a missionary institute in Milan. It was called Pontifical Institute for Foreign Missions (PIME). I wanted to go to work in Brazil in the Amazon, but there were some problems there, so I couldn't go. They kept me in Italy for two years to do some vocational work.

The time was the 1960s when people were starting, even in Italy, to leave the conservative Church and look for some different directions. There were spontaneous groups that were forming outside of the

Church, but still with some religious and spiritual foundations. They were the rebels. I worked with these groups, mainly people from universities, and I liked it. For two years, we organized different things, mainly around the Third World. At the time, the Third World was a big eye-opener, because all the ideas started to come out of how the First World was exploiting the Third World countries—things that we didn't know before.

My work was supposed to bring people into the seminary to become priests. So after two years of nothing, my superiors asked me to make a decision where I wanted to go, out of Italy. I had some friends in Africa working with the leprosy patients, and I wanted to go to Cameroon.

Of course, they don't send you where you like, so they sent me to the Philippines. I had to buy a map and find out where the Philippines were. That was my preparation. After spending nine months in England to learn some English, I went to the Philippines in 1971. I was brought to Tondo to a small house, as small as this room *(gestures),* where three of us lived in a squatter area.

Tondo may be the largest slum area in Southeast Asia. At the time there were two hundred thousand people living in this slum area. Oh, it's incredible! The first thing, of course, was to learn the language. I was living in the community, so that's how I learned Tagalog faster than English because I could hear people talk and, oh, they correct you and everything. It was really fun.

After '71, there was a lot of protest, a lot of uprising in the Philippines, in Manila. A lot of young people, mainly students of the University of the Philippines, were leading a lot of protest against the government, against the Americans, against the foreign interventions. It was really exciting. There were a lot of things going on. I was very new, so I didn't know anything. I don't think I had a direction. I knew I had to do something and my heart was there, you see. I mean, that's why I became a priest, so we can help each other. And that's all I knew. I didn't have any analysis or anything. As soon as I finished the language school and was assigned to this area, I really didn't know what to do.

So going around, you see all these shanties falling apart, and you say, Well, the first thing you might do is to build something. So we started to help the people to rebuild their shanties. After we did one, two, three, ten shanties, then hundreds, thousands of people started to come in. I said, "No, no, it doesn't work."

People in the Philippines need some capital, like to sell fish, to sell vegetables, just to have some income. A couple of pesos a day comes in.

And they borrow from other people called "five sixes." They borrow five pesos and at the end of the day they have to return six. If one day it is raining or there's a typhoon, they don't sell, so they're lost. So we tried to help them with this, but we were not organized, and that failed too.

As a priest, I was looking at the type of religion people were living. There was this old-fashioned stuff, like praying in front of the statues. I [thought], Oh no, this is a lot of superstition. I think we need some good religious education. So I asked the people, "What do you think if you have a Bible study?"

"Oh yeah, sure—why not?"

So the first night there were forty people. Where do you start from? You start from the first page of the Bible so you can go through it, and by the end everybody will know everything. The second night only twenty came; the third night, nobody. I thought it was my language or whatever, so I forgot it. So building houses wasn't working, preaching [wasn't working], so [I might as well] forget everything.

Martial law was declared in September 1972. People started to get arrested and put in jail. Things started to get very hot. That's when we started to look at things in a different way. We started to go house-to-house every night. In 5 acres you have probably fifteen thousand people. So you go to one house—you have three hundred people—[and] you start talking. What are the problems of this area? So the problems started to come out and also the feelings of the people: We cannot do anything with the government, we tried to get the water, we tried to get this, we tried to get that. Nothing! So with the help of a community organization group, we started to get people to go to the community and find out what were the common problems.

After one year of doing this, going around every night and trying to know people and know the problems, we started to organize around small problems. People went to the Department of Health and said, "Hey, we were almost killed in our place because under the house is all this stagnant water." So instead of one person, let's go [with] ten, fifteen, one hundred. They came later that afternoon to spray under the housing. It was a victory for the people, the first time that anybody in the government agencies answered their request.

Well, from there we went to area things. We didn't have water. We had to go collect water with the fifty-five-gallon drum, one mile away. Sometimes we had to pay for it. For three months, we went to the mayor's office in Manila asking for water. The mayor wouldn't come out and talk to the people. He would send out the secretary and the secretary would say to me, "Oh, the mayor wants to talk to you." I would always refuse. We were squatters too—we didn't have the water—but I'm not Filipino. He had to talk to the people.

One day, the mayor came out and talked to the people and promised to bring water—public faucets—to people in the area, and he did. Filipino people are very religious. We made a parallel with what is in the Bible and what was happening out there. When we got the water, the mayor and the bishop came to bless all the faucets. We had a celebration in the church. People brought buckets of water as gifts. The idea was, Christ said that if you give me a glass of water you give to one of the small children: Moses in the desert. We had a big victory. Water is very important for the people. Without food, you can survive for a while; without water, you're lost.

From there we went even bigger—to the land. At the time, [President Ferdinand] Marcos wanted to evict all the people from the area to sell the land. The land is close to the port area. Marcos wanted to sell the land to foreign investors for them to build their warehouses and stuff. We came together with another very strong people's organization in the same area. We joined forces and formed a coalition. In 1974, we had the first march under martial law. Five thousand people joined the march to protest this action. I was arrested that day. At first, Marcos refused to talk to the leaders, but that day was a really strong movement of people, so he finally agreed to talk to the leaders. He promised not to kick the people out, but to start to plan with the people. We put these promises on stones, and we put them like a monument in front of the church. A bishop came and blessed it. We had a big celebration.

The people's organization was using our small church for meetings because under martial law meetings were prohibited. Everybody came to the church. Sometimes there were four hundred people. I was a member of the steering committee, but I didn't have the right to vote. The people decided that I couldn't vote. They resented the Church leadership. Though they knew me and liked me very much, I was an authority, a priest, and a foreigner. I thought that was great because the people were really taking over. It was the same even in our Sunday masses. We never followed the books. Something would happen in the community, so we celebrated that. Somebody was arrested, so the mother, the brother, the sister would come and conduct the ceremony. When we had marches, some people would reflect on them. Our masses were three hours long because they were like having meetings. This was part of organizing. We got involved also with labor. The first strike happened in La Tondena at a liquor-making factory. That was the first factory that went on strike under martial law. Three hundred people were arrested. I was not at home that day, but my name was first on the lists of the police and the military.

In 1976, Imelda was going to kick everybody out who lived along the rivers and drainage areas in order to beautify Manila. These were all squatters. We formed a city-wide coalition—one million people. We went out and organized and trained other organizers. I was training a lot of the nuns who were becoming very radical. We had nuns and priests joining us in demonstrations. They were in fact protecting the people from the military.

One night all the community organizers in Manila were at our church. After we finished the meeting, the military were there outside. They followed some of the people home and arrested them. Some escaped; some were in my house. The military wanted to enter my house. They couldn't come in because there was an agreement with the Church and the military that nobody could enter the house of a priest without a permit from the bishop.

It was night already, not much light. We called back people from their shanties, and they converged on the church. We started to sing to confuse the military. And little by little, we took one or two of the organizers out of the house, and put them in the middle of a group of people who escorted them home. Finally, there was only one left, the tallest one. He was too tall to hide and the military wanted him. I hid him in the sacristy. A friend of mine, another priest, came with a car, gave him some different clothes, snuck him into the car, and left.

At ten o'clock, a colonel and a military chaplain knocked at the door: "Father Gigi, can we come in?"

I said, "Who are you?"

A voice said, "I am Colonel Brazil and I'm with Father Cruz."

"What do you want?"

"Well, we have been told that you didn't let our men come inside the house."

"Well, you make the rules, you follow the rules."

"But we have been told you are hiding some people."

So I said, "Come inside and look. If you find anybody, arrest them." Of course, they didn't find anybody, so they left.

Two days later, the military came back to the house. I saw them when my superior, who was at my house at the time, opened the door and began to leave. I waited for him to come back inside, but he didn't return. So I went out to check, and boom! This guy standing in front of the door said, "Are you Father Gigi?"

I said, "Yeah."

He turned to the chaplain who was there to recognize me. "Is he Father Gigi?"

"Yeah."

"Father Gigi, you are under arrest."

What were the charges?

One was political subversion. I didn't know what it meant. I guess subversion was anything that you were doing that the government didn't like. There was no explanation. The second charge was that I was training persons for the NPA (New People's Army).

They took us from the house to the immigration and deportation office. They read something in Tagalog—a prayer—and said, "Did you understand that?"

"Yeah."

"Did you make that prayer?"

I said, "No, I didn't." But it was a prayer, you know. Our prayers were kind of political, of course, and reflected the reality of the people.

Accompanied by two guards who were holding the passport, we were taken to the airport where they read the charges. They never gave us a copy of anything. We were deported to Italy because the Church collaborated with the military. The bishop of Manila, Bishop Sin, was the one who told the military. We were accused of being communists. We [only had on] pants, sandals, and tee-shirt—that's it.

So when we reached Italy, the reaction of the Church was really against us. In Italy you get good coverage from the extreme left to the extreme right in newspaper and TV: "Communist priest deported from a Catholic country." We did a lot of interviews with the media and showed what was really happening. My superiors in Rome got very upset because of all the details we were exposing. Things got worse and worse with the Church.

To make the story very short, I came to New York where there was another Maryknoll priest, Ed Gerlock, who was deported from the Philippines too, for the same reasons. John Witeck and John Grove invited us to Hawai'i. So we said, "Let's go to Hawai'i and continue to work with Filipinos." Eventually we came to Hawai'i, unwanted by the bishop of Hawai'i and unwanted also by the Maryknoll fathers in

Hawai'i. They didn't even have a room for us. Fortunately, there was this Filipino family who said, "Yeah, stay with us."

After one week, we contacted Jim Albertini and got involved with antinuclear work. Also, the State was kicking leprosy patients out of their facilities in Pearl City. So we got involved in that. At the same time, a parish in Kalihi asked us to do some work with the Filipinos there. That made the bishop very upset. We got involved with People Against Chinatown Evictions (PACE) and Hale Mohalu. We also were involved very much with the antinuclear movement.

After one year, we were asked to come to this parish in Wai'anae. I said, "Okay, but I don't want to live in the rectory." It didn't make sense to live there. The land was all abandoned, it was just bush, and it belonged to the Catholic Church. This Catholic nun, Sister Anna McAnany said, "We have to do something."

I said, "Yeah, okay, I want to live here."

So I started to live in this quonset. After a week, my friend Ed Gerlock also came and lived here.

My first sermon was on Hiroshima Day. On Saturday afternoon we did protests and a march at the West Loch [Pearl Harbor], where there are nuclear bombs. So, of course, my first sermon was about Hiroshima and the military, injustices like Chinatown, what was going on here in Wai'anae. The people started standing up; going out. Well, I thought the people were going out to take a pee, like they do in the Philippines. But they didn't come back. As soon as the first mass ended, oh, the phone calls and everything. So that was Saturday.

Sunday morning, my sermon was even worse—or better. Even more people left. On Monday, ooh, the bishop was furious. He had talked to the Maryknoll superior because people had complained. So I called the bishop on the phone and said, "Eh, let's be fair. Let's sit down and talk to the people who were at the church and see what I said." He said I had embarrassed the United States, the Church, the Maryknoll, everybody.

"What did I say? Just the truth, yeah?"

I was furious, so we really had a big fight on the phone. Some people also sent anonymous letters to immigration, so immigration came and visited me. They sent an Italian guy—smart, no?—who said, "You know, we have these letters, and in case you want to become an American citizen, you will have a hard time."

So I said, "Well, I don't want to become an American citizen; keep the letters."

I went back to Italy for a little while. When I returned to Hawai'i I couldn't come back to this farm because it belonged to the Church. But up in the mountains, there is another farm where a friend of mine, Eric Enos, started to restore all the ancient taro patches in Ka'ala. I started to work there with the young people from high school.

Eventually, I came back over here and we restarted this area. When we were putting down the first pipes for the water, Eric Enos, who is Hawaiian, looked over at the valley and said, "You know, Gigi, there is a *heiau*—a Hawaiian temple—in the valley, but we are not allowed to go and worship."

I said, "Eric, let's go and protest." He looked at me—he had a pipe in his hand—and he said, "We are protesting."

I said, "What do you mean, you are protesting? We are digging."

"No, we are protesting."

Finally, I understood. We were putting down the line for the water and we were going to start planting. We were going to start using this land, and to show that there are other ways.

I had to change my way of looking at organizing. You see, in the Philippines, it was this way: you go around, talk about this or that, organize a plan, go on a demonstration, whatever. Here, you have to build. I learned that you have to build a certain credibility. Also, I think that people look at the culture in a different way. The land is very important. To tell you the truth, I feel strange when I go to town for a demonstration because sometimes it seems like—how do you say— intellectual masturbation. There is no connection with the reality. We just started community organizing. It took a few years.

What's the difference in organizing in the Philippines and organizing in Hawai'i?

I think the socioeconomic situation is different. In Hawai'i, we have a lot of different races. You don't deal with one race. In the Philippines, you deal with Filipinos: one culture, one way of understanding things. Hawai'i is more complex. In the Philippines the people are really at the bottom. Lower than that, you cannot go. Here, they keep people on welfare. In Wai'anae here, from Nānākuli to Mākaha, there are 38 to 40 percent of the people on welfare. Many are indigenous people.

First, you try to deal with a style of life. Welfare is a style of life, like farming or being a doctor or professor. This is the third, fourth genera- tion of people on welfare. So it's really hard to change that. The second thing is that if you protest, if you do something against the government, maybe welfare is going to be cut off. So then what's going to happen? It's hard to organize that way. The situation is different in Hawai'i, so the way of organizing has to be different. Hawaiian people don't confront people usually. They try to talk things over. They can be very confrontational if they understand, but always with some kind of gentleness and kindness.

My experience as a priest and the experience with the land here at Hoa Aina are very much related. One day, a journalist came to write an article about the work that we are doing with the children. We were talking about the philosophy of the land. She looked at me, and said, "What are you?"

I said, "I am a farmer."

She said, "No!"

I said, "I do farming every day. I must be a farmer."

She said, "No. What are you?"

I said, "Well, I used to be a Catholic priest."

"Where is your church?"

She didn't understand. So she repeated the question. I just looked around, and finally she understood. She wrote something like this: "Gigi left the priesthood, but not what the priesthood stands for." And that was a compliment.

There was an older Quaker man who used to live over here. Nice guy. He's dead now. He used to work in Southeast Asia with his wife doing organizing and training. One day, he said, "Gigi, you are more priest now than before."

I said, "Whoa!" I'd like my mother to hear that. *(Laughter.)*

I never got permission from the Vatican to get out. They're supposed to release you. But this pope doesn't allow anybody to get out.

So I got married. My wife was married before, but got divorced. She had two kids, age twenty-one and eighteen. One is married and living outside. The other one is eighteen, living here, and working in an Italian restaurant. You don't see children of farmers doing the farming. *(Laughter.)* My wife and I have a son who is nine years old.

I came to Hawai'i with the intention of going back to the Philippines. I went back after Marcos was deported to Hawai'i, in 1986, and then two more times—in '87 and '88—to check on the possibility of working there. It would have been even more dangerous under Aquino than under Marcos. There was a lot of oppression of people and suppression of community organizing. There were a lot of killings, especially Church workers—more than under Marcos. When I went back in '88 I wanted to go to the place where I was living in Tondo. People were sent to tell me not to come to the area because it was very dangerous. They were arresting people left and right, young people disappearing, being found in a dump area.

The last time I went back to the Philippines was in 1991. I was asked to do some gardening work with some squatters in Caso City. I can go in and out now. I decided, well, I really have to put my mind at peace. It would be hard to come back to the Philippines. I would have to relearn everything. So maybe I should just continue this work in Hawai'i.

This February it will be fifteen years. We just got a twenty-five-year lease from the Church for one dollar a year. The leadership of the Church changed a few years ago. Things really have changed drastically.

Could you describe what you do here?

When we started this project, we never knew what was going to happen. Our idea was, let's plant something to produce food so everybody can eat. Things moved in a very interesting direction. It doesn't work for me to sit down and make a plan and try to fit things into the plan. We knew we had to take care of the land to produce food, but we didn't know how.

We started with these young people who had problems with the police, problems with drugs, problems with high school. Eventually, one of the quonsets in the back was used for a school. Every day they would come here and do some different things: gardening, agriculture, and stuff. We were farming just to produce things to sell. The school next door, after a few years, asked if some of the kids could come and make a garden. Sure, sure, sure. Finally, five years ago, the school asked me, "Would you like to work with all the kids in the school, all eight hundred?"

I said, "Yeah."

Of course, I never was a teacher. The first year was very trying, but it was nice. In the second year, things improved. The third year was even better. So now we are working with all the kids from the school. They come here every day and we do different things. I don't like the word teacher. The Hawaiian word for teacher is *kumu:* "the source." We learned together. I had to learn everything. The idea is to learn with the children how to take care of the land. In Hawaiian, there is no word for "use the land" or "work the land." There are only the words like *mālama,* "taking care," or *mālama o ka 'āina,* or *aloha o ka 'āina,* "take care of the land" or "love the land." 'Aina [without the macron] is not land. 'Ai is to eat, na is what feeds you: 'aina. The English dictionary defines land as the concrete part of the earth, so you can buy it and sell it. But what feeds you cannot be bought and sold. So the learning is not just planting, it's also respect for the land.

When the kids plant, you have them hold the seeds in their hands, and feel that they give life. They plant them in the ground, laying them down nicely without throwing them. Then they cover them. The kids say good night to the seeds. When we harvest, we say "thank you" to the land. And they take home the things that they plant and harvest: "Oh look, Mommy, Daddy, this is what I planted." There are problems in family relationships. A lot of the kids have very low self-esteem. But this is something that they did, so they're very proud of that.

Different grades do different things. Kindergarten is mainly watching the farm and planting the corn, beans, lettuce, and all this stuff. In the first grade, they learn what is needed for germination: the sun, the water, the wind; and they plant.

In the second grade, we do animals. We have all the animals in a mini-zoo over there, so they come every day to take care of them. They feed them and stuff, and we learn the habitat—whatever. We say that the animals have feelings, like if the rabbit is pregnant and it gets scared, it's going to have a miscarriage. So you make the kids understand this.

In the third grade, we do insects. We have the bees now, so we extract the honey and make candles. They take home the honey.

In the fourth grade, we do mainly Hawaiian plants. We start from the migration period and deal with the climate and this kind of thing. We talk of the ahupua'a, the Hawaiian community, from the mountain to the ocean; who was living there; what was growing in the upper land, lower land, and their different uses. We learn to understand that the Hawaiians were self-sufficient people. They were fantastic. We learn of the use of the water and why we don't have water now. We talk about the golf courses and tourists.

In the fifth grade, the first semester we do nutrition, so we plant gardens like vitamin A, vitamin C, protein, and carbohydrates. In the second semester, we go into self-sufficiency. Two kids have one garden to care for, so they have to learn how to work together. If they don't work together, they ruin everything. They learn all the organic stuff from composting. From there we go into the use and control of the land in Hawai'i. We have a big map with small squares. Each square is 1,000 acres. Sugar cane is 180,000 acres, pineapple is 35,000 acres, 5,000 acres in vegetables, 400 acres in taro. Seventy-five percent of the vegetables are imported to Hawai'i, when you can grow everything here. People lost the ability to grow anything.

We also have been teaching people to do gardening at their homes. In a four-square-foot garden you can raise food for two people. Everybody can do that, even if they don't have a big space. So the idea is to relearn how to plant things that we can eat. Yesterday, I was at an area where they just built twelve-by-sixteen-foot houses for the homeless. They have some land around and they asked me to go there and do some gardening. These are the things that really work. It's important to get individual families to raise maybe 20 or 30 percent of their own food. It changes the attitude toward food, toward growing things, toward the land, toward themselves. Self-sufficiency starts with the family.

We organize against the golf courses in Hawai'i. There are 127 of them and they use one million gallons of water a day. The owners say, "The water that is used for golf courses is not fresh water, it's brackish water, so don't complain." Brackish water is salt and fresh water together. With the same amount of water that's used in one day, we can build 6,000 fish tanks, and the fish grow perfectly. You can raise between 300, 400 tilapia fish for families. You don't even change the water every day; you change it every two, three, or four months.

You explain political economy through agriculture.

That's the idea. Here's a great example with the fifth graders. Two years ago, we had twenty-four gardens, with five, six kids in each garden. So I put in twenty-four hoses. I put down all the lines and everything. So during recess, all the twenty-four representatives would come to water their garden. Because they opened twenty-four faucets, the pressure was gone. One day, while watering the gardens, they looked at the golf course in the back and could see the water there going "whoosh!" Lots of pressure. They got upset. I said, "Let's sit down and talk about it." So the kids go home and tell their parents this stuff. The kids become the *kumu*, the source.

When we go into sixth grade, the first semester we do a kind of chemistry. This past two, three years we've been building fish tanks to raise fish. We always continue the discussion of self-sufficiency. Plus, I belong to another organization where I've been building big fish tanks with families. They can sell some of the fish. We teach the kids how to build these tanks. Then we go into alternative energy. We've been building solar ovens to cook in the sun, solar dryers, solar cells to produce electricity, solar water heaters. Some is very low technology, so it doesn't cost too much. There's always the same progression of self-sufficiency.

We discuss things like nuclear power and geothermal. From there we go into pollution. Of course, we have all the military polluting everywhere: Mākua, where they are bombing for practice; Lualualei, where they have these big towers that send out low-intensity electromagnetic radiation.

How do you handle class distinctions between the wealthy and poor?

We go into hunger in the world, but we start with hunger in Hawai'i, the homeless people and everything. When we do self-sufficiency, this comes out, of course. The kids really get very upset about the situation. They ask how can this thing happen? So we go into discussions of our government, who controls what, who the real power is, the multinational corporations.

When we talk about water, we have a fantastic game. We put drop-of-water paper cutouts on the table. We make like a musical chair. In the beginning, well, there are native plants and birds. The kids who are native plants or native birds go down the table and pick up the water. There's plenty of water left. The Hawaiian people come and plant the taro. So taro people—Hawaiian people—go around. Then the white people come and plant the sugarcane and pineapple. The water starts to become scarce. Then come golf courses and tourists. By the end, what's happened is that there is not enough for everybody. Everybody is trying to grab the water. And you know what happens? Sometimes the native people, the Hawaiians, or the taro, or the native birds, don't have water. If by chance somebody—one of the native plants—takes the water, we go there and we say, "Sorry, you cannot have the water. You have to give it to the tourist guy who came."

The interesting thing is that all these things go back to their families. Once a year we get a gathering of the families. We had four hundred people last year. That's the base for our community organizing. So we have been organizing against the golf courses behind here. Now we're organizing against the military. Our group is Hoa Aina O Makaha. Our role is trying to figure out strategies. Now we are in the process of letting the people take over, because otherwise it doesn't make sense. People have been forming their own groups and the leadership is coming out. The role of the community organizer is to facilitate this.

I think that all political movements should have a base on land or something that is concrete. Many times the activist people fight because of different ideologies. I say, "Look, let's go do weeding or something for eight hours under the sun when it's really hot. Afterwards, let's sit down and discuss ideology." I think it's very important that people come together and have a common base. It doesn't matter if you think one way or the other way, as long as you can work together on something. For me, the land is something that is unifying people.

Sometimes when I go to meetings they are too abstract for me. I just leave because it doesn't make sense. It's the everyday stuff, the everyday small thing, if there is a base, that is going to change something. The people we want to live together and to have a better life are the people who don't understand the big ideologies, the big words, the big meetings. But people understand if they see something growing, if they see something concrete, if they see something they can apply to their lives. And that changes the situation, the way of looking at things, even the economy.

John Kelly

A man in his youthful seventies and a longtime activist and spokesperson for Save Our Surf.

I'm the son of two talented and well-known artists in Hawai'i. My mother was a sculptress, my dad an etcher. We live in a house that was built in 1932. From childhood on, I was very much involved in ocean activities, ignorant of the world outside, and had very permissive parents. When I was about fifteen, my mom and dad said to me, "Wouldn't you like to apprentice yourself to your father to learn some of his art skills?" Like many teenagers today, I said, "Nah, I want to do something useful in life." Now it's a big regret of life; I'm doing a lot of political documents in which we need graphics, photographs, and drawings to bring otherwise boring speech to the forefront. I have since discovered how magnificently my parents enshrined the beauty and communal sharing culture of native Hawaiian people, to which we have committed our lives.

I went to Punahou School, Hawai'i's big privileged school, for seven years and then to Roosevelt High School. I don't know how my folks paid for that as poor artists. I graduated from Roosevelt in 1937 and then went to the university for three years until World War II broke out. Before the war, a friend of my parents offered to give me piano lessons. I took them and got really involved with Beethoven, Bach, and all the rest. After the war I went to Juilliard School of Music, graduated there in 1950, and then returned home to Hawai'i.

I was hired as director of the Palama Settlement Music School, which is something like the Henry Street Settlement in New York. It was founded in 1899 to focus on the needs of the youth in one of the most underprivileged working-class districts in Hawai'i. I worked there nine years until I was fired.

In 1959, we received an invitation to attend the fifth world conference against atomic and hydrogen bombs being held in Hiroshima. The invitation came from Dr. Kaoru Yasui, then the head and founder of the international antinuclear movement headquartered in Japan: Japan Council Against A- and H-bombs. There were 25,000 delegates from Japan and 119 from other countries. The other American there was Dr. Linus Pauling, the only person to have been awarded two Nobel prizes—one [in chemistry] and the second for his international work for world peace—a great man. At the end of the conference, I was photographed shaking hands with Dr. Yasui and the chairman of the Russian delegation, over the caption "Coexist or Die." That photograph and the Coexist or Die theme went all over the world. It epitomized the rising antiwar, antimilitarist movement.

When I got home, my boss said, "Give me your keys, you're fired!" I had raised the Palama Settlement Music School from seventeen students to four hundred students, specializing in all the ethnic dancing and ethnic folk songs of the working-class people here. It was a big success. The reason for the firing was that some Palama Settlement board members were big corporate landowners leasing land to the military. They didn't want a peace movement starting up in Hawai'i that would cause them to lose profits from lands being leased to the military.

I couldn't get a job any place here for five years, so I built surfboards and patented a new design board in order to feed my family. I finally got a job as educational director of the United Public Workers union, which was somewhat of a left-wing union here. I worked for them from 1965 to 1969 when the union garbage collectors were betrayed by the Legislature over a 3 percent wage increase. The union's leaders opposed the strike. So the garbage collectors carried out a wildcat strike on Mother's Day, 1969. At 6:00 A.M. on a Sunday, I was sitting on the floor with about sixty of the unit leaders from all over O'ahu, helping them to draw up their plans for a strike the next day. In walks the head of the union. He looked at me and said, "What are you doing here?"

I told him, "I'm taking notes for the next issue of our paper." When first hired, I was asked to start a newspaper for the union. We called it *The UPW Organizer,* which I published for almost five years. It was full of photographs and interviews on all sorts of union issues. It was a good paper, I was told. The union head pointed his finger at me and said, "You're fired."

This was the second time I got fired for doing something worthwhile. Well, we struck the next day. The State Capitol was filled with nearly two thousand striking public workers for the first time in Hawai'i's history. The strike lasted for a week in spite of union officers opposing the strike. The guys won the strike and got a 5 percent increase.

A few years later, I began teaching at the university in the Ethnic Studies Program, which had begun in 1969. The Ethnic Studies Program is unique. The University of Hawai'i was [founded] in 1907 as a technical institution to provide research on sugar and pineapple production, mainly pineapples, which were coming in strong after the turn of the century. Sugar was pretty well established since the late 1830s. But pineapple was new, and it needed all kinds of technical things having to do with soil fertility and all that.

In 1974 the State announced it was not going to fund the Ethnic Studies program any longer. So, a peoples' environmental movement that I had started in the 1960s—called Save Our Surf—got involved. We helped set up all kinds of student/faculty people's committees, with strong outside support, struck the university, and won. The Ethnic Studies Program is now a permanent part of the University of Hawai'i.

During the course of that struggle, something came up that disturbed a few of the scholars who were interested more in their careers than the program. They responded negatively to my suggestion that we go out in the street again and force the governor to come through with the $300,000 he had publicly promised to fund this program. I had suggested we take the entire 650 students and about 100 lab leaders and staff members down and occupy the governor's office.

Imagine: We had a population then of around eight hundred thousand people here, most of whom were indigenous peoples from the Pacific area who had been brought in to do manual labor on sugar and pineapple plantations and later other types of work. And the haole population was beginning to expand. Haole means foreigner in Hawaiian. It has come to mean white skin, but its basic derivation is representing the people from the outside.

We set up a class called the Economic History of Hawaii, which I taught. In 1977, we came to the point again where the administration reneged on their promise to fund the program. I again proposed that we take the entire staff down and occupy the governor's office. Some of these careerist left-wingers in there said, "No, no, no. You mustn't do that! We promised the university we'll never go out in the streets again! We're part of the university system! We're not going to do that kind of thing any longer!" They wanted to put their own damn career objectives ahead of ethnic studies—the most needed and radical program that had ever existed at the university. So we had this big argument about stripping the positions of a few old-timers who'd founded the program and had a real strong policy as to struggle and getting into the research on the ethnic heritage of the Native Hawaiian people. So a few weeks later, the paid staff had a kangaroo court and they threw me out of the program.

So there were three episodes where I'd gotten fired from my job for talking straight and being honest about some of the basic conditions. Well, I have nothing against these people personally now. I deal with them. We've been writing books and doing all sorts of things, but I cannot hold back the explanation that careerism in the professional ranks of the left has been a major debility, a major block against efforts to educate and mobilize the people. When you're a careerist and want to get your degree, or when you've got your degree, you sit back and rely on all the connections that degree has provided for you. Few take chances with strong stands on issues.

Let's back up a bit. A year before World War II, they passed the draft law. We all had to register and join one of the services. I took the navy because it was ocean-oriented and related to my background. I'd been trained in ocean skills, and fishing and surfing by Hawaiians, and I loved it. It was healthy and challenging.

Then the war broke out. I was a lifeguard just before the war, stationed out at Nimitz Beach. It was a remote but brand new facility where navy personnel could enjoy themselves on days off, quite some miles away from downtown Honolulu and Pearl Harbor. We three lifeguards arrived at the beach early on the morning of December 7, 1941. At about 7:30 A.M., we noticed there were suspicious clouds of smoke coming out of Pearl Harbor and planes were flying overhead. We wondered what the heck, maybe it's a mock practice of war. But as the minutes passed, it seemed to be getting worse rapidly, so we jumped in an open car owned by my friend Heideman and drove along a narrow rural road looking for a phone. Suddenly, three Japanese planes flying overhead dived down on us with machine guns blazing. "Nyaaaaa tat-tat-tat-tat!" Well, I got a crease across my head, and another bullet went past my stomach but luckily didn't break the skin! We weren't injured, but the car was filled with machine-gun holes and the gas all poured out onto the road. So, we glided into the sugar field and ran to a little house to call navy headquarters on an old-fashioned crank up phone: "Hey, what the hell's happening?"

And they said, "Return immediately to headquarters. We've been attacked."

We thumbed a ride in a big truck. In about twenty minutes we arrived at Pearl Harbor. Ships were exploding, sinking, and flames were everywhere.

For the next month my assignment was to go out in Pearl Harbor bay with a small navy craft and pick up bodies. Two of us, one on the steering and the other with a hook, would pick up dead bodies, haul 'em into the boat, and take them back to 'Aiea landing. 'Aiea is a small town somewhat leeward of Honolulu. We laid the bodies down on a big cement platform—a temporary morgue. Quite often we would pick up a Japanese pilot who was floating in the water and bring him in too.

Well, the boxes they brought there to put the bodies in were doubles. In this unexpected emergency they didn't have enough normal caskets. So we were putting two bodies in a casket. Not infrequently, we'd put a Japanese pilot and an American boy in the same casket face-to-face in death, close the cover, and nail it up tight. And they'd take these boxes away. Our reaction was, "Who the hell made these decisions that caused these youth—American and Japanese kids from opposite sides of the world who'd never known each other—to kill one another and lie in death together, face-to-face, with all the tragedies to their families back home, and all the bullshit excuses that the government would be making to the people, that they died in fame and glory?" Well, they died in flames, but not glory. It was a horrible thing, and that memory stayed with us. Well, such was the beginning of World War II.

I was then transferred to a navy vessel and did a lot of work at sea. Because of my water experience and knowledge of currents, tides, waves, and more, that I got from my Hawaiian tutors, they put me in charge of the undersea techniques program of the U.S. Navy Frogmen. Frogmen are trained to swim to enemy beaches and do reconnaissance for underwater obstacles that might be encountered on offensive landings. We helped form about thirty teams of fifteen members each. Our headquarters were at Kīhei on the island of Maui—a very rural, distant area in those years—where we were able to carry out mock invasions.

Later I was assigned to a small ship whose assignment was to protect other ships from Japanese submarines. We had underwater sonar to detect the presence of submarines. The ship was captained by Northrop Castle, a local man of the big Castle family here. I was a bos'n's mate then. We were protecting a mine sweeper that had been sent over to the most rugged coast of the Islands, the windward side of Kahoʻolawe, an island that's recently been much in the news over the Hawaiian sovereignty struggles. The navy had fired three torpedoes up against the cliff and one of them failed to explode. This unexploded torpedo was of great importance because of a congenital fault in its design. U.S. subs would get into Tokyo Harbor and fire these torpedoes at Japanese battleships. Some would hit but wouldn't go off. Admiral Nimitz was absolutely [committed] to get that unexploded torpedo back to find out the cause of its malfunction.

On board the minesweeper attempting to find and recover the unexploded torpedo was Captain Momson, the inventor of the Momson lung way back in the thirties, and Admiral Lockwood, who was in command of the entire submarine program in the Pacific. The captain sent a little boat in to try to locate the unexploded torpedo. The boat was run by some haole and a diver wearing a cumbersome headset and an inflated uniform with heavy lead in his shoes. They couldn't get anywhere near the stormy cliff. Huge swells were smashing against it with whitewater extending out a hundred yards from the cliffs. It was obviously a futile effort with inexperience and cumbersome equipment.

I told Northrop Castle, "I'm going to dive off and hunt for that torpedo—these mainland guys don't know what they're doing. They're from the mainland."

He said, "Go ahead!"

So I dived off the ship with my goggles. No swim fins in those days. In about twenty minutes I found the torpedo. It was in about fourteen feet of water, hidden by a large portion of the cliff that comes down underwater. So I swam back to the minesweeper and told Admiral Lockwood. He was ecstatic. Now we had to recover it. He said, "You must be very careful because that thing has been fired already and it's ready to go off any moment. It could explode with any disturbance."

"I'll put a line around the thing," I replied, "but you have to be very careful when you pull it. You have to bring the ship in close so you haul it up almost vertically. There's a big rock just seaward of the torpedo and it's stuck against that rock. You pull it seaward, and you won't be able to get it out. It might damage the torpedo further."

But the captain of the ship was too afraid of these big swells and he refused to get close to the cliffs. So I dived down and put a hauser line around the tail of the torpedo. When they pulled, it hit the rock and eventually the line broke. But the minesweeper had pulled the torpedo into about seventy feet of water, right to the edge of the cliff that goes down 300 fathoms into the deep blue Pacific. So I told them about that and they said, "Well, what are we going to do?"

"I'll dive down," I replied.

So this time they gave me a metal cable with a clamp on the end. I've been deep diving all my life. If you hyperventilate you can oxygenate your body system and hold your breath for much longer. So I hyperventilated, dived down, put the cable on the torpedo, and they hauled it up. The admiral and Captain Momson were holding hands and doing a little jig on the deck, they were so happy. Here was the torpedo lying on the deck. The technicians immediately detached the armed explosive head of the torpedo. When they got into its inner workings, they found that four rods that held the firing mechanism in place were defective. The inertia of certain impacts caused the firing pin to go slightly off the center of the firing cap. They immediately got in touch with the manufacturers and rectified the problem. After that, the U.S. submarine offensives were successful.

A month or so later at Pearl Harbor they had a captain's quarters on my ship and I was told to dress up. When I came out, the President of the United States, through Admiral Nimitz, had awarded me the Navy and Marine Corps Medal, which was like the Medal of Honor, citing heroism in recovering this torpedo, and that a shark had been sighted in the area, and so on. To me, it was just an ordinary thing that any one of our local diver/fishermen could do.

At the end of the war, I was stationed temporarily in Oceanside, California, where we were acclimating our bodies to cold temperature. Twelve of us were preparing to go to Japan. I had designed a Hawaiian surfboard with a depth-finder, a radar screen, and a two-way radio. We had been ordered to develop something that would speed up the frogmen's underwater reconnaissance work. So I was there training with this group. We had bets on who would be the first person to touch foot on Japanese soil. Just before we were to leave, we found out that a new kind of bomb had been exploded over Hiroshima, and that the war was ending. So that was the end of my five years of military service in World War II.

During the war, a noncommissioned, uniformed navy guy walked into the ILWU headquarters in downtown Honolulu where my wife Marion was working. She had quit her job with the Censorship Office and went to work for the International Longshoremen. They had a tiny place with a desk, telephone, and a typewriter. Three unions had to put up the money to pay her a meager salary. The unions were just getting started.

The navy guy who walked in was Dr. Karl Niebyl, a haole from Germany who was fluent in all six major classical languages including English. Dr. Niebyl was a Marxist. He offered his services to the unions to help with some of the things that were going on politically in Honolulu. A lot of concern was felt over workers being brought in from the mainland, with bad housing, poor conditions for children, lack of proper nutritional foods, and more. Dr. Niebyl said to Marion, "Look, if you're going to run for office," as the union had proposed, "I'll help you with your campaign."

He was a fabulous scholar in global working-class studies. He spoke seven languages. He was one of the most intellectual persons we ever met. As our friendship deepened, he began staying here at the house and became very good friends with my parents. He gathered together a group of people who wanted to learn more about world history. So for the next three years or so, Karl was very much a part of our lives, and eight or ten of us had regular classes with him.

He took us back several thousand years to the formation of the first slave societies in Greece and later in Rome. He applied a dialectical analysis to the systemic conditions of whole societies. We began to be aware—me especially, as a dummy—of the fact that there were structural aspects to life that we were never taught in school and of which we had no knowledge. This man had it all. He was incredible.

Every system has its own internal contradictions. In the case of the slave systems, the basic contradiction of both Greece and Rome was that they had exhausted the labor supply. The average slave in Athens lived to his mid-twenties and died of malnutrition and fatigue. So they would send out huge military [campaigns] into central Asia to procure indigenous people and deliver them in chains to the slave market.

Well, they eventually exhausted the slave supply, so the *mana*—the Hawaiian word for power—of the Greeks passed over to Rome. The Roman's military forces marched on the Appian Way up into northern Europe and began taking over indigenous peoples they found there. They went as far as England. Like the Greeks, but in a much shorter time, they exhausted the labor supply. During and after the Christian era, they had to find a solution to the crisis they had created. So ultimately they granted the remaining slaves on their outposts in northern

Europe the right to procreate and change their titles and identification from slaves to serfs. These people then were bonded to the soil. This change gave rise to the feudal system, which lasted another 1,600 years.

The interesting conclusion that we drew from that, and it's more clear now than ever before, is that there is one thing that all three exploitative systems—slavery, feudalism, and capitalism—share, and that is the *competitive privatization of land, labor, and resources.*

The slave system exploited for private ownership the stolen labor of slaves and then sold the products of that labor in the market. The next system—the feudal system of Europe—privatized the products of the serfs. This became the support vehicle of feudalism. The serfs found that the best way they could alleviate pressure on the products they had to produce for the manorial establishment was to have lots of children. So they produced large families that provided their form of social security. Before long, the manorial establishment in Europe found that they had a dangerous surplus population, like Hollywood's romanticized version of Robin Hood where the serfs transformed themselves into revolutionaries.

Thomas Munzer, in the late 1500s, organized huge rebellions in southern Germany and presented a major threat to the manorial establishment. So the kings and manorial establishment began granting serfs the right to leave since they were a danger. Many of these liberated serfs then wandered down to warmer climates in southern Europe. The only thing they had to survive on was their labor, which they sold in the small production and marketing towns that were beginning to spring up. This gave rise to the fundamental needs of the market, or capitalist system, where this newly rising, cheap labor market existed and people had to work because they had no other means of support.

With the newly forming labor force of feudalism, the need for an ideological glue to hang this whole thing together gave rise to the Roman Catholic Church. Dr. Niebyl pointed out to us how everything was in chaos during the downfall of the Greek and Roman systems. People were walking through the streets not knowing what was happening, so they would take flight in their imagination to some other world where they could go and live reasonably. We learned that religion (to "re-live") is something that almost all indigenous people generate because many problems remain. Their minds have developed the capability to think abstractly, but they don't have the technique to fill that abstraction with concrete understanding. So they dream of and sanctify gods in the universe to whom they attribute powers that cause things to happen. Religion arose—the Christian movement particularly—so people could hang on to ideals that would hold them together during times of stress. Today we're faced with a similar phenomenon. Some religious groups are motivated well in political struggle, but most of them claim, "No, no, our god will take care of this." You know, "Jesus Is Coming Soon" is on the big signs of some churches, and that is an extremely negative influence in the real world.

We stress these concepts because we want it to be clear that applicable concepts nurtured our political activism all through the years. Historic conditions arise and implant inherent contradictions within systems. Historic conditions that we're in today have to be analyzed in order to find out what the present prevalent contradictions are in order to properly guide activism. With this background, we and our fellow comrades and friends became very deeply involved in political struggles here.

In 1956 the United States set off an atomic bomb over Johnston Island. It lit up the night sky at one o'clock in the morning here in Hawai'i and everybody was terrified. Johnston Island is about 750 miles southwest of Hawai'i. Patsy Mink, who is now a congresswoman, and I started a group called the Hawaii Committee for a Sane Nuclear Policy. For three years, we did a lot of politicizing of people on the nuclear war danger.

Hawai'i's conquest by the United States military in 1893 was primarily for the purpose of taking over Pearl Harbor as a military base. The United States was a late entry into the world's inter-imperialist rivalries. We had been a slave colony under Great Britain for about two hundred years prior to the Revolution which established the United States. From then until 1865 we were a full-on slave nation. Many Americans have a very distinct heritage of prejudice against indigenous people. The indigenous Hawaiian movement is working on materials that show the extreme racist nature of the capitalist system here in Hawai'i.

In 1893, the U.S. landed troops here and took over Pearl Harbor. A group of haole businessmen formed a clique called the Dole Provisional Government. They patrolled the streets with armed marines and took over the Hawaiian government. They dethroned the queen, and took over Hawai'i in an act of blatant imperialism. They didn't give a damn about the fate of the Hawaiian people.

In addition, the United States took over five other island nations at the same time—Philippines, Guam, American Samoa, Cuba, and Puerto Rico—to have military bastions in both oceans in order to protect and extend their rising investment portfolio that was beginning to penetrate cheap labor areas.

After annexation in 1898, Hawai'i became a territory of the United States by proclamation of Congress. For the next sixty-one years, every damn governor of these islands was appointed by the President of the United States, *on the recommendation of a small group of high corporate officials who were the "owners" of illegally stolen lands here.* Three American foreigners stole the land through an event in 1848, called the Mahele, in which they wrote a law that privatized all the four million acres of Hawai'i's lands into the hands of 251 high chiefs. They had missionized the ruling chiefs' class here, which was not anything that could be compared to a capitalist class. They were chiefs who had certain ritualistic duties, but they didn't exploit their people in the same sense and to the extent that the capitalist system subsequently did.

The result was that these chiefs willingly took the title for all these lands into their own hands, not knowing what it meant to privatize land. For two thousand years, land had been a communally shared resource. Anybody who nurtured the soil and brought forth the products of Mother Nature had natural rights to the land. The products from their labor were shared among the people within what's called an 'ohana. 'Ohana is the large family unit, and the extended 'ohana could include whole villages. Everything here was fundamentally communal, shared with great love. The word *aloha* means love and compassion for one's fellow human beings.

All of this was wiped out by the brutal Calvinists who, upon arriving here in the first missionary landings in 1820, described Native Hawaiians as "savages." From then on, they brainwashed Hawaiians, especially focusing on the chiefs. By the time they overthrew the Hawaiian government in 1893, they had gotten all they needed from the chiefs. In effect, they said to the chiefs, "We're through with you. We've got your land, we've got your labor, we've got everything we need from you. Now, get off the stage of history! We're putting you in jail!" And they did, they put Queen Lili'uokalani in jail and took over the Islands.

January 17, 1993 was the one hundredth anniversary of the illegal overthrow of the Hawaiian government. There is a lot of ferment today among people who are aware of this part of history. But, many Hawaiians do not yet know this history. It's never been taught in schools. It wasn't taught at Punahou School or Roosevelt High School, which I attended. The only thing I learned in school was how to read and write, but no history. We had to dig all of this out in our own research.

In 1960 we found out that the State of Hawai'i had plans that would have destroyed 89 percent of the 140 surfing and fishing areas between the eastern end of this island and Pearl Harbor. One of the plans was to dredge and fill all the coral reef areas around the eastern one-third of this island. For $56 million, Dillingham Corporation, who had the only dredge here, was to dredge those areas and put the money in their pockets. Well, we stopped almost all of those projects from the '60s to the '90s by mobilizing huge groups of people that we called People's Power Bases. We went to the youth because they are primarily interested in surfing. It gives them good health, good bodies, and good contact with the ocean. With many surfing areas threatened, we felt that was a good way to educate and mobilize large numbers of people and awaken their sense of responsibility and love for the ocean, and learn what forces within the economic and political sectors were responsible.

Today, in 1995, the oceans around the Hawaiian Islands, whose major industry is now tourism, are gravely endangered. We have silt and pollution and the dumping into the sea of raw sewage around all the islands. The siltation is shown by this little device here, which I use in hearings. *(Shows holder with three bottles.)* I used them last night. These are three little bottles, each with a tablespoon full of sand and sea water from a different area. The first one is from Nānākuli, an untouched area where there's a clean and natural sand beach and clean sea water. The second is from Waikīkī. The third is from the reef runway area out near the airport, where the Dillingham Company, Hawai'i's largest construction firm, had gotten huge profitable contracts to dredge and fill the ocean areas.

Now, if you shake these bottles you'll see that it takes less than one second for the sand to settle in the natural sand area. The other two remain silted out for several hours. In Mother Nature, normal wave action comes in from wave-generating storms thousands of miles from here in the southern Pacific. These waves come to the Hawaiian Islands and form a great surf that has made Hawai'i world renowned. The world capital of surfing is Waikīkī. But when the waves rise and break near shore, they stir up this sediment, and it floats outward in little currents that are formed in bays. In the middle of the bay are currents that rush back out into deeper water and carry the silt seaward. Silt settles gradually onto the coraline base, which is the foundation of the food chain. When this silt settles on the coral base, the corals die for lack of oxygen and sunlight. As the coral dies, the herbivores and carnivores either die or migrate elsewhere. We humans at the top of the food chain are deprived of one of the most important sources of protein: fish.

Ke'ehi Lagoon, next to the airport, was demolished by Dillingham dredgings during World War II. They dredged out 41 million cubic yards of coral there, which they used to help fill in six square miles of highly sophisticated water delivery systems, built by the Native Hawaiian people 300 years before Captain Cook came here. The Hawaiians had built extensive irrigation networks and decentralized the river valleys during several hundred years prior to the first Western arrivals in 1778, a period of tremendous increase in the population. In what they called 'auwai—little streams—fresh mountain water, with its nutrients, came from the upland forests. Vast areas were nutrified. At the end of the journey of this man-made 'auwai system, there were thirty-eight major fishponds in Waikīkī where they raised mullet, aholehole, and other local fish, which produced their protein. This was one of the most sophisticated and effective developmental projects in the entire Pacific.

The reason the Hawaiians migrated here in the first place is believed to be because the Marquesas, the islands where they originally came from, had severe droughts about every seven to ten years, and the droughts lasted for several years at a time. So some set off in a voyaging canoe about 2,000 years ago and settled here. A long thousand-year period of slow growth was followed by a period of about 300 years of tremendous increase, during which the population doubled about every 113 years.

While some Hawaiians don't like to think about this, the historic evidence shows that the chief's class sold out their people. Very little historical-materialist education has been done anywhere in the Pacific about the chief's class. Chiefs became alienated from their own people and began to exploit them before Cook arrived. When the missionaries came here in 1820, they focused on the chiefs, persuading them to do their bidding, and began the privatization of all the Islands' lands and labor. Some wars took place in which commoners killed some chiefs who were abusing their privileges under the aloha system. It's a sensitive area of history. We're trying our best with educationals to help people understand how, why, and when the chief's class arose and [why they] are not to be relied upon.

In today's sovereignty movement, some are looking toward reviving the chief's class and reconsecrating the queen or king here, as a monarchy.

In Hawai'i the haole (foreigners) have created the most singular monopolistic class in the United States, and probably in the Western world. Ninety-five percent of all Hawai'i's land today is owned by about eighty major landowners. The State and federal governments own 53 percent of the land, all of it stolen property due to the illegal overthrow on January 17, 1893. The other 47 percent of the land is owned by approximately seventy-eight major *private* landowners who own and control the primary base of production in Hawai'i. This is the essence of the privatization of the two single most important resources in human history: *land* and *labor.*

These big capitalist landowners in Hawai'i are land rich, but relatively capital poor. They marry up with transnationals, mainly from Japan today, who are capital rich but land poor. They make their big financial and political deals for the exploitation and plunder of land and labor in Hawai'i to control the tourist industry, which is the overriding industry base. They bring in cheap labor from Southeast Asia and other Pacific Islands, like Tonga and Fiji, to do the shit work for the corporate power structure. We have this tremendous influx of cheap labor. About 80 percent of those concrete-jungle hotels in Waikīkī, one of the world's largest tourism meccas, are owned today in Japan. About 78 percent of the workforce—the people who wash the toilets and serve the drinks—is imported labor.

As a result of this concentration of ownership of land, Hawai'i has the worst housing crisis and highest cost of living in the United States. We have probably the largest number of homeless people. In one respect, homeless means people are living in the bushes or in old derelict automobiles, or in tents along the beaches, all over the Islands. It also means that in the middle-class communities, you've got two or three generations living together. The kids can't earn enough money in today's inflated economy to sustain themselves, so they have to live with pop and mom, or grandma and grandpa.

We know of families in Wai'anae and Nānākuli where twenty-five to thirty people live in small three-bedroom houses built for single families. Now, that's with little children, parents and grandparents, often living together on welfare. You can imagine the stresses that arise in such congested homes.

The result is a tremendous increase in the use of drugs, liquor, religious and other paliatives to relieve stress deriving from the plundering privatized economy that doesn't allow people to solve the many problems it creates. Many of Hawai'i's political, environmental, and Hawaiian sovereignty activists regard these problems as the result of Hawai'i's illegal, but deeply-rooted, oligopoly in land ownership and resulting control of all basic political processes.

A few years ago, during Hawai'i's basic transition from large-scale agriculture (sugar and pineapples) to tourism, a corporate institution called the Oahu Development Conference surfaced and publicized its policy, declaring that *"Concentration of population creates a more intensive market."* In simple words, [they are saying] advertise "Paradise Hawai'i" worldwide to attract tourists by the millions (6.1 million tourists in 1995 compared to 1.1 million residents). This artificially rising demand while the few big landowners restrict the supply of marketable lands causes prices and profits to soar.

As a result, Hawai'i's 1.1 million residents today face the highest cost of living in the U.S. and its worst housing crisis. Homeless Native Hawaiians are living in derelict cars here in their homelands, on beaches, in bushes, hunting in vain for affordable lodgings, while many are jailed for sleeping in public parks!

In Hawai'i's few sky-high-priced holes and narrow spaces between urbanized tourism jungles, residents must elbow their way on beaches, sidewalks, in food stores, on freeways and jammed urban traffic among Hawai'i's 6.1 million tourists and buses today!

The Islands' federal and State lands—all stolen during the illegal overthrow of the sovereign nation of Hawai'i in 1893—are primarily used for infrastructures required and built by the private sector, including tourism harbors, airports, freeways, roads, dumpsites, sewage disposals, and other similarly costly appropriations.

The money that puts politicians in office comes from big landowners and their corporate allies, including Japanese investors in tourism. The result is that corporate Hawai'i runs the whole rotten show. Many locals of both high and low status view today's political system in Hawai'i as totally corrupt.

At the State level, the governor, president of the senate, and speaker of the house control every important piece of legislation on the floor. In defiance of the U.S. and Hawai'i Constitutions requiring separation of the three main branches of government—law making, law administering, and law interpreting—these three . . . politicians control the five-vote majority (the governor has three votes) of the nine-member State Judicial Selection Commission, which appoints every judge in the Islands' judicial system. No judge ever casts a vote on issues that would deprive him of his second and third ten-year reappointments by this clique of three leading politicians whose campaigns are financed by Hawai'i's monopolized corporate power structure.

The next step in the local rising rebellion against corporate domination is building peoples' power bases in constituencies most severely

affected by the capitalist system's ever-privatizing plunder and depreda-
tion. Our Save Our Surf (SOS) movement begun in the 1960s has won
thirty-four major environmental victories totalling over $2 billion dol-
lars in taxpayers' money saved from destructive dredgings and coastal
interventions. The successes were reviewed by Steward Udall, President
John F. Kennedy's secretary of the Interior in his nationally syndicated
column, "Our Environment." Udall visited Hawai'i in 1971 and interviewed SOS teenagers on their aims, methods, and successes. His review
stated that SOS "is undoubtedly the swingingest—and surely one of the
most effective local environmental groups in the whole country."

The movement's thousands of teenage participants based their successes on the simple but profound sequence: EDUCATE, ORGANIZE
and CONFRONT! To accomplish our aims, the basic strategy rests on
three simple concepts: respect the intelligence of people, get the facts to
them, and help them develop an appropriate action program.

Save Our Surf's most recent battle with the State in September 1974
stopped a $30-million, 24-acre parking lot for 687 automobiles planned
to be built *in the ocean* fronting Kaka'ako next to Honolulu Harbor's
entrance channel. To sidestep our opposition, State planners lied to the
public by reducing the true size of the threatened Flies surfing area on
their maps down to less than 2 percent of its actual dimensions!

Today, the Native Hawaiian people's movements are primary and rising. The struggle for restoration of Native Hawaiian sovereignty rests
firmly on Native Hawaiians' two thousand-year history based on communal sharing of land, labor, and resources.

This is the key in educating everyone as to how today's crisis is based
on almost the exact opposite system of values—the competitive corporate privatization of land, labor, and resources that is imposing history's
worst social, economic, political, and environmental crises on these
Islands and their peoples. Today's Hawaiian sovereignty uprising is the
most important moment and movement in Hawai'i's two thousand-year
history.

Guy Nakamoto

An activist in the Waiāhole-Waikāne area and retired.

What food crops that people need can be grown in Hawai'i?

Almost all. Citrus fruits are good. On the cooler higher elevations, like on the Big Island, celery, lettuce, and head cabbages grow good. Most vegetable staples, like onions and beans grow good. We can produce enough meat since we have lots of pastureland. We could produce milk here. We could produce all the chickens and ducks we need here. Every island has a little section that's used for grazing. On the Big Island there is the large Parker Ranch. Then there's the Shipman Ranch and the other small ones.

I'm involved with Life of the Land, Hawai'i's Thousand Friends, the Hawai'i Lai Ika Wai Association, the Waiāhole-Waikāne Community Association, and the neighborhood board.

I first became aware of land monopoly in about 1945 in a *Reader's Digest* story. It described how the people in Hawai'i depended on the Big Five corporations. Everything used in Hawai'i came through the hands of the Big Five: toothpaste, bedding, food. Everything depended on them, other than the local stuff that we could grow. Every home used to have a little garden in the back. They raised their own pigs and chickens and vegetables. But shoyu, rice, and stuff like that had to be imported, and you had to get it through the plantation store. Every community around the Islands used to have a plantation and a plantation store, which was a complete system of monopoly.

In 1954, 1956, when the Democrats began to take over, the veterans of World War II, the nisei—children of the immigrants—began to get involved in the political process. Before that, it was all Republican, Big Five stuff. The new political power, which is made up of these second-generation immigrants' children, are behaving just as badly today as the former Big Five people. *(Chuckles.)* It seems like human greed is the same thing whether you're Big Five or a poor immigrant's son.

Watching all those things happen, I began to see that we need to have education at the grass roots that is different from the stuff taught in public schools. The public school teaches you to become obedient citizens. Protest is a no-no. They don't teach how to change the wrong, how to see a larger picture of society, how to see beyond tomorrow, how to see what is going to happen to your children and your grandchildren.

I watch programs like Phil Donahue. He lines up congressional representatives, and they talk about how can we change this system of politics by money power. They miss the whole picture. The democratic process has to do with the people, but the people are not involved in it. You ask the people to get involved and they don't know what to do. I find educated people with degrees who come to the neighborhood board meetings. They get disturbed. They write letters to the senators which say, "This system doesn't work." They say the senators don't answer their letters. They don't understand that you need to address problems through a community organization. That's where the political power is, and we all miss it.

I just saw in a woman's magazine an article by Barbara Streisand who said that women must get active and make their votes count. So I told a woman at a shop, "You look at this. What she says is true. She just opened the door by saying you must vote. That's the minor part. What happens after you vote is the most important thing. You must tell your sisters, grandmother, mother, daughters, to get involved in this process."

And she says, "How am I going to get in?"

"Don't you have a neighborhood board in your area?"

She says, "There is."

"Did you ever go to those meetings?"

"But, I'm busy."

"You see, that's the problem. Now, when you say you're busy, what does it mean? You don't have time, right? Why don't you have time?"

"Because I have to work."

"Why do you have to work?"

"Because I have to pay my mortgage."

"You missed the point. If you don't go to these meetings and if you don't help correct the problems, you're going to pay for it or your daughter is going to pay for it, or your grandmother is going to pay for it by somebody attacking your family: a criminal incident, a rape, you know. And then you are going to say, 'Chee, this is a rotten system.' But you could prevent that if you spend two hours a month right now. Tell your boss, 'I have to take two hours off; I have a public responsibility; democracy is not free; I'm not going to let somebody else do all the work.' I'm involved with several community organizations where I spend many hours. I never saw you at those meetings. Now, you think that this is a democracy. Do you think you have carried your own responsibility? You haven't. You think about it. You're a mother, right?"

She said, "Yes."

"You have a daughter, right? Look, sooner or later, one of you is going to get caught in a rape situation. Oprah Winfrey the other day had a show with rape victims. And you know what, this rape victim describes what happened with the jurors: six women and two men. All the women voted against that rape victim. They said she asked for it, you know, the way she dressed. Well, what is the next question? Common sense is, 'What kind of clothes should I wear then? Should I go in rags? Should I not groom myself? So if I dress properly, what is properly? On whose standards?' "

I said, "Lady, you've got to get involved and start asking those questions and pound the table so that the attorneys listen to you, so that the judges listen to you. Fifty-two percent of America's population is women and where are they?" So I hope she gets involved.

Then I said, "Take a look at the economic picture. We had banana fields over here, but we destroyed the banana. Where do you buy your bananas from?"

"Oh, Times market."

"Did you ever look at where the bananas come from?"

"Oh yeah. Panama, South America."

"You know how many thousands of miles those bananas have to travel? And you know while they're traveling they're creating air pollution. And tractors, trucks, and steamships are burning fuel. And then we say, 'Wow, we have a black hole in the sky.' "

And everybody says, "Well, what's wrong with the system, with the politicians? We voted for the governor, the mayor, and they're not doing what they're supposed to do."

I say, "You've got the whole picture wrong. Democracy is not like that. You vote for the man, then you have to tell him what to do."

So I start off with that and then I bring it down so that they can handle it. I say, "Look, you're not going to learn everything overnight. It took me eighteen years. First, you've got to get in your mind that this is your responsibility. Then, once a month, check off two hours and go to these meetings and fill yourself with information. If you don't have that information, you're going to get frustrated, and you'll say, 'Ah, this thing doesn't work.' "

What kind of people are you communicating with? Neighbors, everybody?

Everybody, everybody. Strangers I see. Like yesterday, I took my daughter to the self-improvement school, John Robert Powers. I let the woman finish her program for my daughter, and I said, "Listen, I want to talk to you about yourself as a citizen. You see this Barbara Streisand article? Look, she says to go and vote."

She said, "Well, I'm going to talk to my husband. This is very interesting."

I said, "Look, if he wants to come, bring him, but don't go and hustle him. I'm talking about rape issues. You better get on it, not your husband. Get your grandmother involved with it, your mother, your daughter."

Tell me about your background.

I was born and raised on the Big Island, stuck in the sugar plantation. My father came from Japan to work in the plantations, so I'm called a second generation. An agent for the plantation businesspeople would go to Japan and tell them, "Listen, I've got a job over here in Hawai'i, and you're going to be a rich man, so join up." The most that I aspired for in my life was to become a sugarcane truck driver.

As soon as his term of years was fulfilled, my father moved out of there and went on his own. When the first Model-T Fords [were shipped to] the Big Island, he bought one of them. He got into an automobile accident, broke his leg, and was laid off for six months. We had ten children in the family. To feed and doctor them just wiped him out. And then my mother got sick for six months in the process.

In 1941, when the war started, my father owed the grocery store something like fifteen years of unpaid bills. He was lucky because this Japanese store owner was also an immigrant's son, and I guess he was a humane type of person. He said, "Listen, Nakamoto-san, don't worry about the bills. My insurance is your children, so raise your children and they will take care of the bills."

Well, when the war started, the military came in and said, "Listen, all you farmers, whatever you produce comes straight to our military commissary office." There was no squabbling about price and whatnot and no more fooling around with the vegetable brokers. The military became the vegetable brokerage people. My father paid off all the store bills by 1947. Then he moved to Honolulu. So, since 1947 we have been living in this Kahaluʻu, Waiāhole area.

I left the family in late 1940. I came seeking a government job. They were paying the great sum of fifty cents an hour. That was way better than the plantation, which used to pay a dollar a day. While I was working as a laborer in Pearl Harbor, on Ford Island, the Japanese bombed the place. I lost my government job. I went back to the Big Island and got another government job as a laborer. In 1943, when the job was finished, I was transferred back to Honolulu and worked for the U.S. Engineers.

At the end of 1944, I got my "congratulations and welcome to the military service" letter from Uncle Sam and I spent two years with the service, as an interpreter in Japan.

Did you feel sensitive during the war about being of Japanese ancestry?

Yeah. I was working in Pearl Harbor at the time of the bombing. On December 8, we reported back to work. This big haole sailor grabbed me by my pants and threw me in the warehouse. We were all locked in that warehouse for the day. At five o'clock, they had sailors round us up and then put us on the ferry, and got us kicked out of Pearl Harbor. The people outside said, "Oh look at the Japs." Well, I was disturbed with that. When they bombed Pearl Harbor we said, "What the heck, they're calling us Japs and these damn Japs are shooting at us. Where are we?"

When we went to Japan as occupation people, haole soldiers would treat the Japanese citizen, our enemy, better than they would treat us, who were descendants of the immigrants. Before the war, in 1936, I visited Japan and I knew those children did not like us. They looked at us as second-class Japanese. They bowed down to us as conquering soldiers, and yet I felt that they were not honest, knowing how they felt about me during the 1936 visit. So I kind of kept away from them. I saw our local nisei treat the Japanese girls badly.

I came home and got a job as a sales clerk with Sears Roebuck. In five years I was promoted to assistant store manager, and then we went to Maui to open another Sears Roebuck store.

After this I went into the insurance business. In the insurance business, you know, they talk about individualistic effort. I was selling insurance, minding my own business, living in Waiāhole Valley because the rent was cheaper, and trying to raise five kids.

In 1974 the community people had selected Bobby Fernandez as the president of the community association, and he was going around and telling people, "Eh, let's organize." I never paid too much attention. Every night I would go out and sell insurance. On the way home, it's nine, ten, eleven o'clock, the Waiahole School cafeteria is filled with people. There's not much parking; the streets are crowded with cars. And I said, "What the heck's going on here?"

So I went to those meetings. And I said, "Eh, you guys—you guys are crazy. This is the landowner and she has the right to evict us if she's going to do something with the land." But some attorney, and the Revolutionary Communist Party people, said, "Hey, there's another side to this story." At that point, I began to tell myself, "Eh, what these people say makes sense." So I got involved.

Most Americans are afraid of the word communist.

Yes, the devil. I'm sure most of the people had that fear of the big specter of Communism. And yet, on the other side, they had this eviction notice. They were going to lose their house; were going to be evicted from the place they raised their families. The landowner, Mrs. Marks, was going to change the use of land through the zoning process. She was the heir of Mr. McCandless. All of us were renting on a yearly basis; then she changed it to a monthly basis. And she sold the land to a developer, Mr. Powell. There are two valleys over there, Waiāhole Valley and Waikāne Valley. The Waikāne section of the valley was less populated. The developer had developed the strategy of attacking the community. The way to do it is to move into the area where less resistance is likely to develop. So he found an area where it's vacant. He bought 500 acres and he started to bring his bulldozer. And he made requests for zoning change. We protested and we stopped the zoning change. He brought the bulldozers, and the people stopped them.

Mr. Powell said he wanted to build a thousand-house community.

We found out that it was going to be a rich man's community, with a huge marina outside of Waiāhole, and all that stuff. I had a total conversion in the process of stopping this development.

Life of the Land is where I got my education. Hawai'i's Thousand Friends gave me a bigger worldwide perspective. Life of the Land was started in 1970. They were talking about developers making changes for hotels and condominiums. That got people disturbed. And they said, "Look, we've got to do something about this." These were people looking at the environmental picture and trying to slow down development. They asked me to join, so I joined. They were mostly whites who grew up in Hawai'i. I think I'm the only Oriental who got involved with that group. We had Fred Benkel, an attorney. We had Doug Miller. His father is a professor at the university. We had Dr. Art Mori—he's a teacher of chemistry at Chaminade. Our goals at Life of the Land fit with the goals of the Hawaiian community. We say, land use and Hawaiian issues and environment—they're the same.

Hawai'i's Thousand Friends developed in the early 1980s. Mrs. Marilyn Bornhorst, who served several years on the City Council, was on our side. She's a people-oriented politician. She said, "Eh, you guys are spending so much time trying to fight the developers. I think we should organize Hawai'i's Thousand Friends, similar to Oregon's Thousand Friends."

Thousand Friends means that we wanted to get one thousand contributing members, but we never reached that. Anyway, we kept going with whatever we had. It became a powerful political entity. We joined with the Sierra Club Legal Defense Fund. We sued the Mormon Church in Lā'ie, where the Polynesian Cultural Center is. They were polluting the stream, the taro patches, the ocean with their effluent. We sent them a notice and they did not respond, so we took them to court and we got the out-of-court settlement.

With the help of the Sierra Club Legal Defense Fund, we were able to sue polluters in Hawai'i Kai and Kailua. We had the help of Life of the Land and Hawai'i's Thousand Friends working together. Our executive director is doing a good job. She goes to the mainland and has contacted Thousand Friends in seventeen other states. Other organizations are making criss-cross information sharing.

In 1913, Mr. McCandless, the father of Mrs. Marks, used to own 7,000 or more acres. Mr. McCandless and his brother were brought to Hawai'i as well drillers. He drilled water wells for the plantations on the plains out at 'Ewa, the leeward side. The big job he did on this windward side was to create this Waiāhole tunnel system. That tunnel goes through this Koʻolau Range and reaches the other side of the island and feeds the plantation. Today, it still siphons about 30 million gallons a day for the plantation. It's rain runoff from these mountains. He also developed a lateral tunnel that develops more water from the interior of the range. He put in about twenty miles of ditch system. He has about four or five tunnels that go into the mountain. So when he did all of that, he dried up all the water that was going down into these two valleys and destroyed the Hawaiian families' taro fields. There's only two or three acres of taro growing today, a minuscule operation, compared to what was formerly there.

When I look at the history of what happened to Waiāhole Valley, I see a clear picture. The white man comes in with his engineering power and takes away the water resource. Taro is the Hawaiian's staple food, and that's destroyed. So the Hawaiian families leave the valley and go into town and become welfare recipients. You know, they don't know any other lifestyle. So I can see all the families moving out.

I took this little slide show out to convince people to support agriculture and oppose the developers. Then I had more time to think about what comes next. As soon as the devil was pushed out of the way, the community went back to doing the same thing they did before the struggle. And I thought that was dangerous. They don't see the larger picture. You've got to watch the whole system. You may think you have won a little battle over here, but what we're talking about is war with the system. It may be quiet for another five years or ten years, but the same people are going to come back—different personalities, but the same people. The developer is going to come back and swallow you up again and you have to start all over again. So I thought, We need an education process going. I kept pushing this, but there was not much interest. We must keep informing ourselves because it's going to come down on us again.

So, five, six years ago, a Japanese developer came in to begin golf course development. Now the community is a little bit split. You know, there's half of them that want the golf course. We're against it, because it's an extension of tourism. So now we have the Waiāhole-Waikāne Community Association, and we have the Concerned Residents of Waiāhole-Waikāne. So the valley people are split in half. Life of the Land is against golf courses. Hawaiʻi's Thousand Friends is against the golf course. We see a larger picture and all the consequences that come with the golf course. We see the deterioration of the environment. We're a little bit encouraged because the State government is now putting out educational information about how sensitive our environment is, which is already showing signs of stress. So we thought, "Hey, they're coming on our side—that's good." And yet, it won't happen because we're depending on the politicians who have all been fed and kept by the developers.

Well, that takes us into another kind of thinking: how to develop support. And I say, "Look, we must go out and educate."

Others say, "Well, we've got to write up material and send pamphlets out, and a newsletter."

I say that is not going to work, that's what we've been doing. You have to go out personally and deliver the message and grab their hands and get them excited and get moving. The others, they say, "Well, I'm busy."

I'm retired. And I'm in the process now of building my own house on the farm lot. I'm about halfway finished. You see, I was the vice president for the Oahu Self-Help Housing Project that we organized in the middle-'80s with the help of Mr. Donald Hanson.

But Life of the Land, Thousand Friends, [and the] neighborhood board are all wrestling with the political process. We've got to do something to get the right people in office. You don't have the informed grass roots. They get trapped into these advertisements that are pushed by money power; all that flash [on] TV. So I'm trying to fill that gap, not to tell the people what to do, but to help them to think. And I say, "Look, you have to think what's good for you." I want to bring that kind of information.

I guess the insurance industry helped me to become what I am. I left school at eighth grade, and through the insurance industry, I got my degree in personal financing. I was able to enter University of Hawai'i classes. Then I got a little B.A. from Windward Community College. It gave me a philosophy of life.

I go to places like McDonalds, all these fast-food restaurants. If you go over there at seven-thirty in the morning, what do you find? You find retired people who have a whole bunch of experience and knowledge being wasted. That is one of the rich resources that we have. Oh boy, I said, we can hustle these people too. Well, they're saying, "Ah, let the children do it. I worked hard for what I got; time for me to rest now."

I said, "Chee, that's a negative kind of thinking because your life will be revived if you get involved." I say, "We have State psychiatric hospitals overflowing. You are a retired person. Between you and the patient in the hospital, where is the line? You're just one line between being sane and insane. You know how you keep yourself healthy? By getting involved. You stay home and drink all day, and talk nonsense, no contact, no real stuff to talk about. Football, this team won and that team lost. Those things don't stir your adrenaline so that you become healthy. You're a grandfather, you're retired. Do you know what your grandchildren are doing? Why aren't you over there at the day care center helping the children put the jigsaw puzzles together? You will see what it will do for you. All of your aches and pains will go away if you just try it, you know."

And so we have all this information, but we don't know how to put it together. Economics! So, I say to people, "So what if General Motors closes down all their shops and goes to Mexico? They're not making cars to sell to the Mexicans? Mexicans don't have money to buy. Look, you are the buyers of the automobile that they're going to make in Mexico, in Japan, or wherever. The market is zeroed in on the United States, because you have the money. All you have to do is tell General Motors we're not going to buy your car from Mexico. What do you think they're going to do? Why do you let the few bunch of people with money tell you how you have to live, when you have the real power to tell them how to do it? You're not thinking straight. The Japanese [are] coming over here. We can shut them down, if you think straight. Destroying the banana fields to buy bananas from Panama. Does that make sense to you? Come on, you've got to do some thinking. Don't let the senator or the mayor or the governor do the thinking for you. Their agenda is different. You've been shafted every day, and you don't know it."

I make such statements to anybody who will listen.

And how do they respond?

They don't know what to do with it. They listen. And they're wondering, gee, does that makes sense?

I talk about economics. Following after the industrial revolution, mass production saturated our society and now the companies are moving to Third World countries. We're beginning to become a service society. Instead of 150 million people that we [the United States] had at the war, now we have 255 million. And the way we support those people is getting resources from poor countries. We get chrome from Africa to strengthen our iron ore to make good steel. Can we afford to do that, and what do we do with that improved steel? We make new cars every year and we have piles of old automobiles polluting the place. We have people out there in the Third World who don't have a decent home, don't even have a decent pick, don't even have a decent plow to plow their field with the horses. They use a wooden plow.

I think we have to stop [producing] new cars every year. So all the backyard mechanics, I want to get to them and tell them, "Look, repair the old car, put it back on the road." I say, "Look, Mr. Watanabe in Japan, 1945, after the war, he was a ten-year old boy. What did he do? He started to fix old Toyotas and Datsuns. He was selling old cars, and you know what, today he's a 7-billion-dollar man. Now, you're not going to make 7 billion, but I'll tell you what we're going to do. Getting new cars is to get yourself enslaved to the system." I say all that stuff, you know, so they can feel it in their gut. So instead of two cars, we're going to all live with one car. Instead of having five kids, we're all going to have only one child.

We're so brainwashed with capitalism. People like Friedman say, "Capitalism, free enterprise, is the only way to go because it's directly involved with freedom." I thought, what . . . is this? *(Laughter)* The general public must begin to understand what words like *Communism, free enterprise,* and *laissez-faire* mean. One person making a needle will take all day to make one needle. Ten people coordinating their action can make one hundred needles. What do you call that? It's a social function. Okay, now, so you go to school and you learn individualism and your behavior is social behavior. Pretty soon you know why our people are getting schizophrenic behavior. Our fundamentals, I think, are causing these things. So we have to help change that.

Marion Kelly

An associate professor with the Ethnic Studies Program, University of Hawai'i, Mānoa; seventy-something years old.

I started researching land tenure in Hawai'i because it had been brought to my attention rather vigorously that it's important who owns the means of production. If it's important who owns the means of production, then the important thing for a subsistence economy is who controls the land, and what the relationship is between the land and the people. I took a graduate seminar at Columbia University, New York City. The nine or ten students were all majors in anthropology or economics, or something like that. I couldn't figure out what I was going to do for a term paper. At that time, their library wasn't the greatest, particularly the library on the Pacific.

I decided I'd better learn something about the Hawaiian people. Now, I had already gone through the whole public school system here in Hawai'i. I had already gone through the university here, and taken two years of Hawaiian language. I still didn't know anything about Hawaiian people. I guess that's typical of most students in Hawai'i for many years. And some of the historical events that I did learn something about, I found out later when I did my research, were not exactly correct. I had to write to my mother in Hawai'i and ask her to read and take notes for me on certain chapters in certain books that Columbia didn't have. This is pre-Xerox, so it was a struggle to obtain the data and write a paper. I'm not particularly proud of the one I finally produced, but it got me started.

When I came back here, I knew what I wanted to do: focus on Hawai'i. I went to people in anthropology and discovered they were not geared to what I wanted to do. I would have had to study Southeast Asia, India, Afghanistan, or some countries like those. The United States had just taken over all of Micronesia as a strategic Trust Territory. It had sent a large number of scientists out there—anthropologists, sociologists, linguists, and others—who were trying to get a handle on who these people were and what to do with them. To facilitate this whole thing, the University of Hawai'i set up what they called the Pacific Islands Studies, (today the Center for Pacific Islands Studies), hoping that students would eventually go out and do their research in Micronesia and possibly some other areas in the Pacific. I don't think any of the students who got into Pacific Islands Studies ever did that.

I got into their master's program—Hawaiian Studies was not yet established—and wrote a fairly decent thesis on the events in Hawai'i before the Mahele of 1848, when all the land was divided among a few chiefs. I did a lot of research on the impact of outside influences on Hawaiians, and the influences that moved a few chiefs into changing the land tenure system of the Islands into a private property system. The laws were put together by westerners, primarily American missionaries, who went into the government, wrote the laws for the Hawaiian chiefs, and pressured the chiefs into implementing them.

After receiving my M.A., I began working in the Anthropology Department at the Bishop Museum. At that time, there were just two or three of us in the department. Dr. Kenneth Emory, an anthropologist who conducted the first serious archaeology in Hawai'i and Tahiti, hired me as a secretary.

I'd known Kenneth Emory for many years because my father was a sea captain-fisherman, and had taken the Bishop Museum expeditions out in the 1920s and '30s. My mother went to sea with him. I went with them during the summers. When I went to school, I stayed with my grandparents on the Waialua Sugar Plantation. I had been to quite a few atolls before I was twelve. My father fished along the northwest islands up to Midway and as far as 1,000 miles south of here. He was born on Washington Island [modern-day Teraina] and was one-quarter Polynesian, so this makes me one-eighth Polynesian. I was born in Hawai'i and raised here by grandparents who had come here from Cleveland, Ohio in 1913.

In 1934, when my father took the Bishop Museum expedition down to Mangareva, the head of the expedition, Dr. Charles Montague Cook, refused to let my mother go on the expedition, even though she had been to sea with my father for years and years. So, Mrs. Cook saw to it that we had enough funds for my mother and me to go to Tahiti to meet the expedition. I had my fifteenth birthday in New Zealand.

Kenneth Emory went on that expedition. But before I left on that trip, his wife Marguerite wanted to be sure that I had proper clothes to wear for dinner in the evenings on the ship *Niagara*, a British ship, I think. And so, she gave me two or three evening dresses out of her wardrobe. Here I am, fourteen years old, in Marguerite Emory's evening dresses. We were both thin, so they fitted pretty well.

The first thing I ever had published was an article in the *Festschrift* for Kenneth Emory, which was on a portion of my original M.A. thesis that I didn't put in the final manuscript. It was the story of Vancouver and his influence on the history of the island of Hawai'i when he was here in 1794. Another thing I wrote which wasn't published until much later was an analysis of *pu'uhonua*, which are places of sanctuary in Hawai'i. I did a little study on what kind of sanctuaries are found in other cultures in the world and what kinds are here. I compiled a list of sanctuary sites here that were recorded for the Islands by Hawaiians and others. A sanctuary, *pu'uhonua*, is a special type of temple—*heiau*—that is said to be a safe place for anyone who is being pursued for something they presumably did. Apparently, when they sought sanctuary at a *pu'uhonua* they were excused for whatever deed they allegedly did. It has something to do with the concept that the *mana*, the power to forgive, remains in the bones of the chief after death. And so these bones are collected and become part of the sanctuary. They still can dispense forgiveness. Pretty powerful spirit!

About 1961, the Pacific Science Congress (PSC) was held here in Hawai'i, and I became a little bit involved in it. Then, around 1968 they had another congress, this one in Tokyo, Japan, and we all went there. Somehow, the PSC chartered a plane and we could all afford a round-trip ticket on the plane. It was wonderful. So I got to Japan for a while and saw a lot of the early archaeological sites. Dr. Yosihiko Sinoto, in the Department of Anthropology at Bishop Museum, took us on a post-conference tour of many of the sites. At the time, I also studied with Dr. Saul Reisenberg from the Smithsonian, who came here as a Pacific research specialist. I learned a lot about the Micronesian islands and the people from him.

With political interpretation?

Well, that came later on when I realized what the United States was doing in setting off their atomic and hydrogen bombs in the Marshall Islands, and using them for their own military purposes. This was happening with complete disregard for the health and welfare of the Marshallese people. When I began teaching at the university, I was able to provide a lot of information about the people who lived there. I also got information from people involved in Friends of Micronesia. My Micronesian students from Palau, for example, or Belau now—that's at least 2,000 miles away from the Marshall Islands—it's like another world. Palauan people never even knew what was going on in the Marshalls. Nobody ever educated them as to what the United States was doing in the Marshall Islands.

My grandparents raised me. My grandfather was the kind of person who refused to buy "liberty" bonds during World War I at the time when everybody was supposed to buy them. He had some criticisms about what the United States was doing over in Europe. He had a kind of independent flair about him. He was brought up in a small community speaking German as his first language. When he was age six they moved to Ohio, and he went for the first time to an English-speaking school. When they came here, and there were a lot of Germans here, they'd get together on weekends and sing German songs and speak German to each other. When the United States got into World War I, all that had to end. So they did not teach my mother or my uncle to speak German. That was a no-no.

My grandfather came to Hawai'i to work on a plantation as a machinist. He had come from the automobile industry in Cleveland. In Hawai'i there was this whole plantation hierarchy, you know. The manager and all the submanagers were haole. Further down the ladder you [had] a strata of maybe Portuguese, who were considered by the haole bosses to be lesser human beings than the Scotsmen or the Englishmen. Further down were the field workers, the Japanese and Filipinos. So you had this tremendous economic-political hierarchy. Everybody at the top had to be a Republican. My grandfather didn't fit into that too well.

They came here because one of their sons, my uncle, was not a very healthy baby. They were told they better get him away from the Cleveland winters. Over the years, my grandfather worked his way up to become pump engineer, head of the department of fresh water pumps for irrigation water. When the depression came along, he was retired early. My grandparents had to make a lot of sacrifices in order to meet their obligations.

I can remember when the first Japanese was hired as head of a department on the plantation. This was a man who had an engineering degree from the University of Ohio. Of course, he was not immediately welcomed by the other department heads. But my grandparents invited him and his wife over for dinner. I remember this. Oh, dear. Crazy, crazy times. I must have been about ten years old. I remember setting the table, knowing that these people were different from us. But Grandfather was going to do the right thing, welcome them and befriend them.

It's things like that in my background that probably shaped me, when I think about it. My grandparents were not willing to buckle under to the system, but not usually confronting it directly. For my part, I worked my way around it, for example, by becoming an associate professor with only a master's degree. Of course, it did take me seventy-three years. I didn't get hired by Bishop Museum until 1957 or '58. Well, I stuck it out for twenty-four years and then got fired in 1985 with fourteen others. At that point the museum made a big turnaround, cutting back the research budget, and opening themselves up to the tourist industry. Over the years when I was there, the Bishop Museum took contract archaeology for developers. Because I knew a lot about the land, they would write a section into the contract to do a history of the particular land section which would be impacted by the proposed development. I've done lots of those histories. Most were published by the Bishop Museum Anthropology Department in short reports with from two hundred to one thousand copies being made in order to get them out to the public. Sometimes, the people at Bishop Museum were not too happy with what I said about what happened to the indigenous people of the Hawaiian Islands.

When an anthropologist was hired as director of the Bishop Museum, he began to build up the social sciences rather than the previous emphasis on entomology and ichthyology and the other "hard" sciences. Even anthropologists spent a lot of time on archaeology, rather than what's happening in the Hawaiian scene today. But they finally got a social anthropologist by the name of Alan Howard, who now teaches at the university, and we began to do some work with one of the Hawaiian communities. It turned out to be very good research. I got involved in that, too.

How did the Ethnic Studies Program get started?

I think it was influenced by the Black movement of the '60s. The head of the University of Hawai'i at that time had once been in the New York University system. He knew some of what was going on with the Black movement in the United States, so he wanted something related to the Black movement. He wanted to hire a Black man to head up the Ethnic Studies Program here. That didn't work out. So, they hired a Japanese American, Dennis Ogawa, who had a degree in communication. I went to him and convinced him, with the help of some of my Hawaiian friends, that I was the person to be hired to teach Hawaiian culture and history in the Ethnic Studies Program. He hired me, and we had a pretty good start. I taught modern Hawaiian culture and some history, a combination of what's happening today among the Hawaiian population, how they looked at themselves, how they felt about themselves. It was a good course.

Were you part of the Hawaiian movement?

Not really. The way I saw myself, and still do, is that I have been lucky enough to have done a lot of research and study Hawaiian history, and I feel that I have a lot of knowledge and understanding of Hawaiian history and culture. Rather than my being part of a movement, it is more important for me to provide the Hawaiians with this historical information, and they will make their own movement. I don't see myself as a movement person. I don't go out and organize people. In the process of going out and studying the history of different areas of the Islands, I get to know a lot of people. For example, I did several studies of the land history in the district of Ka'ū, on the island of Hawai'i. There was a lot of archaeology going on there at the time, so my history studies got published, with photographs of people and sites, and things like that. Having that history available gave the Hawaiian movement in Ka'ū a boost.

I help to educate people on their background, and provide them with whatever information they need, if I have it. I keep personal contacts—they're my friends, but I don't belong to their particular organizations. I've been to many meetings of their organizations. I'll go over there and spend a couple of nights in the parks with them when they have their meetings and talk to them. They know that they can call me any time. I don't force myself on them. They have their own agendas. They have their own future.

For example, I worked in two constitutional conventions for Ka Lāhui Hawai'i. I've worked in one job or another that they've assigned me. I don't belong to Ka Lāhui. Ka Lāhui Hawai'i is a very important aspect of the indigenous Hawaiian movement for sovereignty. I'm not Hawaiian, but they gave me a job to do. They said, "We need you up here at the computer." [I said,] "Fine, I'll go and I'll bring my grandson who's a computer expert." And so off we went for two days. We worked up there at Kamehameha School where they had one of their constitutional conventions.

And then, I have classes at the university. One is on land tenure changes in Hawai'i. Another one is on modern Polynesia. We talk about Tonga, what's happening there, emigration, and the lack of natural resources to bring cash income into the country. We study and talk about New Zealand—Aotearoa—the Maori movement there, land issues, things like that. We talk about what's happening in Tahiti. Then we go into what's happening here in modern Hawai'i and we talk about the sovereignty movement, Hawai'i's economy, and its people; what it was like in precontact Hawai'i, their subsistence economy, how it worked, what were its primary elements, and then how it got co-opted by the traders and then the missionaries, and then the plantation system. And all the other things that happened to the Hawaiians. I say, "How do you folks feel about this class? Feel depressed?"

"Oh, yeah!"

I say, "Well, good, it's a depressing story, but you should know it."

Have you been into environmentalism as a movement issue?

I was a member of the board of the Natural Resources Defense Council here in Hawai'i. We talk about the environment here in Hawai'i and how it has been overexploited by commercial agriculture and other kinds of commercial ventures. A group of us just completed a video called "Ahupua'a, Fishponds, and Lo'i." *Ahupua'a* is a land section—mountains to the sea—usually a valley; *lo'i* is a wet garden, two or three inches underwater. It is a special way of growing taro that is much more productive than growing it on dry land, because you can continue to plant the wetland. But dryland taro depends on just the natural rain, and the section that it grows on must lay fallow for one, two, or three years; the longer the better.

Is this being grown by Hawaiian people today?

Not too many Hawaiian people are growing it, because they don't have the land. The land has been taken away from them. There are a couple of haole brothers who are growing taro very successfully on the *koʻolau* [windward] side of this island, and they're in this video too. There is a haole man on the island of Molokaʻi who learned from two elderly Hawaiians how to grow taro, and he's growing it on their land. There are others who are not Hawaiian who are growing taro on Maui. The people who are growing it on Kauaʻi are not Hawaiians, they're Japanese. Not too many Hawaiians are growing it. One group tried to get started, but I think that they gave up after a big storm demolished everything they had grown.

I belong to an educational group that is known as the Pro-Hawaiian Sovereignty Working Group (PHSWG). We have met weekly for five years. The largest event we sponsored was an International Tribunal. The PHSWG members, with a lot of help from the community, put on Ka Holo Kolokolonui Kanaka Maoli Tribunal in August 1993. The Tribunal provided a chance for Hawaiians and others on each of the main islands to give testimony before nine international tribunal judges, all dedicated to protect the rights of indigenous peoples throughout the world. The Tribunal was a great boost to the Hawaiian sovereignty movement. We are now supporting educational forums on the issue of a plebiscite that the State of Hawaiʻi is daring to rush the Hawaiians into before they have a chance to understand the implications of such a vote. The State of Hawaiʻi has no business interfering in the Hawaiian sovereignty movement.

George Cooper

Co-author of *Land and Power in Hawai'i;* in his mid-forties.

I am primarily a lawyer right now. I specialize in land and housing issues on behalf of low- to moderate-income people. I'm also a writer. I'm not writing much these days. Last year I co-authored one essay that was published in one of the local newspapers. That was it. I help other people with their work.

I was born in Virginia in 1948. My father was an army officer; a graduate of West Point. From time to time, I've thought about why I became an activist. There wasn't something like a parent who was a community activist or some event that I witnessed. I mean, I'm just thinking about this friend from Poland who described when she was about eighteen, watching soldiers and security forces just pulverize a bunch of students who were protesting. There was never anything like that in my life.

I grew up in a time and place of affluence for college-educated white people. It was at the pinnacle of American wealth and power. It was an enormously secure environment, one that left me not worrying about money. It wasn't that we had that much. My father died when I was seven, and I was conscious of our family having less than other people around us.

My mother had some progressive influence on me. She was just an extremely decent person and really interested in public events. I began working as a golf caddy in my early teenage years. A lot of the other

110

caddies were Black, and I made some really good friends among them. Some of them used to come over to my house in a completely white suburb. No Black people had ever come there before, except for the maids and the garbage collectors. But it was okay with my mom.

I went to Holy Cross College in Massachusetts and always got very high grades. I got selected to represent that school in this around-the-world study tour in the late 1960s. The one-year tour took about thirty students and big-name professors like Daniel Lerner, who held the Ford Chair of Sociology at MIT. We studied in half a dozen countries and it was a really elite thing. It was founded and funded by some very wealthy individual.

I had no political consciousness up until that point. If somebody had asked me in 1966 if I knew there was a war in Vietnam, I don't know if I did. But that trip exposed me to so much. I spent a year going around the world. We were placed with families. One of the main things that happened to me was I got this tremendous sense of my ability to make my life be whatever I wanted it to be, and it could be based on principles that I developed. Up to that point, I thought I was going to become a corporate lawyer. But, given the era and the other people on the trip, I decided that I wanted to get my life channeled into social-political change.

It was like I had been asleep and now I was awake. I gobbled up all kinds of things: books and whatever, lectures, demonstrations, conferences. I just was so hungry for knowledge. I was particularly interested in people changing their lives. At that point, a lot of it was just an interest in changing myself. So the psychological, cultural part of the youth culture of that time interested me. But somehow, I always had this side to me that was practical. I wanted to know how these ideas could be applied to the lives of lots of people, and how the world could be made better. I was always gravitating toward political action.

I moved here to O'ahu in 1970 to do a master's at the University of Hawai'i through the East-West Center, and got involved in the antiwar movement. It was confined so much to white people that I couldn't see where it connected with community people here. Then I noticed what was happening with the natural environment, what development was doing to it, and I also became aware of the mass eviction that was going on in Kalama Valley, in the eastern end of this island. That really grabbed me. I tried to find some support role I could play. A multiethnic organization had been put together to resist the evictions, made up primarily of young activists. Then there came a point when a decision was made to kick out the white people from that organization, which was okay with me. There were a lot of people with Hawaiian blood who were in that organization.

A university student from Kaua'i and I did a study on the effects of the Princeville Resort development on Kaua'i while I was a teaching assistant in the so-called Survival Plus program, an environmental program with the university. A local environmental organization called Save Our Surf published that and we ended up speaking to community college and high school classes on Kaua'i.

I moved over to Kaua'i in 1972, just about the time when a mass eviction was happening. I got involved in that struggle. It was the point I had been heading toward for several years. I was really, really glad to be there. I was positive I could make a contribution. I threw myself into it, and became really close with those people. The two leaders became like my father and mother. I practically lived at their house at times. I was an organizer, a research person, probably because of my personality, but also because I was about the only white person. It was in a community that was not used to white people, except either as bosses or as tourists. And it all meant that I should be someone who helps and advises, and works, but doesn't lead. That's what I did. That's when I really started to do a lot of research. I co-taught a class at the community college, and prepared all the materials for that class. A guy who owned a radio station took note of me and asked me to become the station's newsperson, and I did that. And then the editor of the newspaper asked me to write, and I did that. So I just really took off, in terms of research and organizing. I would gather all the material I thought was necessary in such things as land ownership and zoning. I learned to do research on how deals are put together and maybe how politicians are co-opted, and stuff that could be used in an exposé kind of way.

We had a couple of interesting cases. One involved this company called Leadership Homes, a subsidiary of something called Leadership Housing Systems, which, in the mid-1970s, was one of the nation's major housing developers. They were planning a very large resort on the southeast corner of Kaua'i, on this wild, beautiful coast that had been a kind of preserve of local people for years, for fishing and camping and hunting.

One thing that happened was that six months of weekly status reports that were generated by the executive in charge on Kaua'i to send to his superiors on the mainland, were given to us, and we gave them to the news media. Among other things, they detailed private meetings between the executive and public officials in which they were manipulating the public process so as to get the resort approved, even though there was a lot of public opposition. There were insinuations of bribes. It was hot, and we put it out, and it caused an incredible uproar in Kaua'i and throughout Hawai'i.

We had another one. You remember the LEAA—Law Enforcement Assistance Administration? The guy who was the LEAA rep on Kaua'i was indicted for attempted bribery because he hired himself out as a consultant to this old, rich family that was trying to get a cemetery rezoned. It was an old prisoners' and Japanese cemetery. We were really opposed to that. I mean, that's such an outrage. We got information that he had attempted to bribe these people. It got blown out in the open and he got indicted. Unfortunately, he was acquitted.

All this was my whole world at that time. The intensive development on Kaua'i was just beginning. Kaua'i got the reputation as the most antidevelopment island: the island with the most opposition to development. That movement began before a lot of development became entrenched with all the co-optation of people that that involves. When I got there and all this began, people were still connected to the old ways. It just enriched my life so much. But, a lot of that kind of thing can run through your fingers. You can go over there now and ask, "Where is this feeling?" And it was partly in the canoe club that used to be there, but isn't anymore. And partly in the beach that's still there, but now there's all these tourists. But there's something that's greater than the sum of the parts that's not completely gone. I mean, Kaua'i will always be Kaua'i. But, it's just so diminished.

I left Kaua'i to go to law school here on O'ahu in 1975. I went back to Kaua'i various times, because there were things going on, like the eviction fight. But I think I was burning out on that work, and was wondering about the things that I wanted for myself. I was looking for some kind of balance. It's a constant struggle. I'm absolutely going through that one right now, again.

That all resulted in my staying here, finishing law school, and getting married. I met my wife—I'm divorced now—in law school where we were in a small group of community activists. She's local Chinese and had been working in the Chinatown struggle.

Another thing that I wanted for myself was to go around the world again. I just loved traveling, so my wife and I did that for a year and we went to lots of places. In May of 1981, we went to Poland when Solidarity was first legalized. We met Lech Walesa, Anya Valentinovich, and other kind of mid-level activists in Solidarity. It was a great experience.

So, I came back here and began work on what became *Land and Power*. Gavan Daws, my co-author, had a book underway about H-3, the highway. He had someone else working with him, doing the research work, but it wasn't working out. He asked me if I would like to do it, and I said, "Yeah." I had trouble getting documents from government officials because H-3 was in litigation. Early in the research, I noticed that in a report filed with the government in the late 1950s, this politician—who I thought had really liberal views on controlled growth and even was antidevelopment—was involved in a real estate sales firm. I thought that was kind of surprising and wondered what I would find if I looked at a whole lot of those old reports. So I looked at all the annual partnership reports filed with the territorial and State government between 1954 and about 1981. Partnerships tend to be a more logical vehicle for land development. I looked at nearly fifty-eight thousand of these reports. I found the whole spectrum of the political leadership of that era was investing and developing the land, or representing developers. *Land and Power* came out of that. The book changed to become what it is now.

After the book came out, it was this big deal here. But there was virtually no public criticism. Almost nobody who was named in an unflattering way had anything to say about it for the record. There were whispers that it was anti-Japanese and racist, which I just thought was stupid. I think the reason it was whispered and not said out loud is that it just couldn't stand the light of day. Because my co-author and I are white, it was an easy shot.

I was very careful to do social scientific work for that book. For example, we raised the question, Do applicants for zoning changes from the Honolulu City Council who are politically well-connected do better than nonconnected people? To answer that, I reviewed the City Council logs for a couple of years, and looked at every last land use matter that occurred. I looked at every single applicant: board of directors, attorneys, and so forth. Then I broke it up between people who were politically well-connected—had retired judges, certain legislators, and so forth, involved—and those who didn't. When I looked at the success rates and the degree of involvement of the politically well-connected, it's just what you'd imagine. Truly, every zone change of consequence had somebody who was in the legislature, or something like that, on the payroll. Nearly 100 percent. Because Asians, and particularly Japanese, were dominant in government at that time, they were the ones with the connections, and so they were the ones working the deals. And you know, I didn't create that.

I hate getting in public arguments, unless I know I'm going to win, and I just hate shouting matches. So I really went all out to be thorough, to have lots of facts, and to not be anecdotal. There was very little comeback in the sense of public criticism by people who felt exposed or attacked. There was a great deal of stuff in the media around it. The *Star-Bulletin* ran excerpts [from the book] five nights running on the front page. . . . It was amazing.

In my latest incarnation, I've got a more up-front role. But I'm still heavy on research and organizing. And I still look to work with groups of people; valleys of people. I represent Waiāhole-Waikāne Community Association. Most of the work I do of that kind, it's free. Once in a while, people will just give me money; people who are outsiders and just looking on.

What's the role of law in the "movement" today?

Well, I think law is always a dimension of social movements that are relatively peaceful, where most of the conflict is verbal. That's the case in Hawai'i today. In the short or medium run, there are a whole lot of individual issues that a person could get involved with. I gravitate towards ones having to do with land and housing and things that directly involve people. I made a real conscious choice, when I first got into this, to pick places where there were people—particularly local working people—who were being hit with something: loss of their homes, their farms, their fishing grounds. So there are all these ongoing efforts to deal with housing or health, or whatever matters. It's like a series of conflicts that invariably are resolved in some way. They come to an end. When a particular community problem somehow comes to an end, it's always ratified and kind of summarized in law. So, it's necessary to have a lawyer involved. Because these conflicts are verbal, not physical, the people in power are always using law. Grassroots people are cognizant of the legal processes that affect them; you know, rezoning hearings and whatever. And so a lawyer is just a really useful person.

Having said all that, the primary effort has to be that people organize themselves broadly, democratically, and pull leaders out of the community to be the up-front spokespersons. I do speak more now than I used to, but I still very consciously put myself in a secondary role and work to help bring out leaders among the people I work with. Basically, it's political struggle. A lawyer is somebody who's an adjunct, and when he or she is not, it's a real problem. It stifles the movement.

What might peoples' politics look like in the next period?

Don't really know. It looks to me like conditions today will just get worse. Whatever can be called peoples' politics in Hawai'i today is kind of on the small side; not exactly inconsequential, but not very consequential either. There's just this endless set of issues that arises in land, labor, education, and so forth. I can't think why conditions wouldn't just steadily worsen, unless there's some general collapse of the world economy, and then who knows what things will look like? Resistance today is kind of low level, somewhat isolated, somewhat on the sidelines. It stands to reason that at some point—that I couldn't possibly predict—if all of these conditions do continue to worsen, I could imagine some larger movement coalescing. It's just all so fragmentary now.

But there are people—activists—who just go and do it, and don't step back and try to think, "Where's it going? Are our efforts being put in the right place? What is this whole system about anyway?" and all that sort of thing. When I was younger, I was more into that; now, I'm not as much. I just try to go out and get done what I can. I think that as needs arise, people will organize to try to fill them. The homeless, for sure now. Something could be said, generally, about some quantum of people who feel really screwed by the system, who feel that it could be different, and who are willing to take action. When some critical minimum is hit, a larger organization will be put together. But there just isn't one now.

In the last two years, I've gotten much more involved than I had been for some time. I worked with people to try to put together a couple of statewide organizations, one dealing with tenants' issues and another one dealing with communities affected by golf course development. But it's just so hard to put together an organization around something as specific as one of those two issues. Just as we were getting going on the golf course issue, the economic impetus for golf course construction stopped. Tenants' issues are more pressing today than ever, and yet it's just so hard.

What ultimately I'd want to see is an organization that unites people from all kinds of issue areas, from all over Hawai'i—grass roots, community, labor, education, health—you know—everything. That seems so far off, and that's only talking about a million people on these Islands here. I mean, try to step that up to the whole country, and it's just beyond me, how to put together an organization that is truly rooted in the grass roots, and not a bunch of opportunist politicians or labor leaders.

I support the general sovereignty movement. I see Hawai'i as a foreign country and not part of the United States. I think that non-Hawaiians can and ought to support the general sovereignty movement. There are all kinds of views and objectives within it. I hadn't been involved with Hawaiian rights issues, per se, all these years. I knew a certain amount, and often Hawaiian issues would be raised in the context of larger community issues. But the first time I've been involved in something that's essentially Hawaiian rights had to do with Hālawa Valley and H-3 on this island. A four-lane highway is going to go up the floor of that narrow valley where there are so many archaeological remains. It's not just that the remains are going to be all ground up, but the sanctity and stillness of that valley is going to be completely gone.

I'm one of the lawyers representing the people, primarily Hawaiian women, who were arrested August 30, 1992, for blocking an access road that is used for the construction of H-3. They were conducting a religious ceremony. This has been my first really serious exposure to Hawaiian issues. I love these people I'm working with. They just have so much heart and spirit and commitment.

I got myself . . . in debt actually, because I was doing so much free work and having trouble getting paid by some people. . . . But I get so drawn to certain things. I could barely restrain myself when these people were arrested for protesting the shipping of contaminated soil to the Marshall Islands. I was so thrilled when people took a stand. I really wanted to go. I've been doing some work for them, actually, but I don't represent anybody. If there's some major civil disobedience thing that happens, I'm really tempted to get in it.

HUMAN RIGHTS
AND FREE SPEECH

The subject of this section is tricky, even though people seem to instinctively know what human rights are and free speech is. We think the topic must be placed prudently into a political economy context for it to have meaning. A society like the United States has internal contradictions in its structure and ideology that tend to obfuscate the meaning of human rights and free speech. High-sounding concepts like freedom and the rights of citizenship are promoted by the establishment and generally accepted by the people. On the other hand, the system is unable or unwilling to provide a decent life for all citizens. The result is a continuing social tension. The quest for human rights and free speech has driven the politics of many people in Hawai'i and continues to be the foundation for movements in opposition to imperialism, war, poverty, and environmental degradation. The sovereignty movement is beginning to test the capacity of the establishment to accommodate to the demands of people with Kanaka Maoli blood.

Coming out of the Great Depression, at the prelude of World War II, President Franklin Roosevelt in 1941 announced four freedoms that were the prerogative of all people: freedom from want, freedom from fear, freedom of speech, and freedom of worship. Roosevelt may have felt that his "Four Freedoms" were the most fundamental of human rights. As events unfolded, it became clear that they were more rhetoric than achievable goals in the kind of free enterprise society that Roosevelt and subsequent presidents shepherded. Still, his call was a rallying point for later generations of activists who were distressed by the evolving condition of their fellow humans and by U.S. foreign and domestic policy.

In our developing years, we thought of free speech and human rights as something like two sides of a coin. On the human rights side we saw, over time, a steadily expanding list of rights that became effectively an outline of the left-progressive agenda. Some rights like "dignity" and "social equality" were fairly abstract, while others like income, food, housing, and health were concrete. The most comprehensive statement on rights came from the 1948 Universal Declaration of Human Rights of the United Nations, and the extensions of the declaration that appeared later. Nearly everything a progressive might desire is found in those documents. On the other side of the coin there were historic pronouncements—as in the U.S. Bill of Rights—of the people's freedom to express their conceptions of human rights and peacefully act upon them.

As we matured, we began to see that the two-sides-of-the-coin idea was a beautiful—but mechanical—simplification of a complex process. As we participated in movements for freedom and equality and studied the dynamics of political economy, it became clear that the key question was, *Which* human rights? Roosevelt declared that all people should be free from want and the United Nations stated that all people should be properly fed and housed. But no official declaration from laissez-faire systems tells the people who are not properly fed and housed and free from want how to *gain* their material human rights, other than placing confidence in the free market. Human rights declarations have emerged out of the operations of, and with the guarded blessing of, the ruling class of the day. That class never intended to change its system to the extent needed for a guarantee of *material* comfort to all people.

Promotion of human rights and free speech ideas came from left-progressive thought and practice that was tacitly tolerated by the ruling circles during World War II and the postwar period of abundance. During the war, the United States was forced to deal with fascism's harsh disregard for humanity. And, of course, the United States was allied briefly with the Soviet Union, so it had to temporize its steadfast anticommunism. During the twenty-year period of relative abundance and lack of serious foreign business competition following the war, the ruling circles could afford to share a little more of the pie with the working class, even with minorities and oppressed people, and reluctantly permit more free speech on basic human rights if the subject matter did not seriously challenge the free enterprise system or greatly alter the control of capital. But it was inevitable that the challenge would occur, even without it being a principle goal of the challengers. Civil rights activists found that winning the vote or the right to eat in an integrated restaurant did not provide a decent standard of living for all, but only the right to participate equally in certain U.S. institutions. To win fundamental *material* rights would require a hard look at the system of ownership and control along with a political plan to make change.

Throughout the era of relative abundance—roughly from 1940 to 1970—many left-progressives assumed that equal social and material rights were in sight. It was just a matter of time and struggle. Simultaneously however, the ruling circles had been deathly afraid of the red specter stalking the world since the appearance of the *Communist Manifesto,* and especially since the founding of the Soviet Union in 1917. With the Great Depression, they were alarmed that the workers, who had nothing to lose but their chains, just might unite to meet Marx's challenge.

Following World War II, the worldwide expansion of socialism produced great paranoia among the ruling circles. They found that most civil wars and liberation struggles were driven by some group's aspiration for a decent standard of living and the removal of oppression. Some movements were formed that demanded a redistribution of wealth, which only could mean that a fundamental change in the ownership and control of capital was required. Having been scared out of their wits, the owners of capital assumed a highly defensive, anticollectivist response, an expression of which was McCarthyism in the 1950s. Older residents of Hawai'i know well the anticommunist Smith Act trials of that period.

Then the owning class forged an elaborate institutional mechanism of police, teachers, planners, philosophers, researchers, and clergy, to monitor and "understand" the dissident movements. The ultimate purpose was to subvert and disable those who had strayed into forbidden territory. Activists always were restricted through official policy or informal sanction to philosophy and politics in such "safe" areas as moral opposition to war, civil rights, gender equality, individual liberty, freedom of religion, and so forth. Those who strayed into the *economics* of race or gender or imperialism were ultimately put down unless their quest contributed to the well-being of the free market.

Then, in the late 1960s when the postwar boom was receding, a new right wing began to emerge out of the nooks and crannies into which the older right had crept during the prosperous free-speech '60s. The right wing has exercized near-total free speech on such matters as family values, patriotism, the right to bear arms, crooked government, and the moral superiority of free enterprise. Though some of these overlapped interestingly with left-progressive thought, there was absolutely no overlap on the right of all people to have decent food, shelter, and clothing. What people had, the right wing asserted, was the right to compete in a free labor market and the right to become rich even if others were hurt in the process.

But perhaps even more important, the reemergence of the right wing corresponded with the deepening crisis in the world capitalist system, a development that worried system guardians to the extreme. Their concern was not particularly that another 1930s-like collapse would hurt millions—*that* is the unfortunate spin-off of economic cycles—but that a resurgence of left-oriented human rights demands would be articulated by the victims of the crisis. To try and forestall that possibility, the right wing was given a free hand in setting the terms of the human rights debate. Today, it has unquestionably taken the lead in that struggle. The doctrine of laissez-faire that the right wing sanctifies is about the desirability and moral supremacy of an unregulated market. The left knows that an unregulated market invariably produces major class differences, from great wealth to gross immiseration. However, the left has been stultified in its ability to promote an alternative.

Should free speech and equal protection of the law be accorded to both right-wing and left-wing forces? Free-speech liberalism often agrees with the establishment that "extremes" from both the right and left are undesirable and should be discouraged. They agree to stay the course within a flexible center where both right and left can exercise their freedom of speech and openly present their cases. Essentially, a semblance of this scenario was practiced in the 1960s when times were good in the rich nations, when the average material life of most groups was improving. That period produced an unusual output of left energy and development, a sign that democracy was working somewhat. But times have *not* been good for the last twenty years, and things are getting progressively worse. Now we are in a strange period when the advocates of laissez-faire have free reign to test their theories and there is little effective opposition to them.

Part of the problem is that liberalism—the base of human rights and free speech advocacy—has gone about as far as it can go. Liberalism "went to the mountain" a few times in the performance of its historical mission of temporizing the excesses of free enterprise and building bridges between capitalism and socialism. Liberalism got a glimmer of insight into the idea of material equality, the *most* basic and radical human right of them all. That means in practice that decent food, shelter, clothing, and other essentials are the inherent right of all peoples. Some of the more advanced liberal activists began to realize that race, gender, ethnicity, age, and nationality—social characteristics that *seemed* by many to be most important—might well be equalized one to the other if all people had relatively equal access to the material things of life. If all the Kanaka Maoli, African Americans, Maoris, and Tongans had their material needs met it would mean that they had become equalized somewhere along the way. Instead of deducing such a cause-and-effect logic from its brief journeys to the mountain, liberalism was outmaneuvered, outgunned, or bought off.

Our thoughts on human rights and free speech are straightforwardly applicable to Hawai'i. Few places parallel Hawai'i's unique set of contradictions: a Pacific military outpost amidst the aloha of the Kanaka Maoli; a rapidly evolving have and have-not society with the Kanaka Maoli on the bottom. The speakers in this book tell us that more human rights are being trampled on every day and there is no rational rectification plan afoot. Nearly everyone believes that things will get worse.

So, why isn't the constitutional right of free speech exercised more often and more radically on behalf of material human rights? In addition to the general thoughts above, part of the explanation may be that the glitz of a maturing, synthetic service society has been superimposed on the *mystique* of old Hawai'i. This has stupefied and entrapped a lot of people, especially those who materially benefit. As in the continental United States, there are a lot of bribed people in Hawai'i. Then there is the palpable military presence, quietly representing an omnipotent establishment that has many ways of stifling free speech. Potential protesters may be neutralized before they speak, while experienced activists may be intimidated into relative silence. This tends to be the case throughout the United States.

Also, some have experienced that terrifying and immobilizing idea that there *is* no solution to the dilemma of unequal material rights. If that awesome conclusion is true, then why bother with free speech? If that's not enough, the vision of socialism that once was valued by so many progressives has quickly faded into something like a jaded piece of history. The propaganda agencies of the new right have relegated the socialist experiment to the dustbin of history, and many progressives have been suckered into such cynical thinking.

The speakers that follow do not necessarily address the weighty issues noted thus far. However, they, like everyone in this book, have spoken indirectly to these issues through their activist lives and social priorities. They have acted on their conceptions of human rights and many times have strongly spoken their minds. They have paid their dues and continue to be involved in progressive activities. All the speakers were university students in the United States. They were deeply influenced by the war against poverty and the civil rights and antiwar movements. They brought some of the ideology and energy of these movements to Hawai'i.

Oliver Lee and Setsu Okubo, both educators in Honolulu, were deprived of their freedom of speech because they spoke out against U.S. foreign and domestic policies or tried to inform their students of material that was not complementary to imperialism or free enterprise. Sometimes they did outrageous things like questioning the system, and their hands were slapped hard.

Tracy Takano is a veteran leader of the Rainbow Coalition and active in civil rights issues. Tracy is a co-chair of the Hawai'i Rainbow Coalition, a service worker, and active in Hotel Employees, Restaurant Employees, Local 5. Bill Hoshijo directs Lawyers for the People of Hawai'i, an organization that provides legal services to the poor and does advocacy in the public interest.

Oliver Lee

An associate professor of political science at the University of Hawai'i; sixty-eight years old.

I was born in China in the year 1927. My father was Chinese and my mother was German. My parents got divorced and my mother went back to Germany and took me with her. So that's the second country that I lived in, and then I lived in several other countries during the rest of my childhood and my teens. I lived with different kinds of people: my mother and grandmother in Berlin for six years, my father at another stage, my stepmother at another stage, my uncles in Mauritius for seven years at another stage. So the socialization is complicated because of different countries, different cultures, different kinds of schools, different languages.

I was just talking to a graduate student a few minutes ago who mentioned a book which dealt with a group of Chinese students who, after World War I, were given an opportunity to study in France. A good many of them later became communist leaders in China, like Chou En Lai and Den Shao Ping. Mao Tse Tung stayed home, but he was in touch with these guys. They kind of all knew each other. These guys formed some kind of a socialist party among the Chinese in France that later on became part of the Chinese Communist Party when it got formed in 1921 in Shanghai.

My father was studying sculpture in Europe at the same time these guys were there. That's where he met my mother. They returned to

China and had a very turbulent kind of a life in a turbulent environment—you know, Chinese civil war, warlords, communist revolution, World War II. He stayed in China during World War II, but he sent me out to Mauritius. During World War II he joined the Chinese foreign ministry under Chiang Kai Shek. He was stationed in Iran for five years. My seven years in Mauritius takes us to the end of World War II. In fact, I left on VJ [Victory over Japan] Day to join him in Tehran. That's one of the few times I was in the same place with him.

I was in Tehran for one year and went to an American missionary school; first time I met live Americans. There were a lot of well-to-do kids from all over the Middle East and diplomatic families from all over Europe. Why was I speaking English? Mauritius was a British colony that used to be a French colony. After Napoleon's defeat at the Battle of Waterloo, the British took this among many other places from the French. The common language was Creole, which is kind of a corrupted French, isn't it? In Mauritius nobody spoke English. I was going to a Chinese school most of those seven years. That's where I basically got my Chinese culture, Chinese education, Chinese language. During the war, I listened to BBC [British Broadcasting Corp.] radio. They gave you daily war reports very slowly, and I literally copied down the words. That's how I learned English. In Mauritius I used to keep a diary in German because I wanted to keep up my German. For several years I would translate a German paragraph into English every day. After a while I was able to read *Tarzan*. There were ten volumes of *Tarzan* that were translated into Chinese. So I would read the Chinese and then read the English, and that way improve the English; also, Sherlock Holmes and Mark Twain. It was formal English, but good enough for the American school in Iran.

At the end of that school period I spent four years in New York. My father stayed behind in Iran. I went to the lab school of Columbia Teachers' College—a good school; all kinds of rich kids, smart kids. From New York, I went to Harvard. What to study? My father had pretty fixed ideas. He said, "Well, I'm in the diplomatic service and you've seen some of it in Tehran. It's a pretty good life." He was a very pragmatic sort of person and always concerned about making a living. It was tough in that civil war type of environment. To him, the question of survival was important. So anyway, he said, "I know the ways in the diplomatic service and we could get you in there and you could become a diplomat. To facilitate that, you ought to major in something like political science, or political economy." So that's how I got into that field. *(Laughter.)* But see, during my college years, the Chinese Nationalist government collapsed. So that was that. *(Laughter.)*

I graduated from Harvard in 1950 in the Truman era. After a little while there was McCarthyism. So everything was anticommunist, right? It wasn't begun by McCarthy, it was begun by Truman. The education that you got at Harvard was anticommunist, obviously. Harvard has its own dynamics, you see. The general atmosphere was added to the normal Harvard kind of conservatism. In college there was no introduction, no contact, no nothing with leftism, Marxism, socialism, Communism. It's not among the students, it's not within the faculty, it's not in the recommended readings, it's not in the texts, it's nowhere. Therefore, I had no contact with leftist thinking.

But there was one man named Owen Lattimore who was a guest speaker at Harvard. He was no Marxist. He was a liberal, but a very good scholar and very independent, and of course he became a victim of McCarthyism. I had heard him speak and was impressed. His way of analyzing and being open minded about the Chinese Communist revolution and many other things appealed to me.

After finishing at Harvard, I had an interlude of studying at Boston University [BU]. My wife-to-be was in her senior year at BU and we got married. It's nice, it's happy, we're living right near BU, and I attended BU just to be with her.

Then I went to Johns Hopkins University where Lattimore was professor. I had a whole year of him and that was important to me. He was running off to Washington to defend himself every so often. I was impressed by the man. I would say that's the beginning of my sense that there's something wrong with the mainstream. I mean, shucks, when you talk about McCarthyism and so on, that hits you right on the head. You don't have to be sensitive. But you'd have to be fairly sophisticated to see beyond the veneer of the liberal Democratic Party and Truman's Fair Deal.

When my first child was born I dropped out for a year, took a couple of jobs, and saved up money. Then I went to the University of Chicago. What I said about Harvard applies fairly well to Chicago. You know, this was towards the tail end of the McCarthy period. There were the big McCarthy hearings in 1954. I remember all of us gathering around the radio and listening. Chicago was mainstream, don't rock the boat, and so on. Again, I picked up nothing about Marxism, or socialism, except by way of my studies of China. I wrote my master's thesis and Ph.D. thesis on China. So through that route I got to read things regardless of what the profs were recommending or not recommending. Chicago didn't do any radicalization for me, for sure, except perhaps through the China field. And I was kind of slow because I had this anti-communist baggage, partly from my father.

My father didn't want to go to Taiwan with Chiang Kai Shek so he resigned and then came to America. He knew the damn thing was corrupt and incompetent. He had no love for the nationalist government.

What does a resigned diplomat do when he comes to America?

Well, not too good. It's a sad story. He came to America at about age fifty and died in 1976 at age seventy-six. So that was a third of his life; a wasted third. The first fifty years were okay, because they were kind of vibrant and active and he had accomplishments. But in America he was a fish out of water. He spoke English but not fluently. He had no marketable skills on the American scene, though he could write up a storm in Chinese poetry and Chinese essays.

He had a few thousand bucks saved up. Some other ex-diplomats who had preceded him to New York had gone to Lakewood, New Jersey, and nearby areas and bought chicken farms. So he went and bought a chicken farm. He did that for nine years. At the beginning business was good because of the Korean War, but gradually it declined. In the good times he had taken on too much mortgage to expand the land and chicken coops. He couldn't pay the debts after a while, so he went bankrupt. He had social security and he retired. But he just kind of shriveled up, you know. It was very sad towards the end.

In the middle of my dissertation at Chicago, as my little girl was growing up, I felt the need to have a full-time job. I had worked part-time for years. And so something came through from the University of Maryland. The chairman of government and politics called me on the phone and said, "Mr. Lee, we need an instructor to teach four sections of the introductory course and we're already two weeks into the semester. Are you interested?"

"Yeah."

"Can you come out by Monday?" This is Friday he calls me. *(Laughter.)*

So I said, "Yeah, I'll be there Monday."

So I left my family behind and drove down there. I had no teaching experience, no preparation, no syllabus, no nothing. I hadn't read the textbook which already was ordered, and had to face four sections. Actually, I think my Chineseness rubbed some of the students the wrong way. At that time—1958, in Maryland—there was racial prejudice there.

I did four years of teaching there and completed my dissertation. But Maryland is where my politicization sort of began, partly because later on I taught my own courses in international relations: Soviet foreign policy, Soviet politics, Chinese foreign policy, etc. I had enough understanding of what things were really about by this time.

Were you reading anything on the left by this time?

No, nothing. I didn't know about the *Guardian* or *Monthly Review.* However, the times were changing. This was 1958. And within a few months, the Cuban revolution happened. Eisenhower was making some moves which calmed things down a bit, like inviting [Nikita] Khrushchev over here and treating him nicely. And the guy looked like a human being rather than a demon. He was on TV plenty. So I guess there was a bit of a thaw there. Later on, things tightened up again. Kennedy wanted to be gung ho, you know, and wanted to prove something. Eisenhower didn't need to build up his image. He had authority.

Okay, I was doing some of my own reading about China and Russia. If you're teaching, you'd better try to figure out what makes sense to you. You have to get your shit together. You've got to figure it out. What do all these facts and data mean? You've got to make it make sense.

You see that up there? *(Points.)* That's my FBI file: 690 pages. Some of my students—I was teaching some evening classes and some at military bases—wrote letters to the FBI: "Dear Mr. Hoover, I'm taking this course on international relations and this Mr. Lee, I think his first name is Oliver, was born in China, and he shouldn't be teaching at an American university." That's where the file began. Many years later I asked for the file and they sent it. So I see these letters; no names, of course. I didn't know that they wrote these letters until many years later when I got the goddamn file.

So I'm going along, teaching. A few beginning instructors in the department, and the brighter graduate students, no longer accepted the traditional kind of description of American foreign policy or the American system. Partly this was so because the political atmosphere was changing and partly because enough negative stuff had become known about American foreign policy and domestic politics. Enough had become known so that the brighter students could figure things out. It may be partly also just coincidence, but there was a good collection of bright students who had leftist leanings. We had a study group in which I learned a whole lot more about political reality than I ever learned at Harvard or Chicago. The times were changing by the late 1950s.

Then I quit the job because they were paying very poorly. I had a friend who was working for the Library of Congress in Washington, D.C. There was a branch called the Legislative Reference Service, and they hired me. It was full of Ph.D.'s, and we wrote reports for the congressmen, some speeches, etc. I was doing good work and was evaluated well during a six-month trial period. At the end of that period the personnel director calls me in. And he says, "Well, Mr. Lee"—he didn't beat around the bush—"your work is okay, but we have to ask you to resign. You can resign and things will be okay, but if you don't resign, we have to fire you."

I was stunned and I didn't know what it was about. I had no idea about this stuff, you see *(points to FBI file)*, but that's what it was about. They must have asked for the file early on. During those six months, I was writing some things which were professionally good, but politically touchy, apparently enough for them to get my FBI report. I wrote a long paper about the 1962 China-India border war and I blamed the Indian government for provoking the Chinese. That was totally unacceptable, but it was the truth. I was just about the first one to write that stuff down. Some years later a British guy named Neville Maxwell published a book where he made the same case, but more effectively [and] at greater lengths. Today it's commonly accepted that the Indians provoked that war.

So I was out of a job. I said to myself, okay, you've got a Ph.D., you were sort of trained for academic life, and you have teaching experience. So I figured, okay, I'll go back to academia. Then I ran into a former schoolmate from Johns Hopkins who happened to be from Hawai'i and happened to be from this department. He was on leave of absence, working for Senator Inouye. And he says, "Well, there's this one-year opening while I'm here in Washington, and I'll recommend you." That's how I got here.

I don't think I told them about my leftist leanings. I played it fairly straight. This was a good department and most of these guys were open minded and relaxed and left-liberal at the time. So I came here in September 1963, but on a gamble because it was only a one-year opening. That's how desperate I was. We sold our little house. We drove our old jalopy across the whole continent and we took the slow boat here.

When I was at the Library of Congress I was studying our policies in

Vietnam. We hadn't sent Marines in yet, but we were supporting the South Vietnam regime. I wrote a piece about that, so I knew that the American policies were no good. I gave a few speeches here, I remember, and some of it was covered in the paper—1964. Some people were beginning to notice this guy Oliver Lee. And then in February 1965, [President] Lyndon Johnson started systematically bombing North Vietnam.

So early on we formed the Hawai'i Committee to End the War in Vietnam. We had our first big march in the spring of 1965, and I think it happened at about the same time on the mainland. We were an active group. Every chance we could, we had a demonstration, did leafleting, did picketing, gave the U.S. Army a hard time, got on their bases sometimes, this and that. And we were hassling the churches. Then twice a year we made the major effort, coordinating with the mainland stuff. They had their big thing in Washington or New York or San Francisco, and we had ours. But here it was on a very small scale. I remember on our first demonstration we had 36 people. People cussing at you, gesturing at you. And then we built it up—75, 100, 125—but without compromising the message, you know. Three hundred was the max. It was important to us to never water it down. In fact, we got more and more radical as the events became more harsh. Year after year after year of this war, you know.

And then, of course, after the Tet offensive in spring 1968, Johnson was basically forced to reverse course. The U.S. government by that time basically knew they're going to wind it down. They're not going to continue to escalate, and they're not going to seek victory, at least not the hard way. And the general population was turning against the war. There was one last fling, in terms of the antiwar movement, and that's the invasion of Cambodia, which was spring of 1970. That was about the last gasp, I think, of the antiwar movement. People basically understood that the American government was trying to get out, and partly it was [President] Nixon's "I have a plan" rhetoric. A lot of people bought that.

Then in spring 1971, the U.S. sponsored a South Vietnamese invasion of Laos, which was supposed to be a neutral country. There was some American air cover, and this and that, but not much in the way of American troops. I happened to be in Berkeley at the time on sabbatical. I was in some Berkeley demonstrations, but to me the energy wasn't there; the anger wasn't there. It wasn't the way it used to be. It didn't feel quite right. And then, there was the big march in San Francisco—a quarter million people—and my wife and I were part of it. The numbers were there, but the anger wasn't there. It was too much flower power and "all we are saying is give peace a chance." I just wasn't used to that kind of mellowness. To me, this wasn't the real antiwar movement.

Somewhere early on I said, "Hey, Marxism—that's where it's at. That's the only way to explain American imperialism." That was my turning point. The FBI kept their distance, presumably tapped my phone, kept compiling a file, took my photographs at every demonstration, and so on. But they never directly tried to interview me or anything. So in that sense, there was no harassment that I specifically know about.

How did your issue come up here at the UH?

Oh, well, that's a story. It was a major event in Hawai'i in the late '60s. It was a two-year fight. The establishment took it very seriously. When I say establishment, I mean not just the university administration, but the legislators, the governor, the army, navy, air force, marines, the business community, the social clubs, and so on. They all wanted to get rid of me. I mean, I was a monster. I was the devil incarnate.

In my classroom I taught about China and the American war in Vietnam. So news gets around: this guy is a radical teacher, and he claims to be a Marxist. At a big public meeting, labor union leader Art Rutledge took a mike and thought he would hurt me somehow by saying, "This Oliver Lee, he's a self-confessed Marxist." I'm proud to be a Marxist. *(Laughter.)*

So people began to know and take notice, and the students would talk to their parents, and so on. In 1966 a conservative women's group called We the Women put some pressure on the university president, and he kind of brushed it off. I guess the group was too small. Every now and then he gave a good speech about freedom of speech, academic freedom, and the integrity of the university. But then a year later another group, the Waikiki Lions Club—let's say they were just a front group—took a public position that this Professor Lee should not be teaching at the State university because he's pro-Soviet, pro-Chinese, pro-Viet Cong, or whatever. So they put the pressure on the president. He fended them off because their demand was too blatant, too crude. I remember him saying, "Well, Professor Lee is mainly teaching graduate students, and I think the graduate students are mature enough to be able to figure out how to deal with Professor Lee's teaching." Now, to me, this showed an Achilles' heel. What did he mean, he'll defend me in terms of teaching graduate students? What about defending me in terms of teaching undergraduates?

Then I applied for tenure. In late spring, 1966, my colleagues, who knew I was a Marxist, stood by me and recommended tenure by a seven-to-one vote. Some of the Maryland years of teaching were applicable to the formula that they had at the time, even though I had been here only three years. So then it went to the dean, who didn't like me. He had heard me give a talk about Vietnam. *(Laughter.)* But he said, "Well, Oliver, your department has recommended . . . etc., so here's my letter of intent to grant tenure." The formula was such that you had a one-year waiting period from that day. Then you would automatically get tenure. In the meantime you just do your teaching and do your writing and whatever. Obviously, if you [commit a terrible crime], etc., the letter of intent will automatically be reexamined.

On that same day, one of my students came into my office with a friend who was a member of a small radical group called the Student Partisan Alliance. Later on it transformed into the SDS [Students for a Democratic Society], but this was the beginning of student radicals on this campus. My student says, "Oliver, I got a statement here that we wrote up, two pages, and I'd like you to look at it and then see if you can run it off for us on the ditto machine. We want to pass it out tonight at some meeting. We call it a year-end report from the Student Partisan Alliance."

It was a two-page tirade against American imperialism, American capitalism, for revolution in Africa and everywhere, this and that. There was a passage about the Vietnam war. It said a good many students don't want to go into the draft. They want to go to Canada, or whatever. But we advocate going into the armed services, going to Vietnam, and doing what you can to undermine American aggression, like shooting American officers in combat and divulging military information, and on and on.

So, well, the question was, How do I handle it? It became funny after some years, but at the time it was very serious. I told the student, "This is pretty heavy stuff, and, of course, you know that I agree with most of it." As a matter of fact, I had seen something similar earlier on. This student and I were together on a radio talk show earlier and he already had some version of this; not the shooting of officers, but some other parts about revolution. So I said, "You know I agree with most of it, but some of it I don't agree with. But it's your statement, it's not mine. It's heavy stuff and it borders on sedition. But on the whole, the way you phrase it, I think you're legally in the clear. See you later." That was the end of my technical advice. And then, pretty soon every word of this statement hit the press. Even though my name was not in there, people suspected that Lee had something to do with it.

So they inquired, "Who are these students? Are they officially registered? Who's the faculty advisor?"

"Oliver Lee."

So the dean finds out about it immediately. The dean calls me in. He says, "Okay, the shit has hit the fan. You're the faculty advisor. Just tell me really what happened. Who are the students? How did you get to know them? How often have you been advising them and what kind of advice did you give on this thing?"

So I told him. I told him fairly straight.

So then he says, "Okay, that's what you say you did, and I can't accept that. I want you to come back by noon tomorrow and give me a written statement. Just put down what you told me." So I did that, except I did better. I gave a political analysis to it, in terms of academic freedom; and some technicalities about the functions of the faculty advisor, and some principles, and so forth. I figured I could beat this just by standing firm on academic freedom. But the dean didn't think so, and he was in touch with the university president. They were determined. The dean said, "Remember that letter of intent to grant tenure? I want it back."

I guess physically I handed it back to him, but even if I didn't it was legally null and void. No promise anymore to grant tenure. I had a terminal year, and then out. I said, "Not that fast. At the Library of Congress they kicked me out pretty fast—but here, I'm going to fight."

I had just become more politicized, more radical, more angry.

How did you start your fight?

Well, several things. In general, you're supposed to exhaust the university process. If you ask the AAUP [American Association of University Professors], that's what they'll tell you. So I wrote a thing to the Board of Regents. Of course, it was in the papers every day. Within a couple of weeks they held a big meeting in an auditorium at the East-West Center. All the media were there. One of the regents read this long statement that they were backing up the administration and denying tenure. Their rationale was that Dr. Lee, in giving the advice that he gave to this Student Partisan Alliance, was showing a lack of judgment and maturity and sense of responsibility to the university. From that point onward the Board of Regents took the full responsibility.

I contacted the AAUP, and they said, "It's clearly a major case and it looks to us as if your academic freedom has been violated." But still, there were internal processes continuing. A faculty senate hearing committee took half a year. The AAUP said, "Okay, go to the faculty senate, etc., and keep us informed."

So I kept all the clippings and batches of Xerox and sent them everything. For two years, they followed it and they assigned a guy to follow it. That gave me confidence because I knew they were in my corner. After a while, they put down on paper that the university had violated Dr. Lee's academic freedom and academic due process.

A colleague had a big-time lawyer friend in California who took academic freedom cases for free. So my friend says, "Hey, Vic is a good friend of mine and he happens to be at the lawyer's convention in Waikīkī. Go down and see him. Tell him your story."

I called up the guy and we had dinner together. For about two hours I told him my story. And he said, "I'll take your case. You've got to finish your internal processes at the university, but when the right time comes we'll go to court and we'll win." My friend had told me about this guy's reputation. He was a radical lawyer. Terrific! I felt I couldn't lose legally. I knew enough about the law and the Constitution to figure it out even on my own. But with this guy I couldn't lose.

My fight at the university took nearly two years. In December, just about Christmas Eve, at the faculty senate hearing committee, five senior professors found unanimously in my favor. They were mainstream liberals and conservatives from different disciplines. The university president said, "I cannot accept this report. I thought I was right in withdrawing Dr. Lee's letter of intent, and I still think I'm right. I can't continue as president without enjoying the full confidence of the faculty. Therefore, I'm submitting my resignation, but I'm willing to serve until the university finds a new president."

And then, wow—the community out there and half the campus went crazy: "Dr. Lee is getting the upper hand here in the struggle between good and evil. The president is a wonderful man. He has done great things for the university. He's very popular in the community; with the legislature; with the faculty. Please, Dr. Hamilton, reconsider your resignation."

There was a hullabaloo for some weeks, but he wouldn't change his mind. He knew he had made a mistake. He wanted out. Incidentally, he had been president at one of the big universities on the mainland before. So that was his career. But he was washed up after my clear-cut victory. He never went back to university administration.

The next thing that happened is there were three hundred students, including all of my friends, radical and otherwise, but including a lot of strangers, who decided to make a fight of this. They had a big rally and marched down to the administration building. They went inside and stayed after closing hours. Huge mobs were milling around outside. The press was all over the place. They demanded tenure for Oliver Lee. On the second day I joined the sit-in along with eight or ten other professors. The university didn't quite know how to handle this. It was getting bigger the second day. At about 10:00 P.M. they sent the police: "You're trespassing, but if you walk out now nothing will be said. If you stay, you're going to be arrested."

Half the students walked out and half stayed. One hundred and fifty got arrested, including some faculty and me. We went to jail and then got bailed out in the middle of the night. We went right back to the administration building, but we couldn't get in. So we camped outside for about nine days. It was a great thing for temporarily waking up the students. It got a good many students out of their lethargy. This was the spring of '68 and the Vietnam War was going strong.

The Board of Regents got worried. All nine of them came in person to make a major statement to the students. The whole purpose of this visit was to kill any possibility of this getting out of hand because the students were angry. The university didn't want to back down. The Regents were clever. First they said, "We appreciate your concern with the best interest of the university, so we have an announcement to make. President Hamilton's resignation is accepted and is becoming effective as of now." So that was the end of him.

The students cheered their victory and the media played it up. That's how they often do things. They don't talk about the issues; they focus on personalities, and vilify the bad person. But there was another part to the announcement: "Dr. Lee's letter of intent to grant tenure cannot be restored, so therefore, this coming year will be his terminal year, but he will not be teaching." How about that? That's illegal as all hell. I have a contract! Terminal year, what do you mean no teaching? We continued the sit-in for some more days, continuing our demand for tenure for Dr. Lee. But it was in the middle of May and there were final exams, and then the summer vacation. Okay, so that was the end of that phase of the struggle. After nine days, we folded the tent.

In the fall semester the student movement just didn't build up again on this issue. The students had gotten rid of the president, and Dr. Lee's case seemed to be hopeless. Even some of my faculty friends said,

"Oliver, there's no way in hell that you're going to get reinstatement. Take your money, go to the mainland, get another job."

Should I go back to my lawyer who's still sitting in the background; my ace in the hole? We never had to use him because the AAUP published my case in their journal. You know, they have these violation-of-academic-freedom cases. It was in black and white: the UH violated Dr. Lee's academic freedom and academic due process. These reports are then submitted to the annual AAUP convention and the convention votes whether to censure this university or not. It was clear that the vote would have been for censure; no question about it. So in the days before the convention the pressure was on the regents. The more liberal half of the faculty said, "In the university's best interest, Dr. Lee should be reinstated."

Is that what they did?

Of course, that's why I'm here. It was as hard as hell for the Board of Regents to do that. It was a split vote. From day to day, it was uncertain how they were going: to cave in or not to cave in. The reporters were trying to figure out the lineup. At one time it was five to four *against* Lee. Then it was five to four *for* Lee. With the pressure from the AAUP, the regents finally caved in.

Tell about the Hawaii Union of Socialists (HUS).

Well, I was among the small group of people who founded the organization in 1978. Part of the motivation was to pull people together who couldn't stomach the Revolutionary Communist Party (RCP), which was the most active left group in Hawai'i at that time. Some of our HUS folks had actually been inside the RCP, but got disillusioned. Some people never wanted anything to do with RCP. So a small group got together and said, "Let's form an organization which is nonsectarian, nondogmatic, and nondemocratic centralist." About one year later we created a bookstore. Over the years the bookstore was the main project for HUS, although early on we were fairly active in various community struggles. We supported the Waiāhole-Waikāne land struggle, the struggle that resisted eviction of Chinatown people for urban renewal, and the Hale Mohalu struggle to resist eviction of people with Hansen's disease. We also were part of the antinuclear movement and we opposed intervention in Nicaragua.

At the high point, HUS had about twenty-five members. Some would simply delegate themselves to participate on a regular basis in, say, the

Chinatown struggle. In that way we would have our socialist input in the various struggles and then report back to HUS. If there was going to be a demonstration, all twenty-five of us would be there.

But then, later, the energy level declined. It ended up with the bookstore being the main project. I was a co-manager for the first five years. And then my co-manager dropped out, so I was the only manager. Year by year, business improved. We started from scratch, with no capital and no books, but we built it up and it grew. By 1987 it was getting very burdensome on me. I was always trying to delegate. Some of it worked out and some of it didn't.

Then a person showed up who was willing to do a lot of the work, under my supervision. In return for putting in about twenty hours a week, we allowed him to live in the bookstore. He had no other place. He did that for three years and things were manageable from my point of view. But then he turned out to be a thief, so we got rid of him. Again, the full burden falls on me. I was wanting to shut the thing down, but the other HUS members just hated the idea, as I did. I mean, the bookstore meant something to the movement and it meant something to me. So they twisted my arm to go another year, and hopefully they would find some way of making the thing go by some kind of a team effort, or whatever. But that didn't work out, and finally I said, "No, I've got to quit." It's more complex than that, but basically the energy and the commitment weren't there to continue it.

On a small scale I continued to order textbooks for my own courses and several other instructors. Besides textbooks, there are these kind of political theory, political economy kinds of books which our graduate students like. So I'm running a small bookstore of over one hundred books here in my office.

What are the important issues for future work?

The American economy basically is on a slippery slope. This much I'm very confident about, but what that's going to lead to and within what kind of a time span—that's pretty hard to say. Generally speaking, I agree with [Professor] Wallerstein who is predicting major fundamental collapse of the capitalist system. I agree with him about the collapse, and of course, Marx said the same thing. Wallerstein says the collapse will come about fifty years from now. I'm not that confident about the time frame. I think it could happen a whole lot sooner. The exact contours of this crisis and collapse—that's pretty complicated. Basically we're talking about a worldwide capitalist depression, all right, but how long is it going to last? How deep is it going to be? And above all, what will then follow? How are the different nations and working classes in the world going to react to such a crisis? There are so many imponderables. Struggle yes, but with fascist elements on one side and then leftist elements—Marxist, communist elements—on the other. And how are these class struggles going to intertwine with other things like ethnic movements and nationalism?

Within HUS, some [members] are sort of social democrats, or democratic socialists, and some are not. So there's always been a tension between those who figured, okay, so we're socialist, but we've got to be practical, and there's this election campaign going on and let's make some kind of an impact. Some of us just don't want to bother at all with the normal U.S. political processes. I think this capitalist economy is in very dire straits. Reagan screwed it up during his eight years, worse than it had been before. He left a legacy that's incredibly difficult.

And of course, then there's the whole international scene, which obviously has changed a whole lot in terms of disintegration of the Soviet Union and so on. But at the same time, America has also experienced all kinds of setbacks and limitations and constraints. In the first twenty-five years or so after World War II, America had this enormous reputation for political, military, and economic efficacy. People were kind of scared of it. After our defeat in Vietnam, it was shown that American military power, in spite of all its tens of thousands of nuclear warheads, is actually very much limited. The U.S. government really began to understand that. From that time to this, and into the future, America has been very much hesitant to get into anything similar. But the interventionist impulse and motivations are always there, so the U.S. government kind of picks and chooses now. If it's a big problem, well, we hope it would go away. If it's a small problem, we'll go in there and smash those who are giving us a hard time.

Setsu Okubo

Known as a person who influenced many during her long years as an educator, in and out of the classroom. Her full activist life of demonstrations, marches, meetings, and study groups continues at age eighty-one.

I was born here in the Islands. My parents were immigrants, born on the island of Shikoku in Japan. I grew up speaking Japanese. I'll never forget my first day in first grade. I couldn't understand the teacher. I thought she asked me to write my name on the board, so I started writing. She got a ruler and slapped me on my wrist so hard. I was so embarrassed. I never told anyone in the family about it. It's unthinkable that *that* was my introduction to public school. I was never very appreciative of most of the teachers. *(Laughs.)*

My father was a clerk in a Japanese importing firm and pretty literate in English. When in Japan, my mother had gone to a Christian normal school and become a language teacher. In Hawai'i she was a housewife. When all the children were grown she went to work. I guess my family was bourgeois, a little different from other Japanese. I grew up in Pālama, which was then the area with all the government buildings. Later we moved to Waikīkī, not far from the zoo. Many of the residents there were Hawaiians, but now they're all gone. We were isolated from the neighbors. I remember as a child we got both the morning and evening papers, and we also got two Japanese papers. That was a rarity in the neighborhood. Reading made me more aware of world events.

Later on when I started teaching, I expected the kids to know about contemporary events and I insisted that they read the papers.

After I got my degree I was sent to the Big Island to teach in public school. The principal was Mrs. Duncan, a Scotch woman. Most of the plantation higher-ups were Scotch. She was *so* racist. I couldn't stomach her, so I started sassing her back. The other teachers were horrified. I had learned to swear after my brothers came back from the war. I would tell her off and never bothered to even greet her in the morning. I lived in a cottage with some other teachers. The school secretary, who also lived with us, would tell me what the principal's reaction was to me: "Oh, Mrs. Duncan would say...." I knew very well what she thought, but it didn't bother me.

When I was on the Big Island I learned about Hawai'i's people and how they were treated by the white employers. I would visit the plantation communities. God, the bosses would walk through the Japanese workers' homes with their big boots. You know how the Japanese remove their footwear to keep the floors clean. The workers would take a lot of stuff that the ordinary white person wouldn't take. This is the way they all were treated.

In 1947 I took my first sabbatical and went to Columbia University in New York City. The other teachers didn't take their sabbaticals, but I took every one. There was a left-liberal paper—I think it was called *PM*—that talked about the problems workers faced. I *loved* that paper. I would read it on the bus and people would look at me as if to say, "Who the hell are you?" Back in those days they couldn't stomach anyone reading radical papers like that.

At the university I lodged complaints against some of the professors. They were so unqualified and so stupid in their teaching. I recall going to the dean and saying, "I would like to get out of Dr. Cole's class." He was just one of the English professors I grumbled about. The dean asked, "Why, are you failing?" I said, "No, I just don't respect his teaching." He said, "Well, just take a novel and read it in class." He must have known that my criticism was valid.

However, I was able to get into Greg Sinclair's English classes. He was a lover of books and was outstanding as a teacher of literature. Through him I learned to love books. He introduced the class to Modern Edition books that would cost about one dollar for any classic. I studied the literature of Asia and of other areas, and I think I became more politicized from my reading.

During World War II I met a professor who told me I should read the

Marxist classics. So, in New York I began to do this. These books were not available in stores, so I ordered them from Collets [books]. I read these books and found that there really was something to Marxism.

Several professors at Columbia were offering a tour of Europe to visit the post-World War II countries. So, I took a long tour all over Europe. Later, when Russia was opened to travel I took a tour there. And later, the same thing with China. I learned that so many lies had been told about Communism-Maoism; they're still lying today. I took a year's trip around the world on my own, by myself.

When I began teaching again, it wasn't easy to talk about the things I had discovered because you got labeled. But I wanted the kids to read about the world so I got them to buy student subscriptions to *Time Magazine* (I wouldn't do that today) and insisted they read it cover to cover. Then I would test them. The kids hated me. They kept on failing. They tried to keep out of my class. Even my own niece tried to keep out. I told them about the countries I had visited, but they didn't understand. Everybody else told them, "Oh, she's communist." That's what I was labeled. They would argue with me and I told them, "Well look, I've been there; none of the others have." But that wasn't satisfying to them. I was already a radical.

But a few have told me later that they learned a great deal and appreciated my class. I was just transferring my own experiences to them, but I really couldn't explain about the world to kids who didn't know what was going on.

I didn't take part in any protests until the Bikini Atoll nuclear explosions when the natives were forced to leave the island. I became interested in connecting art to my protests as a way of capturing the attention of kids and passersby. I made so many banners, for everybody.

Just this last semester I took a course at the Center for Hawaiian Studies at the University of Hawai'i. The professor brought two Indians to class, an American Indian (Ward Churchill) and a Canadian Indian. I suddenly realized that in all my education nobody had ever taught me about the American Indians. I thought how hopeless the school system was. I was going to go after them with, "How dare you!" Then I realized that they didn't know themselves. Most of the books were written in the 1970s and '80s. There are new ones just coming out now. Ward Churchill did a book around 1993. So, it wasn't the fault of the teachers—everybody was dumb about American Indians.

God, talk about being colonized. In one of his books Ward Churchill has a chapter called "I Am Indigenous" in which he gives a whole string of American Indian names. And he says, "If you don't know these people you have no social consciousness." I didn't know most of those people. I decided that I've got to learn more about American Indians.

You keep learning all the time; even now.

Yes, though the present semester is the first for a long time that I'm not going to school. But I continue to buy books, and now I'm buying art books. When I was preparing for teaching I didn't have time to learn about art. When I got a job I took art courses in the summer sessions at the university. Little by little, I got into art.

In about 1969 I decided I needed to learn Russian. You don't get enough truth in American newspapers. The only university that offered intensive Russian was the University of California at Berkeley. So I went there for a summer course. At Berkeley I met a woman from Kentucky—a fellow student—who also liked art. Everyday after class we would go to San Francisco. Berkeley was in the heyday of activism. They were always protesting something, and I was part of it.

During the Vietnam War I participated in protests wherever I could. Sometimes some of my students would join in a protest and the school principals didn't like it.

When the sovereignty movement started I could relate to the Hawaiians. They were colonized. I understand this completely. Haunani-Kay Trask, who is highly criticized, is only saying stuff that needs to be said. I was more than ready to agree with the sovereignty movement. I can relate to the most radical of the Hawaiians. I can relate to the Black movement in the big cities because I read Malcolm X, Franz Fanon, and so many others.

Sadly, a number of my friends can't relate to some of these ideas. For example, they won't join the International Emergency Committee for Abimael Guzman. They won't *touch* the Revolutionary Communist Party (RCP). They have a fear of being called ultraradical. God, nobody in Hawai'i knows what's going on in the world except the RCP people, but they are hated by the regular, so-called academics or activists. These people won't even subscribe to RCP publications. God, when you read the local newspapers, you *have* to subscribe to RCP publications.

How do you identify yourself politically?

Marxist-Leninist-Maoist. I'm still quite comfortable with this. A lot of people have given up on Mao because China has taken up capitalism. But still, Marxism-Leninism-Maoism is basic. Of course, something else might be produced later by another analyst or philosopher. When you read about Marxism and Leninism, I don't see how it's possible to say that's not workable.

I don't think Americans are educated enough. You can't even talk to a college graduate; they are just turned off. They don't know the primary facts of socialism because they've been prevented from learning that. They're so brainwashed. And they think they're so superior. Education in our schools is so controlled by the machine—subject matter, textbooks, and everything. When kids graduate from college they haven't learned a damned thing. They've only learned the tenets of imperialism and capitalism.

The Indians of Peru understand. The Russian workers understood earlier, and even today they feel that the dropping of Communism has been bad for them. But the establishment groups in power are so damned powerful. They've got the weapons and control all the institutions.

Children in the United States are dying. I see photographs all the time of children in the big cities who don't get the basic necessities. The politicians and people with power don't give a damn. Look what the Republicans are trying to do now with the help of the Democrats. I don't know how they can legitimize what they're doing.

Do you think the Hawaiian sovereignty movement might lead a general working-class movement in the future?

I would like to think that. At the Center for Hawaiian Studies, when they would show Malcolm X's speeches on video, the Hawaiian kids were just full of spirit. I've never seen kids respond so. Their response is different from the other ethnic groups. They're not only aggressive but they will fight for their rights. Of course, they have been done in by the Office of Hawaiian Affairs, and that's just a scandal.

The people in power go all over the world to kill revolutionary instincts everywhere. They're just not satisfied in their own country. The established nations and their representatives in the United Nations are doing very little because they're controlled by the United States. But the non-self-governing groups are beginning to get organized and demand that they be heard. I feel that's a damned good answer to the United States.

Tracy Takano

A waiter at the Sheraton Waikiki Hotel and co-chair of the Hawai'i Rainbow Coalition; forty-something years old.

I've been working at the Sheraton Waikiki as a waiter for the last fifteen years, so I've been active in the Hotel Employees, Restaurant Employees, Local 5. And I'm the co-chair for the Hawai'i Rainbow Coalition. I have a family of three. I was born in 1954 in Pu'unēnē, Maui, a plantation town.

I guess what got me active in different political things was just the conditions here, just the kind of situations that people were living under. When I was in high school during the Vietnam War, there was a lot of questioning and looking at things. Reading Malcolm X inspired and motivated me to get active in things. I read a lot of stuff from the Black Panthers. Some things were starting to happen at the university and some of the high schools. In my sophomore year, I was kind of messing up at school, like a lot of people, so my parents put me into a private school. I didn't like it that much. I used to spend a lot of time at the library and I just happened upon the *Autobiography of Malcolm X*. It made a lot of sense. It was a different experience. He was talking about African Americans on the mainland, but I could see a lot of the same kind of problems here.

Then I went to the University of California at Berkeley for three years. There was a lot of activity there. The Vietnam War was just about ending, but things were happening there in the Asian American community. There were a lot of evictions. That was something I was really opposed to, and I decided to get active.

I didn't finish school. I guess some people know what they want to do, but a lot of people don't. For a little while, I thought I wanted to be an attorney and considered applying to law school. But then I started to work with people in the community who were facing evictions. A lot of urban renewal was happening during that time. I guess the thing that really upset me was that it was perfectly legal for people to have their communities torn up and forced to move out for these huge developments. And that sort of got me to thinking that the law is not a cure-all.

I was working part time while going to school. Then the gas and electric companies opened up affirmative action positions. I got a pretty good-paying laborer job with the gas company and worked for them for a couple of years. Once, we were digging this trench to put in a new gas service to a subdivision. It hardly ever snows in San Francisco, but these light flakes started coming down and I was freezing. And I thought, Gosh, you know, at home I could go to work in tee-shirts. So my wife and I moved back about 1977.

When my wife and I came back from California we needed a place to live and we needed jobs. So we just started walking from one end of Waikīkī to the other and applied in different hotels. My wife got a job as a waitress at the Sheraton. Then she heard about an opening from somebody else, and that's how I got in.

What's it like to wait tables at an expensive hotel?

Well, the Sheraton Waikiki is not on the high end; it's not a luxury hotel. It's somewhere in the middle-high end, I guess. Most people treat you all right. Most of them are not the real rich. They're not the average person, but they're not really rich either. There're always a few who think they're kings, or some of them really are kings, and they just act like that.

I'm shop steward for my department, so the contract protects me from layoff. The person right below me in seniority started about six months after me, so I think he probably works about three-fourths of the time. The layoff doesn't usually last more than a week, so you can't collect unemployment. Vacation time is not that great. The health plan is pretty good.

I got involved in the Chinatown community where they were fighting evictions and fighting to save their community. I went to see a friend who lived in Chinatown and he asked me to help out. There was a community group there—People Against Chinatown Evictions—so I joined in their work. During the 1970s, a lot of these communities were facing eviction. There was a lot of stuff happening. By the late '70s it was finishing up on this island, and I think Chinatown was one of the last major ones. It was sort of at the tail end of that whole period, and [it] kind of picked up on the neighbor islands after that.

I've always been active in the union. It can be one of the more important organizations.

Is that the largest hotel union?

No, the ILWU actually has more hotel workers than Local 5. Local 5 originally was the largest. But ILWU grew along with the growth of the hotel industry on the neighbor islands, where the ILWU has a lot of roots.

The Local here is about fifty years old. Originally, there was a big struggle to get in. The last major struggle for representation was probably in the mid-'60s with the Ilikai Hotel. The workers struck for representation. The union lost the first time, but won the second time. The Sheraton started to expand. The Hyatt went up. There were other chains that started to expand at that time and the union got recognition. And then, like everything, a lot of things changed when Reagan came in. It got much harder for unions to organize. The employers had a better climate to keep unions out. They learned a lot of new tricks,

People really need unions. For unions to grow I think it would take the kind of leadership that really stands up for the workers, and also can learn. The unions here have to learn how to build coalitions with the community. Unions here also need to learn how to get over their competition with each other.

In the past, the ILWU made it clear that they were standing up for the plantation workers. They did this in the context of, "Look, if the plantations and the large corporations keep control of the plantation workers like this, then nobody is going to have any kind of say, because they dominate politics, housing, economy, everything." In 1990 the union struck the major hotels in Hawai'i. There were about 8,000 people on strike statewide. In the 1990 hotel strike the people understood much clearer, even though they didn't work on the plantation, the importance of what the union was doing. The message was clear why people should support that kind of strike. The economy is a lot more diverse now. Tourism is the largest industry in the state. The hotel business can't dictate such poor wages. I mean, it just holds down the rest of the state. In 1990 we were [about] 20 percent below what hotel chains were paying their mainland workers in other major tourist destinations.

Some unions have the ability to be on the cutting edge of leading the fight for democracy in Hawai'i, like the ILWU was back in the old days. We are in a really dependent kind of status here: the cost of living is higher, the health is poorer, the conditions are a lot worse. It has to do a lot with the way the economy and politics are controlled from the outside; and to me, it's the ugliest in the hotel industry. The ability of the union in that sector of the workforce to become organized and press for the economic and political things we need is going to push the whole movement in Hawai'i forward.

I think there has to be more direct unity between the labor movement and the different community groups out there too, because I think that's what it's going to take to really change things in a deeper kind of way. That means capturing elected office for people who really represent the desires and needs of the people. That also means changing the economy of Hawai'i from outside control to something more home-grown that will benefit people and is controlled by people here. Part of it is giving people more direct control over their lives. Part of it is the promotion of culture. I think it's going to happen on a lot of different levels. The unions can play a big part in this because their people need those kinds of changes. But I think that it's going to have to be in conjunction with people in the different national organizations—Hawaiian, Filipino, whatever—that are trying to push forward the needs of their people.

I think tourism is going to have to continue on some level. I mean, I work in the hotels. I don't want to see it end. In terms of promotion of tourism, the state should give support to the different cultural groups out there and allow them to flourish. That attracts people. They have to protect the environment a lot better. That brings people. It has to be done in a way that respects people's integrity, and not in a way that has hotels on every single square inch of the best beaches out there. Agriculture needs to be supported because the scale is much too small now. Agriculture should be on a more cooperative kind of level. There has to be more attention paid to developing what's here.

Would you see about the same number of people visiting Hawai'i in the future?

I don't think the volume can maintain itself. I think it's too high for the resources we have—water and everything else—especially on some of the neighbor islands. There was this big rush to get hotels on the neighbor islands on the theory that you go for the luxury hotels because the people with the money are going to travel regardless. Even though they aren't full all year round, the rate of profit in the luxury hotels is a lot higher because they charge an arm and a leg. So, those hotels went up all over the place. Some were on sites that were important to people for fishing and some were on burial sites. They're finding now that they don't have the water to support all these hotels and people aren't filling them up. The thing always was that it was going to create more jobs. Even the unions supported all these hotels going up.

But my feeling all along was that it's kind of ridiculous because there's this limited body of tourists. Only so many can come over in a year and you're just spreading them out over that many more properties. I've worked here fifteen years, but I only work if the hotel is full. We work based on the occupancy of the hotel. If the hotel is, say, 85 percent full, then a certain percentage of us are laid off for that week, or whatever. Nobody's guaranteed a forty-hour work week. This has created a lot of instability for unionized workers.

A lot of people work two jobs; some work three jobs. Both the husband and the wife are doing it. The status of the working people here has to do with the way the economy and the politics in this state have been shaped: service industry, low wages, high cost of living, too many people working a second or even a third job. And, of course, it impacts on the home because both parents are working. We're at a point where a lot of things can happen and most of them aren't very good. There has to be a major kind of shift in the way that Hawai'i is run.

What about the Hawai'i Rainbow Coalition?

The local Rainbow started in December of '86. Reverend Jackson had gone to Japan to push the Japanese government and corporations for franchises for minority people in the U.S. And he went to Japan to give support to the Koreans who are an oppressed nationality in Japan. On the way back he wanted to stop here, so I helped arrange different events and meetings for him and the response was really good. We went to the university in the middle of exam week and I told him, "Well, I'm not sure how this is going to turn out," but there were over 1,200 students there. We had a community program in the Pālama Settlement and there were [about] five hundred people there.

We decided it would be important to start a chapter of the Rainbow Coalition here, so in early '87 we started to do the groundwork for it. Then Jackson ran for president in '88 and we ran the local campaign. In the primary, Jackson got 38 percent of the vote here, in spite of the governor and the congressional delegation supporting [Michael] Dukakis. That showed that Jackson's message of hope and empowerment wasn't restricted to people from the mainland or African Americans, or anything like that. The message was something that people were looking for here too.

The Rainbow Coalition has evolved into sort of an umbrella. We're not trying to oversee all these different other movements, but kind of be a place where people can come together, push for their demands and make their needs and their issues known, and a place where people can come together for the common good. It's mainly been involved in election campaigns, State Democratic Party convention issues, and different community issues. We have members on all islands.

It's not a real tight statewide organization since we don't have the resources. I think that it's going to continue to be somewhat loose, but I think we need a lot more interaction between the different islands, between the different kinds of constituencies that are represented by the Rainbow. We have to figure out more of a long-range mission, where we want to go, what kind of things we want to push.

We got our biggest jump in membership during the '88 Jackson campaign. We really started bringing new people into the political process. We targeted certain areas, went door-to-door, and registered people for the Democratic Party. We registered hundreds of people in certain depressed neighborhoods, people who had never voted or never had been part of any kind of political process. We got a really good response from Hawaiians and Filipinos on the strength of Jackson's message. Because of the kind of lives that people had, they were ready for that kind of change. We would say, "I'm with the Jesse Jackson campaign. Would you be interested in registering to be a member of the Democratic Party? This is the way you'll be able to vote for Jesse Jackson in an upcoming primary."

We thought that to really bring people in, we have to define what we mean by the Democratic Party, because right now the Democratic Party is so diverse—it goes from developers to poor people. So we're talking about expanding the Democratic Party among a certain sector of people. We felt that the Jackson choice was the best way to do that.

Is there a potential for a third party here?

Well, there's a potential in the sense that I think that the more conservative forces in the Democratic Party are trying to shut things down, trying to keep the party from expanding. To expand means to let in working people, people of color. That's where the numbers are. So, I think there's a basis for a third party in the sense that people are getting frustrated and see that it's going to take a lot to change the situation. I'm open to it, though it would take a lot to build a third party. The Green Party was on the ballot here this past election. They ran several good candidates, but they didn't really have a party. To me, a party in the real sense has to have a broad base and a mechanism to get people. I don't see the potential for anybody doing that for a while. The best direction for the Rainbow right now is to continue to expand the composition of the Democratic Party and see how things shape up in the next few years.

We have a lot of people that are new to politics. I think in a few years the Rainbow will get to the size as well as the experience level where some Rainbow people have run for office and have won. I'm the co-chair of the Rainbow Coalition, but that's not the only thing I do because I think that it's going to take a lot more to really make things happen. That's why I'm still active in the union and other kinds of things in the community. It's going to take a lot to change things and a big part of it is the basic empowerment of people at the grass roots.

What's the potential for linking Rainbow and the sovereignty movement?

The Rainbow supports the sovereignty movement. There's a lot of different issues and details that have to be worked out. I think that's for the Hawaiian people to decide. The Rainbow Coalition has always stood for empowerment, for self-determination, for people having control over their own lives. It's a pretty basic thing in Hawai'i for Native Hawaiians to have sovereignty. So we're very much in support of it.

The labor movement has a lot of debate on where it wants to go. In every movement there's difference of opinion. Very few have a clear view of what the future is going to look like in twenty years. That's why I see the importance of building more alliances between the labor movement and the movements among the different nationalities. Questions on the role of labor or the role of Hawaiians will have to be debated in an atmosphere of mutual respect and trust. All these different progressive movements agree that something's wrong, but I don't think any of them have quite defined their ideal solution that will work for the good of all the other people in the state.

Things are really changing quickly. Not long ago, sovereignty was something that nobody knew about or talked about, and now it's become a topic of discussion every day. To me, the struggle for democracy in Hawai'i is really on the cutting edge of things. I think that working people need democracy, that different nationality movements need it, and the Hawaiians need it. The further we can push democracy along here, the more that's going to open up the possibilities for everybody advancing.

[Since the completion of the interview Tracy Takano resigned from the Sheraton as a waiter to take a position with the ILWU. He now works in the organizing and housing programs of the union.]

Bill Hoshijo

A lawyer in his forties.

I am the executive director of Na Loio no na Kanaka, the Lawyers for the People of Hawai'i. We're a nonprofit, public interest law firm with an office at Pālama Settlement here in Honolulu. Our program work is primarily in the area of legal services for the poor and advocacy in the public interest.

I was born and raised here in Honolulu and attended Kalani High School. Hawai'i is one of the places where people still ask where you went to high school; it has a special significance here. I guess it's kind of a small town in a lot of ways. I am third generation Japanese American. My father was born and raised on the Big Island in a plantation camp called 'Amauulu, outside of Hilo town. His parents came to Hawai'i from Okinawa, so I'm half Okinawan. My mom was born in Japan and raised in Portland, Oregon. During the war as a teenager she was interned at [the] Minnedoka, Idaho, camp. Toward the end of the war she was furloughed and relocated to Chicago, where she met my father, who was a member of the Varsity Victory Volunteers, 442nd. After the war, he came back to Hawai'i.

My father had a colorful early adulthood. He was a professional boxer. He was a seaman. He boxed and he shipped out. He got stuck in San Francisco by the great longshoreman strike a couple years after the war. He remembered being at a rally where he saw Paul Robeson [left-wing Black singer]. He said there was such a big crowd that he could barely see or hear. Then he went to Chicago and reunited with my mom there. They got married and he went to school there on the GI Bill. He got his master's in business. My mom just recently got reparations under the reparations legislation. My brother and sister were both born in Chicago. I was born here after they moved back to Hawai'i. I was the third and youngest child, and didn't have that remarkable a childhood.

When I was in junior high school, at the height of the Vietnam War, my brother went away to Antioch [University] on the mainland. In terms of how I was politicized, I think that he had a lot to do with it. He was involved in a lot of the early ethnic studies activism and the very beginnings of Asian American studies. A lot of it stemmed from the Black Civil Rights Movement and the Vietnam War. He always brought stuff home for me to read. When he would show up he'd say, "Well, have you read the stuff I gave you?" If I hadn't read it, he was pretty much of a taskmaster, and he'd sit there and have me read it to him. After a while I got tired of that and I'd read the stuff that he sent me on Asian American studies, labor history, stuff about the war.

When I was in high school, he came back a couple of times to do his work term. Antioch has a work-study program. He had been involved in some labor organizing and some other things. I remember one time when he came back, he took me out and had me walk a picket line down at Dole Cannery. That made a big impression on me. It really taught me what picket lines are about.

After I graduated from high school, I went to the University of Hawai'i for three years and took some ethnic studies courses while I was up there. For me, that first year in college was a lot like still being in high school. I didn't take it very seriously. So I went to San Francisco State for three years, encouraged by my parents and brother. By the time I got to San Francisco State, all of the real hot and heavy activism and confrontation was over. All those people were blacklisted already. So again, I was on the tail end. But while I was there, I took a lot of ethnic studies courses. It was one of the few programs in the country where various ethnic and racial groups had an ethnic studies program housed under one roof. I got to meet and deal with a lot of different people and all kinds of different political perspectives.

And you know, it's funny, when we first started this organization the young lawyers that got together noticed that pretty much everyone had gone away to school and come back. For a long time we didn't see that much interest in public interest work—Hawaiian issues, environment, civil rights, human rights—from local students who just stayed here. But that's changed for the better.

In recent years there's been a lot more interest from people who have come out of the University of Hawaiʻi law school. Even while they were in school, they sought out opportunities to do this kind of work. In the last few years, there's been a lot of energy coming out of the school from students who want to get involved. They're not all interested in exactly the type of work that we do, but there's an increased interest in pro bono [without fee] or public interest work. I'm really not sure what's behind it.

I've been teaching at the Ethnic Studies Program at UH since 1984, and all the time we talk about whether students have a broader consciousness. Are they more willing to make a commitment? And it's hard to say. From what I've seen, it's been kind of up and down. I think one of the things that's been happening is that a lot of the interest in public interest law is in response to the growth of the Hawaiian movement, the sovereignty movement in particular. There's just more of a sense of justice and injustice, but I don't know that the law school is doing anything exceptional to encourage that.

I went to law school at the University of California, Davis from 1979 to 1982. As a relatively young school, it had a reputation for being innovative and not tradition-bound. Unfortunately, when I got there I found that it wasn't that much different from any other law school. Although I wasn't around for it, there had been a purge. At some point, all of the progressive, radical faculty left in disgust. My class had a fair number of nonwhite, nontraditional students. People had to band together. It was a pretty effective Third World coalition that formed. There were ongoing battles with the administration over admissions and retention.

The Bakke ["reverse discrimination"] case was decided in 1978, and I saw its effects. During the time that I was in Davis there were no Black or Latino medical students enrolled in the medical school. So once they did away with the task force on affirmative action, they pretty much did away with all the target groups. Through our admissions work, we worked with alumni, and I had the opportunity to meet a lot of the young attorneys who were out in the community trying to do public interest work with groups like the Asian Law Caucus and La Rasa Central Legale.

There was one particular faculty member—Jim Smith—who encouraged students to do community stuff. He started an immigration law clinic at Davis, and that's how I got involved in immigration law. Jim was kind of an outcast on the faculty. He was an old movement lawyer who was kind of a burnout, but he really took an interest in students. So I was exposed to the various small community law organizations and worked in the immigration and prison law clinics.

In 1982, I graduated and came back to Honolulu. I talked to anyone who would sit down and talk with me. And I saw what I thought was a pretty limited choice. If you were interested in doing anything that was remotely public interest, you only had a handful of choices. There were probably twenty-five attorneys statewide at the time who were working full time doing public interest law. Nineteen of them were at Legal Aid. There was no Sierra Club Legal Defense Fund here. Native Hawaiian Legal Corporation was just a couple of attorneys. It was really a pretty limited field.

That summer while I was studying for the bar I talked to my handful of friends in town who had been practicing labor law or were with Legal Aid. We thought there was a void that needed to be filled and decided that we would start a new organization. I don't think we were really aware of what would be involved, but we just jumped in. For about a year I worked with this group in organizing the office and took contract jobs on the side from time to time. I worked in the House majority attorney's office during the session, so I had a little exposure to how the Legislature worked.

When we first started the office, we had a very involved board of directors. We'd call meetings and everyone would have to pitch in. We've been in this space since August 1983. This building is part of the Pālama Settlement, a private, nonprofit organization. They're best known for their youth programs, which are housed in other buildings. This building houses various community organizations. They try to get a pretty broad spectrum of services: dental, Catholic charities, senior programs, and so forth.

When we were looking for a place and I was checking out office space, I came in here and met the executive director, Bobby Bachino. His office was right across the hallway from us here. I walked in and he was this older guy wearing a pink aloha-print jumpsuit. He didn't know me from anyone. I talked about what we wanted to do, and he said, "If you want an office, we'll give it to you rent-free," so he gave us this space here. And you know, for years, that's the only way we could survive.

At the beginning, I was making a thousand a month, if we had the money, and I'd get the salary in increments. For a while, it was really touch-and-go. You're trying to establish a track record so you can get funding to do the work you really want to do. Then at a certain point, a window of opportunity opens and you've got a caseload. People begin to look and see that you've been around so long that they think you're an institution. You get funding because people know that you're just starting, but you're serious about what you're doing.

I think the turning point was really the Immigration Reform and Control Act of 1986 —the Simpson, Mazoli, Rodino bill. We had been involved in immigrant rights advocacy; fighting the legislation. We had been involved in some immigrant rights coalitions here. It's ironic, but because of the passage of the legislation, there was this need for services. That led to our first stable funding because there was a need for both education and representation for people affected by the legislation.

I think a fair summary would be that it was a law enforcement bill. The sentiment behind it was regaining control of our borders, so it was an anti-immigrant piece of legislation. It was meant to control illegal immigration from Mexico and Central America into the American Southwest. There were two major components of the bill. One was the so-called amnesty provision which provided for legalization of undocumented residents who could prove that they had been continuously in the United States illegally prior to January 1, 1982. The other linchpin of the legislation was the employer sanctions provision. Up until that time, it wasn't a violation of law to hire an undocumented immigrant. But the new law said that employers are required to verify identity and authorization to work, and to keep records of it. The idea behind all of that was that if the magnet was taken away, then people would stop crossing our borders.

What's the applicability to Hawai'i?

Most of our clients are Pacific Islanders, Filipinos, and Asians. So we see a kind of a strange application of the law here. For instance, because of the history of Samoa, there can be one household where some members of the immediate family are born in Western Samoa, so they're aliens; some are born in American Samoa, so they're U.S. citizens. Problems are a little different in Hawai'i because there aren't that many immigrants who have entered without inspection. For the most part, they come in with some form of documentation and then they overstay. I'd say 90 percent of our work has been working with immigrants from fifty or sixty different countries. The other 10 percent are civil rights cases. It's really a mixed bag.

We have four professional staff—three lawyers and one legal secretary. I think we're pretty stable at what we're doing now. I don't see any expansion in our immigration law project. We can't take every case, but I don't see justification for chasing funds to expand that particular service. And we really are at a point where our board is taking a step back, looking around and deciding where we should go next.

When we first started out, a colleague and I went to talk to a former director of the Asian Law Caucus. We had a lot of ideas about what we wanted to do. At most of our organizing meetings we'd talk about things like whether lawyers should be involved in organizing, what the role of a law organization was, how you balance political advocacy and organizing against being a legal technician, and all these kinds of things. We sat down with this guy, and he said, "Okay, where's your one-year plan? What do you want to get done?"

"Well, we want to establish a law office and represent poor people," and we had all these things we wanted to do.

And he said, "Make a list of all the things you want to do and then where you're going to get the money to do the first thing on your list." So he helped us draw out this timeline, and he said, "At the end of your first year, your goal is to still be alive." At the end of five years, if we had stabilized one project and were handling a full caseload and doing the legal work that we wanted to do, then that would be, he felt, a good five-year plan. I think we managed to do that. At the same time, we have that sort of bread-and-butter work that we do. Then there's civil rights and all the political stuff that we do that's, I guess, just for love.

One of the things that we decided early on was that it's hard to make a distinction between a service case and an impact case. One of our debates was whether an effective legal organization should concentrate on providing strictly individual case services: people with entitlement problems, or housing, or whatever their immediate needs are. This is opposed to the impact litigation approach where you go with broad impact cases—sort of the *Brown v. Board* ["separate but equal" civil rights case] approach. There are some organizations that do their work almost exclusively in the area of impact litigation. One example is San Francisco Public Advocates. We resolved the dilemma by really just not dealing with it. One thing we found is that it's a mix, and there's not a clear line. You don't get good issues for any so-called impact work unless you're providing services. When we work with immigrant community groups, providing the services is really important because you can't get your foot in the door otherwise.

The law firm Bouslog and Symonds were the lawyers for the ILWU in the 1950s, defending union officers and organizers in the Smith Act trials. One thing about Hawai'i that I think is unique is that the civil rights movement has historically been very closely tied to the labor movement. The victories of the labor movement were the civil rights victories on a range of issues like the right to trial by jury of your peers and the right to vote.

We look at civil rights as being a very broad category. We're not looking at it technically, meaning Bill of Rights advocacy like the ACLU [American Civil Liberties Union], or civil rights advocacy under the various civil rights acts. In this sort of loose definition, we really include human rights. It's not strictly protection accorded under law to particular protected classes. We're looking at it as a broad area of law tied to some of the human rights concepts under international law.

Another question that we talked about for a long time at the beginning was what the role of lawyers would be in trying to support social change. And one of the things that we did kind of come around to, not formally, was that when it came to cases that were political in nature, we would get involved primarily if there was either a community organization in place or there was the pretty good potential for organizing around the issue. We might take an individual case if it presented an issue that people in the community were interested in enough to organize around and make it into a political case.

One of the things that's coming up, where there are political organizations already out there doing the work, is in the sovereignty movement. We've been working with a few other organizations and individuals who are trying to put together a defense team that can share resources and provide representation and work with the various political groups.

There's a newly formed Hawaiian lawyers association. There's a core group of attorneys that has done pro bono community work; political work. It's never really been institutionalized, but there is this network of people who can call each other on the phone and get together and form teams or coalitions. And it's always sort of been that way. We hope to institutionalize that to some extent so that we don't have this up and down pattern where we have to reinvent the wheel every time something comes up.

Standard of Living: Housing, Health, Welfare

Recurrent visitors to Hawai'i will complain how it's changing; how things are getting more tacky, commercial, crowded, less friendly. Many residents of Honolulu, including some speakers in this book, note with disdain that home is not what it used to be. They never used to lock their doors at night. Rush-hour traffic jams now rival Los Angeles. They miss a favorite ocean view that's been blocked by a new condominium or hotel. There is a chilling apprehension about sitting on a nuclear arsenal and radioactive waste dumps. Underground sewer breaks are causing street cave-ins. Housing costs continue to soar. Good jobs are harder to get. More people are begging and sleeping on the streets. Unheard of drive-by shootings occasionally happen. Commerce is winning over aloha. Honolulu looks and acts every day more like a typical U.S. city. Residents notice a gradually declining *material* quality of life that seems to be getting worse, accompanied by lower morale.

Hawai'i residents live in the middle of the Pacific Ocean. It is more likely that their attention will be focused on activities in Manila, Tokyo, and Tahiti than New York or Atlanta. There is an intriguing love-hate relationship with the "mainland," and often a sense of estrangement. Perhaps Hawai'i's low record of voting for U.S. presidents (about 44 percent of eligible voters) could come from some level of "alienation." Along with five states in the deep South, Hawai'i shares the distinction of participating *least* in presidential elections.

When one compares social and economic data for Hawai'i with comparable composite data for all fifty U.S. states, one finds an occasional important difference on some factor, but most variables on health, jobs, income, housing, or crime show comparable U.S.-Hawai'i scores, with Hawai'i often slightly above the average. For example, the infant mortality rate per 1,000 live births is about ten for the United States and nine for Hawai'i, a difference of one. The standard of living in a U.S. state is greatly determined by its being a unit of the whole: as goes the whole, so goes the part. Do Hawai'i's unique characteristics—weather, aloha, isolation, diversity—modify this proposition? We will see what conclusions might be drawn through a look at comparative U.S.-Hawai'i statistics from such sources as the *Statistical Abstract of the United States* and *The State of Hawaii Data Book 1993–94*.

In 1992, for every $20.00 of value generated in Hawai'i's gross state product (GSP), $17.00 came from the service and government sectors where wages often are lower and work longevity may be tenuous. 1992 was the year the GSP had reached about $30 billion, a resounding climb of 231 percent since 1980. Currently Hawai'i—indeed, the United States and most other places—is the product of economic, political, and social precursors from the 1970s and 1980s. Since the '80s, a disproportionate share of GSP is finding its way into the accounts of the wealthy and those 20-odd percent in Hawai'i who still are upwardly mobile. This is the "trickle-up" process, a quintessence of the rich-poor relationship and the very nature of the current political economy.

In 1960, Hawai'i's population was 633,000. With double-digit growth in the next decades, the population reached about 1,110,000 in 1995, a 73 percent increase in 35 years, far higher than the United States average. Most newcomers to the Islands concentrated themselves in already populated areas, particularly Honolulu, where job opportunities were better. Since 1960, population density more than doubled that in the United States. In part due to increased density and the need to share high housing costs, Hawai'i has led all other states in the average number of persons per household. This may reveal a touch of Eastern culture and aloha in housing, but it also suggests housing scarcity.

It shocks many to learn that the cost of housing in Hawai'i exceeds nearly every other place in the country, with a median house cost of $360,000 and a median monthly rental of $1,100. As the cost of housing skyrockets, the younger generation (the first to be worse off than its parents) vainly seeks ways to scrape up $72,000 for a 20 percent down payment on a median-priced house, followed by a $2,000 monthly mortgage payment. Let's assume that a young couple found the down payment and bought a median-priced house. If both persons worked full time at the median wage of about $12.00 per hour, their take-home pay would be about $35,000 per year. The first $24,000 (69 percent) pays the mortgage, leaving $11,000 (31 percent) for house repair, utilities, food, clothing, auto, insurance, giving, savings, and other necessities. The couple brilliantly juggles their budget, but never can make ends meet. They delay having children because of the additional cost.

The median household income today in Hawai'i is over $42,000 per year before deductions. That *seems* pretty high, especially if you are poor, but it still is pretty close to the U.S. average. The *real* problem is that the cost of living is roughly 40 percent higher than the United States. Hawai'i's median household income is far beneath the 1992 annual "intermediate" budget of $58,374 set by the U.S. government for a family of four in O'ahu. That figure is more than four times the budget set for 1971. In the past ten years the cost of fruits and vegetables, shelter, and medical care have nearly doubled. Working people just aren't making it.

The wages paid Hawai'i's 600,000-member workforce are generally not a lot higher than the national average. In the private sector a laborer, hostperson, and data entry clerk—typical jobs being created today—earn about $9.00 per hour, or $19,000 per year if they work full time. Many workers must work longer and harder to make a living. The forty-hour week, rapidly becoming a relic of the past, applies to only 43 percent of the workforce in Hawai'i. The average hours per week for full-time workers now exceeds fifty. The 33 percent who work less than forty hours per week represent the rapidly growing trend of involuntary part-time work with low wages and few benefits.

Like the United States, where every day the job market gets more unfriendly to workers, Hawai'i has a significant and expanding poverty population. In 1992 there were officially 130,000 people in poverty (11 percent of the population), those who fell beneath $17,000 per year for an urban family of four. This is an ominous rise since 1987, and likely an undercount since a lot of poor people blend into neighborhoods or beaches, and become invisible. The 100,000 recipients of Medicaid, a U.S. health insurance program for the poor, may find benefits drastically cut if the 104th U.S. Congress has its way. Congress is also poised, at this writing, to slash benefits to some 50,000 poor women and their children in Hawai'i who receive Aid to Families with Dependent Children (AFDC). The average yearly AFDC income for poor families does not exceed $6,000, a bit above the U.S. average, but not adequate at all.

Even more telling, Hawai'i authorities estimate that 176,433 people missed meals for economic reasons in 1992.

A lowering material quality of life for an increasingly underemployed population with considerable doubt about the future surely affects the social behavior of some people. Those who turn to street crime usually come from material deprivation. Their "deviant" behavior in making a living is somewhat consistent with their material circumstances. They have plenty of white-collar criminal role models. The culture imposed by the rich is characterized by greed and a couldn't-care-less-about-you attitude. In general, we would judge that most working-class crime is clinically normal behavior. Street crime in gentle Hawai'i is increasing. Signs of a frightened and defensive population abound: burglar alarms, double bolts, guard dogs, rent-a-cop agencies. More police are hired and the prisons are full. But interestingly, Hawai'i's violent crime rate is nearly three times less than the United States, while *property* crimes are about 15 percent higher. Aloha seems to prevail in one dimension of criminal behavior, but material need in another.

Robert H. Stauffer said, "With the exception of the decimation of the native population during the eighteenth and nineteenth centuries (caused primarily by the introduction of biological agents), never before in the history of Hawai'i has the standard of living declined to such a degree and in such a relatively short time as statistics show for the 1970–1982 period" ("The Tragic Maturing of Hawai'i's Economy," *Social Process in Hawai'i*, Peter Manicas, ed. [McGraw-Hill, 1993], 187). Our review of statistics since then shows that the decline has continued to the present and undoubtedly is accelerating.

It is tempting to speculate on the total number of Hawai'i residents who are "at risk." No data we know have done this successfully, and the likely reason is that the establishment *knows* how gloomy the picture would be so it authorizes no such studies. We think that between one-quarter and one-half of the U.S. population is at serious risk, based on welfare, unemployment, working poor, crime, health, homeless, and other data; and on our assumption that most "official" data are undercounts. We do not think the situation is much different in Hawai'i; maybe just a bit slower in coming because of lag time. One thing is for certain, the class structure is dynamic: the rich are getting richer while the poor and middle classes are getting poorer.

These unfortunate developments should trigger a storm of popular protest and demands to the political leaders for a different allocation of public resources and a better management of the social system. The 1960s certainly showed how mobilized people could get things done. But the progressive movements of that era that patched up and added to the safety net were unable to hold sway for many reasons, including the rise of the new right.

By the end of the '70s the restive right was making a call for a new "social contract" in America. *Business Week* devoted three of its issues at the beginning of the Reagan "revolution" to presenting and justifying the new right's case. The particulars, based on supply-side economics, were socially far reaching: all social sectors—labor, women, minorities, elderly, urban dwellers—must sacrifice previous gains made in order for more investment capital to be generated. Of course, the call was framed in patriotic terms—the need to sacrifice for your country—which effectively hid the clear economic and class character of this right-wing movement.

Then, when *all* major quality of life indicators were showing more people going down the slippery slope—created by the free market and twenty years of governmental benign neglect—lo and behold, the radical right slinked into national power. The call for a new social contract two decades earlier became institutionalized as the mean-spirited "Contract with America." People "naturally" slipping down the slope now were *pushed* with a vengeance. As of this writing the safety net is being dismantled, insidious racism is surfacing, and a new chaos is entering the lives of the working class.

Leaders in and out of government are falling over themselves to reduce the costs of services and business, which of course means lowering the standard of living of working people. Rather than budgeting for an *expansion* of services and jobs at a time when they're more needed than ever, all efforts are being made to *cut*. In Hawai'i, as elsewhere, politicians play a game of blaming previous administrations for covering up major budget deficits; this, in a state whose balanced budget used to lead the United States.

One of the more insidious illustrations of commodification and privatization in human services—very fashionable in the United States today—is health care. Some 40 million U.S. residents have no health insurance. Skyrocketing health expenditures are caused by some 2,400 competing insurance companies, record pharmaceutical profits, overuse of medical procedures, inflated hospital and physician incomes—costs which are unregulated by federal or state authorities. Current efforts to force physicians and patients into profit-making health maintenance organizations and managed care networks is further eroding the quality of health care. Some patients are denied emergency care by insurance carriers, while others are responsible for large medical bills upon discharge. Among the industrialized nations, the United States alone promotes profit from illness and health care.

The good news is that Hawai'i has led the United States in life expectancy and has had the lowest death rates from cancer, diabetes, and accidents, as well as heart, pulmonary, and liver problems. The bad news comes from the developing trends discussed above, which are putting more people at risk and eventually will result in more illness in the population. The great contradiction of Hawai'i is the precarious state of health of the Kanaka Maoli, clearly expressed in a life expectancy of seventy years compared to the eighty years for whites, and in a doubled infant mortality rate. The indigenous people once were very healthy. Kekuni Blaisdell, a Kanaka Maoli physician appearing in part 7, notes, "[Our people have] the highest of rates for the major causes of death such as heart disease, cancer, stroke, diabetes, automobile accidents, and even suicide." Public health professional Ku'umeaaloha Gomes, also appearing in part 7, is critical of the narrow vision and undercounts by the public health establishment whose statistics are skewed toward the more healthy Hawaiians with jobs and more money.

In part 6 of this book, Ah Quon McElrath relates the little-known history of how health care was brought to Hawai'i. The Kaiser Medical Plan was initiated in the 1950s by the ILWU in spite of strong objections by the Hawai'i Medical Association, then known as the Hospital Association. Hawai'i is covered by a health insurance plan considered one of the best by some U.S. health activists anxiously grasping for a good working model. South Dakota Senator Thomas Daschle sent his staff to study the system in Hawai'i. The two largest plans, the Hawai'i Medical Service Association [HMSA] and the Kaiser Foundation Health Plan, provide both group settings and private physicians, and cover everyone who works at least twenty hours per week. Activists tell us that many workers are contracted to work less than twenty hours by employers wishing to escape this obligation. There is little doubt that Hawai'i's plan is an improvement, but it is far from perfect. Like the United States, Hawai'i suffers from increasing hospital costs and unregulated prescription drug costs.

1995 marked yet another year of failed attempts by U.S. activists to get a national health system. This battle has been waged for seventy-nine years, beginning in 1906 with a coalition of labor and, shockingly, the American Medical Association. The AMA now leads the fight *against* a national health plan. It is estimated that switching to a single-payer, federally managed program would save enough in bureaucratic costs to insure the 40 million Americans currently uninsured.

The speakers grouped into this part are veterans of struggles for improvements in health, welfare, housing, and other life necessities. Their backgrounds reflect the diversity of Hawai'i. Most of them are searching for solutions to the downward spiral in quality of life and for a framework to unite activists in the coming battles.

Rick Rothschiller, one of two serious surfers in this book, has a growing class perspective and multinational experience in China and the Philippines. The many forms of oppression are worrying preoccupations which he describes. Mary Choy, born in San Francisco of Korean parents, has a political perspective that impels her toward many forms of peoples' struggles. She was arrested at Kalama Valley, protested the Chinatown evictions, joined Kōkua Hawai'i, and currently works with the Pro-Kanaka Maoli Sovereignty Working Group.

A daughter of the Islands is Christine (Kalahiki) Brown, who works with tenant associations such as People Against Chinatown Evictions and those committed to affordable housing and rent control. She is a member of a neighborhood board and keeps her activism firmly fixed on important local needs. Will Butler is a physician who grew up in Louisiana and has lived and practiced medicine in Hawai'i since the 1950s. An active member of Physicians for Social Responsibility and other groups, his activism is well known in the fight for justice and equality undertaken by the left.

Jim Brewer is a leader in the League of Employees for Economic and Democratic Advancement (LEEDA). He and his fellow activists can be seen each Wednesday outside the State buildings in support of the rights of workers and other causes. Rachel Saiki has a long and rich history in the struggle of workers to achieve a decent standard of living. Today, she continues her commitment to various progressive causes.

Rick Rothschiller

The executive director of the People's Fund in Honolulu; about forty years old.

My great-grandparents were immigrants to the United States: three sets from Germany, one set from Russia. My paternal grandfather owned a small scrap metal reclamation company and had eleven children. My maternal grandfather was a farmer and a small businessman in North Dakota. My parents were married in 1954 and I was born a year later. I consider myself as being from a working-class family because my parents moved to California where my father worked in a fish market, studied plumbing after work, and became a plumber. He's still doing that today—blue-collar worker in a union. My mother became a licensed vocational nurse. That's as far as she got. She did nursing off and on while we were growing up, but mostly she was a housewife.

My father was Catholic, and I went to Catholic schools for sixteen years. Even though our income was not high, education was very important to my parents and they sent all three of their children to Catholic schools. So I think that was a big impact on who I am. But in my teens I stopped attending church services and wasn't feeling moved by institutional Catholicism, although I think some of the morals were implanted. You know: justice, equality, it's harder for a rich man to get into heaven than the camel through the eye of a needle, the meek shall inherit—that kind of thing. I think those things affected me and also made me open to Marxism later on.

166

I grew up in the white suburbs around Los Angeles and was kind of sheltered from a lot of the world. I entered high school in 1969, the time of the student movement, antiwar movement, Civil Rights movement. All these things were having an effect on me. I was a good student, studied really hard, and was always near the top of my class. In 1973 when I graduated from Chaminade High School, the Marianist brothers offered to send me to Chaminade College here in Honolulu on a full-tuition scholarship. I was not really politicized much at all, just very superficially. It was when I entered college, when I came to Hawai'i, that I started paying attention to what was going on and seeing how world events affected me and others.

I had never been here before. It was just a real new wild experience which helped open me up to various cultures and different communities. At home I experienced racism in a different way. I didn't call it racism; I didn't know what it was. I just knew that there were only one or two people in my high school graduating class who were not white. There were more and more Hispanics coming up from Mexico and then there was a Black population. I remember the Watts riots in 1965. My father took us on a kind of tourist trip to see Watts afterwards. It conflicted with what I was being taught morally in school and what my family professed: everybody's equal and all this kind of stuff.

When I came here I experienced a situation where I was not of the majority race, and I think that was very healthy for me. By then, the antiwar movement was winding down, but there was still a lot around. The Weather Underground was still happening and I was aware of it. The other part of the '60s—the countercultural dimension, experimentation with mind-altering substances—I think actually influenced my behavior more; and I even inhaled, I have to admit that. *(Laughter.)*

Eastern philosophy had affected California and it was all over Hawai'i. In high school and college I studied comparative religions. I was looking around spiritually and I even tried to check out Catholicism again, but I couldn't. Zen [Buddhism] was the religious philosophy that most impacted me, and I've held it to this day. And of course, it fit in with the experimentation and psychedelic experience of the day. Catholicism was something I learned: catechism and ritual and ceremony and hierarchy. Zen is something that I sought and found, and experienced in a completely different way. I don't do any Zen ritual or ceremony, or I don't attend any Zen activities. It's more or less a personal philosophy.

While in college I worked twenty hours per week for three years out of the four, and the other time I got by on unemployment or whatever. I started out studying accounting because accountants out of college were highly paid. So I had a kind of conservative orientation. But I think my life experiences then started to change that. I became more interested in psychology and philosophy.

After my second year of college, I spent most of the summer in Europe, traveling around by train with a backpack. That opened me up to the world. After that I paid more attention to foreign news and cultural differences. My understanding of the world was so limited compared to people there. Many people spoke several languages. They knew more about what was going on in the U.S. than I knew.

When I came back from Europe I changed my major from accounting to psychology. I read Freud and Jung and Carl Rogers—the phenomenological orientation. I read Erich Fromm, Camus, Dostoevsky. Those people made me think. And even the Bhagavad Gita (sort of the Hindu Bible), and Krishnamurti (Hindu philosopher), and Lao Tzu (founder of Chinese Taoism). I feel fortunate to have grown up at that time, rather than, say, in the late '50s, because there were so many opportunities to explore the inner and outer world and look for alternatives. I think it had a deep effect on me. The way Chaminade dealt with religion was to present opportunities for people to develop their Catholicism or Christianity or to explore alternatives. My teacher who taught Philosophy of Religion was an Indian from India. He was a real global person.

Then I started surfing regularly, three or four times a week. I still surf four or five times a week when I can fit it in. And I think that also influenced me because it put me in a very intimate relationship with nature in the past twenty years of rapidly declining environmental health. Surfing is exciting and challenging. Surfing is like snow skiing, plus the medium is constantly moving. It takes an absolute concentration and abandonment of reason for split seconds of time. At the same time, it takes putting one's self in rhythm with nature: getting used to when and from what direction the sets are going to come, how big are they going to be, where the bottom is, how the bottom is now, where the sand is. All these things affect how the wave will break, and that's important. But also, what are the tides? What is the tide doing today? What times of the year are the winds coming from certain directions? Where will the surf be? All these kinds of things. When I'm outside I'm looking at the clouds to see which way the winds are or feeling the temperature. It's very intense, and it's an incredible rush. In skiing you can get a lot of speed. In surfing, speed is not the main thing, but it's the acceleration which is more of a rush.

There are women surfers, but not many. In a past issue of *Surfer* there was an article by a professional woman surfer about sexism in professional surfing and about discrimination, those kinds of things. Surfing has become very aggressive. As the surf gets more and more crowded with people scrambling for waves, sometimes there are fights and things like this. When I first started surfing the era was different and the attitude was different. It was more like what they called soul surfing: being in touch with nature, appreciating it, riding the wave, being one. Now, there's a lot of money involved. Several pro surfers are making over $100,000 a year, so it's very competitive and commodified—name brand this and that. So it's changed very much.

No politics in surfing?

No, it would be nice if there were, and there should be. Like in most areas of life, I think there's potential there, especially people who are in touch with nature everyday, and what's happening to nature, and what's happening to the oceans. There is potential there, but it's not tapped, it's still commodified. Surfing is important to me too because of the work I do. I've been mostly a full-time activist since 1976. There are few people on this island who have the opportunity to do that, but it's burn-out work. Before that, I was doing social work a lot, and that's burn-out work too. Many people I know have found that it's good to have some kind of completely different release. It helps me to maintain some kind of perspective and balance in my life.

I graduated with a bachelor's in psychology and applied to Ph.D. programs at UH, Stanford, and Berkeley, but was not accepted even though my GRE scores were pretty high. My advisor at Chaminade said, "It's probably because of the school you're graduating from, and your classes." I looked briefly for a job here but didn't find one, so I went back to California because I wanted to live on the coast and surf. I ended up in Ventura, California, working for two and a half years as a bookkeeper for a group of thirteen psychiatrists. But my values had changed enough by that point that I wanted to do something more meaningful. That's when I started, in the late '70s, on political activism.

The first group I belonged to was People for a Nuclear-free Future, which was the Ventura County chapter of the Alliance for Survival. We were working primarily on stopping the start-up of the Diablo Canyon nuclear power plant. That's when I started reading things like *The Nation* and *The Progressive*. I was introduced to people who had been in the movement a long time and who had perspectives on what was necessary to make a more equitable and just environmental society.

Around 1980, I gravitated to the Ventura County Progressive Coalition, an anti-Reagan kind of coalition that was dominated by liberalism, but had some communists and socialists also.

At that time, I also went back to school. I didn't like the way I was making a living and I actually lost my job because they started to computerize their bookkeeping system. I went full time into a master's in community/clinical psychology at Cal State Northridge. Clinical psychology is what most people associate with psychology, which is individual therapy. Community psychology came out of the '60s, and part of it is community mental health and another part is looking at the effect of social institutions on individual well-being, and looking for methods of intervening to change those institutions.

Central America was heating up around that time, so I helped to start a Ventura County Coalition for Human Rights in Central America to protest U.S. policy in Central America. Nicaragua was the society where we could get firsthand information, and we could see how it was forming itself after the revolution. I began to look for alternative forms of economic relations in society. I started to get access to left papers and was introduced to Marxism. I looked at the Soviet Union, China, and other postrevolutionary societies. So I think what I was learning was, as Joseph Collins titled his book, *What Difference Could a Revolution Make?* or how can things change?

At the same time, I was getting some experience testifying at city council hearings and lobbying on this and that. You know, what's going to happen working within the system and asking politicians to make changes. Then I started learning about nuclear weapons, and that whole issue became important to me. I also was becoming conscious of global rivalry and arms buildup. Watergate and Vietnam were important for me early on. I became conscious of how it seemed like the ruling elites were willing to use nuclear weapons. I mean, they used nukes in Japan, in World War II, so they might use the things again. All this was giving me some idea about who's running things, what kind of people they are, and what they might be willing to do to get what they want. I began looking more and more for alternatives.

I was working during the summers as a counselor in a CETA [Comprehensive Education Training Act] program, working with disadvantaged communities—primarily Hispanic and African American—in Ventura county. That was my first experience of actually working closely with communities of color, and especially oppressed communities, and it was a very valuable experience. I was putting that together with my studies about community psychology, the justice system, the educational system—how biased and racist and class oppressive our social institutions are—and experiencing on a daily basis how people are dealing with it. I came to understand what the CETA program was: it alleviated a little bit of suffering for a little while for some people, but it was a Band-Aid and it wasn't going to solve the problem. There wasn't going to be any means to change things structurally for the better. So that was a valuable experience.

In my last year of graduate school, the husband of my thesis advisor had led the first delegation of psychologists to China. They had wanted me to go on to Ph.D., but I felt like I needed more broadening. My advisor found an opportunity for me to teach English in China. This was an opportunity to give to the Chinese what they wanted at that time—to learn English. It was an opportunity to live for nearly a year in an entirely different economic system and a 3,000-year-old culture. I had started reading Chinese Marxism, Mao and stuff. There were the two dominant paradigms on the planet, it seemed to me, for how to organize a society, how to make a society more just and equitable, and to meet the needs of the people. I already was quite aware that a lot of the mainstream media [coverage] about communist countries was propaganda and lies. So I wanted to experience it for myself. Before I went, I was told by a man in his seventies who had been beaten up in the early 1920s as a labor organizer, "You're going to learn a lot more there than you're going to teach," and he was absolutely correct. Every day that happened. China was an incredibly moving experience.

What struck me about China was that pretty much everybody had food, clothing, housing, and a job. But there were serious problems. China is a very poor country and it seemed to me that a lot of people were unhappy with what happened under Mao and a lot of people were still unhappy under Deng. I saw that the Communist Party was monolithic and very top-down and not living up to its ideals. I was talking mostly to intellectuals, although I had a girlfriend who was working class and couldn't speak English. Some people lost faith in the revolution in the '50s and others in the '60s, during the cultural revolution, and then others since Mao died. . . .

I don't know how to summarize. You know, it persuaded me that an alternative is possible, that we don't have to live with capitalism the way that we have it in the United States, that the radical alternative is possible. And I think it motivated me to look seriously at how to make that kind of change in the U.S. I had been learning more and more that a lot of the problems with attempts to make revolutionary change in other parts of the world resulted from interventions by the U.S. and other capitalist countries. It seemed then, and it still seems today, that things were becoming more and more global and the solutions have to be more and more global. It's the global capitalist economy, global imperialism, my own country. I'm in the belly of the beast, although in Hawai'i we like to hope that maybe we'll be a different country. But for now....

It's connected to the beast.

Yeah, yeah. *(Laughter.)*
When I came back from China I stopped in Hawai'i and threw out some résumés. Within a week I was offered a job as a social worker. I thought, Well it's a job, and I like Hawai'i and I remember how beautiful it is. I worked for over a year as a social worker in Kalihi at Susannah Wesley Community Center. Kalihi is the location of the largest housing projects in the state, where 80 percent of the immigrants to the U.S. in Hawai'i were coming first; a very poor area, kind of the ghetto, near downtown. I worked with adjudicated teens and their families, a category that is overpopulated with native Hawaiians, Filipinos, and Samoans. It was a valuable experience for me to work with and learn from the most oppressed people in the most oppressive communities in Hawai'i. I got another look at Hawai'i itself, different from when I was here going to college. My eyes started to open up as to actually what was going on here.

I looked around for groups to get involved in. I checked out Greenpeace and a couple other groups. I went to some forums of the HUS [Hawai'i Union of Socialists] at their bookstore, Modern Times. Those were good, but I didn't join Modern Times. I wasn't invited to join and I was poor. The most active group was LACASA, the Latin American Caribbean Solidarity Association. I got involved with LACASA because they were the most active and they were politically left. I also did a little media work with the Native Hawaiian group called Ka Hea, "The Call." I needed to learn a lot more about the Hawaiians; I still need to learn a lot more.

And then I got a job for a semester teaching at Honolulu Community College as a counselor and teacher of human development. It has the highest percentage of working-class people of all colleges in the state, so that was valuable. Then I audited some political science classes at UH: political philosophy, taught by a conservative; Marxism, taught by a sympathetic critic of Marxism; nuclear war, taught by a right-wing peace-through-strength guy; and a graduate course on exterminism which looked at genocide.

In 1986 I visited a friend in Oregon who had helped open a SANE [National Committee for a Sane Nuclear Policy] office there. We thought, Why can't we open one in Hawai'i? He and I put together a small funding proposal to national SANE. They ended up giving us a couple thousand dollars to open a canvassing office. Though I was excited about SANE's canvassing tactics, its liberalism was hard for me to deal with. Even though there were some progressives like Jesse Jackson, Marcus Raskin, and Seymore Melman in SANE, I saw that it was a primarily East Coast, upper-middle-class, liberal kind of group and seldom asked the kind of questions that I would like asked.

But what struck me was the canvassing. This wasn't just having another forum or demo on peace and nuclear stuff with the same fifty people, which is what we were doing in Hawai'i, but going out and looking for people and finding out where people were at. I had a lot of hopes for it and it was working well across the country. I got some canvassing training in Oregon and Pittsburgh for a couple of weeks. Then they sent an organizer to Hawai'i to help open an office. We hired staff, [and] kept it going for about six months, but it didn't work too well. It was a lot harder to canvass here. One, the cost of living is higher so people have less disposable income. Two, SANE lobbied Congress and stuff, and it's a long way from here to Washington, D.C. Three, there is a huge military presence and influence on local politics.

We went door-to-door, collected signatures on petitions to send to politicians, tried to raise money, looked for members for SANE, and looked for activists. When I came to the door, I would ask people if they were concerned about the issue. Before I would ask for money I would ask them if they would do something: get involved, come to a meeting, come to an action. Well, very few people would do those things. But what was really fascinating to me was to be able to talk with such a variety of people on an issue that I had to learn intimately. Some people would open the door and say, "Bless you son, come on in," and offer me something to eat and drink, and bring out their checkbook. Others would slam the door in my face, or curse at me, or call the cops, or sic their dog on me. There was a political spectrum from alienated leftists to alienated fascists. I had to figure out where they were coming from, try to approach them, and see if we could develop something together. It was a challenge and a very valuable experience. Again, I learned more than I taught.

All the staff quit because it was too hard, but I kept doing it myself. I guess I was more committed, was older, and knew the issue better. I canvassed off and on for four years. In 1988 the INF [Intermediate-Range Nuclear Forces] Treaty was [ratified] and people started to think, "Oh, the problem is going to be solved," or, "I gave you guys twenty-five bucks, didn't you solve that problem yet?" I couldn't compete with the bombardment that was coming out of the newspaper and the propaganda on television every day. Then, of course, concern went downhill as other problems became important and as the Soviet Union and Europe began to change radically. It was harder to make a living at it, because I was being paid out of the proceeds from canvassing. I was living on the margin.

So I went back to working part time in social work, this time working intensely with families, ten hours a week per family, with a partner. These were also predominantly poor people in communities of color, but all over the island this time, instead of just Kalihi.

At about this time I met a woman with whom I later lived for a few years here. She was an American woman who had returned from China where she had taught for two years. She was a strong feminist and really helped to give me a woman's perspective and to understand the oppression of women. She pointed me in the right directions of what to read and what to see and who to hear. So that was a big impact on me.

By now you were totally purified. Was there anything left? (Laughter.)

It's not to say that I've overcome my blind spots or my problems, but I'm making a conscious effort in my life. You know what I mean?

I worked as an administrator for six months at the UH Institute for Peace while they found someone else. That exposed me to the academic range of opinion on peace and world order studies, and stuff like that, and it was valuable.

Then I worked at Gigi's [Cocquio] farm [Hoa Aina O Makaha] for six months as an administrator. I didn't do much farm work. I didn't get my hands that dirty, but I got to work out there and Mākaha is different. It is an experience in developing an alternative living arrangement.

At that time there was the buildup to the Gulf War, another crucial experience for me. Having been the only full-time peace activist in the Islands since '86, when the Gulf War happened I really tried to develop a coalition between the RCP [Revolutionary Communist Party] on the left and the liberals on the right. This was going to be a coalition which would call not for Maoist revolution on the one hand, not for sanctions on the other, but somewhere in between, which was to bring the troops home *unconditionally.* The factions had their differences, but they both had the same slogan for the January demos. Even so, we couldn't get that off the ground.

I learned some lessons there. I learned that I had a little bit too much trust in the old new left people. I should have gone on my own. I wish I hadn't been quite so burned out from four years of canvassing and organizing. But you know, it became clear to me that the anti-Gulf War movement in the U.S. was a joke. When the elite started getting onto what the movement was talking about, most of the movement was manipulated and marginalized. "Bring the troops home" wasn't even spoken on television. It's what Noam Chomsky called "the boundaries of acceptable discourse." *Bring the troops home* was outside of that. We had no effect on breaking that boundary.

It is true that the war moved fast. We couldn't get anybody to do any work until late December when people started coming to meetings. A lot of the old new left were saying, "Well, we need to start going into the schools and educating people," and stuff like this. Some younger people were saying, "We've got to get out on the streets January 26," and they wanted to build an organization, have elections and stuff in December and January. Granted, nobody could judge that the war would be that short, but we had indications. Months before, Secretary of Defense Cheney had said it would last four to six weeks. He was right, you know. The firepower that was being sent over there and the knowledge that Iraq is a Third World country—I was disappointed in the movement.

We're struggling. The arms race was one place where I became aware of the nature of the problem. It's not a question of some minor reforms to stop testing nuclear weapons. It's a lot deeper: it's historical, it's cultural, it's ideological. The Gulf War pointed up what we really have to deal with and how incapable we are of doing it.

During that time I started reading such world systems theorists [as] Andre Gunder Frank and Immanuel Wallerstein. I also was reading the Frankfurt school to go back and see how they dealt with the crisis of Western Marxism in the early '30s. A lot of those questions have not been answered. I was really looking around; I'm still looking. I still don't have answers.

And then I went to the Philippines. In 1990 the local Philippine support movement sent me there as a peace activist to attend an antibases conference. Filipinos have been trying to get the U.S. bases out since

1898. Instead of just going to the conference, I stayed for a month and had what they call exposure experiences. Then I went back in March of '91 and worked with the antibases movement for six months—until September, when the Philippines was going to have to decide if they wanted to renew the bases treaty. I was involved in the campaign to defeat the treaty and we were successful in the Senate. As it turns out, the U.S. is developing some access arrangements. U.S. officials have said publicly that they expect to have at least as much or a greater presence in the region [as] they do now. They'll have access to the harbors and Philippine air space. It's being worked out now. The U.S. has more control of Philippine air space than the Philippine government does.

While I was there, I was able to spend most of June in an NPA [New People's Army] camp in the hills outside of Manila. I was able to experience the revolutionary mass movement. It was a very moving experience for me to see the kind of poverty that people are living in, the kind of oppression, the kind of lives that they lead, and their willingness to sacrifice to make social change. Some people I met in the NPA camp had college degrees and were from bourgeois families. They could have had servants; everything they wanted. They gave that up to live in the hills to make social change for the country. That was very impressive to me. Here in Hawai'i, some people think they're activists if they put a couple of bumper stickers on their car and go to a meeting a couple times a year. You know what I'm saying? In the Philippines I was able to be among people who have the spirit and hope and potential. I was encouraged by being able to work with a real mass movement, never having worked with one before.

I came back from the Philippines to the best job that I could get in Hawai'i, which is working full time with the People's Fund, being in touch with the movement, helping the various social movements in some way. The question I'm coming to is how long I will be willing to make the sacrifices—the few that I'm making, compared to people in the Philippines—to continue to work in the movement. I don't know. These are questions I have to work out personally.

I'd probably like to get married and have children someday, and maybe buy a house so I don't have to worry about being a bag man. I like the People's Fund because a lot of people here—from their mid-forties to their seventies—have been around a lot longer than I have. That gives me perspective and helps me see how they've dealt with their lives; how they've stayed active. They inspire me too, you know.

And then I see other people are no longer active at all; others who are promoting the mainstream parties and electoral politics. I read an article a couple years ago about Tom Hayden, who was running for reelection in the California Assembly. It was a tight race and he was apologizing for his activities during the Vietnam War, saying that he was wrong. I hope this doesn't happen to me, but we never know. We never know.

What do you see coming? Are you cynical? Realistic?

Well, there is some cynicism. There is also realism, maybe. I think the more I'm into it, the more understanding I have of the gravity of the issues. The ecosystem is being destroyed from under us. Oppression increases. There are forty thousand children dying every day on this planet from malnourishment or preventable diseases. We see a growing Third World inside the United States. We see the U.S. using the same kind of tactics inside the United States that previously had been reserved for the Third World. They use the same SWAT team in Los Angeles that they use to arrest Noriega. They use the same army troops in Iraq that they use in Los Angeles. I try to be global in perspective, which is to say that it doesn't matter to me whether workers in the U.S. or in Japan or wherever are making cars.

There's enough on this planet to go around, and what's preventing that is greed and exploitation. It's becoming clear now. As conditions for the lower strata continue to decline in the U.S., there may be some opportunity for them to become more aware of what they have in common with workers, poor people, and women in the Third World. Maybe that will provide some solidarity and some opening for developing a more global international solidarity movement. I understand that there have been some meetings recently by workers in Mexico and Canada and the U.S. regarding NAFTA [North American Free Trade Agreement]. So that's a possibility. I have a ray of hope that's coming through clouds.

Things are deteriorating rapidly for most people, and the current indications to me are that things are not going to get better in the short term. The society is stratified all the way down. Certain sectors and classes, especially the technocratic elite, are bribed by the top 1 percent of the financial and political elite, while people at the bottom are forced to blame themselves. You know what I mean. All this kind of stuff has to be dealt with. So in the short term, I don't see a lot of room for optimism, except in the grassroots work that's being done.

I have a basic attitude toward human beings. A lot of people talk about human nature. I don't buy this human "nature." I prefer the idea of human potential. It seems to me that we—including the most oppressed people—have the potential to right the wrongs, to overcome racism, to provide homes and shelter and food for everybody, to educate people, to provide health care for everybody on this planet. It can be done. There are people who are working for it, and a lot of people are making tremendous sacrifices to try to catalyze the kind of change that's necessary. And I think it will happen. But I don't think it can be done within capitalism. I think it has to be a radical—in some sense revolutionary—kind of change that needs to take place. I don't know how it's going to happen, for sure.

What we have as a movement is so limited. The movement, especially in the core countries, especially in the U.S., is backward, it lacks clarity, it's small, it's sectarian in a lot of ways. Because it's small, it's easily co-opted and marginalized by the dominant political institutions, including the electoral system. Activists are co-opted, visions are co-opted or watered down, people are bribed. So it really seems like a vast problem.

The vast problems may generate vast solutions.

Yeah, that's my hope. When the poverty and misery that people experience become so great and people rebel—how great is that? And then, are the elites willing to use fascist or repressive techniques to put that down? Look what's happening in the U.S.—for instance in L.A. Since the rebellion there, I understand that twenty-some communities within the first month set up armed communities. In other words, you can't go in there. Now, that's getting like Manila—a city of 8 million, plus 4 million squatters—where there are sectors where rich people live completely separated from the tremendous poverty. They drive in tinted-window, chauffeur-driven cars to their work in the business district, which is usually close by. They read or watch television, and aren't exposed to the poverty. Meanwhile, the oppression goes on. And I see that this is one way the U.S. can go. In Chicago I heard that there's a tenement housing project where the people have asked for armed guards, fences, ID cards, and frisking. It scares me that the most oppressed people are asking for more repression. I understand the reasons for that—the violence, the crime, the crack—but that's not solving those problems.

Mary Choy

Continues a full activist life that began many years ago; around retirement age.

I was born in San Francisco, California. My parents emigrated to California from Pyongyang, North Korea, to escape political oppression under Japanese colonial rule. Their home was in Uiju, on the shores of the Amnok (Yalu) River, overlooking China. One winter, when the river was frozen over, mother and father—disguised as Russian refugees—walked over the ice to China and thence to America.

Unable to support his family as a Methodist minister, literally "poor as a church mouse," father opened a tailoring and cleaning shop to supplement his wages. The church served as a social and spiritual center for the Korean community of mostly single men. It was a heavy responsibility, especially for mother. Burdened with the nurturing of her family and of the church community, she was overworked, became ill and died when I was just five. Father was left with three young children.

My father had a younger sister, Ha Soo Whang, living in Hawai'i at the time of mother's death. She was educated in Korea, came to America, and attended Athens Women's College in Alabama. When she completed her American education, she stopped off in Hawai'i on her way back to Korea and was offered a job as a social worker for the International Institute of the YWCA. She worked with the "picture brides" from Korea and with other young families. Working alongside with my aunty were other women social workers of Japanese, Chinese, and Filipina ethnicities. The International Institute was a beehive of activity for the young and older women, offering classes in cooking, English, folk dancing, mothers' clubs, etc.

When my mother died, Aunt Ha Soo went to San Francisco for a visit. At that time she and my father decided that my sister and I would come to Hawai'i for a short stay while father recovered from his bereavement. Our short visit extended into years! Aunt Ha Soo became family. With her meager salary she set up a household and educated us through our college years. Korean women of that generation seemed to have an unusual sense of dealing with finances and aunty was no exception. She eventually accumulated enough money to purchase a small house. Self-reliant, unselfish, and compassionate—that was my Aunt Ha Soo.

My father, his elder brother (we called him "Big Uncle"), and aunty were patriotic to the bone and never gave up hope that Korea would some day become independent from Japan. Father and Aunty were politically progressive, but Big Uncle was the revolutionary. I am happy to say that progressive politics has not died with them, but is continuing through the third and fourth generations of our lineage.

Although lifelong desires to return to the ancestral home were never realized by father, Big Uncle, and Aunt Ha Soo, I take great comfort in the fact that I did visit North Korea, stood on the edge of the Amnok River, [and] looked over into China from their hometown of Uiju. Uiju is now called *Sin*uiju (new), rebuilt after complete destruction by U.S. bombs during the Korean Civil War, 1950–1953.

The immigrants came to work on the plantations?

Right. The ninetieth anniversary of the first Korean immigrants who came to these Island shores was celebrated in January, 1993. The plantation workers were recruited in Korea by plantation owners with the assistance of the Japanese government. They were usually single, and if married were not allowed to bring their wives. Women were matched by pictures with their future husbands in Hawai'i, thus the term "picture bride." As I mentioned before, these were the women my aunty worked with, giving them aid and comfort, often in abusive situations, and easing their "assimilation" into American culture.

My sister and I often accompanied aunty as she made her rounds visiting the families, skillful as interpreter, mediator, teacher. An outstanding contribution she has made were her pioneering efforts to keep Korean culture alive. She organized Korean young womens' clubs where Korean music and dance were taught by the elders in the community. She created dramatic stage productions based on Korean folktales, which were presented in the beautiful setting of the central court of the Honolulu Academy of Arts. With this connection to my Korean heritage, I have never lost sight of understanding and appreciating my identity. But at the same time, I now realize that I was caught in the process of American "assimilation."

The International Institute was finally closed by the YWCA and aunty was retired. But ever active, she lived to a ripe old age of ninety-two. Her life of commitment and compassion for her people was without a doubt a great influence on me.

Were Korean women outstandingly strong, compared to other ethnic women?

I can't say for sure. The women who worked alongside my aunty were equally as strong and committed, and well respected in their communities. I remember them so well: Mrs. Kishimoto, Mrs. Yee, Mrs. Avecilla. Traditionally, Korean women keep their own surnames when they are married. They play a major role in family decisions. In my aunty's family, the eldest of the eight siblings was a sister. When both parents died at an early age, she became the undisputed head of the family.

My activist tendencies flourished during the Vietnam War. Our younger children were involved in the Save Our Surf movement and a growing disenchantment with the Vietnam War. We were members of a Methodist church with a very progressive minister. He led us in study, opening our eyes to the injustices of that racist war. When he was assigned to another church, the church became irrelevant. In a search for relevance, we were led to the Church of the Crossroads, which was deeply involved in the issues of the war. It established a sanctuary for the soldiers refusing to serve in the war.

In 1971 I was involved in the formation of the Ethnic Studies Program at the University of Hawai'i. Soon after, the administration decided to shut down the program, and that was a mistake. There was a tremendous outpouring of support from the students and community to continue the program. The innovative approach for academia and community to work together paid off. After weeks of intense struggle with the administration, the program was saved.

In 1971 I also became involved in the eviction struggle in Kalama Valley on Bishop Estate land. This was one of the earliest land struggles in Hawai'i. We were there to support George Santos, a pig farmer. George took a stand, refused to move, and got tired of being pushed around from place to place. The Ethnic Studies struggle had been a preview. The students and community responded to George's plight. The desire to know the true history of the people of Hawai'i became intense. Why were local people being evicted and relocated time and time again? To know the truth about labor history and the dislocation of people from their homes were the burning questions being raised.

On Mother's Day, May 21, 1971, the showdown between George and other Hawaiian tenants on the land and the Bishop Estate began. The State of Hawai'i's special force was there in full battle dress and assault weapons. Ironically, many of the force were men of Hawaiian ancestry. Following a discussion of who would stay and be arrested or leave, thirty-six of us decided to stay. The young people then climbed to the rooftop of George's house, to be brought down one-by-one by the police, fingerprinted on the spot, [and] driven away in police cars to the old police station on Young Street. George was the first to be dragged out of his house. His pigs, including piglets, were removed, many to die later from the inhumane treatment.

Being in jail for the day was an experience! We nine women were led into a large cell, happy to be together for support and solidarity. Lunch was pork and beans, a slice of white bread, served on a tin plate.

The three-week trial was explosive, devoid of courtroom decorum. The two local lawyers raised every political question, only to be denied by the judge as irrelevant. We were found guilty of trespassing. We appealed to a higher court, asking for a jury trial. The State, wary of another political trial, dropped all charges against us, refunded our fines, and cleared our court records.

Was there an organization? Did you study together?

Yes, it was called Kōkua Hawai'i. We studied Mao, liberalism, monopoly capitalism, etc. Our inspiration came from the Black and Puerto Rican movements. Leaders from the revolutionary Black Panthers and the Young Lords parties were invited by the Ethnic Studies Program to come to Hawai'i to share their experiences with us. What a consciousness-raising time that was!

With the Kalama Valley and the Ethnic Studies Program conflicts still vivid in our memories, some young people gathered their forces to help the Chinatown community people to contend with the problems of urban redevelopment—in other words, the destruction of their communities. Our daughter, recently graduated from the University of Wisconsin, a hotbed of antiwar protest, helped to organize The Third Arm. She enlisted the help of her father to open a Free Chinatown Medical Clinic. It became the center for Third Arm activities, a walk-in clinic plus a center for political education. It was a stimulating experience for us. We had parties, fundraisers, potlucks, forums—Chinatown and the wide communities coming together as comrades.

In later years, Third Arm evolved into an organization called People Against Chinatown Evictions (PACE). The clinic and outreach work continued. A first stunning victory for the people of Chinatown and PACE was the construction of an affordable, sanitary apartment building on River Street. It was unofficially named in memory of one of the gallant fighters, the Teddy Duncan Apartments.

After fourteen years, the Free Medical Clinic in Chinatown was closed, but the clinic in Ota Camp continued to function. To retrace my steps a bit, let me tell you about Ota Camp. It was a solid, family-oriented community of Filipino families. Their homes, gardens were immaculate. They were given eviction notices by the owner of the land, Mr. Ota. How was a community of two hundred or more people going to preserve their lifestyle and homes? Where were they to move? With strong leadership emerging, a strong steering committee, and strong support from the community, Ota Camp was victorious in securing an alternative piece of land to build affordable homes, keeping their community intact. We were proud to be part of the Ota Camp struggle.

Joining the Kalama Valley, Chinatown, and Ota Camp efforts for housing rights was the Hale Mohalu patients' movement in Waimalu, Pearl City. The facility was an intermediate care center for leprosy patients. It was a home away from home (home is Kalaupapa, Moloka‘i). The patients felt very comfortable in the Waimalu community. After a decade of ownership, the U.S. Navy turned the facility over to the State of Hawai‘i with the stipulation that it would continue to be used as some kind of health care facility. The State said it was too valuable a piece of property for that kind of usage. The patients were then given notice of eviction. The State's alternative housing was to be carted off to Leahi Hospital into a sterile, curtained bed-ward environment and maybe thrust into a hostile community. For months the patients and their supporters defied the State. But again, the showdown with the State was inevitable. The day of eviction, patients and some supporters resisted arrest and were unceremoniously carried and dumped into the hot sun. Although the patients were evicted from their "home" and lost the Hale Mohalu site, the struggle for alternate housing was carried on by new forces. After ten more years the State finally compromised and split the Hale Mohalu land into two: one for a home for people with health disabilities and the other for a baseball field. It's so sad to see how State power is used against the people rather than for them.

How is that?

Well, to go back to Kalama Valley, we saw there a State police force made up mostly of Hawaiians arresting their Hawaiian brothers who were fighting to stay on the land. Hale Mohalu was the same: pitting brother against brother. Many of the patients also were Hawaiian. It must be an old plantation mentality, and the colonial system of divide and conquer, which persists in Hawai'i. On the other hand, this may be breaking down. If so, I attribute it partly to the present Kanaka Maoli (the first people) sovereignty movement in Hawai'i. There is a growing realization that Kanaka Maoli and non-Kanaka Maoli must come together in support of independence for the Hawaiian nation, which includes complete control of their lands and resources. It affects us all and I am glad to be a supporter.

For the first time in the history of Hawai'i, a Kanaka Maoli People's International Tribunal was held on O'ahu, then moving on to Maui, Moloka'i, Kaua'i, and the Big Island. A panel of nine international judges [was] invited to hear testimony from Kanaka Maoli and other indigenous peoples from the nations of Cuba, Puerto Rico, Guam, and the Philippines. These nations, like Hawai'i, were also taken over by the U.S. imperialists in the year 1898. Global networking and solidarity!

The sovereignty movement has become an essential part of my life. It has helped me to take a look at my own decolonization process. I may not in my lifetime see independence for the Hawaiian nation come full circle, but I know that my children and their children will.

Christine Brown

Head of the Smith-Beretania Tenants Association; age forty-something.

I'm Hawaiian-Spanish-Portuguese. My name is Christine Brown, but my maiden name is Kalahiki. I was born and raised on the island of Oʻahu, and I lived in Kapahulu. When I was young we used to walk down to the Natatorium, but there was no high-rise. You could see only the Moana Hotel. That was it. It was beautiful then. We're getting more crowded. Things are really, really going down.

My father had a hard life, and he always believed in honesty. He was very active with the Democratic Party. He knew the higher-ups, but he didn't go for any of the lip service. Things were hard and everything, but we always had a decent meal on the table. My mother and father raised chickens, rabbits, ducks. She had a garden. We never starved like I hear people do now. I mean, we were really very fortunate.

My husband deserted me and my three daughters, so I went back to my parents' home. I would ask myself what was wrong with me as a woman. And I would go outside and walk around the yard and I'd cry and I'd feel so hurt. And my father called me, and said, "Come girl, come."

So I went to him, and I said, "Yes, Daddy?"

He turned to me and said, "You're a Kalahiki, and I don't ever want to see you walking around with your head down. You keep it high, girl, and you remember who you are."

And from that day on, I never did put my head down. It's been a little too high at times.

I was something like twenty-six years old and I had never voted. My father used to tell me to vote. And I told him, "No way," that all crooks get in, that I was not going to vote at all. But then when it was election time, he just put his paper down and told me, "Vote girl." I'm living with my parents and I just had to vote.

He got me involved with Kalihi Valley Community Association. They helped the different organizations to get on their feet or get things they needed. My father was the president, and he put me on the board. I had no say in it at all. I mean, when my father spoke, you listened. That was the way we were brought up. You didn't talk back.

Whenever my mother and father would be invited to shindigs, my father would always take me to keep my mother company. I would watch my father tell a lot of big shots, "Don't give me that. I'm not a kid. You can tell it to the others, but don't give me that." And my father would walk away.

I told myself, "Oh, my goodness."

And they'd go to my father and they'd say, "You know how it is. We just have to play it out."

And my father would say, "Don't give me that."

And I used to feel proud of him, that he stood up for what he believed in. So, my father made a big, big powerful spot in my life.

I moved into this building eight years ago. It's a low-income, HUD [Housing and Urban Development] building. The management treated the tenants here real poorly. There was an association here and I joined it. But then the association kind of broke up. And I noticed that the elderly Chinese tenants here were getting pulled around. I mean, they weren't called into the office, they were dragged into the office. I felt, these are old people, you don't do this to old people. I mean, someday I'm going to be there, and when I get there I don't want to be pulled or dragged. I want to be asked nicely to come in.

Why was the management doing this?

Because they're Koreans, and see, the Koreans do not get along with the Chinese. This goes way back. The Koreans are poor people and so actually they hate the Chinese. I mean, they can't see the Chinese having anything. They won't put their hands on me. But the elderly, like seventy and eighty years old, I mean, they just pulled them by the shirt.

Then I got deeply involved with the association. We had to stop it. We had to let the tenants know their rights. And I didn't know how to do it. I started, but it didn't come into shape. And then through one of the tenants here, I got to meet experienced activists like Brahim [Aoudé] and Mari [McCaig]. They told us so much: how to organize, how to band together, how to keep together. And then, from there they asked me to continue. We fought for our rights. We got them. I guess I was ready to be molded correctly.

Then they asked me to join PACE, People Against Chinatown Evictions. So I belong to that too. And I am the president of our association here, the Smith-Beretania Tenants' Association. Somebody from PACE asked me if they could come to our meeting. We were more than grateful that they would come and listen in. We weren't too proud. You learn from this; you don't turn your back on it. PACE is something like twenty years old. We're just babies compared to them. So they came in and they showed us how to go about doing things.

And then, afterward, we showed the building management what we wanted, and we got it! We didn't ask for things that were unreasonable. It was where it was right for them and right for us. The landlord has rights, but so do the tenants. You can't come into my apartment anytime you feel like it—things like this. We'll give them another chance on that count. We even got reimbursements. We had nine demands. Out of the nine, we got eight. The only one we didn't get was new management. *(Laughter.)*

The owner is Schull Builders, whose headquarters are in Ohio, and we demanded them to come down here. Mr. Asho came down and met with us, and then we gave him our demands. And, oh, we had the media here and everything. That really did it. We passed out fliers to the whole building and let the people also speak for themselves, because they were the ones that wanted help. They didn't know how to do it, so we got them all together.

Then I also got involved with the neighborhood board, and I also got involved with Citizens for Rent Control. We need rent control so badly.

Being a local person, born and raised on this island, watching what used to be in the old days—you know, you never locked your doors. In Kapahulu, where I was born and raised, you didn't lock your doors. Then, my mother sold the home in Kapahulu, and we moved down to Wai'alae-Kāhala. We still didn't lock the doors. That's the way it was. But now, I mean, it's pathetic, and the rent is so high.

Do the people talk about solutions?

We know what the solution is. We need more housing. Rent control is just a second step. Since we don't have any more housing, this is the best thing right now. The only ones that are against us are the real estate [people]. They're the only ones. I went in front of Pali Safeway market myself with petitions for rent control. Within a month and a half, I myself got three thousand signatures. Those people were willing to sign it. And you don't have to go and twist their arm or anything. I tell them I have a petition for rent control. And they know right off the bat what that means. They say, "Why didn't you folks start something like this sooner?"

I give them a fact sheet. And I do tell them what it's all about. It is for the landlords and it is for the tenant. It isn't strictly for the tenant. They've got to understand that when the taxes go up, so will the rent go up. No tenant or no landlord should lose their property because of the land tax. This has to be passed on. If the landlord makes improvements, the rent has to go up a little. I mean, you can't live slummy all the time. You have your apartment painted and whatnot. They do understand these things, and they sign with no problem.

I get to meet people and I get to talk to them. I have met landlords and the only thing they want to know is if it's going to affect them so they can't raise their rent. People that own their home are willing to sign it because they know what it was like before they bought their home, and they know that their children can't buy homes now because it's so high. So this is one thing I really believe in. It's needed so badly down here.

What do you think the chances are of rent control passing someday?

Well, we would try to get it on the ballot, but you have to realize that when they got us together there were around twenty-five of us and it was only two months before the election to get 26,000 or 27,000 signatures. We got to almost 12,000, but we didn't make it. So we're still continuing it, and we will until our problem of housing is solved.

We never had people sleeping on the beaches. You know, the rents are so high. It's pitiful. They're using the parks even. Our mayor let them live in tents in 'A'ala Park. Our Islands were never like that. It just went out of control. I believe that rent control can help the people. There's no way we will give up this struggle. To me, it's a dream. But see, rent control won't affect me in any way. I'm subsidized by HUD; I'm under SSI [Supplementary Security Income]. But that doesn't mean, because I have it nice, that I can sit back and say, "Oh, that's not my problem, give it to the next person." That's not fair.

There aren't enough people like you.

Oh there is, there is. I do believe there is. I believe the people are standing up now. I think they even had a petition signed against a city councilman because he voted one way and the district wanted him to vote another. I looked at that and felt good about it because the people are saying what they wanted. But I do believe the people are speaking up more so and want to be heard.

If it wasn't because of my being under HUD, I would never be able to rent my place. I have to be grateful. I have gotten really independent and I enjoy my life. I've been granted so much. I feel like I've been put here for a reason. My place is to go out and help others. That's the way I feel.

I get called by tenants who are still having trouble with the manager and whatnot. And I don't understand them—they're Chinese. We have our interpreter and we've told them that if they have any trouble to call my number and tell me to come meet them. I'll get a call, say, like eight o'clock, "Come, you come, come now." You know, it's the Chinese. "I come, I come." I know they're downstairs. I'll get dressed and take off, and I'll take them to the interpreter. They'll speak Chinese and it will be translated back to me. Then I'll go in the office and I'll fight with the manager if the tenant is right. Then the tenant will be happy.

What do you see in the next five to ten years?

Well, we'll consider ourselves getting elderly, right? There will be the young generation. The young generation will come up and grow. I look forward [to the day] that they'll start organizing. They'll start learning what we have learned. I'll pass on to others what I have learned.

My father is seventy-nine years old. Okay, I got myself active. My father was a boxing commissioner for four and a half years. I used to see him on TV and whatnot and felt so proud, you know. Then when we got in the movement, I'd call my father: "Daddy, see, I'm taking over your place." And I'd say, "I'm on channel 4," and they would watch. Or when we had our hearing for rent control, "Daddy, I'm on TV. Oh Daddy, I should have lost weight." *(Laughter.)*

Do you think those in Congress are really representing the people?

Not the people. I wish we never became a state. I think it's the biggest mistake. If we had stayed a territory, it would have been okay. It happened when I was a child. Things are more uncontrolled now, the way they're doing it. They're running things the way they want it, you know. Our land has been taken away from us. It was a dirty shame what they did to the Hawaiians. The Hawaiians want the land, and they have no right to that land. Look what they did to our Islands. They said high-rises were needed and whatnot. We never had high-rises. More people are coming in and the locals aren't even thought of. Some of these new people say, "If the local people can't afford to live on this island, then why don't they go to the mainland where the land is cheap?" It is so unfair, and so many actually are moving out.

Could you talk about the neighborhood board?

The neighborhood board is supposed to represent the district and it helps the people if they have problems. It goes to the City Council and they have hearings and whatnot, and they speak of all these problems. People who want to build high-rises have to take the plans to the neighborhood board and the neighborhood board has got to approve it. If they don't approve them, it can't be built. If you want to serve on the neighborhood board you have to go and fill out an application, and then you have to run and everyone that votes then gets a ballot. Then they mail in these ballots. If you get enough votes, you get in. Then you belong on the board. I got voted in. I believe that getting voted in is to represent the people, not yourselves. Because if you speak out for yourself, you don't belong there. Get out!

I'm proud to say that I am a mother of three. I have three beautiful daughters and I have seven grandchildren. I have one daughter in Kaua'i, and my other two daughters are here.

I started a teenage girls' club for my daughters. I had around seventeen girls. Once they worked the carnival and got something like $125. They wanted to go camping. I asked them how many had ever gone to the outside islands. And they went, "Wow!" you know. We decided to raise more money to go to Kaua'i. So we did. The next year we raised 2,000-something dollars and went to Hilo. The club paid for all the meals, the hotel bill, we had two cars and everything, and they could eat whatever they wanted. But all I asked of the girls is that they go to one good restaurant. The last night we went to a good restaurant. Most of the girls came from Kalihi Valley housing. In the restaurant they had to sit down and learn to eat like ladies.

I asked my brother-in-law to help me, and we had a volleyball team. We went to different parks and challenged different teams. This kept my daughters busy and active. When my oldest one graduated, she had a scholarship to go to the University of Hawai'i. Oh, I was so proud, I cried. My second daughter . . . didn't get [a] scholarship, but she went on to community college. I was still proud of her. And my baby, she got a scholarship and she went to the University of Hawai'i also. I was proud that they went forward and they made something of themselves.

Then they got married and started having children. My first had a little girl and named her Christy. And I was so proud—my name is Christine. And I said, "Me, Wendy?"

And she told me, "Yeah, Mommy."

And I said, "Well, what if it was a boy?"

She said, "It couldn't be a boy, Mommy, 'cause I had the name all picked already."

My second daughter has four children. Her last child was a girl. She named it Kristin. When my oldest daughter was around twenty-seven and had my grandson, I talked to her on the phone, and I asked, "What did you name him, sweetheart?"

And she told me, "If my sisters can do it, I can do it also—it's Christopher." *(Laughter.)*

A retired physician in his seventies who is still an activist.

I'm a physician. Barbara and I have lived in Hawai'i since 1952. We've lived here in Kailua since 1959 in the same house. I've practiced medicine the entire time that I've been in Hawai'i. The first seven years were in Moloka'i. The organization that I'm most identified with is the Latin American and Caribbean Solidarity Association, LACASA. We've been in business since 1982, and continuously have published a newsletter, held meetings, organized lectures, and brought visitors here, mostly focusing around our opposition to U.S. foreign policy in Central America.

I have been a member of Physicians for Social Responsibility (PSR) since 1962. It was organized by a group of physicians, mostly Harvard-based in the Boston area. The entire May 31, 1962 issue of the *New England Journal of Medicine* was devoted to a PSR symposium on the effects of nuclear war, particularly the effects of a hypothetical explosion over the Boston area. This created my interest, and I became a member nationally and I've remained so since. After a hiatus in PSR due to détente between the Soviet Union and the United States, and energies diverted to the struggle against U.S. aggression in Vietnam, in the late 1970s the dormant organization came to life again. At that point, I organized and founded a Hawai'i chapter of PSR and we have been active ever since.

Dr. John I. Frederick Reppun was my mentor and employer for a year in Moloka'i, because under Hawai'i law I had to work under a licensed physician. We had a parting of the ways at the end of a year because I wanted to go into private practice for myself in Moloka'i, and we had some differences in philosophy. Fred was very conservative, and I'm obviously not to the right of the spectrum. He made me a very generous offer, but I was a young buck who said, "Thanks, but no thanks."

The PSR experience taught me a very important thing, which I've also seen repeated in other contexts: People can continue to grow and change even after they're fifty or sixty years of age. Fred was a good example of that. In the 1960s, I had come over to O'ahu and renewed our acquaintance. I referred him some patients and did things that I could to kind of smooth things over with him. And little by little, he moved to the left politically and we worked together in PSR. That was an illumination to me. Here was this man who had even tried to use the FBI and the medical society and other agencies to get rid of me a generation earlier. Here he was my ally and one of my good friends in the PSR movement.

Another fellow, a Kaiser Health Plan colleague, Dr. Cliff Straehley, was my main nemesis during the years of the Vietnam War struggle and tried to get me kicked off the executive committee of the Kaiser group here. He was just horribly hostile to me. He was a thoracic surgeon and a very prominent member of our Kaiser group here. He too changed his views about what was going on in Vietnam and what the meaning of U.S. policy there was. When I decided to bring life again to the Hawai'i chapter of PSR, I put out a letter to all of my colleagues in Kaiser. The next morning, Cliff was the first one in my office with a handshake and a check for PSR. Without being explicit about it, he was telling me that he regretted some of the things that he had done. This revealed to me that political alliances like that can improve personal relationships if you just hunker down, hold tight, and let a little time go by. Much later, in 1994, Cliff actually said, "I was wrong and you were right." None of my other colleague/opponents ever did so much.

During the struggles over Vietnam, civil rights, and Central America, the strongest feelings of contempt that I experienced toward people around me were directed at people who would sidle up to me and say, "Gee, you're sure right about this, I certainly agree with you. In fact, here's a check made out to cash for your organization, but just don't quote me because I work at Pearl Harbor," or, "I'm a member of the Medical Society," or, "My wife works for the military," or something of that sort. I just can't stand it. I'd rather somebody would come out and say, "You're an SOB, you're a slimeball, I don't agree with you at all!" I'd much rather they do it that way.

Tell about your background.

I was probably converted in the delivery room where my mother had me. It happened pretty early, anyway. I'm from a middle-class white family, born and raised in north Louisiana. That always strikes people as a little unusual, especially if they don't know that there are an awful lot of really good, decent progressive people in that part of the world. But I was a rambunctious, rebellious teenager, and my mother and I never got along well at all. I came to feel sorry for her in later years, because as I learned her history, I saw that she had been oppressed and taken advantage of in a lot of ways. Both of my parents came from very humble backgrounds. Their families were dirt farmers.

My father became a very distinguished forensic pathologist with a national reputation. He died a year or two ago at 103 and he was still just as vigorous as he could be. He functioned as a medical examiner and held elective public office for sixty-four years—some sort of record, I guess. In the last forty or fifty years, nobody ran against him. He was a great influence on my life.

I frightened and worried my mother. I don't think I ever worried my father that much because he was a man who had a great capacity for trust. His idea of making people trustworthy was to trust them. You take a chance, you win some and lose some, but in the long run it's the best way to go. My mother was a little more naive. She was bitter. She didn't like men. She was the youngest of eleven children and the only girl. Her brother, who's name was Dodd, was president of the Southern Baptist Convention—a big job; big man. He went around the world and, among other people, interviewed Gandhi. When he came back he wrote a book called *Girdling the Globe for God,* which we immediately transmuted into *Girdling the Globe for Dodd, by God.* That was a family joke for a while. I hate pomposity.

When I was sixteen years old—about 1933—one of my earliest maverick activities was forming, along with some Black friends, an interracial group in Shreveport, Louisiana, where I grew up. Later, this became the core of the NAACP, which was, I think, the first chapter of the NAACP in Louisiana. In those days, the NAACP was considered a fairly radical organization. Hell, I got buckshot in my rear end one time in Shreveport from a Black friend, because the Blacks were very much afraid of us, even though we were about half Black and half white.

In my father's work as forensic pathologist and medical examiner, he was a very good and just man. His work gave him opportunity to save more than one Black life in those days, just by giving some guy thirty bucks in cash and putting him on a freight train, literally. I mean, that's the way life was in Shreveport. Everybody carried guns. It was almost like the Wild West in those days.

Later, at the Tulane Medical School, there was a little cadre of left-wingers and civil rights people before there was much of a civil rights movement. We'd go up to Mississippi, and go into restaurants and say, "Y'all got grits?" That was our cachet, or ID, that we needed to get in and out of the town all in one piece. Barbara and I were in the thick of the thing in 1965 in Alabama. We lost friends there—killed. We were scared to death. You know, you walk down the streets toward dusk and a car comes along slowly behind you and you're so relieved to see all those Black faces looking out instead of cops. Once about 2 A.M. we were chased by a Klan car on a lonely road and had to go maybe 80 to outrun them.

I have simply always despised injustice and inequality. I can't identify a beginning for it. It didn't have religious roots. I've never had a religious experience in my life and I detested being dragged to church. I detected as a child that the men in our community went to church to make business deals, and the women went to see who was dressed how. My favorite book, which I must have read over twenty times as a school-ager, was *Robin Hood*. I had one big well-illustrated copy of the book and I just loved it. I read it over and over again, and ran around our trees there with a little bow and arrow and imagined myself as Robin Hood. And I've always hated bullies. I've hated big guys beating up on little guys. That, to me, is a sin, a crime. And so wherever it came from, those were my early feelings as a child and adolescent, and I still feel that way. That's Vietnam; it's the U.S. and Central America; it's a big guy beating up on a little guy. That's a thread that runs through my whole life.

The nearest I've come to waffling was back in the '60s when there were groups like the Weathermen. The big question that we debated endlessly in our organizations and meetings was the role of violence in social revolution. What's the nature of the revolution going to be and how are we going to bring it about? I had inner conflicts on some of those subjects. I've never put myself forward as a total pacifist, and I get impatient with idiotic questions about "what would you do if your wife or mother were being raped and murdered," or something. I think those have nothing to do with the question of war between nations. I'm against militarism. I despise militarism.

Anyway, to go back, I had gotten a good high school education at

Webb School in Tennessee—very stern academic discipline, but I did well with it. Bell Buckle, Tennessee: three hundred people then and three hundred people today. Then I went to Duke University, got a first-rate education, and graduated in 1939. I've told very few people this, but I declined Phi Beta Kappa at Duke because I discovered in a little library research that Phi Beta Kappa discriminated quite widely against both women and racial minorities. So I said, "Thanks, but no thanks." I mention that to illustrate that I didn't care a damn about the badge. If an organization is guilty of things that I don't approve of, then I really don't want anything to do with that organization.

My first marriage occurred when I was still a student at Duke. We had a daughter who now lives in the Netherlands. My then-wife and I went out to Stanford University and I enrolled on a scholarship to take a master's degree in literature. Dr. Harden Craig was, according to the catalog, chair of the School of Letters, and I sought him out. He's a Shakespearean scholar and president of MLA [Modern Language Association]. I introduced myself, and said, "I'm here to take a master's degree in the School of Letters."

And he said, "Oh, dear me, why did you come to me?"

And I said, "Well, you're chair of the School of Letters, Professor Craig."

And he said, "Oh, I am?" And he went and got a catalog off a shelf and he said, "Yes, you're absolutely right. You know, I think I've been that for eight years and you're the first student who's ever wanted to register for graduate work in the School of Letters. Why on earth are you doing that? Why not English or German or philosophy, or something? Here in Stanford, the boys and girls take care of their own, you know. Your English Department is going to take care of you, but you'll be an orphan in the School of Letters."

And I said, "That's exactly what I want. I love being an orphan." And they left me alone.

At Duke one or two good teachers had sicced me onto some radical writers and philosophers. I discovered Bertrand Russell, and he was one of my heroes. At that time, Russell was teaching at City College of New York [CCNY]. World War II was looming. I think everybody felt it was around the corner and Russell was well known for his dissenting views on almost everything, including personal life and sex, and politics, and so forth. The board of regents abruptly withdrew his appointment at CCNY and it became a rather celebrated case.

I got in trouble at Stanford because of Russell. I was teaching freshman English and I thought that was a good subject for my students to get acquainted with. I told them to go to the library and find out who Bertrand Russell was; what he thought, said, and wrote; and how come CCNY was going back on their contract with him. Oh, the irate letters from parents of my students that started pouring in: "Who is this young asshole who wants to sic our precious young ones on this awful monster?"

Well, I finished my work. My first marriage was breaking up at that time and I went down to Mexico. My wife very promptly went back to the United States and left our two-year-old daughter with me, and I took care of her for close to a year. And there I was, barely 21, just beginning to learn the language, and feeling a little bit at loose ends. I wanted to travel and be a big writer. But I got stuck in Guadalajara and never got any further. My first wife came down and took the child back to California, and we had an amicable separation.

A few months later, I met Barb on a tennis court. She and I have been together fifty-one years. We celebrated our fifty-first wedding anniversary a few months ago and didn't even have any celebration, except a very private one. I've loved it. We've been so together on everything, that's the remarkable and joyous thing about it. Not always harmony—that's boring—but love, and unity. She's had five primary cancers and beaten them all.

I introduced Barb to some very subversive reading material. I had been turned on more through reading and academic contacts. She had experience with some working-class people and it had affected her. When we came together in Mexico, we saw things very much the same way and we hit it off right away. We played tennis and drank tequila much of the time.

Three weeks after we met we took off from Guadalajara. There was an amusing incident. Her sister, mother, and her sister's husband—a Spaniard from Astorias, northern Spain, who was very conscious of family honor and all that—didn't like me much. I had met her father before I met her. He and I had drunk some rum together in Guadalajara, and we hit it off great. So he was kind of sympathetic, but the rest of the family didn't like me and didn't trust me. The family had decided that Barbara was going to go to nursing school in Chicago. They were putting her on the train and the family was trotting along on one side of the train and I was trotting along on the other side so that they wouldn't see me. I hopped up on the platform and banged on the door until the porter let me in. I said, "Is she alone?"

He ran and looked and then came back and said, "Sí, sí señor. Está sola."

Barbara and I traveled around the north of Mexico for about six months, on foot much of the time. We crossed the western Sierra, the second-highest mountains in Mexico, in about a seven-week trek. We were so in love, we didn't know what the hell was going on. We were too dumb to realize the danger we were in a lot of the time, but the people treated us magnificently. We had a homemade sleeping bag, canvas, a quilt, and a knife. We had a .410 shotgun over-and-under .22, but somebody stole that fairly promptly. Everywhere we went in the tiny villages—sometimes they were just one or two little huts up in the mountains—the Indians would treat us splendidly within the limits of their humble resources. But they would warn us against the people *otrolado,* as they say: "It's okay here, but on the other side you're in danger. They're going to cut your throat. How awful these people." Then we'd go over there and they would treat us just as well and tell us how bad the other people were.

Barbara was pregnant with our first child, a daughter, and we decided we'd better go back to Guadalajara and mend our fences with her family. We were warmly received and eventually became very close with her family. Then I started teaching at the American School of Guadalajara and held that job for a few years.

Along came World War II. My draft board in Shreveport were decent people, but they didn't understand my views at all. I wrote them a letter when I first registered and explained that I didn't believe in burning bushes and the word of God being brought down from a mountain on stone tablets. I said I was sorry, but I couldn't apply for a draft exemption on narrow Christian pacifist grounds. Those were the only grounds that were acceptable to draft boards at that time. I said I had strong philosophic objections to war between nations because I think war invariably does more harm than good. They didn't understand that, but they were very nice and gave me an occupational deferment for several years because of my work with the American School in Mexico. In a fit of prescience I told my draft board that if the U.S. and the U.S.S.R. won, they would be at each other's throat at once.

But finally I got my greetings letter from the draft board and I decided that I had to go back. So I joined the Maritime Service, which at that time was a branch of the Coast Guard, and I wanted to get on a merchant ship. That was the one kind of service that was philosophically acceptable to me. At that time, merchant ships were taking food to liberated areas in Europe and bringing injured troops back. But instead of putting me on a merchant ship, they put me in a receiving unit in Sheepshead Bay in Brooklyn and made a hospital corpsman out of me. That's where I sat out the last year or so of the war.

After the war, I decided I was going to be a big-shot writer. Barb and I spent a year in Rockland County, north of New York City, and I did some writing. I did one hell of a good article for *Science Illustrated,* a magazine that was just getting off the ground, on the use of ultraviolet rays in operating rooms to try to sterilize the ambient. Damn, if somebody didn't come out in the *Reader's Digest* or the *Saturday Evening Post* with an article on exactly the same subject. Absolutely killed it flat.

So Barb and I said, This ain't gonna work too good. We loved the West and we love horses, so we put an ad in the *Saturday Review of Literature:* "Young couple wants job on dude ranch or hustling horses, west of the Rockies." We gave a box number and got a bite from some people in Wyoming. What we failed to tell them, and this is where we cheated, was that we had two small children. So we went out to Wyoming and wrangled horses and dudes, and I built bunkhouses and all, for about six months. I got fired from two very good jobs because I couldn't get along with the bosses, nor Barb with their wives when they abused our kids. We basically were just sort of drifting around and having a ball, you know.

So I said, "Let's go back down to Mexico and see if my old job with the American School is still there," and we did that, and it was still there. But there was a new owner of the school who had a lot of rules that didn't appeal to me. And also, on general principles, I have always felt suspicious of the effort to try to go back. You can't unring a bell, and you can't go back in your life very successfully. That has been my experience.

So I said, "Oh hell, let's go to medical school." I needed one credit in physical chemistry, so we went back to my hometown and I taught Spanish and English literature in the local college there and at the same time took physical chemistry. Our third child was born there during that year. Then I entered Tulane Medical School. The next four or five years are a blur of no sleep and just hitting the books.

Still, we did some political action in New Orleans. There was a cadre of left-wingers there. Some of my Tulane classmates were members of the Communist Party [CP] who tried to recruit me into the party. I worked very, very closely with them, and collaborated with just about everything they were doing. This was the height of the McCarthy era, you see, and another of my activities was opposing McCarthyism in its various aspects. But I could never see joining the CP. I didn't like their regimentation and the discipline they subjected their members to. But I contrived ways to work closely with them, especially those who were personal friends. Of course, our left-wing activities alienated 95 percent of my classmates, who were these young doctors-to-be. They were very malicious. We'd come out after a party in the French Quarter or something, and find our tires slashed by my classmates. Once they took the rotor out of our car.

I had a foretaste of what I was going to catch many years later from my full-grown medical colleagues during the Vietnam years. Back in medical school, I didn't realize how vicious these guys could be. But on the other hand, I didn't realize that some of them could be educated. I didn't even try to educate my classmates in Tulane. I was just rather contemptuous of them, I suppose, which was immature on my part, but some of them were contemptible people.

We came out to Moloka'i, more or less straight from hospital training in New Orleans. Every small town was looking for a doctor, so there were a lot of opportunities. I had a stack of brochures on the station wagon seat, and we made a ten-week, 10,000-mile junket through western states looking at places. I saw a real cross-section from the best to the worst of U.S. medicine. We had the four children with us. We had a built-in babysitter—a young Cajun girl whom we put through nursing school. We had the dog and a Siamese cat with kittens in the car. That was an exciting trip.

We had gotten down to one brochure, and that was in Moloka'i. I called the guy from a drugstore pay phone in Ventura, California. The connection was terrible. I said, "Is that job still there?"

And I thought he said, "Yes it is."

I said, "Hold it, I'm coming out. My name is Butler."

We took just about our last $200 to ship the car out to Moloka'i.

So we came to Moloka'i and we loved it. The nearly seven years we spent there were a delight for our children. I had one great political battle there during those years. I immediately became known as the union doctor. After Fred Reppun, who was the only other doctor on the island at that time, and I parted company, I said, "If I'm the union doctor, Fred, that must make you the confederate doctor." I don't know whether he liked that.

In 1921 or 1922, the U.S. Congress passed what was called the Hawaiian Homestead Act. It was an empty shell and never imple-

mented. Tens of thousands of Hawaiians sat around for two generations waiting for land to be given to them, which is what the act called
for, and getting very little of it. What they got was very bad, marginal
land with little or no water. On Moloka'i, a lot of the homesteaders
rented their land out, which the act permitted, to the pineapple companies for about $40 an acre a year. The homesteaders—men and women
and children—took jobs with the company picking pineapple. That's
how they made ends meet. Those were the people who constituted a lot
of my patients, and they were all ILWU union members.

Barb and I lived the first year in the guest house of the Hawaiian
Homes Commission, which is the State agency charged with implementing the Hawaiian Homes Act. As soon as I terminated my employment
with Fred and went in practice on my own, we were told that we had to
get out of that house. They were trying to get me off the island, see,
because of my close ties with the workers. When word got around
among the workers, they said, "Doc, we talked this over and there is a
house down in Kaunakakai that's available and the down payment is
not too much. We will lend you the down payment at 1 percent interest,
if you're interested."

I said, "I'll take it, I'll take it."

The day we were supposed to vacate, they turned up at our house
with a big flatbed pineapple truck and moved all our furniture into the
new house. With quite a few cases of beer, there was a big celebration
for two or three days. No pineapple was picked during that entire
period. We appreciated the aloha of the workers there. Some of them, to
this day, are still very close friends.

The great political case that I had there against management was a
case of a company nurse badly neglecting a patient whose name was
Domingo. He had cut his Achilles tendon with a hoe. I don't know how
you do that; he must have been a contortionist. The nurse mistreated
him by giving him inadequate doses of penicillin and doing nothing
with the wound for three days. The infection ascended in the Achilles's
tendon sheath and became very serious, at which point she called me in.
I had to hospitalize him. Under general anesthesia, I made a very wide
excision in the tendon sheath to let the pus out, and put him on high
intravenous doses of penicillin.

When he went back to go to work, he discovered that he had been
fired. So I had to go to bat for him on that. They claimed that he hadn't
properly notified them of his workman's comp status. It was just a real
brazen effort to get rid of a worker. The ironical thing was that Do-

mingo was absolutely loathed by everybody: management, his camp
buddies, his union brothers. He was extremely dirty, very stupid, can-
tankerous, irascible. He was a thief. Everybody hated Domingo. The
lesson I learned in this was that you go to bat for a guy on principle no
matter how unlovable and how unlovely he is. If he suffers an injustice,
you go to bat for him exactly like you would go to bat for Sir Galahad
or somebody.

I testified on this notorious workman's comp case when it went to
the second level of arbitration. The union fought it vigorously and had
a couple of good lawyers who later became close personal friends of
ours. My testimony was crucial to that case. One day we were all down
in a bar in Kaunakakai, drinking up with the lawyers. The lawyer for
the company accosted the union lawyer: "Eh, Meyer, when are you
going to send that doctor back to law school?" He knew I was right.

So after the union won the case, a very honest arbitrator named Bill
Cobb was so irate he was quoted in the press as saying, "This is the
worst case of abuse of a pineapple employee by the company that I have
ever seen in twenty years of arbitration," or something like that.

I called Torkildson, the company lawyer, on the phone. I said,
"Torkildson, when are you going back to law school?"

He said, "You son of a bitch," and he hung up on me.

As a result of that good fight, I lost my clinic privileges up in Libby.
Libby called me the very next day and said, "You can't use our dispensary for your office up there any more."

And the same damn thing happened as when we got kicked out of
our house. When my dispensary privileges were jerked because of the
workman's comp case, the workers just didn't pick any pineapple. They
went out in the fields, they took their decks of playing cards, their cases
of beer, and sat down. This was July, the height of the picking season,
and they let the supervisors know that when Dr. Butler has a place to
practice in Maunaloa, you get some pineapple picked. Pineapple doesn't
last long in the hot sun, once it's ready to be picked. That lasted 48
hours. Harry Larson, the manager, called me on the phone and he said,
"You son of a bitch, I guess you win this one. Your people in Honolulu
are stronger than ours." A lot of telephoning had gone back and forth
from the ILWU people to the management people. Management said,
"Get that doctor a place to work." They rented me a little house at a
reasonable fee which I made into a clinic.

Moloka'i, from time to time, had occasion to ask a specialist from
Honolulu to come over to do a case that I was not qualified to do—

complicated orthopedics, for example. The orthopedist that I usually called over was a man named Dick Dodge. Around 1958, Henry J. Kaiser had been out here looking over real estate, which he later got into very heavily in Hawai'i. He was in the hotel, fell in the bathtub, and broke his hip. Dick Dodge happened to take care of him. Mr. Kaiser decided that Dodge was fine, but that the hospital and health care facilities were not up to snuff in Hawai'i, and that he ought to move in with a health plan here. His health plan was already pretty well established in California. So he decided to move into Hawai'i. He hired five physicians, including Dodge and four others, to be the initial partners in the enterprise. Dick said, "Do you want to join with us?"

And I said, "Why, sure!"

We were ready to leave Moloka'i at that time anyway because our kids were getting into secondary school. Elementary school was fine in Moloka'i, but secondary school wasn't that good. Also, I had done what I went over there to do: prove that a doctor can relate to working-class people at their level and in their context. So I came over to O'ahu as a hired hand for the five partners. They lasted one year because they were stupid. They thought the Kaiser Plan was a way to make a financial killing for themselves. That wasn't Mr. Kaiser's idea, or anybody else's idea. Toward the end of a year, they started negotiating a new contract and made astronomical demands. Then they made the mistake of offering an ultimatum to Mr. Kaiser. You don't do that unless you are fully prepared to back it up, and they weren't.

They said, "We want this or else."

And he said, "That's fine; it will be or else," and he paid them off.

While that was going on, a senior Kaiser medical man from Oakland came over here and sought me out. He also went to our very competent cardiologist, T. K. Lin, and also Phil Chu, who later was our chairman. All three of us were just hired hands. He said, "Will you take over the group and run it? Because we just can't get along with these guys."

We immediately said, "Sure!" The five partners were paid off and disappeared, and we organized the group over again. The three of us ran it out of our hip pocket for the first couple years. At that time, we had about twenty doctors and twenty thousand members. Then we decided we should be more formal, especially when we got a big contract with the federal employees, and another one with State employees. We were beginning to grow and feel like we might make it.

The hostility in the medical profession was ponderous. Our initial hospital on Ala Moana was originally built as a hotel by Henry Kaiser.

I'm sure doctors here would drive past there and look the other way. Wives stopped speaking to wives, and all of that kind of crap. Club memberships were cancelled.

We expanded our executive committee by adding two rotating members on two- or three-year rotating tenures. The three of us more or less declared ourselves lifetime members of the executive committee. All the doctors approved that in general meeting. Later, we enlarged the executive committee to seven.

The boys tried to kick me off the executive committee ten years later, during the Vietnam years, because they didn't like my political activities. They didn't question my competency and my right to continue as a member of the group. They didn't want me on the executive committee because I created a bad image in the public eye. I have to admit I didn't lean over backwards to cater to these guys. I demonstrated, I lectured, I yelled, I went in sit-ins, and all the rest. I had a lot of notorious collisions with police and other authorities, and got arrested over and over again.

But I think the news story that irritated my medical brethren most was the column head on the front page that said, "Dr. Butler says Bishop Kennedy is either senile or a liar." There were two Bishop Kennedys here, a Catholic and an Episcopal. I'm not sure which this was. What happened was that this jerk went over to Vietnam and came back with a big press release saying, "There's no napalm being used in Vietnam, especially on children. That's ridiculous. It's just a story that these people have cooked up."

I discovered that he had stayed with General Westmoreland. That's what I went to the press with. I said, "He's either senile or he's a liar. He was a guest in Westmoreland's villa and I am inclined to agree that there probably were no napalm children in Westmoreland's villa, but that doesn't mean he couldn't have gone out and found some if he looked for 'em."

My medical brethren were upset. "You have to say it that way? Can't you find some other way?"

The thing that really got to them was the famous effigy case. That's what it's known as here. It was a good case because it went all the way to the Hawaii Supreme Court where we finally won it. Lyndon Johnson himself was coming through on his way to southeast Asia, and he was going to speak in the open air at the University of Hawai'i, Mānoa Campus, and boy, we were just licking our chops. That was a made-to-order opportunity. There were six thousand people out there on the campus. We had a huge effigy—one figure dressed up cowboy style, labeled LBJ, and the other figure in military things, clearly labeled the Pentagon. One thing we were very careful to do was not go against the GIs. In fact, we had GI support groups here. We had meetings of GI support groups in *this* house. We always figured that if there were twenty people here, at least three of them were agents. But that's all right, we could live with that, you know. You can figure out who they are and feed 'em false information, but be nice to 'em in the meantime.

Anyway, there was this huge effigy up there and six thousand people. The place was teeming with undercover cops and uniform cops, and especially secret service people. I was standing next to a Honolulu police sergeant, and I heard his walkie-talkie squawking, "They are at the airport and will be there in minutes. Get that thing down." I knew what "that thing"was. I went over and put my hand on the thing, along with another person or two. I wanted to make sure that I wasn't going to let someone else take the rap for my doing. Moments later, the police rushed us, knocked the effigy over, and beat us up. They arrested three of us and charged us with disorderly conduct. That's the usual routine, and that was the case. We fought it all the way to the Supreme Court.

Dempsey Hewitt, a pediatrician colleague and real born-again Christer, in a general meeting where the subject of "what are we going to do about Butler?" came up, scolded me about giving such a bad image to the group. And I said, "Dempsey, you're a pediatrician, charged with the care and the welfare and the safety and health of living flesh and blood children. Here, you're upset because we did something with figures made out of papier-mâché. Where are your values?" And he didn't utter a word in response. He just sat down. I used to get so mad.

I first got in the Vietnam thing when Madame Ngu made her famous statement, "Every time a Buddhist monk barbecues himself, I clap my hands with joy." That was one of her famous utterances that made all the press. That was as early as '62 or '63, I guess. And so I'd been writing letters to the editor and trying to get an organization started. We started with five people demonstrating in front of the Federal Building: Barb and me, Oliver Lee and his wife, and Madeline Murray O'Hare, the famous atheist. We built up our group until we could call five hundred or six hundred people out in the streets on six hours notice. I don't recall how O'Hare got involved. I guess she was just passing through.

Oliver and I remained for the whole duration of the Vietnam struggle as co-chairs of the Hawai'i Committee to Stop the War in Vietnam. We met once a week. We had to stay on our toes, figuring out who were the agents and what do we do with them, and planning demonstrations and sit-ins, and so forth.

In the beginning, the pitch was the brutality of the war, the atrocities, get a truce, get negotiations started. A typical meeting of our group would involve twenty to thirty people. And then it developed that six or eight of them thought that we were going a little too far when the litmus test became, "Are you supporting the NLF and Hanoi?" Oliver and I and a lot of others quite frankly said, "Hell, yes. We're supporting the NLF and Hanoi and the communists in Southeast Asia." The six or eight moderates left our group at that point and formed their own organization, which lasted, I think, about six months.

We had wanted to go to Cuba right after the revolution was culminated, or at least after Fidel's people entered Havana in 1959. I had some early fights with the State Department about that. They kept saying, "No," and I kept saying, "I am, too!" We had to table that because we got involved in the Vietnam thing. Years later, in 1968 specifically, we were able to go to Cuba, and again in '72. We were never sanctioned in any way, just inconvenienced.

Barb and I had a connection, Alberto Bayo, who was a *coronel* in the Spanish Loyalist Army. He had sought refuge in Mexico, as many Spanish Loyalists did, and we made his acquaintance in Guadalajara. Bayo was an old lecher who was on the make for Barbara's mother, which was a personal connection that we capitalized on a little bit. I used to play chess with him at the Casa de Democracia in Guadalajara, a Loyalist hangout. Now, Bayo was the man who taught the elements of guerilla warfare to Fidel [Castro] and Che [Guevara] in Mexico. I don't know how they hooked up with him, but he was the guy that had shown them the ropes. They were both green as hell. He stayed on in Mexico after Che and Fidel had gone to Cuba. Later he moved to Cuba where he was promoted to *general*. I had exchanged some letters with him and his letters from Cuba were always franked—he didn't bother with postage. He was kind of an elder statesman to the Cuban Revolution. In 1968 he was all set to receive us, and he would have been a great entré into the inner circles in Cuba, but unfortunately he died just about a month before we got there.

Our first visit to Cuba was extremely interesting, and people did receive us very warmly, despite the fact that our sponsor had passed away. We were terribly impressed with what they were doing, and things they were trying to do, but had not yet succeeded in doing. Their spirit was admirable. I knew what to expect because I had done my homework and was well briefed on the Cuban Revolution. But we still were taken aback at some of the realities of what they had been able to do, especially in health and education. I took about 700 slides and we took some moving picture film. I interviewed a lot of people, especially in medicine, and I wrote an article for *The American Journal of Medical Education* on Cuban medical education. And I wrote an article for *Ramparts* magazine, which was very popular at that time. That was a great experience. We enjoyed every bit of it.

We took a Cuban freighter to Canada and landed in the snow up in Banff. We both had Hawaiian rubber sandals on. Barb got frostbite, which she still suffers occasionally from to this day. That was fun. When we came back, we were interviewed by the press and we talked very freely and had pretty good stories. We had a couple of close personal friends on both local dailies, and so we got good press. Of course my medical colleagues in Kaiser scolded me. They were such nitpickers. I had put in for a vacation and I had said I was going to Latin America. When I got back, they said, "Why didn't you tell us you were going to Cuba?"

I said, "You get a map and you look and you see where Cuba is. It's in Latin America."

During the Vietnam War, they tried to kick me off the executive committee, and asked me to resign. I said, "No, I'm not going to do your dirty work for you. You want me off of the executive committee, you kick me off." I even offered to meet with my main critics. I said, "I'll meet with you and talk about Vietnam as long as you want to," but they would never meet with me formally. A year later, at the next meeting of the general membership, they got the vote they needed to kick me off the executive committee. It made quite a play in the newspapers here. Jack Hall, who was regional director of the ILWU at that time, was one of our closest personal friends. He and a couple of other big shots, including Walter Johnson, went to bat for us and issued press releases. That was a good battle.

I got involved in dissident activities at an early stage of my life. Now, at the other end of my life, I am not real sure what's going to happen. I'm not a good prophet. I have no crystal ball. I do not have much hope for the Clinton administration. I am profoundly worried about the global aspects of the assault on our natural resources. I don't have to elaborate on that, but we simply cannot go on. In fact, we may already have passed the point of no return. I've told friends frequently that we have no guarantee that our species is even going to prevail. Why should we?

Millions of other species have come and gone—what is so different about ours in the long run? A species which behaves as atrociously toward our planet as our species has. So if you accept that as a possibility at least, then the question becomes, What is the going-away process going to look like? Once in a speech at the university, I said, "Is it going to be the sudden and merciful nuclear bullet to the head, or is it going to be chronic tuberculosis for the species and the world population that takes us down?" And I really don't know. We have grandchildren that mean a lot to us and human life means a lot to us in general. I prefer humans to cockroaches, all other things being equal. Cockroaches, however, are three hundred times more radio-resistant than human beings, and they have a better chance of being around one thousand years from now than we have. I don't know what form it'll take. I think this country's glamour and prosperity will vanish over a period of fifty years or so; maybe twenty-five. I'm not optimistic, I must say. I just don't know what form it'll take.

Jim
Brewer

An activist with the League of Employees for Economic and Democratic Advancement (LEEDA) and the editor of its newsletter, *Employees Today;* in his mid-fifties.

I strongly suspect that a lot of people become politicized at a very early age, and I feel that I was one of those people. I was born in 1939 in a remote area of Missouri in the swamps along the Mississippi River. It was at a time when they were building the levees and draining the swamps. My grandfather had been a sawyer in a sawmill that was part of the cutting down of all the cypress and hardwoods in that area of the country.

Because he was a farmer, my father was exempt from the military in World War II. It was a time when farming was becoming mechanized, so there was a large displacement of farmers from the soil into the cities. My dad was trying to make a living off a twenty-acre farm, and you just couldn't do it. So he went to Memphis to try to find a new livelihood. He worked at first, like farm immigrants to the city usually do, mowing lawns and trimming trees and bushes.

My mother was left with me, and later my newborn brother, on the farm. We were living kind of isolated in little better than a tar-paper shack, a very small cabin with no indoor plumbing. My mother washed our clothes in an iron kettle, over a fire, and the ashes under the fire were then made into lye soap. We made our own cottage cheese and canned everything for the winter. When I was about four years old my dad and mother broke up. My mother went to work in Michigan, which was booming because of the automobile industry. My dad stayed in Memphis and became an insurance salesman, working door-to-door, collecting insurance premiums once a week on a route.

I stayed there in the southeastern tip of Missouri living with aunts and uncles after that. The aunt that I lived with the majority of the time taught school for forty-one years. Her husband, who was my dad's brother—and a union man—was a retired lumberjack and railroad worker who had run away to the Northwest when he was 16. He helped cut the forests and lay the ties, and built and repaired trestles and huge bridges for the Union Pacific Railroad. He came back at age 38 and married my aunt. Soon after that when Dad and Mom broke up they kind of adopted my brother and me. All of this was a very disruptive kind of childhood. I felt like I was an orphan. The fundamentalist Christian atmosphere stigmatized you if you belonged to a broken home. I think that sensitized me to the feelings of other people.

My schoolteacher aunt gave me a love of learning. I remember she bought a set of encyclopedias for my brother and myself, and I basically read them all. I became a bookworm. After I was in the navy and went back to this little town I grew up in, the librarians were getting older, but they all remembered me because I was that guy who read almost every book in the little library there.

I had moved to Memphis to live with my dad. I was kind of a rebellious student. Those times were James Dean times. Everybody was kind of a "rebel without a cause." My last two years of high school were at the same school Elvis Presley went to, in Memphis. I was always giving the teachers a hard time. I could make an F in one class and get the science medal in another class. I flunked the senior year of school by a half a credit or so, so I did not graduate from high school. Shortly after that I got my dad to sign the papers, because I was under eighteen, and I was inducted into the navy in Little Rock on June 6, 1957. I wanted to get out of there because it was such a hateful environment growing up in the South in those days of segregation.

You were sensitive to the racial situation?

Yes. As a result of being a bookworm, I had been very impressed by the biography of Toussaint L'Ouverture, the Black Haitian general who led the successful revolution against Haiti. As a kid, I also worked for a dry cleaner and picked up dirty clothes in the African American section of town. I got to know a lot of Black people, and a lot of the racist stuff that we were fed on the white side of town was just totally negated by my work over there. Funny thing is that the guy who owned the dry cleaner had moved down from Detroit, and he was a civil-rights-minded white guy. He hired a guy from Detroit who was African American, and he and I got to be really good friends.

I did basic training in San Diego, California. Then I went to the Far East. On the way there I came to Hawai'i in 1958. I had a cousin who lived here and he took me all around. I remember thinking, Well, you know, this might be a good place to live. Then I went to Japan and then to Formosa (now called Taiwan), where I spent about three months on a station ship for the ferrying of ammunition and stuff to the Quemoy and Matsu Islands. The Chinese Nationalists on Taiwan and the communists on mainland China were firing heavy guns at each other at that time.

I spent two years in the Philippines, from 1958 to 1960. I got married there and we had six children. I helped rear three older daughters and three younger sons. My youngest son was stabbed to death in Waikīkī about eight years ago. I consider him a victim of a violent society based on greed and narrow self-interest. The grief I felt from his loss cannot be described with words. I have eleven grandchildren who all live on the U.S. mainland. My oldest daughter and her husband moved to the Seattle area last year in 1994 after twice having tried to make a go of it here in Hawai'i and live near me. But the high cost of living and low pay prevented it. They are the last of my children to live here. I feel very lonely sometimes.

I had been born and reared in the segregated South, but I had worked with Black people and came to view them as equals. And then going to the Far East and Pacific just expanded all of that. And of course, my children are half Filipino. My first wife and I split up in the late 1970s. The three older ones, the teenaged daughters, stayed in Texas with their mom. Then the oldest son went back, too, after less than a year here in Hawai'i with me.

I had the younger boys with me here. Each year I put the two sons who stayed with me in a summer program at the University of Hawai'i called Operation Manong, a cultural program for kids to understand their Philippine heritage. My surviving son still remembers all those songs that he learned, and he knows Philippine culture and understands that side of his heritage.

I went to submarine school and became a Polaris submarine navigation computer technician. I got out of the navy as a chief petty officer. I always felt uncomfortable in the military. The Vietnam War was continuing and the debate back here at home was heating up. I had a lot of really mixed feelings about what I was doing. The movie *On the Beach,* about a nuclear submarine crew which returned to desolation after a nuclear war, made a deep impression on me. I really became concerned about the necessity for peace. Each submarine I had been on could, for all intents and purposes, have destroyed the Soviet Union as a civilization, because all the major cities could have been whacked by just one submarine. When we went to battle stations we didn't know whether it was a drill or the real thing. And then you start thinking, Well, do I really want to participate in any way in the destruction of the world or another civilization? That was a politicizing experience. In 1970 I was medically discharged from the navy after serving twelve and a half years.

I took my family to the Philippines for two or three months, thinking that we might just live there. That was just before the Marcos takeover, a very unstable time. I soon realized that if we stayed there my family might be in some jeopardy. It was really polarized. If you were an American citizen you were going to have to take one side or the other, and I wasn't going to take a side against the Filipino people. So, the family and I came back to Hawai'i.

Just before being discharged, I worked at the Pearl Harbor sub base for about six months and started looking for a job, anticipating that we would make Hawai'i our home after my discharge. I answered an ad in the paper which said, "Make $3,000 a month." In 1970, that was big money. It turned out to be the International Marketplace, which owned one of the big memorial parks here. I went to work for them selling family funeral plans and burial plots. The sales pitch is very persuasive: If you're going to buy a funeral plan or a cemetery plot one day, why not buy it before you need it? That way you can get what you want and not be pressured into some stupid high-priced deal at the time of family grief. Actually, I was very good at it and they made me a sales manager. I never did make $3,000 a month on a regular basis. After more than three years, I got fed up with it. I didn't like marketing. I didn't like the sales process.

Then a sales motivation group hired me away from the cemetery and made me the general manager. A psychologist came from Florida. We were to remake peoples' ways of thinking so that they could become successful salespeople. You remolded their ideas and their values and everything. That was where I began to realize that people can really change, even as adults.

Then a couple of guys I knew—ex-submariners—started an estate planning firm which sold life insurance and mutual funds and stuff like that. They hired me to teach people how to sell. They were convincing people to drop their whole-life policies, which are part savings account and part insurance. The savings account part pays very little interest, but the companies make big profits by investing your money. A lot of people don't realize that insurance companies are the biggest banks in this country. I really began to question the economic system we live in.

I hadn't been around union activists, nor had I ever met anybody who called themselves a socialist or a radical. And I was already nearly thirty-five. I began to realize that a lot of the racism stuff that I had been taught as a kid had to do with stratification in the South. I realized that we really don't have a true democracy. I've heard it called a "cash-register" democracy, heavily slanted in favor of the people who have money and power. You can see the ways they hang on to it and transmit it to their cronies and relatives.

At some point, most people come to the realization that we are inherently interdependent social creatures whether we like it or not. The individualistic person is only fooling him- or herself. I came to believe that we all *could* live in a society that would be socially responsible and need-driven instead of greed-driven. And the best vehicle for this is *true* democracy among equal people. Those kind of thoughts started falling in place for me. My idea now is, Why can't we work together and all get rich together? If we live in societies where everyone is trying to make everyone else happy and well off, then you will be well taken care of yourself. I am not talking about a pie-in-the-sky utopia. Everybody would have a decent-paying job and [be] expected to carry a fair share of the workload.

I'm amazed at how many people I've met, in their sixties and seventies, who've said to me, "Jim, you know, the problem with living in our dog-eat-dog society is that by the time you figure out what's going on, it's too late." I feel I was fortunate that by the time I was forty years old, I had some idea of what was going on. Around age thirty-five, I started to get some inklings. You know, it seems like I've learned everything the hard way. That's the story of working people. We have to learn everything the hard way because there are so many blockages to our learning it the easy way.

Around 1974 I decided to become an activist as a Christian minister and, through the pulpit, try to help make this world become humane and need-driven instead of greed-driven. I decided that there needed to be fundamental social change in this country, and a good forum to do it from would be from the pulpit. When people ask me what I am politically, I tell them that I'm a part of the religious left. To this day I consider my activism as a humanistic religious ministry, but not connected to any particular church.

Anyway, I went one semester to this fundamentalist born-again Christian school in Lubbock, Texas. It wasn't a seminary, it was a school of preaching. I had kind of rationalized that you could be a minister and not be a believer. Like I said, I do everything the hard way. Anybody who was a thinker or a questioner in that school became a pariah within a very short time. They liked my being good at speaking and convincing people and working door-to-door, but somehow or another I was too. . .

You weren't preaching the Word of God?

. . . I was too much of a free thinker, I guess. So I dropped out of school. I said I was going to go on a "quest for human unity" and form a secular kind of humanistic religion by the same name. So I enrolled at Texas Tech and started taking sociology and anthropology and political science, and whatnot. This was the beginning of my social activism. I went to Texas Tech for about three years, worked at various part-time jobs, and drew my VA benefits to go to school. While I was there I came into contact with some Unitarian feminists involved with NOW (the National Organization for Women). And out of that—for about a year and a half—I became a member of a weekly men's feminist consciousness-raising group based in the local Unitarian Universalist Church. Then I met some Iranian students, some of them Marxists and radicals. I also met some Mexican American activists, specifically a group called the Brown Berets, and I went to a few meetings. For one of my political science classes, I wrote a paper on Mao Tse Tung and ended up reading about fifty books on China and Mao. I began to realize that there were people who had been working for a long time for a need-driven, humane society. I wasn't sure whether they were on the right track or not. I also began to realize that I didn't really want to be a religious guru or anything like that . . . too undemocratic for me.

About that time—1978—my wife and I broke up and I came back to Hawai'i with my three youngest children, the boys. The first thing I did here was to get a job in the Greenpeace office. I worked as a fund-raiser for Save the Whales, Hawai'i, using my training as a salesman. The kind of sales that I was trained in was person-to-person and door-to-door. That kind of thing is really good in precinct organizing and things like that.

Right away, I started school at the University of Hawai'i. I'm not sure that I ever finished a course because we would get involved in some kind of struggle. It seemed like I was having to drop my classes so I wouldn't fail them. Close to the university was the nonprofit Modern Times Bookstore. It was a place where you could join political discussion groups and work as a volunteer clerk for the bookstore. Another bookstore that opened close by was called the Asian-Pacific Books. Roland Kotani and some other folks and I opened that bookstore.

I was taking some courses in political science and then doing a lot of outside reading. In this so-called free society, you can become thirty-five years old—like I did—and never have the remotest inkling of what Marxism, socialism, feminism, nationalism, and the other "isms" are about. These are legitimate ideas and everybody in a democratic society has a right to be able to know and examine them. People should be able to analyze where we've been and where we could be going; to paint visions and dreams and see if they can come true.

So I became involved in the activist scene in Hawai'i, mainly centered around the University of Hawai'i. I got involved in Hawaiian rights and struggles at Sand Island. I wasn't a main organizer, but I was there and supportive, and people knew who I was. I wrote a grant proposal which got several thousand dollars for the startup of the Pacific Concerns Resource Center, which is based in Fiji now. It is the center for the Nuclear-Free and Independent Pacific movement.

I also was involved with environmental stuff. We formed groups like the antinuclear Opihi Alliance, where Don White of Greenpeace and I helped play a leadership role to stop nuclear waste ships from stopping in Honolulu Harbor on the way from Japan to France and Germany for reprocessing. We successfully stopped them and now they go around the Cape of Good Hope, a long trip that way.

Around 1980 I was arrested at Nukoli'i on Kaua'i, along with thirty-three others. We called ourselves the Nukoli'i Thirty-three. By a two-thirds majority, the people of Kaua'i had voted against the hotel development there, but the State and county governments sided with the developers and the project continued. So some of us went to help stop it. To me it was a fundamental question of democracy for Hawai'i. If they could ignore the majority vote on Kaua'i, they could do it here in Honolulu and elsewhere.

It was also about that time, too, that I got kicked and beaten up by thugs working for the Korean dictator, Chun Do Whan, at the Korean consulate up on the Pali Highway. Some twenty-odd of us from the Modern Times Bookstore group were holding signs protesting his visit to get $14 billion worth of jet fighters from Jimmy Carter. About the time he arrived in his limousine, about fifty of his bodyguards attacked four of us. That was an important event for me personally. My head had been smashed by a wooden club and required several stitches. Afterwards, I remember looking up into the concerned and loving eyes of my activist partner, Renee Ing, as she clutched my hand while the doctor stitched my head. Right then I realized that we were bonded for life. Today she is my wife and best friend.

When I first came back here in 1978, I lived on the North Shore. I took the bus home from the Greenpeace office in Honolulu. I began seeing these Mao posters from the Revolutionary Communist Party along the bus route. That was just one of the many groups on the campus that you couldn't avoid meeting at times. There also were various socialist and communist and radicalist and nationalist groups and women's liberation groups. I called it alphabet soup, because these folks all had these names with initials, like RCP [Revolutionary Communist Party], CPML [Communist Party, Marxist-Leninist], HUS [Hawai'i Union of Socialists], and whatever. Those are the kinds of associations that were in the activist community at that time.

Do you think of them as the "isms" that you don't like?

No, not necessarily. The negative "isms" that I'm mostly talking about are the fundamental "isms" that people can understand on a daily basis. I'm talking about racism, for example, and negative nationalism and negative feminism. I believe that the Hawaiian and Native American movements are legitimate national movements. These are nations of people and they have a right to their identity and their heritage. If feminism means women's equality, then I'm a feminist. But if it means turning the world upside down into a matriarchy where women would be superior, then I call that negative feminism. The "isms" that I'm talking about are antidemocracy: classism, racism, religious fundamentalism, rabid nationalism, sexism, and ageism. In a broader sense, these create division, which I call "divisionism."

Classism is the most important negative "ism" that we have to fight against. I first became an activist in the years leading up to Reagan and Bush. Then Reagan and Bush launched a real class attack. Those were years of privatization of things like public housing or bus transportation on the mainland. These were years of deprogressivization of the income tax. During the Reagan years, they cut taxes for the highest income bracket by more than one-half, helping to create the budget deficits, the huge national debt, and many of this country's present economic problems. I'll never forget the attack on working people when Reagan appointed Thorn Auchter to be head of OSHA [Occupational Safety and Health Administration]. The first thing this guy did when he came into office was burn tens of thousands of brown lung posters, which warned people who worked around cotton gins and in spinning mills that they were in danger of getting brown lung.

A lot of people pretended that Ronald Reagan was kind of an insensitive, sometimes-doddering fool. But the truth of the matter was that Reagan knew what he was doing and was backed up by right-wing think tanks like the Heritage Foundation, the American Enterprise Institute, the Coors family, and the Hoover Institution at Stanford University. Things were very much thought out. It was a class-conscious attack on working-class people, and the result of it was that we had a considerable widening of the gap between the richest and the poorest. It was all conscious.

It was the time of a great shell game, which showed how knowledge in our society can be manipulated. Most of us were living in a depression or a recession during those twelve Reagan-Bush years; things got harder and harder for us. But they constantly used cooked-up, one-sided statistics to show that there was a recovery and a boom. They would show the Dow-Jones average and what was happening on Wall Street, but they weren't showing what was happening to us on main street. During that time, there was a great restructuring of the economy. Industrial manufacturing jobs were being replaced by service jobs. And investment capital ran away to chase cheap labor, taking many of our better-paying jobs to other places supported by our tax dollars where dictators keep union-free environments—like the Philippines and El Salvador.

They were able to do all of this on borrowed money. In two hundred years of existence, this country had built up a $1-trillion debt. Within eight years, Reagan had quadrupled the national debt to $4 trillion. That was part of the shell game to make it look like we were living in good economic times. Our kids will pay for this huge debt, not just in tax dollars but in lost education, lost opportunities, loss of standard of living, and a thousand other ways.

This also was a time of militarization and dehumanization. Reagan cut taxes for the rich in half, losing hundreds of billions of budget dollars each year. He also doubled the military budget, creating the need for hundreds of billions of new tax dollars each year. To make up for the skyrocketing debt, they saved money by throwing the mentally ill, blind people, and children out on the street to be homeless. Can you imagine such deliberate government policies? The federal housing budget was cut 75 percent during the Reagan-Bush years. That represents housing stock that was never built to keep up with the growing demand for housing.

During the Reagan-Bush years, somewhere between one-half and one million family farmers were displaced from the land. In addition to what this meant just in terms of rural economics, it meant another exodus from rural areas to urban areas that put further strains on the cities. This was an environmental disaster, because these family farmers took care of the land and preserved the soil. Agri-business chemicalizes the soil and lets it blow or wash away. This country has lost half of its topsoil.

Reagan-Bush attacked our unions, starting off with the Air Traffic Controllers. The union movement has continued to become smaller. They watered down and understaffed the National Labor Relations Board. Grievances, strikes, or organizing drives were rendered nearly impotent.

Racism had such a resurgence under Reagan and Bush. Reagan never had an independent Black leader visit him during his whole eight years in the White House. Jesse Jackson never set foot in his office. George Bush used the racist Willie Horton ads to help get himself elected. Their policy was to turn back the gains of affirmative action. They used quotas and reverse-racism as inflammatory terms to stop the movement towards racial equality.

So we live in a terrible time. It is a legacy of arch-criminals.

Today, activism has changed from the streets to the mainstream. Patsy Mink, for instance, has been an activist for the working people most of her adult life, but now she is a member of the U.S. Congress. A lot of activists are lobbying. . . . A lot of people changed. They not only say what they are against, but they also speak out for what they are for. They have moved from just resisting injustice to insisting on concrete programs to build a just society. That's how it's been for me. At a certain point, I quit being an *anti*nuclear activist and became a peace activist. Things just don't work out politically when all you're doing is just being negative.

This is actually what we're doing now with LEEDA, which we formed in 1989. We are an employees' organization developing a pro-employee political platform. We're proactive, setting out initiatives that we are *for*. We're not going to be like Olive Oyl in the Popeye cartoons, always helplessly beating on Bluto's chest, waiting to be rescued by Popeye. We're *not* going to be raising hell *after* something's already been done and decided. By going after a positive platform of change we will reverse things and then help start building a just and equitable society.

Over the years, the heart of the so-called American dream, which became a reality for a lot of families, was that one person in a two-parent household, working forty hours a week, could make a decent living for that family. That has been eroded to the point where most two-parent households are working two jobs outside the home. So the work-week has been lengthened—from forty to eighty hours—for one household with both parents working. This can result in child care problems. The education crisis in this country revolves around the preceding basic economic fact, rather than, say, poorly trained teachers or bad school boards. It really revolves around how much time parents no longer can spend with their kids. Somebody has to spend the time with these kids. They know they have to have that attention. If they don't get it, they act up. Teachers are spending time disciplining—and mothering and fathering—rather than teaching. We need effective after-school programs where kids get attention, smaller classrooms, more classrooms, more teachers.

You ran for mayor of Honolulu? _____

I ran for mayor. That was just our way of taking the housing struggle to City Hall at the time. We had just stood a sixty-two-day vigil in front of the State Capitol offices calling for *Housing Now!* But beyond that one issue, we're working for full democracy. Someday we'll get away from the class society we live in now, where elections and political appointments are bought and sold. We need an employees' political party and a political program for working peoples' everyday needs. We need to work person-to-person and door-to-door for housing, education, health care.

Unlike much of the eclectic and spontaneous activism of the '60s and '70s, we need continuity. With a political party, you can have some continuity. You can build up a history and you can have a reservoir of experience, and you can cover all bases instead of fighting one struggle at a time in isolation from other vital issues. It's important that we have a party of employees—a labor party—because we represent about 75 percent of the population.

The two major political parties are compromised by the fact that they let the rich minority contribute money to them. All money has strings attached to it. We believe in having an organization in which we raise money through dues and donations and fund-raisers amongst working people. We're the people who every day, when we go to work, produce the actual wealth that we consume. We provide the services that make the world go 'round. We should have the dignity, pride, and prosperity that goes with that.

I'll tell you a little funny story. When we were holding the sixty-two-day vigil in front of the State Capitol for affordable housing and to house the homeless, a lot of people would honk and wave. Once in a while though, some Mercedes, or other rich person's car, would go by and somebody would sarcastically yell, "Get a job!" Most of us were people from the Church, retired, whatnot. One day I turned to Tom Shields and said, "Tom, we ought to tell *those* guys to get a job!"

There are too many people in this society who spend their days going around the golf courses and tennis courts, wearing their California aloha shirts and figuring out how they can get more for themselves and screw the average working person. They're landowners, bankers, employers, who take advantage of us. While they play, they've got us working too many hours, and paying too much for housing, interest on installment credit, health care, and everything. And they're paying us low pay. We've been losing that struggle, and we have to turn that around. We have to tell *them,* "Get a job!"

Rachel Saiki

An activist in her seventies who still continues her activism of many years.

Father was only nineteen when he came to work in the sugar plantation on the Big Island. I remember him telling us that they used to go and catch *'o'opu,* which is a freshwater fish, up in 'Akaka Falls. He said the head was the size of a clenched fist—real big, yeah? Somewhere along the way, he learned how to cut hair. While he was working at the plantation, the boss' wife—or somebody—taught him English. My father didn't want to stay in the plantation, so as soon as the contract was over he came here and established himself as a barber and had a barber shop someplace by Central Union Church. The second barber shop, where I was born, was in a building that is still standing at the end of Fort Street.

My mother was a picture bride and didn't get here until my father was in his mid-thirties. She was fourteen years younger. So, he was a bachelor for many years and that must have been hard for my mother . . . by then he must have had set ways. I have an older brother, born at the first shop, and two younger brothers born where I was, in the second shop at the end of Fort Street, a building still standing today.

My father loved plants. The owner of the building where my father had his shop was a yardman. He used to work up in Pacific Heights, which is close to where we live. He got very annoyed at my father for having lots of plants because [in] those days the landlord paid the water bill, and the water bill was high. My father wanted to get out of there so he bought this property we're in right now. The last day he was supposed to go to his shop he had a stroke. He was in his early fifties.

I was just finishing eighth grade. When I was ready to go into ninth grade, my father got sick. On top of that, from ninth grade up a $10 tuition had just begun. We couldn't afford it, you know, so I had to do babysitting work at a family friend's home. I stayed with the family, got room and board, and got $5 for each term—$10 total. This was way back in the 1930s, during the depression.

Then I worked by the day with another family, mostly helping with the baby and doing the laundry. In those days, we had no washing machine and had to wash by hand. . . . Then I got a summer job in a pineapple cannery. After that, I went to work in a garment place. They used to do a lot of khaki pants. I knew somebody who worked there and they used to make about $20 a week—piecework. [The] first time, you know, you have to learn how to use the power sewing machine, which was really fast. Whatever we earned was not enough to cover the expenses for the day. We had to pay 15 cents for bus fare and about 15 cents for a sandwich, so I didn't pick up my 50-something cents. But anyhow, the lady said, "I think you are too young."

So, that's when I went to S. H. Kress and Co. They just tore down the building where Kress used to be. On one side is Fort Street Mall and on the other side is the Union Mall, right in the heart of town. I think I started work in 1938. The girls that worked just before me were under NRA . . . and they had a minimum wage of $12, but when I went in it was $9 a week, and we worked eight hours a day.

I worked there maybe a year in the hardware department. The supervisor of the cafeteria department, a local Chinese guy, was taking advantage of the girls in that store if they didn't give him a date. He gave them a bad time and so they quit. . . . Just at that time, the haole manager of the store—they all came from the mainland—was [fired]. . . . So a new manager was brought in.

The workers didn't know too much about the ILWU. They had gotten a lawyer and then got all the workers in the cafeteria side to sign a petition asking the new manager to get rid of the supervisor. So at that time, then, the ILWU came over and talked to some of the key guys in the cafeteria and told them the way to do it. The ILWU was organized industrially, you know, so they said you have to get the whole store organized.

Word got to us that they wanted us to come to the union hall for a meeting. I was interested, so I went down and it sounded good to me. I got elected as one of the trustees. That was on a Sunday. We went to work on Monday, and found out that about seventeen of us from all over the store had been fired. And so, that's how I got to be involved in the union.

So they had the NLRB [National Labor Relations Board] hearing, and John Reinecke was one of the local people that helped with organizing after we got fired and we went into negotiations. I don't think we had anybody from the ILWU, but we had guys from the ship. I don't know if they were firemen or whatever department, but they knew their stuff. Two of them used to come and help us with our negotiation. And I remember one guy would kind of get after the new manager and get him all riled up. He got him so annoyed that he would say something that the company's attorneys didn't want him to say.

In the first decision, I was the only one not reinstated. Some had other jobs and those that went back didn't stay very long. John went through all the transcripts and found they had mixed my testimony and somebody else's testimony and were really going for me. It took a whole year before I was called back. I used to hang around the ILWU office every day. I came home really late when we had to do picketing. That's when I got my real education in the union. I saw why it was important that you organize and stick together.

The war had started, and so a lot of the non-Japanese who worked at the Kress store started getting better-paying jobs at Pearl Harbor and [places] like that. The matron at Kress was part-Hawaiian. She got a job at Pearl Harbor. Not very many people would take a matron's job. You know, you have to clean the public toilets and girls' toilets and stuff like that. But they didn't know that not only was I hard-headed, but I also had worked in private homes, so scrubbing toilets is not going to faze me. So, I had a job.

Sometime later, we went to see the head of the local NLRB, a former New Zealander, and told him that before I was fired I had done some time on the sales floor. The company then allowed me to work most of my time handling small boxes of glasses and working as a salesperson on Saturdays.

But I got pregnant, so I finally had to leave. Many people admired me for the stand I took, but nobody would stick their necks out and get into organizing.

Some years later, the Marine Cooks and Stewards—that's a department on a ship that does the cooking and the waiting—started a shore-side division and started organizing workers. I was hired by them.

American Sanitary Laundry was one of the larger laundries here. Just before they had a certification election, I got a job there. I was a watcher for the union when they had the election. I became a chief steward and would take grievances to the boss.

The organizing was done by progressive people here, and I just went in after the organization was already started. If I had really learned how to be an organizer, my job would have been to train people who were going to stay there. I wasn't going to be staying there, you know. I had better things to do than work in the laundry, but I wasn't smart enough, or nobody told me, to organize people to take over the job that I was doing. So, of course, the boss was real happy when I left. My boyfriend was going into a vegetable business. The boss said, "Yeah, we'll come over and buy stuff from you"—all that kind of baloney. But what happened was the guys at the Marine Cooks and Stewards didn't service the members. That was the first union in Hawai'i to ever have a decertification election, so you can see how green I was.

I was out of the labor movement for awhile because I had my son to raise. My son's father—my boyfriend—was an ILWU member. He was married. By the time his wife gave him a divorce, I decided I didn't want to get married to him, so I came home and took care of my son and myself. Since he was pure Japanese, there were many people who were interested in adopting him. But I said, "That's my son and I'm going to take care of him."

My oldest brother was a brewery worker. During the war, they had some kind of electrical thing at the brewery, so a Japanese American couldn't work there. So he had to work outside, as an electrician's helper. But after the war ended, he went back to work and he was in the brewery workers' union. In those days, the unions were working close together. When they had conventions on the mainland, the seamen's union would have other union delegates go to the mainland, working their way on the ship and back. My brother liked that, so later on he became a sailor.

He was a little bit more open-minded. He used to take my son all over. Some of the places, maybe it was better that he hadn't. He used to take him to bars. He drank a lot just like my father. He taught my son some Japanese songs. And then he would make a little money singing at the bars.

My youngest brother passed away about five years ago from a heart attack. He worked most of his life as an auditor for the PX accounting system. The army had called him in and questioned him about me. If he had any good sense, he would have told them, "My sister has her own mind. Go ask her, don't ask me about her." But he would tell my mother, and my mother would get annoyed and take it out on my son instead of me. So I had to take care of that. My father was a little bit more sympathetic, I guess, because he had gone through the sugar plantation. My mother never was, because she came from a farm and she didn't have any experience. She did work at the tuna factory when she came here, but in those days they didn't have a union.

Then I went to business school for two and a half years, and my folks were happy. They thought that I would get a job and bring in some money, but that wasn't to be. *(Laughter.)*

The first job I took was working for the Oahu County Committee of the Democratic Party. The head of it was the man who later became the governor of Hawai'i—John Burns. Yeah, I worked under him. I never worked for the ILWU, though everybody thinks I did. What I did was go over to the ILWU office and copy all the names of active members of the ILWU to help form the Democratic clubs. And then I got involved— I guess maybe because of my boyfriend—in the women's auxiliary of the ILWU.

After a while, I guess they didn't have enough money, so I went for the first time on unemployment compensation. When my unemployment ran out, I went to work for the *Honolulu Record,* which was a labor paper.

Was any particular union behind it?

Well, the base was the ILWU membership. They supported the paper and all the conventions. I took care of the subscriptions, helped with the mailings, and helped run the offset presses. We had a really small staff. Most of us got about $90 a month, and we would sacrifice. But that's how we kept the paper going for ten years. Then the ILWU took over, and I think the paper only lasted two or three years at the most after that.

My job on the paper became mostly taking subscriptions on the neighbor islands, where I spent about 60 percent of my time. I would go to each island twice: once for subscriptions and once to get advertisements for the anniversary issue. My job was mostly on the outside. We would fly to the islands and ship the company Jeep over. I used to stay a whole month with friends on Kaua'i, you know, and work the whole island.

On O'ahu we had newspaper stands. A lot of people were scared to subscribe to the paper, so they would buy it on the stand. But many people subscribed on the neighbor islands. All the mayors of the neighbor islands would subscribe. They were supportive because the base was the union guys, and that's where they got their votes. All the little business places and plantation stores would take ads and that's how we kept going, along with the subscriptions. Some Filipino guys who couldn't read took subscriptions because they realized how the union had helped them get better wages and working conditions.

And they treated me royally. I used to work the Filipino camps and other English-speaking camps. I would always work with the secondary leadership and they would take me around to the different camps. The Filipino guys from different camps would cook something for me—special. Once I was at the cockfights and this guy won the fight, which means he won the dead chicken, too. So he made stew, and oh, that thing was so tough, you know! I said, "Hey, more tough than me!" *(Laughter.)* I had some fun, you know.

One of my co-workers at the *Honolulu Record* didn't want to work under the ILWU when it took over the paper, so he started a business of his own—a little print shop—and I worked with him for a few years. Then, a friend referred me to the Honolulu Board of Realtors, who wanted someone in their print shop. So I worked there as an offset printer for eight years. When the print shop closed, I left.

I had to wait a year or so till I was sixty-two to get my social security. But that's when I got back into the movement again. Aiko Reinecke would see to it that if there was anything going on, she would hit me for a contribution. So I was contributing to all of these causes. Whenever there was any kind of labor dispute, or they needed somebody on the picket line, I was a volunteer for that. So I've been in many, many things.

One of the things that I got involved in was the case of Yu Hsi Chen. He went to the university here. He was from Taiwan, but he was more for Mainland China politics. He went to Japan where he worked for a progressive paper. He was fluent in Chinese, Japanese, and English. Then the Japanese government, in cahoots with the Taiwanese government, deported him to Taiwan where he was held in jail for treason. All of us who knew him went to bat for him, all over the world. So finally, with all the protest, he was released. John and Aiko Reinecke were his sponsors. He came back here and he went to the university and got his doctorate.

I've been active in the Philippine movement, too. We picketed the Philippine consulate. I went to the KMU conference in Manila in 1985. Kilosan Maya Uno [KMU]—they call that the Communist union—is the most progressive union in the Philippines. Today, KMU has worldwide support. I went to Manila when the Philippines was still under Marcos, so I saw what a country could be under a dictator like him.

Fortunately for me, I can pass as a Filipina, so I went on bus rides where military guys with guns would come aboard and check around. I had a letter from our infamous Senator Inouye, who was buddy-buddy with Marcos, requesting that I be allowed to go and visit the labor leaders in prison, in Mindanao. A labor attorney who took me to visit with the labor leaders in prison told me not to say anything when we were passing the guards. I asked him later what he had told the guards. He told them that I was the labor leader's grandmother. Later, he took a job with the Aquino government.

I went to Japan almost five years ago when my brother passed away. I had met Ron Fujiyoshi, the minister who protested the fingerprinting of the Koreans while he was stationed in Japan. I had met him at a picket line before I went to Japan, so I said, "Oh, I'm going to be in Japan; I'll come to your trial." So I took the train from where I was staying and went to Osaka and listened in on his trial. I got interviewed. . . . I figured I'd give moral support for a local person making a stand like that. It was really interesting. Ron Fujiyoshi has me on his mailing list. His trial has been going on for twenty years. They have amnesty for all the protesters, but he refuses to go in on that. He wants to make his point that if they want to be leaders in the world, they better start at home and clean up some of that stuff.

5

Women's Struggles

Gender movements in Hawai'i are not a mirror image of those in the continental United States. That they are not is part of the paradoxical side of Hawai'i: it is at once the very essence of U.S. corporate society; and also, in the growing indigenous peoples movement, its vision of an antidote. As the most recent state in the Union, it could profit from its knowledge of immigrant history in the other states, how industrialization shaped its cities, and then abandoned them with despoiled land and air. The vision of the sovereignty movement could deliver it from the ruined infrastructure of rusted steel and decaying bridges, its specter of teeming cities of the unemployed—all this with no plans to fix them. The vision delivers a reuse of the land, clean waters, and people working in harmony and a sense of collectivity. Part 7 of this book discusses sovereignty at length.

At the same time, Hawai'i has been—as recently as the mid-twentieth century—a contract-labor agricultural system, with its many workers siphoned from underdeveloped Asian homelands. The new generation of these people seems both grateful for its Americanization and rapid intergenerational social mobility, and perhaps fearful of its future. How women were used in the workforce and on the plantations presents a different pattern from the "pioneer woman" settling the United States and becoming an owner of new lands. The women of Hawai'i were the chattels of the chattels, the underlings of the paternal lords of the plantation. This unique cultural and social history, the presence of a distinct indigenous population, and the other ethnic groups that assimilated in the more recent past—all must provide a different mix for the discussion and solution of women's classic inequality. Perhaps the statements by the speakers who follow will provide the opportunity to hear part of this history firsthand. Speakers in other sections of the book, such as Rachel Saiki and Mary Choy (part 4) and Lynette Cruz (part 7) should also be seen as part of this history.

The backlash of the women's movement described so well in Susan Faludi's book, *Backlash: The Undeclared War Against American Women* (New York: Crown, 1991) is not missing today in the lives of women in Hawai'i. The vivid picture of popular culture from the U.S. media is instantly available on TV and in print—no lag time here. Thus, women in Hawai'i get the same reactionary and anxious picture as women in the continental United States: women have lost out to the "equality trap," the barren womb is causing mental illness, neglected children and women's freedom spawn crime, and the large number of women in the workforce causes unemployment. And all this is the result of too much feminism!

Our speakers in this book would seriously doubt whether gender equality ever grew beyond infancy. Women still earn on average 70 percent of the income of males, and women with bachelor's degrees are likely to earn the same as a male high school graduate. Most women are still found in low-wage service occupations that have been traditionally cast as a "woman's role" in the definition of woman-the-server. These occupations are more available in today's service economies. More than three-quarters of U.S. women are employed in just twenty of the 427 U.S. Department of Labor job categories. According to the U.S. census, women represent 95 percent of secretaries, 94 percent of nurses, 85 percent of elementary school teachers—but only 6 percent of engineers, 4 percent of dentists, and 5 percent of senior executives.

The feminist scapegoat theory seeks the facile "psychologistic" explanation: laying the blame on wrong-thinking individuals—the mental abberations of a generation of Betty Friedans. The civil rights approach to gender inequality says that strong implementation of anti-discrimination laws will make the difference. The political right says that victims who are poor, on welfare, elderly, or otherwise weakened by an unrelenting economic system are responsible for a failing economy. Females, of course, fill these social categories in greater proportions than males.

Entirely bypassed are the political and economic causes of today's badly skewed distribution of wealth and power. In the economic climate of the 1990s, women must work outside of the home, particularly in Hawai'i where the cost of living is so high. Buying a median-priced home requires a minimum down payment of $70,000, about double the average annual income. Without two earners, this would be virtually impossible. Even two earners often require financial input from their better-off previous generation, who purchased their home at a 400 to 500 percent lower price.

Women workers also have been victimized by the vicissitudes of the economy and profit-oriented corporate decisions. At times of recession, when industries are glutted with products, women—and other expendables—are the first to go. Today, a large part of the national economic activity consists of leveraged buyouts, which result in corporate downsizing and the firing of workers. Downsizing, the chosen method to increase the value of a corporate stock, means that the less productive white-collar workers will be dropped, such as women who served administrators and workers who produced inadequate dollars for the company or inadequate grants for the university. Meanwhile, blue-collar workers are replaced by machines and older workers are let go before retirement eligibility. A company may declare bankruptcy, dump its workers, and open afresh in Mexico with a benign, poverty-driven workforce—all perfectly legal. And who is hired if the company reopens in the United States? Answer: that portion of the unemployed who are happy (forced) to receive a much lower rate of pay. And what about the working conditions?

The conditions of low-paid workers are often unclean, unsafe, and unregulated. The twenty-five African American women who died in 1991 of smoke inhalation from a fire at the Imperial Food Products chicken-processing plant in North Carolina could tell the story, if they had lived. They were locked inside during working hours to prevent coffee or cigarette breaks, and the facility had not been inspected for six years by the inadequately staffed U.S. Occupational Safety and Health Agency. The fate of low-paid workers is to work in often marginal and unregulated facilities; the American equivalent of the Mexican or Filipino factory .

Women around the world have been plagued for centuries with other malefactions and inequities. There are notable examples when one examines the question internationally and interculturally. The learning of "gender-appropriate" behavior exists in every country, and begins in infancy. The practice of body mutilation continues all over the world. In countries like the United States, it is expressed in breast enhancement, liposuctions, facial surgeries, and skeletal weight reductions. In other countries, women may fatten themselves to obesity for enhanced marriageability. Among some North African peoples, women may be forced to undergo brutal surgery to remove their clitoris, which—it is claimed—serves to reduce their sexual appetites and keep them more faithful to their husbands.

Violence against women, particularly wife beating, is still rampant as a form of social control. Anti- and pro-abortion laws in the United States prescribe or proscribe matters of childbearing. The well-known practice of female infanticide in India—the subject of a recent public TV documentary—is used as the method of choice for solving economic and cultural problems, such as the unquestioned necessity of a dowry when a young woman (but not a young man) marries. The problem is removed by killing the new daughter. In Thailand, the selling of pubescent girls into prostitution is considered the wisest choice available to large families whose lives are threatened by poverty. These practices are rooted in dogma and traditions passed down from ancient times. Many attitudes are preserved in sacred documents, such as the Bible and the Koran.

Today, these attitudes toward gender range from intact, virtually uncontested norms, to hidden, vestigial thoughts which are likely to emerge in cases of assault, harassment, or rape. One way or the other, in the latter twentieth century, perhaps it is believed that women must be kept under some control lest they take over as a group in phalanx formation. Lesbianism is often singled out as an extreme example of female takeover. It could be conjectured that there is more latent worry over this than a takeover by fascists. Few oppressors seem to worry about takeovers by poor and disenfranchised groups over which the ruling elites seem to have placed their centuries-old power imprimatur. Will *that* oppression ever end, much less that of the formerly weakened one-half called women?

The many cultural manifestations of gender problems are present in varying degrees in Hawai'i and show up among our oral histories. Sometimes they are more virulent and threateningly present, such as the often "horrendous, brutal" sexual harassment cases coming to the attention of Susan Hippensteele, advocacy officer in the Student Affairs Office at the University of Hawai'i. She has been involved in some three hundred complaints involving students, faculty, and staff in the past three years. We have no speakers on this topic from the broader community in Hawai'i, but we suspect the same situation prevails in the general population.

That harassment is charged at the highest levels of education and government—purveyors of truth and knowledge, the makers and watchdogs of law and order—is evident not only in Hippensteele's heavy caseload, but also in recent charges of sexual harassment against Senator Daniel Inouye. This is outlined briefly in the following testimony of Meda Chesney-Lind and was also a subject of energetic activism by Frances Viglielmo. Chesney-Lind, as a social and political analyst, understands the power relationships inherent in the charge against Inouye: decades of entrenched power create an iron wall protecting the harasser from the accusations of the complainant. Troublemaking at this level is dangerous to one's job, and who knows what else.

The women's movement today is by no means dead. The National Organization for Women (NOW) is part of the landscape in the United States, with staffed offices in many states that respond to proposed legislation and have the political experience to organize large demonstrations. Pro-choice and sexuality issues have been championed with great effectiveness. Recent efforts have centered on the need to organize a third party, and a tentative start was made with the formation of the Twenty-First Century Party. More uniquely, the process of uniting women of all social classes and races has begun. NOW began principally as a white woman's organization, heavily skewed toward professional and middle-class membership. With today's attacks on liberalism and the accelerating thrust to destroy yesterday's social gains, the fight back is taking new forms in feminist organizing. During the past year or two, NOW began new alliances with women's welfare and poverty organizations, such as Up and Out of Poverty Now. This could inject new fire into the movement.

The women's movement has not burned out since the 1960s when the first large-scale, post-suffrage movement took place. While other movements of that creative decade have come and gone, the women's movement has changed only its current emphases, its succession of members, its group names, and at times its rhythm and pace.

Hawai'i has produced recent women's formations and collectives. The Pacific Women's Network, formed in 1994, is committed to self-determination, advocacy for the disempowered, education, and community organizing. It was asked by international women's groups to sponsor the Seventh International Cross-Cultural Black Women's Summer Institute in 1995, which drew women from Africa, South America, Asia, and other areas around the world. This was a stepping-stone to the United Nations Women's International Conference, held in Beijing in September 1995 and attended by over fifty thousand women. Hawai'i is singularly located for such worldwide conferences and dialogue.

Nā Mamo o Hawai'i ("descendants of Hawai'i, for posterity")

began in 1993 as a reaction to testimony in legislative hearings from Kanaka Maoli against same-sex marriage. The group's countering that gays have a revered place in Native Hawaiian society spawned a series of forums and educational events. Today, this organization includes all people who have been marginalized because of race and class, both male and female. Now new questions are being raised about the effects of the missionary patriarchal society on the Kanaka Maoli: What are Hawaiian values? Did the missionaries convince the people to be nice (*'olu'olu*) and to be humble (*ha'aha'a*)? Did this colonial status seek to destroy the strengths of the ancestors who were never afraid to stand up and speak?

Na Mamo was asked to present panels at the Pacific Island Women's Conference held in Honolulu in 1995. This drew women and men from the entire Pacific region and the United States. The attendance was principally nonwhite.

The problem areas that were taken up by this conference are very contemporary in spirit and reflect the emerging issues of the sovereignty movements in the Pacific. The dominant theme, not dealt with before by groups of this kind, was the need to move away from the Western paradigm of land ownership and *private property*. They stated that "private property is what did us in as Hawaiians and resulted in our lower status." This issue has remained somewhat cloistered in the political forums of the U.S. left and has appeared as a nineteenth-century idea whose time had never come in the United States. The lifeblood, energy, and spirit of the sovereignty movement should open up new directions and new fire.

All kinds of support groups have become part of institutionalized gender consciousness in Hawai'i. College students become familiar with women's and gender issues in course offerings provided by the UH Women's Studies Program and a number of community colleges. An uncommon emphasis addressing Asian, Pacific Island, and Third World women is a part of the Hawaiian intellectual establishment. *Voices*, the Hawaiian women's news journal, is notable in its enlightened coverage of the abortion issue and problems of the entire Asian-Pacific women's social system.

Chesney-Lind calls attention to the women's watchdog and advocate caucuses in the State Legislature. They grew out of opportunities for women to achieve legal careers with the opening of the UH Law School in the early 1970s. But, she feels that too much reliance has been placed on the Women's Caucus because of its effectiveness in the past. This had led to a scarcity of a strong women's leadership when crises occur, such as the Inouye case.

Women are leading many progressive, reformist organizations today, such as welfare rights. It is appropriate that womens' commitment to family survival is also channeled into related problems like homelessness, housing, education, and the environment, all capturing effective female leadership. Strong "taro-roots" women in Hawai'i are very visible in the sovereignty movement, taking leadership in the 'ohana groups (those based on family membership), and leading in the preservation of the language, culture, and spirituality of the ancient Kanaka Maoli traditions.

Issues usually categorized under "the woman question"—equal pay, affirmative action, sexual harassment, abortion rights, education, child care—do not claim all of the time and organizing skills of activist women. But the full consciousness of how these problems relate to the need for political power is not yet a consensus among women.

In addition to those of Chesney-Lind and Hippensteele, the oral histories that follow paint a striking picture of the involvement of energetic activist women. Ho'oipo DeCambra struggles hard in the difficult areas of education and its new consumerist accent. Lucy Witeck fights for fairness in all arenas, and her cross-racial experience as a former VISTA worker serves her well in activism of the Islands. Frances Viglielmo owes much of her activist awakening to having grown up in the sexist military society of American-held Panama. Today she never fails to exert enlightened leadership in Hawai'i's antinuclear, environmental campaigns that stem from the use, dumping, and storing of that same military establishment, this time in the Pacific.

Meda
Chesney-Lind

Director of the Women's Studies Program at the University of Hawai'i at
Mānoa at the time of the interview; in her forties.

The Women's Studies Program began at UH in the early 1970s. I was
still a graduate student in sociology. Of course, as soon as the Women's
Studies Program appeared, they were automatically on the first hit list
that was generated when a budget cut was rumored. My first involvement with the program was to be part of a committee to defend it, both
on the campus and downtown, and basically rattling whatever cages we
could to protect it from the budget cuts.

I have long been interested in women's issues. I taught in community
colleges from 1974 to 1985. I got a research appointment at UH in
1979, so I was back on campus in a quasi-faculty role from '79 on. So
in '85, when a position opened up in Women's Studies, I hopped over
and it worked wonderfully. When I came here the program had suffered
from an excess of success, and many of the faculty had moved into
administrative positions. The former director of the program is now the
interim vice president for Academic Affairs for the campus. A whole
bunch of us came in '85 and wanted to reshape what was essentially a
pretty strong program. We have tenure in the program, which is an
unusual state of affairs. That is a really important thing for women's
studies programs around the country. You have security in your work,

and this means the people judging your work are not hostile to feminism. There are all kinds of ways that universities can silence us if we are split between different departments. We sort of had a friend in the administration who is herself a feminist—Amy Agbayani—and she knew that programs like ours were always going to be vulnerable to budget cutting unless there was tenure in the program. When she got in the position to be able to do something, they made a bureaucratic change and now there are warm bodies in these positions, so they can't easily do away with you when times get hard.

The degree of activism of the faculty varies by faculty member. In the early days the program was quite an activist program. Then there was the fear that if you do that, you would somehow not be seen as academically respectable. Fortunately now, a number of us, for whatever reasons, are able to trot out vitae that are as "respectable" as the boys, but who also have a deep commitment to women's issues. We're basically the academic activists of the women's movement. We see our role as being the people who the women's movement can come to for information, for data, for policy, and for support. Kathy Ferguson, who's another member of the faculty here, has said it very eloquently: "We are a part of the women's movement." That's the way we think of ourselves in the program, so we do get involved locally.

Most recently I've gotten involved in the sexual harassment allegations involving Senator Daniel K. Inouye. [State] Representative Annelle Amaral—a wonderful person, a Native Hawaiian, a deep and committed friend of the women's movement, a great activist—had the courage to come forward and say that she believed Lenore Kwock and her allegations about the senator. The Women's Studies Program saw that she was taking a lot of punishment for taking that position. So I think we were the first women's organization in the state to issue a formal letter of support—we all signed it—to her and then distributed copies to all the members of the State Legislature. When the senator was going to be speaking at our commencement, it fell again to us to come out and say we were deeply troubled about the appearance of support that such a forum was going to give the senator, that the university was behind him in some kind of symbolic way by giving him this audience.

Dan Inouye was pretty much assured of reelection before these charges surfaced. And even though 60 percent of the state believed the allegations against him, they went ahead and reelected him, although by the lowest margin that he's ever had. I think there is a considerable undercurrent of discontent in the community. But he counts on the power of the Democratic machine in this state to be able to silence almost everybody. That's why it's so essential that people like us [with tenure] speak up, because almost everybody else is vulnerable. I've told the women in the Women's Studies Program that I am prepared instantaneously to resign as director when it becomes clear to me that my activism could jeopardize the program. And I think we have to look realistically at that possibility. I mean, I'll still be employed, but I know that he has a very long reach in this town, and there's every possibility that they'll come after us. But, you know, you can't live your life looking over your shoulder.

This gets back to a broader issue about courage versus cowardice. My view of the world has always been that the people sniff you out; and in this town they sniff you out early. Are you somebody that they can walk over, or are you somebody that's going to cause 'em trouble if they start pushing? I've taken what people have regarded as very risky stances. I think the worry is that, "God, if she does that with no prodding, what's she capable of if we really make her mad, if we go after her?" I actually think they're probably unwise, though, because if they went after me personally it would be harder for me to defend myself. But if they go after my friends or things that I believe in, it's easier for me. Like when they went after Annelle for saying what everybody believed and saying it in a community where it took incredible courage to say it, it just made me furious.

You know, in some ways this Inouye thing captures the kinds of challenges this community faces. We don't have a women's movement to speak of in this town. It's a very tight little town. It's a plantation community in a lot of ways. Even though the current oligarchy were the victims of the plantation system, the fact that they're now in control means that they have learned some very ugly lessons about blacklists, about how you can drive people out of town—just hope that they won't be able to find a job and will have to leave. In the old days, of course, the plantations could deport people, so it was a little easier. But they come as close to that as they can. A few of us escaped that by some sort of mix of career craziness. My good luck is that my work has a national audience, and so they can't totally control my voice. The standards they've developed to measure success for academics are standards that I've been able to meet.

I think these are basically the people who initially started out as labor radicals of the '50s and '40s, and who have benefited mightily by the development and by the control of, particularly, State government.

There has been this explosion of land value. The kinds of contracts that they have been able to give to their friends have created an oligarchy of people who initially had a quite progressive view of the world. After you've been in power for thirty or forty years, you're very, very powerful, and that's essentially been the story. Inouye has that kind of power. In some ways this is a challenge to the whole community, and it's not been met adequately. The silence of women leaders like Patsy Mink on this case has been appalling and discouraging. The man has so much power. The net result of it is silence, and then this surly demand that the women victims come forward.

How is women's abuse handled?

We've been working with a friend of mine, Nancy Kriedman, who's the executive director of the Domestic Violence Clearinghouse. Just this Wednesday I went to talk with her about the possibility of interns with the Women's Studies Program going out as crisis workers in cases of domestic violence. Victims of domestic violence basically have nobody now. The police respond to the calls, but nobody is there for the woman after the officers leave or if they make an arrest or whatever. The Police Department recognizes the need for there to be somebody who can be with the women to sort of say, "Okay, well now, do you know the way to the shelter? Do you want to get your clothes together? Do you want to stay here?"

My research area is women and crime, and I've worked with a lot of community groups to block the construction of a new women's prison, or to downsize it. They were going to build a huge one and we worked to make sure that didn't happen. They're building a much smaller facility so they're going to have to use alternatives to women's incarceration and get programs out in the community.

A friend and I published a little policy monograph for the National Council of Crime and Delinquency that went out to seventy thousand folks. It showed that there are model programs around the country that they could be using, like halfway houses for mothers with young children. Mothers can serve out a portion of their term while going to school or while working in the community.

I was trained as a sociologist. Just two years ago I stopped taking *The American Sociological Review*. I actually wrote them and said that I think sociology lost its heart and soul, and it probably lost it as a result of the politics of the Reagan-Bush years. When I was making my early "career" decisions, I saw people being driven out of departments and realized at that point that I did not want to get into a traditional academic career. Some women talk to me now and ask me to mentor them, and I have to warn them, especially young criminologists, "You must realize that I've had nothing like a traditional career." Early on I saw the purges going on in those departments around the country. I realized there was no way in hell, given my personal history and background, that I would ever be hired.

Criminology is making the same stupid mistakes that sociology did, becoming so esoteric and using models and statistical methodologies that are totally inappropriate. No policy maker could ever understand anything we were talking about. All the good sociology is being done by journalists. Look at that wonderful series in the *Philadelphia Inquirer,* "What Happened to America?" That was excellent sociology, and it was done by journalists.

There's no life left in our work. The people who were writing at the time when I first wanted to become a sociologist provided a way of understanding your world so that you could get control over it and do something to change it.

The other danger to sociology comes from the direction of postmodernists. I think that perspective was another coping strategy developed by intellectual radicals during the last ten years, when we weren't being listened to. I think they would just rather like to go to the back of the plane. If the plane is crashing, there are two places you want to be. You either want to be in the cockpit, knowing what you're going to run into, or you want to be in the back, having a little picnic basket and champagne. I think this is the picnic basket and champagne crowd, back there, deconstructing everybody, and themselves.

And I think the feminist movement is deeply challenged by this. I worry so much about Women's Studies getting into this. I have great differences with one of my close friends on precisely this point because she feels that it's not a threat to our political activism. If you start telling people that woman is a social construct and that we should not talk about women anymore—you know, I remember a time when we did that; there was a time in my intellectual life when we were never mentioned. This is very dangerous.

What's happening on pro-choice?

Oh, this community is very good. We were the first state in the country to pass what amounted to legal abortion in 1973. The religious and ethnic diversity is a great gift here. There isn't that stranglehold that

Christianity has on some other communities. Eternal vigilance, of course, is important and we're certainly very concerned whenever there's a person put in a key position in the legislative committee. You know, they're trying to erode things. Of course, the girls are always the first to lose their rights, so the "parental notification" is a constant threat here. But basically my reading is that we're okay on this because of the diversity in our community.

Is there a pro-life movement here?

The military and the Caucasian community—the two groups from which those things are drawn—are pretty marginal politically in the community. They're more or less ignored and the Legislature is not going to be drawn into these kinds of things. There's a healthy suspicion of Caucasians who come in and tell you they know everything.

If we go down the longer list of women's issues here in the Islands, we're doing well on abortion rights. We're doing pretty well on things like domestic violence, but it's a constant struggle. We're pretty well represented in the State Legislature. Up until this crisis with Senator Inouye, both the House and Senate women's caucuses in our Legislature were very effective champions of women's issues. There are a lot of women in our law school, which has been one of the breeding grounds of women legislators. When our law school opened in the early '70s, half of the students were women. The professions that are the pipeline for political life, like law, have been open to women fairly early on. Many of the women who are in the Legislature were around the edges of the first wave of feminism and are good women. But a grassroots feminist community is not much in evidence here. I think one reason the women's community has been kind of lackadaisical is that we have relied on those women for leadership and for good work, so we haven't needed a grassroots kind of activism.

These women legislators have been in long enough now to have seniority in both the House and Senate, and they were shrewd enough politicians to get themselves in line for key committees. In some cases there were enough of them so they were voting as a bloc. Tragically, the last two rounds of leadership fights in the last Legislature have fractured some of this, and we're trying to heal some of those wounds. The Inouye thing was a tremendous pressure on this group. I think that experience helped us discover that we got a little bit lazy as women leaders. We were counting on a group of people who were really quite vulnerable to someone like Dan Inouye. I think an honest thing to say is that they simply were incapable of taking the initiative on this issue. They simply were risking so much to do it that other people needed to step in. Then we discovered there was a real void. When you start looking around for the other people to step in, it's a very short list. So we've learned an important lesson in this whole experience.

What got you into the movement?

I got involved in college in civil rights work. I was then in Walla Walla, Washington. When I was finishing college I had gotten involved in the antiwar movement. You know, it was 1969 and what else could you do? I am immensely grateful for the time that I was born and the time that I was able to come of age. It forced my age-group to face these kinds of moral dilemmas. In our early twenties, both my husband and I were having to deal with his potentially going to prison, challenging authorities as *manini*, the Island word for kind of small [or stingy]. But our formative years were arguing with university bureaucrats over things like: Could we have crosses in the courtyard as a mock graveyard? and fighting all these devious ways they found to tell us we couldn't. Early in our lives, I think we learned some very powerful lessons about might making right.

The great blessing of the antiwar work was that it brought me together with other women who were activists and concerned about what was going on. While we were doing the kitchen work, we began talking, and eventually a women's movement began on the campus. My radical career as an activist is just sort of a sketch of any woman who is forty-six years old and is an activist in America.

The one personal difference might be that my father was abusive to me. I think my interest in young woman offenders—which is kind of a deviant thing, even for most feminists—was that I came from an abusive family. As soon as I started reading the stories of young women who were running away from home, I understood why they do that.

In the early days of the women's movement there was the understanding that many women were going to jail because of the war. There was a sisterhood with women who were in jails and detention centers. But that was lost once we started going for the Equal Rights Amendment. I'm constantly going to [the] women's community to try and talk to them about the issues of women offenders. I get a polite, "Oh-that's-very-interesting" kind of response. But never the real, "And so, now we have to do something." It takes an extraordinary woman to realize that there but for the grace of God went she.

242 MEDA CHESNEY-LINDMEDA CHESNEY-LIND

Some of the women whom I have talked to as adults in prison had been runaways. I discovered how you got into prostitution and all those kinds of things. It has enriched my life tremendously to have friends who had been in prison and to try and help where I could. I began to understand that often so much damage had been done to them that they were not going to make it, and that's really hard to watch. Women's health issues have extended to women on the streets—things like AIDS. There's a death threat associated with prostitution and drug use that there wasn't before. There are some very powerful things going on in this area that I wish I could pull the feminist movement into.

We have been more successful in the last few years because the number of women in prison in America more than tripled. People couldn't avoid the soaring number of women in prison, and we've been getting some attention on the part of policy makers. We've been going to policy makers and saying, "The number of women in prison has gone up threefold. Did you accept that in the 1980s?" Well, no they didn't. "Well, did you understand that almost all of that is a function of your war on drugs?" And you know, these are women doing mandatory sentences for trafficking. This is not Manuel Noriega; this is an economically marginal—usually minority—woman, who probably is a mother.

A friend and I wrote a book that we worked on forever, on girls and delinquency. It was written with all of these different audiences in mind. We didn't do anything the right way, but we got off really lucky. I insisted that it have a chapter on programs, and that we have a chapter in which we talk about our interviews with girls. This is back to the whole question about what we are doing and who we are talking to. I'm kicking myself that we didn't do the book more popularly so that there would be an even greater impact. But certainly, we want our colleagues and students to read this stuff. I want it to be a part of everybody's understanding that the experiences of girls matter. We have to rethink and constantly reanalyze the work we do. We've got to be able to talk to people with a language that makes sense to them.

I got involved in youth gang research because I was worried about the racist way the issue was being framed. I've been doing a lot of research work in the community, and I certainly ask about girls in gangs. I'm not sure gangs are criminogenic. Our research suggested, that, yeah, there are kids, and they are in gangs, but at least in Honolulu they don't differ significantly from their counterparts who are members of minority groups with arrest records who are not in gangs. So whatever the gang is, at least in this community, it's not necessarily more criminogenic than simply being poor, a minority, and occasionally in trouble with the law.

I've worked with the State Legislature looking at delinquency prevention and intervention in the neighborhoods. Now, all policy makers represent constituencies and neighborhoods. I had never really thought this through in a Machiavellian sense, but I now understand very clearly that if you start talking to legislators about neighborhoods that have problems, this is something they can relate to. And if you tell them, "Look, here are your schools in Hawai'i and I'm ranking them by how many troubles they have," everybody's interested in that. Over the last couple of years I've been trying to talk with the State Legislature about problems from a neighborhood perspective, and get them to think about doing neighborhood-based work, particularly in the most troubled neighborhoods. And they've been buying that because it's a way out of the pork-barrel mentality that they sometimes fall into by default.

The biggest challenges, I think, to the women's community will be the degree to which we can respond to the diversity that is characteristic of women in America and women in the world. One of the good things about living in Hawai'i is that Caucasians are a minority here. You're daily reminded of your status in the world here, because we're a microcosm of the world. When many Caucasians come here, they discover they're haole; they're outsiders. Your race is salient here. It's wonderful, but it is humbling and troubling for some people. Some people don't like it and they leave because they like to be where white is normal. It's still a colonial place in that sense.

Will we, as a nation, be able to advance women's issues after a very long and terrible period of backlash? I think we have our work cut out for us.

One of the best things about Women's Studies is that it's the most interesting place to be on campus. It's been a hotbed of wonderful ideas, and the students have been a tremendous gift to us. The campus is half female, and we get the brightest and the best. The boys are very nervous about this. There's an anarchist phrase: "We build a new society in the vacant lots of the old." Women's Studies, I think, really did do that. We took on topics and issues that they didn't care about. Initially they paid us no attention, and then I think what has happened now is that the young women are resonating to it. We're inured to a certain amount of discrimination in our lives. We were educated in basically a male-oriented universe and sort of stumbled on women's issues.

Feminism and academic feminism has thrived in part because they ignored us. They thought our work was so marginal and so unimportant that they left us alone. There's great freedom in that marginality. Looking at these young women coming up, I worry that as we get more acceptable that we might lose some of the honesty that humility forces on you. I hope this doesn't happen. Of course, given the current backlash, it's unlikely the young women coming up will lack challenges and opportunities to make a difference.

Lucy Witeck

A working mother of two who has been a serious activist; in her forties.

I work as an assistant supervisor at the Hawai'i Newspaper Agency that's owned by Gannett and the Persis Corporation. I am active in the local Newspaper Guild and presently its treasurer. I'm also on the board of the People's Fund, a nonprofit funding organization for social change projects. I'm a mother of two children: Matthew, 22, and Lia, 19.

Both my parents are nisei, the second generation of immigrants to Hawai'i. I am sansei—third generation. My father is what they call *nai-chi*—Japan Japanese—and my mother is Okinawan. The Japanese don't consider Okinawans to be pure Japanese, so they rarely intermarry with an Okinawan person. How my parents got together, I still don't know. My mother's father was a plantation worker. They lived out in 'Ewa at a plantation camp. My mother finished high school. She caught the train from 'Ewa to go to Farrington High School, right down the street from us now. I think she was in the first graduating class at Farrington. My father's family had a rice farm in Waipahu. They had water buffalo, and there was some kind of a spring that provided a source of constant water. They were considered real country bumpkins by the so-called city people. When my dad went to school, he would get into a lot of fights because they would treat him like he was stupid or slow. By trade, he is a master carpenter. A lot of it was self-taught or learned from some of the older artists. He had an eighth grade education. For him, education was very, very important. He constantly stressed to us, "You have to go to college. You have to go to college." He would stay up late at night with algebra and geometry books, and also taught himself how to read blueprints.

That sort of determination and stick-to-it-iveness was an influence for us. If something has to be done, you kind of see it through. He thought justice is justice, fair is fair, and right is right. You need to stand up for your own rights. We had a lot of controversy during the Bachman Hall (University of Hawai'i) sit-in. My parents really gave [my husband] John and me a hard time. My father was more reasonable about it. While he did not always agree with me, he could see that I was doing what he taught me to do, which was to stand up for what I believed was right. It didn't matter if what you were opposing was bigger than you or stronger than you, you need to stand up for yourself. I guess because I've always been smaller than the average person—I mean, I don't even hit five feet—you develop a kind of offensive defense. A lot of times people wouldn't push me into a fight as a child, because I was so bad tempered that they didn't want to mess with me. It's not that I was a good fighter—I would just get so enraged.

I grew up believing in the American dream. Anybody can be whatever they want to be. It doesn't matter if you're male or female, Asian or white, or whatever. Our family was sort of working poor, middle class. My mom worked as a seamstress in a sweatshop for minimum wage for many years, until illness caused her retirement. My dad retired with an eye injury. They've worked hard all their lives. It wasn't until I was out of high school and joined VISTA [Volunteers in Service to America] that I began to look at things any differently than what I'd read in the books all my life.

I was not ready to go to college, although I did go a year to the University of Hawai'i, did nothing, and got kicked out. To this day, I think it was a psychological way of saying, "Okay, Mom, I can't go to college because they kicked me out. Now I can do what I want to do." And that's when I applied to and was accepted by VISTA. I had the attitude that I should do something for my country that supported me, fed me, and gave me an education. For the Peace Corps you needed a college degree. And I said, "Well, I'd rather do something for our country first anyway." I mean, clean up your own backyard before you go somewhere else and say, "Hey, this is what's wrong with you. I'm going to help you." Many years earlier, I had read some Zane Grey book about some social worker going and doing good somewhere in the Smokies. So I had this vision of maybe going and helping somebody on an Indian reservation or elsewhere.

To my amazement, they accepted me. I went to Wolf County, Kentucky, for six weeks of training among poor whites in Appalachia. The week before I arrived, they had run out of the county the one and only Black family that lived there. I asked the Appalachian volunteers who were conducting the training program, "How come nobody told me that they ran—?" I mean, I look very different and my hair was down past my waist, and obviously I wasn't white and I wasn't Black. People were very nice to me. They'd always come up to me, "How ah ya, how ah ya," and I never could figure out if they were asking, "How are you?" or saying, "Hawai'i."

So I trained there, thinking my assignment would be among poor whites. Then they turned around and assigned me in a Black community in Glade Spring, Virginia, which is near Bristol. I spent a year there working primarily with youth. The schools had been integrated just in the school year before I got there. So the Black kids were going to the white school down in town and their three-room schoolhouse had been purchased by the community to be used for a community center. My job was to organize programs and stock a library and do projects with the kids. There I was, fresh out of training, from Hawai'i, never been away from home, in the middle of a lot of strange people.

Did you have associations with Blacks in Hawai'i?

I had a few friends in high school, but they were so assimilated into our groups that you don't think of people as being Black or whatever. There are so many different kinds of people here, you don't know what anybody is. We have a neighbor up the street who's Black Filipino; he looks Hawaiian. You just don't really think about it. You don't base your friendships on what people are—at least we didn't in high school—except we didn't like the military haoles because they really thought they were a lot better than us.

It slowly dawned on me at Glade Spring, around 1966, that there were no Black men there between the ages of eighteen and twenty-five. And it slowly began to dawn on me that that's because they were in the military. Bodies would come back because of the Vietnam War. They had no other opportunities. And it started to become clearer to me that you can't be whatever you want to be if you're Black, and in many cases, if you're a woman.

I used to write things to myself back then because there were so many contradictions. One of the things I wrote when I was 19 years old was, How can you pull yourself up by your bootstraps if you don't even have bootstraps? I'm not one who sits down and analyzes everything in a political sense. You just look at what's around you and ask, What's fair and what's not fair?

Getting back to my VISTA assignment, my supervisor was white. When we were refurbishing the schoolhouse, one of the things he said that really offended me was that they would build an outhouse for the community center because the Black people didn't need indoor plumbing. And I went, "What do you mean? When it's snowing out there, it's cold!" So we got into this huge fight, and the community got extremely offended by his attitude that they didn't need indoor plumbing.

A pure example of racism.

But I never said, "Oh, that's racist." You don't think about it. It's just not fair. I learned a lot of things that year. A lot of my own ideas changed. I mean, I looked back at Hawai'i and I said, you know, we're always taught that it was a melting pot and everybody is equal, et cetera. That's not true. I mean, you look at what goes on here and it's not all that rosy.

About four miles down the road from Glade Spring was Emory College. They would send volunteers to help with the community center. These were all white kids, and that was fine, and we got along okay. They were nice kids and they meant to do good. They weren't snotty or superior or anything like that. They were in the spirit of the '60s, really wanting to help. They would invite me to things. I went to one college dance with them and I felt so out of place. I thought, What am I doing here? I mean, they're nice people, but I don't really belong here.

So I got right back in the Black community: my social base, my entertainment, my community. One day I was sitting around and talking with some of the kids, and they asked, "How come you hang around us so much when you can go hang out with the white kids at Emory College?" Since I wasn't Black, since I had a choice to be with either the Blacks or the whites, they couldn't understand why I didn't choose the whites. It never was a conscious decision, it was just where I belonged. Those were the people I was comfortable with. When I told them, "Because I'm happier here," it amazed them that they were more interesting to me, or I was more comfortable with them, than the white kids. I think they felt that if anybody in their right minds had a choice, they would go with the whites.

I did some pretty dumb things while I was there. Once I had one of the white students and about four of the Black kids in my car and we went to a carnival in Abington, and it was cold. So after we got back in the car I said, "Let's stop for cocoa."

And they didn't say much, but at first they said, "Oh yeah, okay."

And then I said, "Oh, let's stop there!"

And they go, "Oh no, no! We're not that cold. We don't want any."

And I got all this negative stuff from the kids, but nobody would tell me that this was a restaurant where you didn't mix racially. But I didn't think anything. I parked the car, herded them all in, and the only table open was the one way down at the end. We sat down, and I turned to look for the waitress, and every single head in that restaurant was turned toward us. I couldn't figure out what was wrong. They made us wait, but they served us. Yeah, they did! The kids and the white student were too embarrassed to tell me that we're not supposed to do this. I think it was a major turning point for my life in terms of how I look at society and what I was to do about it.

I came back to Hawai'i to finish school and to learn a skill that would be helpful. I went into sociology, thinking I would go into social work. By the time I finished my degree in 1973, I came to feel that social work was more Band-Aid work, rather than empowering anybody to change their situation. So I just let the degree kind of dangle, nine years and two kids after I first started.

When I was finishing up school, I got involved in a women's group. One of our projects was prison work and visitations. I had a course on criminology, and it began to make some sense when we started to look at the prison population and who's there and what they're there for. Things again seemed a little skewed to me. I kind of looked at everything with a bit of a jaundiced eye.

I met my husband John in 1968 at the time of the Bachman Hall sit-in. Of course, the men were saying they were all going to go to jail and women just had to support them and stand by their man. We got pretty involved with the antiwar stuff. I would say primarily that's what changed my focus. There's a lot of things I probably wouldn't do if I wasn't married to him. He used to come home and tell me about this rally or that rally.

He was a real "troublemaker."

Oh, definitely. Should have seen my mom when I took him home. Oh, gosh! She went, "Oh!" And some of my relatives, when they met him, said, "You know, he doesn't have horns—the way you read about him in the paper, you'd expect horns and a tail." And they were also surprised at how nice he was. And he is, he's a very nice person. Not everybody believes that a person can be a radical and still be nice. I'm bothered by people who claim to be so political but sometimes are so ugly. They're not necessarily motivated by caring or by love, but some agenda that they have to get through, some guilt they have to work through, or whatever it is. I don't feel comfortable with people like that because they're so hateful. I can't remember the quote—it might have been Che Guevara—but it was that the true revolutionary is motivated by love, or something along those lines. You need to have that as the base, otherwise you become as ugly as what you're fighting.

Back in the '70s, they would have these study groups and they'd read Mao and this and that, and they'd discuss it, and I'd say, "I don't have time for that. If there's a demo, if you want me to make the sign, I'll do that. But I will not sit through hours and hours dissecting something that was written, no matter how good it might be for me. I don't have the patience for it."

Common sense tells me you don't treat people in ugly ways if what you're trying to do is change society. Everybody has good in them, even people that I think are doing awful, horrendous things. There is a basic humanity. A lot of activists forget that and just see the enemy in big letters. They lose sight of that humanity and the fact that a person can change. Some of the radicals used to say that they weren't going to have kids because this is such a shitty society to bring them into; you know, that whole mindset. And I said, "Well, if you're not doing it for the kids, who are you doing it for? And if you refuse to have kids, then you have no hope. And if you have no hope, what are you doing this for?"

John was involved in just about everything. Were you there with him?

For parts of it. Some of it I thought was too stupid to do. Well, what is it, the crazies that started out with this revolutionary organization that I came to? While I would work on certain things, like the newspaper, or I would hold signs and stuff, John was very much involved with them. I never did as much as he did, mainly because by that time we had two fairly small children and I felt they were much more important. I have the strong belief that if you have children, you have a responsibility to them. You cannot say, "Well, I must save the world. Sorry, I don't have time for you." The first five years are so critical. You have to be there. And besides, I'd rather take care of the kids than go save the world. I watched sort of secondhand what was going on and how people were behaving. One of my observations to John was they were self-righteous, we-know-all-the-answers, arrogant. If I wasn't right there with them, then there's something lacking in me, that I wasn't committed enough or political enough, or whatever the criteria was at that point. And I said, "Screw that, I don't need that kind of—." I mean, I had that in the cliques in high school. If somebody displeased them, they would snub them. I said, "You know, I got out of all the cliques in high school because of that kind of stupidity. Five to ten years later, I don't need this. When they grow up, maybe I'll listen more seriously to what they say, but to me, they're playing games."

Some of them would come out with some absolute, like—and I'm sure a lot of relationships are strained because of it—if one partner was more political than the other, then you should dump the other. I mean, forget about change or bringing them along, or whatever, they're so superior. I think there was a sufficient number of couples who received that kind of pressure. Some split up and others managed to stay together.

I think the thing about many left organizations is that there's good things and bad things. The bad thing is feeding on other people's insecurities and forcing them to kind of prove themselves politically all the time. I felt that a lot of people got involved with movement things oftentimes out of a need for an identity, and not necessarily that they really saw things that were wrong that they needed to help correct. I think that's why some people are so rabid when you have any criticism. You know, they take it so personally. It's their identity you're challenging.

You were serving a need to be a good mother. What about the role of women?

Well, we thought the usual stuff back in the resistance days. I started to say earlier about the little woman who had to stay at home and be supportive while the guys get marched off to jail. It was the guys who were in jeopardy. You know, women could only be supportive. But as that whole arena grew from antiwar stuff into community struggles in Kōkua Kalama, Kōkua Hawai'i, and those efforts, women began to demand a greater role. There were criticisms of the guys, saying the women are always taking care of the kids. The guys had to help with the child care. Another thing was the double standard stuff, where the guys could have affairs and fool around, but women were not supposed to.

John has always been someone who's right there behind me, pushing. He says, "You can do this, you can do that." And he says, "You're local, you're female, you can be a spokesperson." And there were people who would criticize him, saying, "Why don't you let Lucy do this, that, or the other?"

And John would say, "I try, I really do." Nobody would believe him.

And so I would tell them, "Lucy is doing what Lucy wants to do. Just because I'm female doesn't mean I have to take the leadership role." I mean, it's like the women's lib people saying, "Oh, you can't stay home and bake cookies. You can't take care of children. This is not fulfilling your destiny." Some of us want to do that. So why impinge upon my right to choose what I prefer to do? And they say, "No, you're just brainwashed into thinking that's what you want to do."

And I say, "No, that's really what I want to do. I don't want to be out there in the forefront."

Struggles for survival seem to be increasingly led by women.

I think when it comes to putting food on the table and a roof over your children's heads, women will get a lot more involved than if it's for something elsewhere. When it comes to basics, they will be a lot more outspoken, a lot more demanding, for what their kids need. There're a lot of women coming out and taking positions and taking leadership in struggles like that here. A lot of them are single-parent families. They're the ones living out on the beaches with the kids.

I'm very optimistic about people. I think people are basically good and I think they care about what goes on in the world, what happens to other people. When you have some degree of success in one area, you might be led to apply that energy into another area, anything that would make it better for our fellow human beings or animals on the earth. That's how we got involved with Kōkua Kalama. We started out as a student movement, and then right near the university was this farming area where people were getting kicked out. I would say that a lot of things are related. You learn so much from this activity, and then you look around and other things become a little clearer to you.

Could you speculate on the future?

Let me get my crystal ball. I know that there will be change. I mean, life is change. There is an ebb and flow of activism which is related directly to the conditions people have to fight with. I really would hesitate to predict what would happen. I would hope that it would be a new generation of people—the kids that we've raised—to look at real issues, and to take steps to better things.

Have the activists produced progressive children?

Yes and no. There were some parents, I felt, who laid their own trips on their kids. "You have to do this, you have to do that." I always felt that they should have a choice. I think their instincts and their feelings are good, but they're not necessarily political activists at this time. That doesn't mean they won't be in the future, when an issue comes up that they feel strongly enough about. And I feel like they have a right to make those choices. There are some kids of activists who are political and getting involved in women's issues, AIDS demos, things like that. When my kids were growing up, my requirements were that they be decent human beings, that they care about other people, and that they don't hurt others. It's never been a requirement that they be politically active unless they choose to.

**Hoʻoipo
DeCambra**

A recent program coordinator with the American Friends Service Committee; in her fifties.

I would identify myself as a Hawaiian feminist activist engaged in creating authentic Hawaiian community for my family, friends, and others. Until recently I was a program coordinator with the American Friends Service Committee. With the help of a lot of volunteers, I designed programs for women of color, indigenous women. We did workshops that are called "training for transformation."

I was born in Papakōlea, a Hawaiian homestead in urban Honolulu. And I was raised there until about age nine. We were surrounded by other Hawaiian families. My Hawaiian mother and neighbors were my significant role models. I remember strikingly that we used to pick all of our flowers. I remember that because of the scent of all the plumerias and how beautiful that was. We used to go and market the leis at the Aloha Tower. I was a small tyke then, and I was told to sell those leis to the tourists. I could never understand why we were selling flowers that were free, that were available for anyone who could go to the tree and pick them and string them. And so I had this early contradiction in my life. I gave away all the leis because I refused to sell something that was free. I just didn't know how to engage in that money economy; and then, going home and seeing mother practice subsistence and fishing, and living off of the ocean and the land. I grew up on the seashore. Life came to us through the 'āina and the sea. Mother fished and picked *limu,* and prepared that for her family. And she taught her children to do this also. And so there was this real contradiction in experiences. I could never understand it as a child. I don't think I quite understand it as an adult either.

In my adult years, I've chosen to be Hawaiian. I was raised to be Christian and American. I was raised to disown Hawaiian rituals, disown our Hawaiian gods. I was brought up in the Catholic Church and raised in a Catholic school. All their rules were imposed on me over my Hawaiianness. Even Mother resisted teaching us Hawaiian things. When I reached my thirties, I started reflecting on that because I had my own children. I was thinking, "What is going to be my role with my children? Am I not going to encourage Hawaiian ways?" There was this renaissance awakening in the larger society around me that was saying we have to choose and study the Hawaiian things. We have to go back to learn our language and all of the things that were not taught to me.

At the same time, there was this inner unrest of reflection. There were so many contradictions in what my mother had to do in order to survive. I've had to work through those so that I don't condemn her. She did the very best she could as a Hawaiian parent. She did what she had to do in order to survive in those times. The politics of those days were just horrendously Western and moving towards American thinking more and more.

Can you pinpoint a specific influence on you?

One person stands out for me—Anna McAnany, a Maryknoll sister—and the way she conducted her Bible studies; the liberation theology. She invited lots of people to our community where I now reside, in Wai'anae. We got to meet these different-thinking people who really respected people who were suffering. People who respected Blacks and minorities—and women. I got to meet all these wonderful people in small house meetings. That influenced me greatly to rethink my ideas about myself. I never thought highly of myself as a woman and I never thought anything about myself being Hawaiian. This was in the late '70s when my children were older. I was just becoming aware of the impact of policies and politics on our lives, on my children's school, on women, on the poor, on Hawaiians.

I ventured out in the arenas that were closest to me. With Sister Anna's help, I had the courage to start a women's support group. The women and I were asking questions like, "How come our men aren't working? Why is there this unemployment? Why can't we put enough food on the table? Why is rent so high?" Just all of these very down-to-earth, basic questions.

We also questioned the school curriculum. Our children were being asked to go window shopping in Waikīkī? They came home and said, "We have to have $60 so we can go on a field trip to Waikīkī and window-shop." Why were the schools promoting this? We don't even have money! Why do they encourage our kids to become consumers? I mean, it just raised all kinds of flags.

And we went, "What? Wait a minute, we're Hawaiian, we're in a Hawaiian community. We're not in Waikīkī!" And we started raising questions with the Department of Education as a group of concerned mothers. We wrote letters to the editor. We started to raise very political questions. Our children shouldn't have the kind of curriculum that dipped into the little finances we had. Schools should be helping us to design programs that would help our children become producers of products that we need, that are local, that are used to increase the quality of our lives instead of families on the [West] Coast. We started challenging the institutions and made a lot of ruckus.

Then there was this big strike in Hawaiʻi by the United Public Workers. None of the schools could run. Then the Department of Education had the nerve to open up schools in ʻĀina Haina and Kāhala, in the more affluent communities, and left Waiʻanae and Nānākuli schools closed in the poor communities. That just put up another red flag, and I said, "I will not stand for this discrimination. Why are they doing that? Why do they have school there and not here?" I thought there's a civil violation here of somebody's rights, and I'm going to challenge that. I remember picking up the phone and calling the civil rights office in region 9, and saying on the phone, "I want to file a complaint; something's terribly wrong. I want an investigation." And I remember the news media picking that up and wanting to get it out into the airways. The fact that I was willing to talk on public radio triggered the Department of Education quickly to retract what they were doing and close all the schools.

That was an education for you.

Yeah, but it scared the daylights out of me, because I was talking to very powerful people. I also felt like I was putting myself at risk.

I was part of the women's group at that time. Over the last decade they have been a sounding board where things are tested and tried. We can act on things with the support and thinking of the whole group, rather than just as an individual. The women were working class and many on State assistance. They were mixed: Hawaiians, Filipinos, Japanese, whites. They are and were women struggling. And that's why they could raise those questions about putting food on the table and paying their rent and how difficult that was. And why couldn't our men have jobs that paid well? Why was there this slump in the workforce? You'd work some time and then you wouldn't work.

With the help of experienced people, we formed cooperatives so that we could buy food in bulk. We joined forces and talked about it, and planned, and decided who was going to do what and issued out tasks, and shared all the jobs. A lot of local people found that really foreign. The haole people found it really natural, because they did it somewhere on the continent. The menu was real Western. They'd order vegetables, and cheese and flour, and all these kinds of stuff. We were used to rice and poi, so there was this contradiction in the menu. But the essence of what we were doing was right. The people of color were quiet participants who got haole food, but we learned that you could do a cooperative, and that was the value of it. Years later, when we did a diet program that showed the Hawaiian diet increased our healthiness, we said, "Well, we've got to buy taro and sweet potato in bulk."

The families were poor families, you know: some haole women married to Filipino men who worked at one job, and raising five kids; a lot of people living in rental housing, moving from place to place, sometimes dealing with menfolks who were violent. Some of our women and men were illiterate. How do you cope with the illiteracy in your community, in this day and age of high tech? How does the person shop who cannot read any labels in the store? Our wide range of concerns moved us women to go and explore new horizons and to go on to learn more and be exposed to more information. A lot of our women went on to school, and some even got Ph.D.'s.

I think the first awakening in my consciousness was that of being a woman. I was a mother, I was a wife. What did all that mean and what did that mean in the context of the larger Hawaiian society? I remember the stigma, as an adult woman, of being told that Hawaiians cannot write. I think that carried probably from childhood into my adult life. So when I realized that people assumed I couldn't write, I realized I had to do something about it. The women formed writing groups. I asked a poet writer to teach me to write. I thought that would help me build up my experience and confidence and I wouldn't have this thing hanging over that I didn't know how to write. It was in those writing groups where I saw my Hawaiian thinking coming through. My Hawaiian consciousness came out on paper, in short poems. I saw me in the writings, and I saw my mother, and I saw my hope for my children.

I saw other Hawaiian women in the writing group who were writing Hawaiian themes. A consciousness of what it meant to be Hawaiian was emerging in our writings. We realized we had to write and read more and then tell other people, so they could understand who we were as we were emerging in our own awareness about ourselves.

Can you summarize that awareness?

Well, I think one thing is that we're connected in the present time to the people who've come before us: our mothers, mothers before that, and that Hawaiian ancestry. We're connected to our *piko*—to our present-time children. And we're connected to the future—what our children will bring. That clarity of connectiveness to generations comes through. We weren't allowed to know this about ourselves. We were taught about the present time. Everything was compartmentalized, and everything was separate and individual. We weren't allowed to know that we did things differently, and that we even planned things differently. Geographically, we lived differently than other people. We had different concepts about the world. All of this wonderful knowledge is deep inside of us.

One story I like to tell is when my son was sixteen, he came to me in the living room and said, "Mom, I want to quit school."

And I thought, well, I'll be a tough parent: "You quit school, you have to go to work. That's all there is in life, boy."

And he said to me, "But Mom, I want to go fishing and diving for a year. I want to go to the mountains for a year." He said, "Mom, I've seen waterfalls and rainbows that you will never see. I want to do this."

I sat there in awe, thinking, this is a Hawaiian boy asking a Hawaiian mother for time to go to the mountains and the sea. And I thought, What am I going to do? I'm so confused. And then my husband and I lay in bed that night and said, "The boy is asking—he wants to go do this." And he saw his father hunt. He saw his father dive. And my husband said, "We gotta let the boy do it. We have to support him."

So we let him quit school and go to the sea and the mountains for a year, and we supported him in doing that. This child built up his confidence, he built up his manliness, he built up his ability to hike steep cliffs and carry 100-pound pigs down. He brought the pigs home, cleaned them, and we made *laulau.* He went diving, brought home the *he'e*—the squid—and the *limu,* and we made food for the family. He did what was the role of the Hawaiian man. And he developed his Hawaiian manliness.

I think that's the same way we Hawaiian women were feeling: we cannot do things Hawaiian any more. But that's not true. We *can* be Hawaiian women, and we can do the things Hawaiian. We have to name them and then have the courage to act and live it out. Yeah, live that Hawaiianness. If that means that our boys and our girls go to the sea and the mountains, then that's what it means. Then we have to create the industries, the activities, so that they can go to those places. This is our culture; this is our life. We thrive in those environments. We don't thrive in the environment where they stick our noses in a book and tell our kids, "This is what you have to learn." It has to have more life to it. Our Hawaiian children have done poorly in public schools. In many, many ways, the whole community is challenging that.

The job of every adult in my Hawaiian community is to provide hope and opportunity for our sons and daughters. That translates into programs and projects that we Hawaiians design, with our intellect, our resources, our ability, our knowledge. But we have to be smart enough to figure out how to do that.

I realized that my son was a Hawaiian child who learned from his peers. The school never let him learn from his peers. So I created an opportunity for him to learn working skills with his peers. I said to him, "Your year is up. I have this opportunity for you to go and study and be an apprentice in this laborers' school to learn about work and how to earn some cash." And I said, "And the best thing is you can do it with your friends. And I'll give you my car, I'll fill it up with gas. You can have it for the time of the apprenticeship program." So I removed all the barriers. He learned a skill in the laborer's apprenticeship program and went to work immediately after the eight weeks. Since that day, my son, who's now twenty-five, has been a working man providing for himself and his family.

In the last few years, I've "gone back home." I decided that my priorities in whatever life I have left should be focused on giving to my own people: my family, my community. I've reprioritized my efforts and I've decided that I'm going to work for Hawaiians. Now I can say I work for Hawaiians, and I work particularly for the improvement of the quality of life of women. We're coming back home. I think that's part of the process of the struggle for self-determination. We're looking within ourselves as individual women, and we're looking around outside of us at our resources.

This is our Hawaiʻi. We have not claimed it as publicly and vocally as we are doing in this decade. And I think that's going to change policy and political direction. It's already happening. Sometime ago I saw in the newspaper that Judge Kukulu—I can't even say his Hawaiian name—resigned being a judge in Hawaiʻi. He said he wants to go work for his people. I said, "Right on, you know, if you are truthfully coming from the deepest part of who you are as a Hawaiian man; hopefully that's what it is and you're not just going to be part of the establishment." I worried whether he was going home, as I am going home, as many of my Hawaiian friends are going home. I'd like to believe that about him. Going home means we're finding work for Hawaiian people, we're developing our Hawaiian communities, and we're going to find the resources to do it. That means pulling out the new vocabulary for ourselves and our Hawaiian-bound values. They're only surfacing as we dive deeper and deeper into this self-definition of who we are as Hawaiians: Hawaiian society, Hawaiian politics, Hawaiian government, Hawaiian community. I think we're being born new again. We have to find the resources and we have to convince the establishment that we need the resources to do this work.

We are dreamers. We are dreaming with our ancestral people and with those people not yet born that there will be this new society in Hawaiʻi which will encompass a lot of our wonderful Hawaiian values that have never been allowed to emerge as a new, wonderful civilization in the world. It's been suppressed, it's been aborted. It's an opportunity for everyone in Hawaiʻi to benefit.

As your movement becomes more and more successful, will it not threaten the powers that be?

Yes! Yes! Yes! How do I react to that? That's a hard one. I can react to my third-generation Japanese friend who says, "What's going to happen to me and my children, 'cause we were born here? This is all we know. We don't know Japan." I will say, "What a good question! We need to talk about this. You need to say what you think your role is here in Hawaiʻi, what purpose. You know, what do you want to see for yourself and your children. What is it you need?"

I have a harder time reacting to these corporate power people. But I think maybe we can say to the corporate world, "If your purpose and goals serve the needs of the people in Hawai'i, then maybe we have something in common that we can start discussing. Maybe you can benefit and so can the people who reside here." But I think if there's not a willingness to understand what each other needs in order to exist in this Hawaiian society, then I think there is only going to be a dominance from people who think they have a lot of power over people who don't have the power. If the powers that be are frightened and they don't understand who we are as Hawaiian people and what we're asking for, then they will only react, and that could be very dangerous. We've seen what's happened with Native American communities and groups that have risen to a level of group power, and how much violence and force that has been put upon them by the people in power.

You are one of the new leaders in the movement.

I'd be embarrassed, or maybe too afraid, to say yes. *(Laughs.)* You know, it takes a lot out of you to question injustice and try to find alternative solutions to that injustice. It takes everything you have, but then, you know, what is life all about? When I was around forty or forty-five, I realized I'm going to die, so what have you done in your life, you know? It's a motivating thing.

My very first protest as a Hawaiian woman was in the late '70s when I walked out of church one morning, and I said to myself, "I can't remain here. I have to go to the streets. I have to go where my people are." My people were protesting the bombing of Kaho'olawe. I jumped in my car and drove all the way down to Barbers Point. I picked up the biggest sign I could find. It said "Stop the Bombing of Kaho'olawe." I hid behind the sign because I did not want anyone to recognize me. You could only see my feet. I thought, "Oh, I'm doing something really great!" This car went by and they beeped their horn and they yelled out my name. I nearly died. I thought, "They're going to tell my mother-in-law, they're going to tell my husband, everybody will know I was here protesting. I will never be allowed out of the house again. I will be locked up for the rest of my married life!"—all of these false fears about engaging in activism and speaking your mind. For days I worried, and nothing ever came of it. Even though I did this act rather cowardly, it was a breakthrough for me. I wonder, where does the motivation to take those risks come from? I must have felt linked to other Hawaiians.

There've been other incidents where I've gone to protests; for example, the geothermal drilling into Pele. I just caught the plane and went out to the volcano and I joined in the protest. I was not going to go over the line. Yet when I stood on the other side of the fence and I saw all the armed police on the other side, I thought, How dare they? How dare they? So when other Hawaiians went over the fence, I went too. I was arrested in protest of the geothermal drilling of the volcano and of the sacrilege against Pele, our Hawaiian goddess. And you know, I was scared to death when I got over on the other side, and I was humiliated by the police and the way they handled us. But I scrambled to get over on the other side to say, "No! No! You cannot do this to us." Those are very important acts in our life, and they increase with intensity as we keep doing them.

Do you expect to do some protesting in the activities around the one hundredth anniversary of the overthrow?

Yes, and it will all be legal. *(Laughs.)* I am coordinating my women's group. We're going to do what we call a liturgy and we're going to lay down the American flag and the cross, the Siamese twins of power that have oppressed us. We're going to take the symbols of *kalo*—Hawaiian taro—the water of the *kai*—the salt seawater—and the fresh water, and the Hawaiian salt. We're going to place those symbols on an *ahu,* an altar that we erect at Iolani Palace made up of *pōhaku*—rocks—that we've all brought as Hawaiian leaders, from all the different islands.

This liturgy was created by Hawaiian women in 1985 for Church Women United. It has had a spirit and life of its own. It has affected the Christian community and the churches, in particular the United Church of Christ where the three white men are coming here to apologize to the Hawaiians on Sunday for their part in the overthrow. This Waiʻanae women's support group liturgy has caused so much controversy over the last half decade because it has challenged symbols of the American flag and the Christian cross that have made people so off-balanced.

Frances Viglielmo

An antiwar, antinuclear, pro-underdog activist in her sixties who still can be seen at the head of the march or demonstration carrying her protest signs, and sometimes she is there alone.

I think probably one of the most important things in getting me politicized was to have been born in 1931 at the beginning of the Great Depression. My father was born in Mississippi. My mother was Eleanor Grace Kelly Farrell McQueary. Although she was Roman Catholic, she married and divorced twice. Her first marriage in 1930 to my father was legit, according to the Roman Catholic Church. They were married in the Panama Canal Zone, where my mother was working for the dredging division of the Panama Canal Company. My father traveled Central America as an accountant for Singer Sewing Machine Company.

If I had been born in Panama under the laws then existing, I could have opted either for American or Panamanian citizenship when I reached twenty-one. My mother did not want to take a chance of my not being an American citizen, so she asked for a leave of absence and went back to her family home in Brooklyn, New York, where I was born. My father gave up his job in 1931 and followed her to New York. But a rift between my parents had opened up, so she went back to the Canal Zone and took up her job. I now recognize that my mother simply made the decision that she couldn't abort me, but she could abort her husband. In 1941 he divorced her for abandoning the home which he had provided, which was exactly what she did. But she got no child

263

support. My mother was the primary influence in my life: an extremely strong, very independent, very determined woman who was willing to risk being the black sheep of her family.

I was fortunate that she had three sisters. I was raised by women. Very seldom in the early years of my life was any man in the house with me. I think that accounts for some of my behavior today—namely, that I have no fear. Intellectually I know that I'm supposed to be afraid of men. In our culture many women have had painful early experiences of strong men dominating them. But I had this strong woman and her sisters. I became the pet, the adored one, because there were no other girls in that generation of family.

I was raised where my mother worked. We moved from one little company town to another, depending on where the headquarters of the dredging division shipped her. The U.S. government literally owned the Panama Canal Company. Our school, our hospitals, and every aspect of our life was directly funded by Congress and we were administered by a military governor. We had absolutely no experience of democracy as the average American would know it. I read an article in the November 1991 issue of the *Smithsonian* by a fellow Zonian—we called ourselves Zonians—named Carl Posey. He wrote about how he realizes now that we lived under socialism, which makes me laugh. I want to scream at him, "No, you dummy, it was fascism!" People often don't know that Nazi is short for German National Socialism, and National Socialism is fascism. Even the socialist republics of the former Soviet Union and east Europe did not have military governors; that's fascism.

We lived in an enclave of total care, if you behaved yourself. It was tremendously sexist. The United States instituted apartheid in the Canal Zone before the Afrikaaners of South Africa got around to it. I mean, you had to have identification, an internal passport, to get into the Canal Zone to attend your work. So my early childhood experience of American life is fascism. Oh, fascism with a friendly face, if your skin is white, but not if you were Black. The penetration of our minds was total.

There were always more Black West Indian laborers than white Americans. According to David McCullough, in *The Path Between the Seas*, the U.S. government looked around for cheap labor. The situation in the isthmus was so horrible that the emperor of China and the emperor of Japan, at the turn of the century, said, "No way, you can't have our people. It's not healthy." They made the discoveries about malaria and yellow fever.

We were surrounded by a sea of Black imported laborers, speaking a very colorful and delightful variation of English. In my early childhood, I had a Black woman caretaker—Iris—who had been in our extended family in the Canal Zone for forty years. She was our laundress back in the days when there was no air conditioning. When I was five, Iris said to my mother, "I can't handle her anymore. She called me a nigger and she won't obey me. Frances is not a baby any more, at five."

So my mother scrambled around madly and finally decided to place me in a Roman Catholic convent boarding school in Panama City during the work week. I learned Spanish at five. My feeling is when you learn another language that young, you have another eye, or another two eyes, on the world around you. I read all the graffiti on the wall as we would go through Panama City from the Canal Zone to where my convent boarding school was. I would read *Imperialismo, Yanquis afuera*. I didn't know the concepts, but I could read it: "Imperialism, Yankees out." So I was raised in the context of periodic uprisings in Panama City. Frequently there were coups by one branch of the ruling elite against the other: musical chairs, playing president.

I was raised with a lot of scorn and contempt by the Americans for the Panamanians. Their elections were corrupt and bogus. There was no real democracy. As a Roman Catholic, I was always part of a distinct minority to the Protestant majority. I could never participate in the activities of the Rainbow Girls, which is part of the Masons. However, like all the children in that very, very hot climate, I did join the Red, White, and Blue Troupe, a group of children organized by coach Henry Greezer. He capitalized on the fact that we always had swimming pools. He organized a swimming and diving group for exhibition and competition for the purpose of entertaining the troops. When I was ten through fourteen—the period of the Second World War—practically every other weekend I was at a U.S. military base swimming and diving in exhibitions for the servicemen. That's how I spent World War II.

Racism was rampant in the Canal Zone; they established apartheid. I catch myself now in racist thought patterns or even in actions. It's like trying to exorcise individual cells from your body. You have to keep struggling against racist thoughts and feelings. It's very, very hard, especially if you've been in the dominant group, and it pays off to be in the dominant group. I find many aspects of American life today very scary. I've lived under fascism and the Americans that I knew never made one peep until Jimmy Carter threatened to hand over their homeland to the Panamanians. Then you begin to get the protests. Americans in the

Canal Zone never voted. We never organized political parties. It was all forbidden and they didn't care.

I was raised in a religious minority group by a single working mother in a divorced family. That was very unusual in the 1930s. My mother was one of the few American women employees of the Canal for years. The Second World War changed things. They needed many more women workers because they had to keep the canal open twenty-four hours a day. Once in the summer of 1942, I found how the world can be turned upside down when my mother came to get me from school in Brooklyn. She had to have priority travel to return to the Canal Zone. When we got to LaGuardia Airport my mother was told, "You've been bumped. You can't get on."

And she said, "Oh, no you don't." She said, "I don't care if it's a four-star general."

So she went to whoever was handling protocol and said, "The canal will not work without me." And she proved it. She said, "I'm the chief stenographer to the chief of the dredging division. I know every man in that division. If you don't put me on that plane, that division will not work as well and you will not get your ships through the canal."

I don't know who she bumped, but we got on that plane. She knew the value of her work. Any time she had any aspect of the law on her side, and somebody was trying to cut her down, she would use that.

I went two years to the Canal Zone Junior College, which was funded by Congress. Where do you go next? I had applied to Swarthmore, Duke University, and Vassar, and was accepted by all three. I said to my mother, "I want to go to Swarthmore because Jenny Lee went there." Jenny was my school friend. Her father was a general, a West Point military officer.

And my mother said, "But it's a Quaker college."

I said, "Yeah, but General Lee let his daughter go there."

So I went to Swarthmore in 1951. It was awesome. The intelligence was so great. I heard Norman Thomas, who spoke at one of our "collections," where people gathered together and began with a silent meditation—typical Quaker rite. I was tremendously impressed by him, especially when he put his arms way out.

And he said, "Oh, you're laughing now, you're smiling now. You think I'm wonderful." He said, "But just you wait. Thirty years from now, you'll be out there in the business world and you'll spend all day and night worrying about cree-ping socialism." *(Laughter.)*

And, of course, my religion was challenged. I had to take Philosophy

100, because it wasn't offered at the Canal Zone Junior College. That was a tremendous task for me. I had to work nine times harder than anybody else. So the seed was planted in Swarthmore College to question the Roman Catholic Church. Swarthmore was very progressive. It had a lot of secular Jews from New York, so it was an intellectually stimulating place. They all had mononucleosis by the end; they were so worn out. Most of us were under unrelenting pressure. It was very threatening to your ego.

Then I went off to get a teaching degree. My roommates and I decided to sign up to do volunteer teaching at Framingham Women's Reformatory. We taught English composition at night for the prison inmates. That was an eye-opener, a very valuable experience. We learned more than we taught.

When I finished that year I tried to live again with my mother, but it was a disaster. By that time, I had a personality and I was virtually on the edge of leaving the Roman Catholic Church. I could not tell this woman who had raised me and had done everything for me that I could not live with her. So I literally clammed up with psychosomatic laryngitis, literally could not get the words out. The doctor hospitalized me so that he could talk to me, and he said, "Well, you know what you have to do."

And I said, "Yes I do."

You could talk to other people?

I could talk to anybody else. If she'd walk in the room, the muscles just shut right down. It was bizarre.

Val and I were married in 1959. We had to go off immediately because Val was due back to teach at his job at a Japanese women's college in Tokyo. In 1960, the antibases movement of the Japanese went into high gear and there were these nasty demonstrations. Eisenhower was supposed to come on an official visit, but Haggerty was roughed up at the airport, and the visit was canceled. Val wanted to see these demonstrations and I was terrified, as indeed I should have been. They were very heavy and, of course, one girl died. I was in a foreign country where I didn't understand the language or the issues. To a certain extent, I was like most Americans there who said, "What do you mean they don't want American bases here? We're protecting them," just as I would have said about Panama.

When we finally got here to Hawai'i in 1965, I went into deep suburban housewife and motherland. We moved into this house in 1967. My political activities—or my activities in defense of myself, my children, my family—were very close to home. Two doors down there was a Scientology theological seminary, and they were making themselves a nuisance in the neighborhood, particularly about parking, which was dangerous. If you have both sides of the street lined with cars, and little children run in and out, you've got a problem. So we organized a housewives' picket. I think that was the very first time I organized anything like that. And we got noticed in the paper on page three, the classic page for local news if it doesn't make the front page. The first real political organizing I did was in defense of the safety of the children on this street. That's classically me. It's going to have something to do with children.

Then I joined the PTA at Aina Haina School and at Niu Valley School. At about that same time I tried to get a teaching job where my hours would be somewhat similar to my children's. I started with the Hawai'i Department of Education [DOE]. Well, welcome to big party machine, political patronage. The DOE is a patronage plum for those who win the elections, mainly the Japanese Americans, which is the dominant group within the Democratic Party in Hawai'i. I taught as a substitute teacher in Punahou and later worked for the community colleges in their outreach to the bases.

Then I got it into my head to start running for office. I ran for the Board of Education three times in the O'ahu at-large race. By that time I had been writing protest letters to the editor about the patronage system in the Department of Education. Japanese American women are chosen to be the teachers and Japanese American men are chosen to be the educational officers and the principals and the researchers. I ran three times for the Board of Education. Then I ran for the neighborhood board here. I was defeated all four times. But in the meanwhile, I had come to be a figure that they recognized down at the Board of Education, and to this day, when I walk into that room, you know, "She's here."

Then the whole affirmative action thing came along. A group of us who had been complaining from different perspectives got together with Professor Michael Haas at the university here, who has done statistical studies of institutional racism in government in Hawai'i. We formed a group called FRESHA (Foundation for Race and Sex Equality, Survival of Hawaiian Aloha) and we filed with the federal government. Our only success was in encouraging the federal government to set up money for limited-English-speaking students.

In 1979 I participated in some organizing. It was pure home-and-hearth activism. Carter reinstituted draft registration subsequent to the Soviet invasion of Afghanistan. My son was eighteen and about to graduate from high school. A very broad political spectrum of people organized a committee for action against registration for the draft. We were at that stage of being pretty classic conscientious objectors, with religious or moral objections to war. There was no left analysis whatsoever at that point. But I was out on the street with people protesting another move towards war as we understood it. You discover that you're out there with socialists, some who flat-out called themselves communists, as well as the traditional Quakers and other elements. I also was exposed to the world of Roman Catholic and Protestant liberals, progressives, or radicals, and Sister Anna.

Having spent three years of very impressionable early childhood in the care of Roman Catholic sisters and also having been taught by them in the parochial school, my essential response to a nun is one of respect. Then when it's a nun in ordinary clothes and you discover that she's planning a march of protest to Camp Smith on Good Friday to protest there being a giant cross at a place capable of destroying 60 percent of the earth's surface—this is, you know, awesome. For me, all of the moral authority of the Church is on her side, certainly not on the side of the military chaplains. I'm of the generation that remembers that famous poster of the five or six chaplains in World War II who offered their places on the raft to soldiers, and they died. But you had only to read about or see what the atomic bombs can do, and you're on Sister Anna's side.

I had taken conscientious objector and civil disobedience training under the Quakers in connection with the draft registration. I began to do what is my classic style, which drives my husband crazy—the solo demonstration.

The bearing of witness?

It's definitely within that tradition—the tradition of [activist] Jim Albertini. Before Vatican II, I used to go to church on Sunday and read John the Baptist and, of course, the prophets. Very heavy stuff. I didn't know my Bible very well. Catholics in those days knew the catechism and the rules of the Church, but we didn't know the Bible nearly as well as many Protestants. But the example is there. So I started doing these solo demonstrations and then turning to the ACLU [American Civil Liberties Union] and saying, "They tell me I can't stand here. How come the government can register these youth and I can't protest?"

You would go out on the street with signs?

Yes. I stood one time at the post office inside the Ala Moana Shopping Center with a sign which said, "Register here against the draft, any age, all sexes." And I had a clipboard, and I just stood there. Well, of course, it was no time before the security guards came and started bothering me, telling me I had to leave. Meanwhile, some people had already registered against the draft. They asked, "Well, what is it really for?" And I said, "It's a contact sheet. When we have a demonstration, you may want to participate, and you'll be contacted. We've got to stop this thing. It's just the first step towards another Vietnam." And then these security guards are around me, and I said, "Well, what's your problem? Nobody was crowding around me. The crowd is here now because of you. Look, you want bad publicity for your shopping center? Just leave me alone and you're not going to have any trouble. Why don't you go away and leave me alone?" And they did. Then I called the ACLU and they said, "You were dead wrong, Frances—it's illegal." *(Laughter.)*

During the Vietnam War I had been out to lunch. I was busy raising my children. But in 1973 I became interested in one of the groups assisting the half-American children who were being left behind in Vietnam; children abandoned, lying in the street. I ran into some very fine human beings who I still keep in contact with.

My husband had joined the Hawai'i Union of Socialists, and a member recruited me; they were consciously seeking more women. I began attending meetings regularly and once their community service project—Modern Times Bookstore—was established, I threw myself into work behind the counter, fund-raising, and, of course, buying books and reading voluminously. What a glorious ten years of activism!

The bookstore became the hub of a tremendous ferment in the islands—particularly on O'ahu—of antiwar, antinuclear, antieviction struggles, and support of the beleagured ordinary people of Hawai'i. There were forums, fund-raisers, book autographing sessions. Even the quietest day of the bookstore—I was putting in between 8 and 15 hours a week—would be brightened by the delight and amazement on peoples' faces as they walked in. "My God, I had no idea there was such a place in the Islands!"

In those ten years, I certainly got the equivalent of an undergraduate education in political science—on the hoof, so to speak. But it was made more meaningful by the direct-action struggles in which we all participated: support for the Hansen's Disease patients ("lepers") under seige by the State Department of Health, draft registration protests, Chinatown eviction protests, and on and on.

The closing of the bookstore in August 1991 was a blow that none of us has recovered from. A precious community asset was lost, but the struggle goes on. Thank God we've got the photos of our many activities there. Best volunteer job I ever had. It was a tribute to Oliver Lee's extraordinary dedication and devotion to the cause of educating and supporting many struggles.

Did you go out solo because you couldn't get a group together?

I think it's always a question of tremendous rage and frustration. I know what it takes to organize a big demonstration. It isn't that I don't join others; I do. As far as support groups go, sure, there are the people who you know in the AFSC [American Friends Service Committee], the people you know among the Maryknollers, and the very active people in Catholic action, like Jim Albertini, Wally Inglis, Gigi Cocquio, and Sister Anna. These people were organizing open demonstrations against ultimate power. It's John the Baptist; it's all the prophets all over again. Christians Against Nuclear Arms (CANA) was a very inspirational group. I regarded them, and my husband, as my support group.

But I'm also very aware of the moral impact of a solo demonstration if the timing is right. The media might come for a solo, so I know that there's an attractiveness about that, and there's a moral witness aspect. But it's also a question of Mother Nature. You do not mess around with the mother of young, because the mother lion will take on a male lion. I'm not saying I'm intellectually conscious of it. Initially, it's just instinct. If I think I'm going to have to spend six months arguing with fellow demonstrators about time or place, then I'll do it alone.

Most of my arrests have occurred when I'm alone. The last one was December 6, 1991. I was trying so hard to be a good girl. Forty thousand veterans had come in for the big Pearl Harbor 50th anniversary. Val asked, "What are you going to do today?"

And I said, "Oh, I'm going to run this media release out to Pearl Harbor."

He said, "What! I don't want you going anywhere near Pearl Harbor."

I said, "Val, they set up a whole van which is exclusively for the media. It's just set up for us to go."

He said, "They'll arrest you if you get within smelling distance of Pearl Harbor."

I said, "Okay, I won't go to Pearl Harbor, I'll see if there's some other way to get this release to the media. The international media are here. We have to get the message out about the danger of plutonium emissions at Pearl Harbor."

He said, "Not Pearl Harbor, don't go anywhere near Pearl Harbor."

I had heard rumors that most of the media coming in to cover the occasion were going to be lodging at the Hilton Hawaiian Village, so I headed there and I parked. I started to wander on the grounds—tada!—I heard military music. I said, "Oh, you fool, of course! Everybody is in the Pearl Harbor Survivors' Association parade, down Kalākaua, in Waikīkī, which is not a military base. That's where I should be," so off I go. There will be a reviewing stand with important people—maybe even Bush will be on the reviewing stand.

I had my death mask and I had my tee shirt: "Make Hawai'i Nuclear-free." This was left over from the great struggle of Jim Albertini and Sister Anna and Christians Against Nuclear Arms. I had my sign which says, "Plutonium Peril at Pearl," and my leaflets. I had a black shawl over my head and a paper death mask on. Cheapo. I knew I had to hit 'em right away with something very recognizable.

As I approached on the *mauka* side—that's the side near the mountains—of Kalākaua Avenue, I saw the reviewing stand ahead on the military base side of the street. There's a rest and recreation base in Waikīkī called Fort DeRussy where they staged many parades. I saw a group of people I knew from Refuse and Resist, which was an antiwar organization, mainland venue. I think there were all women that day. They had a huge banner which said, "Stop the U.S. War Machine." So I approached them and they said, "Hi, Frances." The mask meant nothing to them; they knew who would do this. I said, "Do you folks mind if I stand in front of your banner?"

And they said, "No, go ahead."

So I wiggled through the onlookers in front of them—of course, they were already receiving a lot of hostility—and I got to the front of the crowd, not a big crowd. The parade was just starting. Some of the crowd turned to look at me. Of course, with the mask and the black shawl and the sign, "Make Hawai'i Nuclear Free," they started attacking me. They grabbed my rain jacket from around my neck and then tore away my sign from my hands. You know: "Get out of here! Go away! We don't want your kind," and all that kind of stuff.

At this point, two or three policemen noticed and they come barreling towards me, saying, "Get back, get out of the roadway!" They must have gotten to me just at the point where the back of my heels got to the curb. The next thing I know, I'm slammed down to the sidewalk very hard and there's a knee at my back, and I'm being handcuffed, and my hands put through excruciating pain. Then they picked me up by my wrists and I'm screaming in pain. Meanwhile, my friends in Refuse and Resist were saying, "Police brutality! Let her go! Are you crazy?" Fortunately, it was all on camera—two commercial stations and a Coast Guard photographer.

So they dragged me off to the police station. They lost one of my sandals along the way. Then I got in the car with them, and got, "Shut up, bitch!" I'm screaming, "Take me to the hospital! You've hurt me. Take me to the hospital."

We got to the police station, and as they started to book me, the sergeant in charge said, "And take that thing off her head."

So they yank the thing off my head, and all of a sudden this gasp of horror: "Jesus Christ, it's an old lady!" *(Laughter.)*

The shit just hit the fan. The headline in the paper the next day read, "Sixty-year-old antinuclear activist arrested." [There were] two counts against me: standing in the roadway and harassment. I am alleged to have hit a policeman. See, I was groping, trying to find my sign—who took my sign? So my hands were out like this when the policemen reached me. I had a terrible time.

Finally, I said, "I demand to be taken to the hospital right now." So they took me to the hospital. When I got there, I got this peculiar behavior on the part of the admitting nurse. I was exhausted by the ordeal at this point and feeling at the absolute bottom of energy. And so we start, "What's your name?"

I was giving information in a very low voice because I was exhausted. I thought at least I was on friendly or neutral territory. No. She kept screaming at me, "I can't hear you, raise your voice." Finally, on the tenth time, she said, "I'm going to report that you are not cooperative, that you are resisting and refusing treatment."

At that point, I got up like a shot and I walked to the center of the general area, where people were coming in and out, and I said, "I want a nurse who is going to treat me like a patient and not a criminal, and I want one right now." This was in self-defense. So another nurse goes over and puts her hand on the nurse and calms her down, and we go back in to try again. So eventually, I was seen by a doctor: contusions of the wrist from the handcuffs. I thought the doctor's examination was quite perfunctory. After I got dressed and came out, I said to the nurse, "Now I would like to use the bathroom, please."

And the policeman said, "Don't lock the door. I'll be right at the front."

I turned to the nurse and said, "I'm going into the bathroom and I'm going to lock the door, and would you please stand just outside the door?" Which is how it happened.

So then I came out and we were ready to go back to the police station. He said, "Now, if you promise to behave—"

I said, "What do you mean behave? Who do you think you're talking to?"

He said, "Okay, that's it." Handcuffs go back on. So I thought, well, I'm not out of neutral territory yet, so I raise my voice, "Where's my shoe? I left the house with two shoes this morning. Where's my other shoe? I have to walk outside now." And this is while a lot of people were looking.

All the way to the police station, I just wanted them to know that, boy, people are going to remember me. They're going to remember that there was a sixty-year-old woman here and she was complaining about police treatment back to the police station. It suddenly overwhelmed me—nobody talks about this in Hawai'i—that in that place, a woman I knew—Grace Kotani—had committed suicide, according to the police, after an interrogation in that building for the murder of her husband, who was also an activist. Suddenly it just overwhelmed me, and I dug in my heels as we got to the door, and I started screaming, "I don't want to go in there. I'm afraid of that place. Do you beat people in there? Grace Kotani died in there."

I was put way in the back in a cell. So I did what I usually do when I'm in prison and have to get control of myself. I start singing. I usually try to find a song which is going to bother the bejesus out of them. So I sang "We shall overcome." I kept singing it over and over. I drove everybody nuts, especially since those cells are echo chambers.

They'll never forget you.

No, they won't forget me.

The women here have put on three demonstrations against Inouye. A woman called a friend of mine and said, "Didn't I see you on television yesterday, protesting against Inouye?"

And my friend said, "Yeah, I was out there with Frances Viglielmo."

And the woman at the other end of the phone said, "Oh, she's crazy. My son's in the police and they all know she's a crazy." I tell them when they arrest me, "Boy, before you go through the business of booking me, you better look up my arrest record. You're going to see that I win every time in court."

What am I known for now? The Kwock-Inouye controversy. I'd already been out on the streets demonstrating with two other women at an Inouye rally. I decided there's got to be a voice inside the Democratic Party. Val asked, "Oh? What are you going to do?"

I said, "I'm going to hold a sign in the middle of their party, because I'm a Democrat, and I'm going to ask people to sign up to picket Inouye."

So I went and I sat down right in the middle of it, and the sign says on one side, "Inouye = abuse of power," and on the other side it said, "Inouye Resign!"

I had a clipboard. And I sat there for four hours, in the middle of their party. Towards the end, one woman came up to me, and said, "Frances, you've been a troublemaker for fifteen years—nobody is going to pay any attention to you. Nobody is going to sign up to picket Inouye, so go home. Who needs you?"

And I said, "Thank you so much. I know the day was worth it."

And, of course, one very irate party member behind me had the policeman come. I said, "You're going to call the police on me? Go ahead, make my day. I can hardly wait to see the newspapers."

So she went and she got the policeman. And the policeman came up and said, "Do you think that you could move over a little to the left?"

And I looked behind me and I said, "Why should I move? I'm sitting right in front of an aisle, an aisle between two sets of benches. So they can sit on the benches and they'll be able to see past my sign."

"Well, not from every angle."

I said, "Well, it's a very large park and they can move. I was here first."

And he said, "No, they want you to move." He said, "Just move over a little to the left."

And I said, "Any time anybody wants me to move just a little to the left, I'll be glad to." I see myself as sort of a Cassandra, the Greek woman who prophesied the forthcoming doom and destruction of Troy. I have a long-range pessimistic view of the chances for the democratic ideals of America actually coming to pass.

Susan
Hippensteele

University of Hawai'i advocate for victims of sexual assault, harassment, and discrimination; in her mid-thirties.

I entered graduate school at the University of Hawai'i at Mānoa (UHM) in 1986. Tailhook and the Clarence Thomas fiasco had not yet occurred and the UHM community had paid only scant attention to the problem of sexual harassment since implementing its first sexual harassment policy in 1983.

During my first year at UHM, my graduate advisor began "bothering" me. At the time, I had no name for what was going on. I was only able to detail the things he did and said that made me uncomfortable. I tried to speak with another faculty member I thought I could trust and was told that my "problems with my advisor were personal." Several older women graduate students began making remarks about my being "easy prey" and another "fresh, young thing" for my adviser's pleasure and I began to realize that people really did know what he had been doing to me. I began to get angry about my situation but also felt unable to do much to change it. That others were aware and considered the whole situation funny only compounded my frustration. After about a year of this, I made the decision to quit school, believing my only other option was to comply with my adviser's sexual overtures.

It was fortuitous that I had met a faculty member, new to the department, who knew a bit about sexual harassment. I mentioned to her that I was planning to leave graduate school and she immediately asked me if I was having problems with my adviser. I told her I was and described what the problems were. She labeled my experience as "sexual harassment." But like most college students at that time, I had some fairly strong stereotypes about sexual harassment, most of which were consistent with the image of a stranger rape. Sexual harassment by a trusted, respected, college professor simply did not fit my stereotype and I had a hard time accepting what was going on.

I'm not sure what was more traumatic for me at the time, the actual incidents of harassment or the challenge to my "ivory tower" ideals about academia. It took a while, but with the new faculty member's help and support, I eventually changed advisers and began making academic progress again, expecting to put the whole experience behind me.

A couple of months later though, I was told by another faculty member that my former adviser was taking a group of undergraduate students (mostly women) overseas as part of a university-affiliated program. Somehow, word had spread outside my department about my reasons for switching advisers, and I was asked to meet with a couple of UH administrators to tell them what had occurred. I was told the UH administration was planning to remove him from the overseas program, so I agreed to the meeting after receiving assurances that "telling my story" would be all they needed me to do.

The situation snowballed quickly. After the first meeting, I was asked to speak to another administrator, then another, and finally, I ended up in the EEO office with a complaint form in front of me. At no point did any administrator sit down with me and explain that in order for the University to take any action to prevent my adviser from taking students overseas, I would have to "complain" formally about the way I had been treated. I was utterly confused and quite angry. I felt as though I had been tricked. My first year while the harassment was occurring had been very difficult, and I had a tough time getting back on my feet academically afterwards, so the seemingly endless revisiting of the incidents themselves was painful. But it was the lack of information from the administration and what I experienced as disingenuousness on the part of several of them that finally became intolerable to me. It was a classic case of "revictimization by the process." After winning the formal University complaint against my former adviser, I filed a complaint with the federal Office for Civil Rights against the University itself for systematic procedural violations of students' rights under Title IX.

The Office for Civil Rights decision confirmed my allegations, and the University received a mandate to rewrite its policy and procedures to provide better access, information, and assistance to students alleging sexual harassment on campus. Former UH President Al Simone created a task force of students, faculty, staff, and administrators in 1990 to rewrite the University procedures, and over the course of a year or so, our group developed a document that was really quite exceptional in its scope and detail. Part of our proposal was for an advocacy office to assist and support students who were experiencing sexual harassment, and in 1992 the University created the advocate position that I currently hold.

I was on television and in the papers quite a bit during the late 1980s while my case against UH was unfolding, and the hostility directed at me in those days was incredible. On campus, many students I had known for years refused to speak to me, and faculty I depended on academically often completely ignored me. But at home, it was worse. I received violent threatening phone calls detailing how the caller intended to rape me and my baby daughter, or threatening to kill me every time I appeared on TV or was quoted in the papers. I must have changed my phone number three or four times—I always used an unlisted number, but people ended up getting hold of it anyway. Sexual harassment is still a volatile issue, but on the whole, we are much more aware of it as a social problem. I am still occasionally accused of promoting my "personal agenda" by advocating for victims and during preventive education seminars, but more and more people are accepting sexual harassment as a legitimate concern for the entire campus. To this day, I still jump when the phone rings at home.

A lot has changed here at UHM since my first years as a graduate student. I was shocked when I was offered the position of victim's advocate at UHM in 1992. I had applied knowing I was professionally qualified but certain that my student activism would have disqualified me for this or any other work at the University.

The transition from student to faculty member has not been easy. I hear between eighty and one hundred complaints a year and often wish I had available strategies I used to protest injustice as a student. It's easy to protest when you're telling your own story, but what do you do when the story is not yours to tell? I wish I could sit down with those who still want to believe that sexual harassment is not a serious problem on campus and tell them some of the stories I've heard these last few years. It's incredibly frustrating sometimes.

I guess I've replaced protest strategies I had as a student with some I've acquired as the victim's advocate. Soon after I was hired, I began conducting campus ethnoviolence research. It was immediately clear to me that significant numbers of UHM students were experiencing other forms of discrimination besides, or in addition to, sexual harassment on campus. Because there were so few studies examining the intersections between, for example, sexism and racism, I had a difficult time convincing administrators of the seriousness of these other problems using only anecdotal data. The early findings from the University of Hawaiʻi Harassment Research Project showed that the most common form of discrimination UHM students experienced is racism. These findings were surprising to a lot of people because the stereotype of UHM is that we are a "melting pot" kind of place and that racial and ethnic tension is non-existent here on campus because our community is so diverse.

Do you see a lot of "backlash" against students who speak out on the UHM campus?

There is a lot of fear, on the part of students *and* faculty, about protesting discriminatory treatment on campus. I think there are several reasons for this. First, most people are pretty realistic and recognize that academia has always frowned on those who don't "make the grade" in some way. Victims of discrimination are often viewed as deserving of their fate; they're not as smart, not as competent, etc., and are targeted for ill treatment because of these "inadequacies." Second, those opposing affirmative action and civil rights enforcement have become increasingly sophisticated in promoting the liberal form of white supremacy; "reverse discrimination," "freedom of speech," and "freedom of association" arguments, among others, are used with increasing success to silence and even persecute women and minorities who object to biased treatment on campus. Third, media images continue to glamorize violence against women, but at the same time, have begun to present sexualized images of women as strong and powerful—a new twist on the old myth that women must "fight back" in order to state a valid claim of assault. So when women are sexually victimized and unable to fight back or object effectively, they see themselves as deserving of blame. This is a really huge step backwards for us. This was pretty much the assumption in the sixties and seventies, but rape laws have evolved quite differently since then. Now media images are contributing to a new form of peer pressure that really undermines the progress victim's rights advocates have made during the past couple of decades. I'm beginning to see more and more of this among young women students on campus.

Are students aware that there is an advocacy office on campus?

I don't know what percentage of students, staff, and faculty know about my office. I would guess a large percentage do not. Even so, I get more complaints on an annual basis than I can effectively handle. From the beginning I've received eighty to one hundred complaints per year. From 1992 through the beginning of 1995, I worked exclusively with students, but beginning in March 1995, my job was expanded to provide similar assistance to staff and faculty alleging sexual harassment and related discrimination, as well.

You are a one-person office, and from the outside it almost looks as though the creation of your position was a token gesture. At the same time, I would guess that most campuses don't provide this kind of assistance at all.

That's correct. There are various ways that victim support services are provided on many campuses—through women's centers, student services programs, etc.—but I know of no other campus that provides the type of formal *complainant* advocacy that we do. I have been contacted by several colleagues recently who are interested in using the model we have created, or a variation of it, on their own campuses.

It's heartening to note that, as we track the rise in political conservatism around the country, we can also observe a very strong response from informal victim advocates on campuses where problems of discrimination are becoming more visible. Many informal advocates do their work surreptitiously and do not necessarily want attention drawn to their efforts for fear of backlash, or loss of whatever structure has enabled them to act informally in the past. Right now though, folks are beginning to recognize that we are absolutely going to lose what we have gained if we don't put up a fight, so many advocates are upping the ante, so to speak, and pushing for increased resource allocation to affirmative action and civil rights enforcement efforts as a way of strengthening their positions.

Tell me something about your earlier life. Who were your role models?

I have early memories of my mother's involvement in the anti-war and civil rights movements of the sixties. She was very active with Women's International League for Peace and Freedom, and I remember being hauled up and down Telegraph Avenue in Berkeley in a red wagon with my brother and sister, to and from demonstrations at People's Park. I sat in that wagon looking up at animated faces engaged in arguments and protest and can still feel the strength of their convictions and the visceral response I had to their anger.

When I was nine or ten my mom gave me her dog-eared copies of the speeches and autobiography of Malcolm X to read. I remember to myself that my mom must have read and reread his words to help her stay clear about what she was fighting for. I still have those books and use them the same way myself.

My father is a "hard science type" college professor, a neurophysiologist teaching currently in the midwest. My dad taught me to stick up for myself and demanded that I never make a statement I can't support with facts. He was engaged in some battle or another with colleagues about academic standards or institutional policies, but it is his passion regarding the importance of maintaining professional ethics in academia that I remember most clearly. Sometimes I can get really depressed working with victims of campus ethnoviolence. But I am very grounded in what I call my "academic ideal." I have my dad to thank for this. I think of him every day.

Given how pervasive sexual harassment is on campus and the relatively few people you are able to assist through your office, do you think the work you do makes a difference?

Whew. Tough question. I used to believe that the individual cases themselves would provide the impetus for dramatic institutional change on campus, but in reality very few cases have that kind of impact. For every step forward it seems we take a step back. Yet the opening of this office has offered the first opportunity we've had at UHM to create institutional memory relating to sexual harassment on campus. We now have documentation, written records. In the long run, this documentation will help generate the changes we have to make in order to move toward preventing sexual violence and harassment on campus. Each time a student, staff, or faculty member comes forward with a report or grievance, they make history. Progress is slow, but I can feel it is happening.

Even when I'm feeling the most discouraged, I *know* what I do here is important. I get calls every semester from students I've had in class or assisted through the office who want me to know the impact my being here had for them. I've gotten calls from young women who have just been accepted to law school or graduate school who said the mere existence of my position on campus was the inspiration they needed to make that choice. I also get calls from women who tell me that if I had not been here to help them deal with a sexual assault or harassment on campus, they would not have been able to stay in school.

Yes, I think my work does make a difference.

6

ORGANIZED LABOR

The subject of this chapter bears upon the ability of all our fellow humans to earn a decent living and enjoy a decent quality of life. This simple-appearing matter is not so easily resolved in the real world of capital and labor, of jobs and income. "Earning a living" is a subject that can only be approached in a political-economy context, and so we shall try to do that. In this period of declining labor clout, some observers are writing organized labor's epilogue. Fewer and fewer people are unionized and existing unions are more and more powerless as capital pursues a relentless course to break the labor movement. The world is going through rapid changes in technology and political economy that are dramatically altering the work, well-being, and relationships of working people, and the pace of change seems to be increasing.

In 1990, Hawai'i's labor force numbered a little over 600,000, which was over 70 percent of persons aged sixteen-plus. About 28 percent, or 166,000 workers, belonged to unions. The median household income in Hawai'i approached $39,000 in that year. The 1994 poverty level for a four-person household in Hawai'i was over $17,000 per year. These percentages—unionization rate, median income, poverty level—are about the highest among the fifty U.S. states. There must be something unique about the political economy of Hawai'i.

Most of today's "industrialized" countries moved through four major economic periods—hunting and gathering (subsistence), agriculture, manufacturing, and service—over a very long time span. Hawai'i was a bit different from other places in its historical time frame and labor-management experience. Once the plantation system took hold in the mid-nineteenth century, Hawai'i's *next* economic phases were relatively time compressed. The agricultural period (principally sugar and pineapple) and the manufacturing period (principally fruit canning and mineral extraction) came and went in a span of about a hundred years. Unlike many other societies, Hawai'i missed the slave and sharecropping systems. So, there were time compressions and historical avoidances that contributed to the shape of things today.

The plantation system in the early days was labor-intensive, absorbing a large number of Kanaka Maoli displaced from their traditional subsistence means of livelihood. In 1872, some 85 percent of the plantation workforce was Kanaka Maoli. But the Hawaiian population had been decimated by imported diseases and the loss of their land through manipulations of the haole oligarchy. Thus, there were too few local workers for the expanding and profitable sugar and pineapple industries. The corporations made up the labor deficit by importing wave upon wave of agricultural workers from China, Japan, Korea, the Philippines, and other countries. That produced an Island society whose workers were mixed ethnically and whose capitalists invested simultaneously in agriculture, manufacturing, and service—a very interesting coming together of labor and capital.

The left-leaning International Longshoremen's and Warehousemen's Union (ILWU), taking advantage of the high profits that capital was generating in Hawai'i in the post–World War II period, organized *both* agricultural and manufacturing workers. There was a substantial improvement in the workers' standard of living, and a number of today's entrepreneurs and professionals are descended from plantation workers. When the ILWU later organized hotel workers, an unusual feat was accomplished in the annals of labor history. In effect, workers from three separate economic periods, running nearly concurrently in Hawai'i, were being organized. Traditional ethnic rivalries, craft jealousies, or different worldviews were modified or overcome by a broader solidarity. This was the organizing model of the Congress of Industrial Organizations for all hourly positions at a work site. Concurrently, unions like the Hotel Employees and Restaurant Employees Local 5, the American Federation of State, County, and Municipal Employees, and the United Public Workers also began successful organizing drives. Since Hawai'i was rapidly becoming a provider of services instead of a producer of commodities, most of the targets for organizing were service workers who directly or indirectly served the tourist industry.

The scene is modern Hawai'i, but it could be "Any-Urban-Place, USA." Hawai'i's exaggerated case is repeated in hundreds of U.S. urban areas in the ongoing tug-of-war for the direct dollars of tourists along with the exchange activity that spins off in local economic infrastructures. The official Hawai'i statistics for 1993 show that 6,124,000 visitors accounted for $1.2 billion in tax revenues and were in some way responsible for the existence of 251,000 jobs.

The tourist industry is one dramatic illustration of the profound shifts in markets, technology, jobs, wages, and the organization of work that have come together recently into what some sociologists call the "service society." Eighty percent of all new jobs today are in the service sector, the majority being paid on average just a bit above minimum wage. The service society has emerged in tandem with a potent right-wing political movement. A major objective of the right wing is to curtail the power of organized labor and remove many of the gains won for working people by an earlier labor movement.

The prime motivation for the new-right formation was an ominous, to-the-mat economic factor that began poking out its head in the late 1950s: The rate of corporate profit was falling. This was a very dangerous problem for owners. The movers and shakers came up with a solution in several parts. First, the costs of labor would be dramatically reduced by computerizing, robotizing, automating, streamlining, and *downsizing* all work systems. Next, organized labor would be eliminated as a power contender. Next, more of the national product would be directed toward capital and less toward the working class. Finally, government could be captured to facilitate the above. An intense propaganda war was initiated by pre-Ronald Reagan advance men (with a facsimile in every "developed" nation) to "unite" the American (or British, Japanese, Australian) people around a common goal: Make national (U.S.) capital more "productive" in this day of intense international competition.

The big organizing drives of ILWU and other unions ended as massive changes took place in the local, national, and world economies. Among the changes affecting Hawai'i was a gradual abandonment of plantation production in favor of union-free, labor-cheap places like Thailand and the Philippines. This did not mean that official joblessness soared—when the U.S. unemployment rate is 6 percent, the rate for Hawai'i is 3 percent. The immigrant and indigenous labor force simply was absorbed into the rapidly growing tourist industry. Simultaneously, a number of displaced workers left for the American continent where the jobs would not be better, but the cost of living would be lower. Workers who remained were impressed into jobs like waiter, entertainer, bellperson, driver, maid, secretary, and salesperson; and most jobs paid low wages. Others served the needs of the expanding affluent class of locals as well as retirees from distant places. Hawai'i became a mature service society, with a social structure composed of a small class of rich, a large class of poor, and a "middle" class moving downward.

The term *service society* is a euphemism for a political economy in which the owning class puts its ever-advancing technology to work streamlining and "downsizing" nearly everything. Increasing numbers of workers are squeezed out of often well-paying agricultural and manufacturing jobs as production systems become automated. Likewise, workers in labor-intensive service jobs are squeezed out when service systems are automated and downsized, producing fewer salesclerks and bus drivers. For example, in the year 1956 there were some 256,000 telephone operators in the United States; today, only 60,000. Meanwhile, the remaining employees are forced to work harder and longer for lower wages and benefits, and are functionally unable to provide the necessary services that we all need in a complex world.

The service society is led by an owner/ruler class with members who have no compunction against shifting capital to low-wage areas anywhere in the world. The very class that dictates the prevailing standards of patriotism for its nation, for its workers, has continually shifted its loyalties to *only* those flags that represent profits. Capital needed for local investment in infrastructure, education, urban renewal, and health care flies all over the globe. This class orchestrates a complex symphony of cost cutters, legal beagles, financiers, publicists, politicians, and systems analysts to "rationalize" and privatize the production of goods and services. The music being played in Honolulu, San Francisco, and New York is sweet to the ears of stockholders and corporate managers.

The attack on organized labor has been brutal. Capital-labor battles were waged in private negotiations, the courts, the legislatures, and everywhere. Capital made good use of the communist hysteria that it generated and sustained in the Cold War era as it made deals with an increasingly compliant labor leadership. In exchange for labor "peace," ridding unions of left-wingers, and freely automating the work systems, capital would share some of its profits with the now-decreasing ranks of labor. It is estimated that 20,000 workers were fired each year for union organizing. Then there were the deals between capital and politicians to keep in check or decrease the growth and power of organized labor: Smith Act, Taft-Hartley Act, Landrum-Griffin Act. Federal labor-management oversight changed from a mildly pro-labor stance to a staunchly antilabor focus, and the administrative apparatus that protected workers rights was put into a dismantling mode.

To say that the attack on labor was successful would be an understatement. Percent unionization of the workforce hit its peak of about 35 percent in the early 1950s. It was down to 25 percent by 1980. Today, it is about 18 percent for labor as a whole and less than 12 percent in the private sector. Statisticians estimate that if present trends continue, organized labor will go down to between 5 and 2 percent by 2005—just ten years from now. In 1970, in places employing more than 1,000 workers, there were nearly 400 officially recorded work stoppages involving about 2,500,000 workers; by 1990, stoppages had decreased to 40 involving only 118,000 workers. Roughly thirteen times fewer workers went on strike in 1990 than in 1970. To show further the decline of organized labor, collective bargaining settlements in large workplaces resulted in workers getting nearly 12 percent wage improvements in 1975, dropping to less than 3 percent by 1990. Of course, *these* workers had jobs.

The result of this one-sided process has been a sharp alteration in income flow and the general quality of life of working people. In the last twenty years, the buying power of U.S. workers has fallen by 25 percent. Contradictorily, productivity rose over 30 percent between 1982 and 1991. Squeeze and automate! Over 25 million workers are jobless today or on involuntary short time. In a labor force of some 110,000,000, this comes close to a 25 percent under-employment rate—a return to depression days for the working class.

But there's another side to the story. Hawai'i's labor experience emerged out of a unique set of historical and cultural conditions in the evolution of modern capitalism. The astute and progressive ILWU, setting the course in an earlier period, helped shape a political consciousness on the part of the working class. Join that with the aloha factor in social relations, and one better understands why Hawai'i produced the highest rate of unionization in the United States, approaching 40 percent at its peak. Even in 1988, Hawai'i's unionization rate was 42 percent in manufacturing, admittedly with a small base, while the rate for the United States as a whole was only 25 percent. There are labor unions and employee associations with a membership exceeding 165,000. Unionism is ensconced: the base is there. Perhaps creative organizing techniques will emerge from these experienced union people.

Surely creative leaders will ponder deeply on ways to organize that great mass of unorganized workers that has arisen. Will they look again at the CIO model, which earlier threw an organizing net over an entire factory or industry, to find what might be applicable today? Perhaps the net could envelop the *entire* Ala Moana Shopping Center and all the nonmanagement employees therein. What a set of skills and trades that would bring together! What a rich mix of the world's peoples! Creative leaders may discover ways to resolve inter-union competition as they think more about a movement of workers and less about narrow trade unionism. Perhaps they may investigate the formation of a labor party, such as the Labor Party of the United States, founded June 6, 1996, at a convention in Cleveland, Ohio. Some people think a return to labor militancy will come when workers finally say "enough" to an unacceptable decline in their quality of life and "enough" to prospects of a bleak future. Perhaps a mild but potentially significant beginning is seen in the recent merger agreement by the United Auto Workers, the International Association of Machinists, and the United Steelworkers.

Some labor spokespersons challenge their members to build coalitions with community groups and movements that seek redress of grievances in housing, environment, and other issues addressed by many in this book. Tracy Takano of the Hotel Employees and Restaurant Employees Local 5 illustrates this in part 3, "Human Rights and Free Speech." Such leaders see the need to fashion political and organizing strategies that respond to deteriorating conditions among *all* working people. The sovereignty movement may be a natural force with which labor can coalesce, because of the difficulties Kanaka Maoli people face in making a living. Issues of common interest should not be too hard to find if a principled search for them is made.

Edward D. Beechert summed it up: "In a capitalist political economy, the workers do not dictate the terms of struggle. The only point about which we can be certain is that the class struggle will continue. There is no guarantee of short term victory. . . . Out of this situation can come a new level of struggle and working class unity" ("The Political Economy of Hawai'i and Working Class Consciousness," in *Social Process in Hawai'i: A Reader,* Peter Manicas, ed. [New York: McGraw-Hill, 1993] 163). We suspect that some old-fashioned class-consciousness may emerge as the jobs of workers disappear and their standard of living deteriorates.

There can be no return to shovel-and-hoe labor intensity to put people to work. Technology cannot be reversed, but it can be used to dramatically improve the condition of life of all working people, meaning nearly all people. Many analysts say that the only solution is a rationally designed national plan with *people* priorities, such as a shorter work week with decent wages and benefits. One can call such a socioeconomic arrangement anything one wants. The point is, something new must be forged. Even a Kanaka Maoli-led independent Hawai'i would need a national plan to set socioeconomic goals and manage the flow of materials and labor.

The five speakers that follow are veterans of the Hawaiian labor scene who have been toughened and made wise by many struggles. They may not agree with every word above, but they would unite around the need for a tough rethinking of today's role of organized labor. Previously an active member of the Hawai'i State Teachers Association, Bill Puette provides a perceptive overview of the current challenges to organized labor and calls for an enormous legal-structural overhaul of labor relations. Author of several books on labor struggles, including *The Hilo Massacre*, Puette serves as director of the Center for Labor Education and Research at UH.

We also present two retired ILWU veterans. Ah Quon McElrath fought for workers' rights to health and welfare in the early "radical" days of the ILWU. Today she remains a leading figure in the fight for welfare reform on the State level, often testifying and often quoted in the daily newspaper. Tommy Trask, a nuts-and-bolts leader, shepherded the ILWU as it headed full speed into the service society.

Liana Petranek, who worked at politicizing the Association of Flight Attendants and was active in national anticoncessions struggles, eventually became president of her union local. Concurrent with her doctoral work at UH, she has been a leader in many progressive community movements involving housing, tenants' rights, and Kanaka Maoli rights. John Witeck of the United Public Workers rode the tides of most social movements in the last three decades and knows the importance of labor-community coalitions.

Bill Puette

A labor education specialist and director of the University of Hawai'i Center for Labor Education and Research (CLEAR); age forty-something.

What is CLEAR?

In response to the expressed need and desire for specialized education and training by workers and leaders of the labor movement to improve their professional competence, the State Legislature in 1976 established CLEAR—the acronym for the Center for Labor Education and Research—as part of the University of Hawai'i's College of Continuing Education and Community Service, as the statute says, "to improve their ability to intervene wisely in shaping their environment on the job, in their unions, and in the community." In fact, there are about fifty CLEAR centers throughout the country. Most of them, like the one here at the UH, offer labor studies classes in a wide variety of subject areas to the members and officers of labor unions. About half of the nation's labor studies programs also have credit classes open to the undergraduates at the university as well, but at present the UH program is only a noncredit outreach service to the labor community. Ironically, though Hawai'i has the largest percentage of its workforce unionized, we don't have a labor studies degree program here. Our job is to give union members and their representatives the opportunity to learn what they need to do their jobs legally and effectively.

Often in this day and age, unions are up against labor relations professionals who are trained at the university and may have degrees in business, human resource management, or industrial relations. Generally the union representatives are just rank-and-file unionists, and they must deal with these professionally trained specialists, or even sometimes labor attorneys. I mean, they're almost always outgunned. It's not fair to them or the workers they must represent. CLEAR centers offer programs to give these people a chance to know what their rights are, to be able to understand the laws, how to file grievances, how to represent somebody in an arbitration case, how to file a workers' compensation claim. That's our core curriculum and I think it's real important.

What's your background?

I was born in Cleveland, Ohio, and grew up in that area. Two of my brothers are sort of corporate mentalities. One of them does audiovisual programs for all different types of companies. Every now and then we have major arguments when I go back and visit, since his attitudes are very different from mine. I know he has even done some "union avoidance" videotapes. Our father was an electrical engineer with Clark Controller. I had a very neutral upbringing with respect to most liberal causes. My father is a dyed-in-the-wool Republican, while my mother was an Irish Democrat. When I was growing up, every presidential election saw an in-house battle between my mother's Democratic leanings and my father's Republican sentiments. I was not particularly moved one way or the other.

I came to Hawai'i in 1969 when I was hired as an English teacher in the public schools at Maui High School. I was hot out of college and hired by a recruiting team. There was a teacher shortage back then, so they used to actively go out and recruit on the mainland. I was interviewed in Pennsylvania, and it was the nicest job interview I ever had. He just rolled out a map of Hawai'i and asked, "Where would you like to teach?" I ended up teaching on Maui.

A delegation from the Maui Education Association met me at the airport. The Legislature had just passed the collective bargaining law for public employees, including the school teachers. Before long the teachers were knee-deep in a classic rivalry between the Hawaii Federation of Teachers (affiliated with the American Federation of Teachers) and the Hawaii State Teachers Association (affiliated with the National Education Association). I signed up with the Maui Education Association, the NEA affiliate in my school, mostly because of those three teachers who met me at the airport and helped me get settled. As it turned out, though, there were only three other NEA people in that school, and two of them were about to retire. All the rest were American Federation of Teachers people. I guess I've always been a stubborn guy. I honestly didn't see much of a difference between the two organizations at that time, and I had given my word to the folks who helped me.

I agreed to be the NEA representative because nobody else wanted to be it. Within two months of arriving in Hawai'i, I found myself at the founding convention of the Hawaii State Teachers Association in Honolulu. I vaguely recall it as a blur, you know: sit down, stand up, time to vote, finding out what the right vote is. But it was really just a call to dissolve all of these little island education associations and set up a statewide union to bargain for the state's schoolteachers. The old Hawaii Education Association was little more than a mutual benefit association concerned with professional standards and status, and only occasionally involved in political action. In the old days, your principal used to evaluate you and expect you to belong to the education association, and the principals belonged as well as teachers. About all it could offer was a chance to meet and talk with teachers outside your own school and group rates on insurance policies, but there was no collective bargaining done by the association whatsoever. So in that founding convention we dissolved all the old associations, ejected the principals, and began to prepare for the new age of collective bargaining. Spirits were high and everyone wanted to win representation for the public school teachers and start bargaining in earnest with the Department of Education.

The representation election, however, was so close that they had to have a rerun. The rerun was even more bitter than the original. In my naivety, I thought [that] after the election everybody would put their differences aside, but that was not the case. It was horrible. Of all the collective bargaining units, only the teachers have had three or four representation elections in their history. The worst possible thing for a union is a representation election with another union. I hated it: good union members fighting each other. It was no better than the early days when there were different unions on the plantations for the different races. It was the worst and most self-destructive use of resources I've ever seen.

Right after the second election we sat down and negotiated with the department. The first public union in Hawai'i to go on strike was the teachers. In my first two years of teaching, I participated in two repre-

sentation elections and a strike. I ended up being the picket captain at
Maui High School during the first teachers' strike. I really think that's
where everything changed in my life. You get on a picket line, and you
aren't the same again. When you go out on strike, you don't know if it's
going to be a short or long strike. Every day you're out there, for all you
know, you could be out for two years with no income. No one goes on
strike readily or happily, and it drives me crazy when the press portrays
unions as strike-happy. Anyway, it was a defining experience for me.

The Hawai'i Public Employment Relations Act was a law that was
mandated by the constitutional convention that first required Hawai'i
to grant collective bargaining rights to all State and county workers.
The interesting thing about the Hawai'i law, compared to all other bargaining laws, is that it statutorily defined thirteen bargaining units. Virtually every other bargaining law in the United States, private or public
sector, permits the employees to define the bargaining unit at the time
the petition is submitted. A union has to petition the whole statutory
unit, whatever it is, and all the workers in the bargaining unit select
only one union to represent them. All of the thirteen bargaining units
became represented by labor unions from pretty much the very beginning. So, for instance, all the secretaries in all State and county offices in
Hawai'i belong to a single bargaining unit.

Another thing that's very unusual about Hawai'i is that it's one of the
only states with a single statewide Department of Education and statewide teacher contract. All of the schools in Hawai'i are controlled by
one Department of Education. It's paid for through State excise and
general taxes, not by property taxes at the local level. I've always
believed that this system is the best system. I did student teaching in
Pennsylvania and Ohio and I saw how horrible it was. Ghetto schools
are created by the structure of public school education in this country,
which is largely reliant upon the property taxes of different counties.
When the state has control, you avoid most of that and things can be
done a lot more equally, across the board. People in Hawai'i complain
that schools in poorer districts don't get as much money as schools in
richer districts. But what they are seeing here is nothing compared to
what happens in most of the mainland. It's a great idea for teachers too,
because there's a statewide agreement. Teachers can transfer statewide.
If you move from this island to another island, you can theoretically
transfer your position, keep your service record, your pension, and your
position on the salary scale. It's really a terrific idea. The salary scale is
uniform, so at least as far as salary is concerned there is no disincentive

to teaching in schools in poor neighborhoods. Personally, I've always felt that there should be wage incentives offered to teachers teaching in depressed neighborhoods. On most of the mainland, it goes the other way around.

What is it about Hawai'i that permitted this statewide approach?

It has a lot to do with the history. Neighbor island representatives in the Legislature from the beginning were sensitive to the potential for inequity that a county-funded system would have created. Lawrence Fuch's book *Hawai'i Pono* has a whole section on how the school system developed during the plantation era. When schools finally developed, it just didn't make any sense to do it on a locality based system. The territorial-appointed governors had a lot more control, and—for whatever reason—they built a system with a lot of centralized control. The net effect was that this universal system in Hawai'i is much superior. Hawai'i has always labored under the apprehension that its school system is inferior. When I was teaching on Maui, the students felt, well, they have pidgin English here so you can't expect the same. I can remember the principal telling me not to expect mainland standards from these up-country Maui kids. Well, I just sort of developed standards that seemed appropriate at the time and I didn't think anything of it.

After a few years on Maui, I went back to the mainland for one year to get my master's degree at Edinboro State University in Pennsylvania. The university serves a large community with an economy mostly agricultural and industrial. As part of my fellowship, I had to teach four or five sections of freshman English, and I soon realized that my students at Maui High School were in many cases superior to the freshman college students from this basically middle-class area in Pennsylvania. So to me, it completely burst the myth that Hawai'i has an inferior school system. I also have a very strong belief that smaller schools are superior to larger schools under any circumstance. The idea that the Island educational system is inferior is still very prominent. I had two students in my senior English class at Maui High School who went to Ivy League colleges and graduated cum laude. They were good students, there's no doubt about it, but it wasn't like they were geniuses that stood above everybody else; they were just good students.

I worry that school community-based management—the latest craze in Hawai'i's educational anxiety—may end up being a Pandora's box. Giving each locality too much control of what's going on in the school could backfire. I don't want to see the evil of "ghetto schools" controlled, patronized, or abandoned by local communities as moods and budgets swing this way and that.

I can see some good for a local group to try to influence or work with the local school principal and so forth. But one of the latent issues hiding behind this whole thing is that there are always some people who want to control what the teachers are teaching. Curriculum should not be set by local political, religious, or cultural biases. In 1973 I went to Japan, and it was very interesting to me to see a primary and secondary educational system which was intensely regulated by the federal government. It is ironic that so much admiration is paid to the Japanese educational system at the same time and by the same people who would move our educational system even further away from the kind of centralization that Japanese schools are renowned for.

I went to Japan because I was always interested in Asian studies and was hoping to get a degree in it. A small school in Kyoto—Notre Dame Women's College—hired me to teach English. I got to meet some people. I was also writing poetry and got active in the literary community there. It was a transitional period for me.

After a couple of years there I was ready to come back, and in 1975 I was offered a full-time job teaching at Honolulu Community College. As I was on the plane, Governor Ariyoshi announced a hiring freeze on all State departments. When I went to the college to sign my contract they said, "Well, if you look at the thing we sent you and you signed, it says pending funding. The governor has cut funding for all new positions, so we're sorry but your position has been cut."

I had to work as a lecturer. A lecturer, as opposed to a regular faculty position, is paid by the course. They don't process your pay until after the course has actually met and they're convinced that it's going to go, and that no regular faculty has lost their course. You don't get a paycheck until after you're teaching for a month and a half to two months, as a general rule, a blatant violation of the State's payment of wages statute. I suspect these are the kinds of injustices that turn a lot of people into labor activists.

I did everything that I could do to get the next full-time position. I was quiet as a mouse. I tried to be as good and loyal as I could be. When a position finally opened up, they hired somebody else even though I was the first pick of the department—no reason given. So that was a very bad experience for me. I had the equivalent of a nervous breakdown, I think. I was experiencing all kinds of nausea and stress-related symptoms. I didn't have any medical insurance. It was a nightmare.

Finally, I was offered a job with the Hawaii State Teachers Association as a business representative for the teachers of central Oʻahu. One of the things that I think made me a good union representative is that I had incredible sympathy for anybody who was suffering. I worked with a lot of teachers who were going through the same kind of stress that I had experienced. I got better just by being employed. All of my symptoms went away. I was mostly doing grievances and workers' compensation cases.

The only thing you can strike over is contract bargaining. Everything else has to be handled on a different route. And the strike procedures laid out by the public worker law are very complex and give the State a huge amount of power to make the strike illegal at almost any turn. You cannot strike over bad faith bargaining or unfair labor practices like private sector workers can, and there are many things which are excluded from the scope of bargaining. Many of the things excluded from bargaining by our public workers are, in fact, mandatory subjects in the private sector.

Bargaining for a statewide unit is definitely a good thing for the teachers. It's interesting that some State and county workers don't like that largeness of their bargaining unit. A small group with a special interest tends to feel that their own union negotiators don't give their interests a high enough priority, and they long to be cut loose to negotiate on their own, but I don't think that's a very good idea. It may feel good when you're at the table bargaining, but if you have to go out on strike, the smaller your unit is, the easier it is for you to be run over and forgotten. When I went out with the teachers in the '70s, I took a lot of comfort from the fact the teachers from Kauaʻi to Hilo were out there with me.

How do you get solidarity with such a large geographic and occupational mix?

How do you build solidarity out of anything? I think the airline pilots have the same problem; they're all over the place. The biggest problem with teacher solidarity was that for a long time there were teachers, particularly in the high schools, who felt that there should be a separate bargaining unit for secondary and for elementary. Generally a higher percentage of men were in secondary education and a higher percentage of women were teaching in the elementary schools. Back before the strike, I remember listening to some of those men teaching in the high schools grumbling about being in the same unit with the K through

8 [kindergarten through eighth grade] teachers. "The wahines won't strike," they would say. "They'll hold us back and screw everything up." The thing that always got me was that when push came to shove, when there was a strike, guess who was the strongest? The women! They were out virtually 99 percent. Everyone was out pretty solid, but where we did have problems, it was more often in the secondary schools, with the men.

When we first started, the teachers tended to think of themselves as different from other unionists; there was a certain elitism. For a lot of teachers, it was hard to think of themselves as unionists at first. Many of them at that time were the first generation in their families to get a college education and achieve a status that, at least subconsciously, they felt put them above other workers. But the amazing thing is the growth of the teacher since. There is no question in virtually all of the teachers' minds that they are represented by a union, and a union that has a lot in common with the other labor unions. It was a process of growth for them to internalize that, and it just took some time to figure out that they could still be a professional while being a unionist and sharing some sense of concern with other workers. When you're on strike and another union decides it's going to support you by not crossing your line, that's a lesson. But then after the strike when you realize that these same people supported you—now you drive by, you honk your horn, you put the old shaka sign out to them and let them know you're with them. And maybe you'll stop by and drop off some canned goods or something at the picket line; take that extra step. When UPW (United Public Workers) went on strike after the teachers went on strike, the teachers had a canned goods drive for them and were very sympathetic generally. The solidarity was suddenly something that was real.

Doesn't Hawai'i's labor orientation go back to the ILWU?

There have been AFL [American Federation of Labor] unions in Hawai'i for a long period of time, but the ILWU has been absolutely the major one for years and years. They started with longshore, as their name betokens, and then they expanded into sugar and pineapple. So they had the major workforce and the major piece of the economy. Now we, like the rest of the country, have been evolving away from an industrial into a service economy. For us, that means away from industrial agriculture into hotel and tourism. As far as sheer numbers go, ILWU's only rival in Hawai'i is AFSCME [American Federation of State, County, and Municipal Employees], because AFSCME has HGEA [Hawaii Gov-

ernment Employees Association] and UPW [United Public Workers].
AFSCME also has been very active in building associate memberships,
which is a good idea. An associate member is somebody who the union
does not represent for collective bargaining, but who can join the union
for special service programs like credit card discounts. HGEA would be
the largest union in the state if you count associate members. But if you
define unionization only in terms of the people who are represented by
and covered under collective bargaining agreements, then I expect the
ILWU would still be the largest representative.

The percentage of the labor force that's organized in Hawai'i is the
highest of any state in the United States today—close to 30 percent.
And why? Besides the fact that they have a CIO past, the ILWU was the
most active union in the state politically. Back in the days when the AFL
still held a philosophy of voluntarism by which you stay out of politics
and just do the best you can in collective bargaining, the ILWU held a
totally opposite point of view. Their feeling was, do what you can, get
involved with it, get waist deep in it by any and all means. They were
very much responsible for getting Burns in as governor and for the
Democratic Party revolution in the state in 1954, a landmark year in
Hawai'i's politics. Prior to 1954, Hawai'i was Republican country; after
1954 it became Democratic country. It's an absolute lights-are-out,
lights-are-on phenomenon. People ask why the Democrats and labor
have such a strong hold. I think the answer is universal: the greater the
repression that has been suffered by labor and by people generally, the
stronger and more committed they become.

If you look at what labor went through in its early organizing, it was
horrible. The history of the labor movement in Hawai'i was incredibly
racist. They had racial wage differentials: the Japanese wage rate, the
Filipino wage rate, the Portuguese wage rate. And when there were
plantation strikes, they were played off against each other. Do you
remember the stories of *Uncle Tom's Cabin* and the horrible overseer?
The reputation of the overseers here in Hawai'i is no better. They were
called *luna,* and they were mostly brutal and widely despised. There are
pictures of them sitting on their horse with whips; they were mean. A
lot of those early plantation strikes were caused because of the horrible
treatment by the *luna,* who were either Caucasian or Hawaiian, or
sometimes Portuguese, while the people in the fields were Filipino and
Japanese. The treatment they suffered was just horrible. We owe it to
the children of Hawai'i to describe how bad it was, and not paint over
that past record with nostalgia and half-remembered truths. Hawaii's

unions were forged in repression and decades of often violent struggles brutally suppressed.

The other thing that was really bad was that virtually the entire state was owned by five major companies which were haole owned and dominated. The Big Five, as they were called, even had their own school to send their children to so they wouldn't be contaminated by local contact. When the unions tried to organize, you talk about blacklisting—hell, if you're blacklisted in New Jersey, you can get on the interstate and hitch a ride two or three states away and they don't know you anymore. But when you were blacklisted in Hawai'i, they know you and there was hardly any place you could go to escape retaliation. Leaving Hawai'i was not really an option. It's not like they share a culture with the rest of the United States—the culture of Hawai'i is home to most of the people who live here.

The longshoremen were the first to be able to successfully organize for a lot of different reasons. Certainly the Wagner Act [National Labor Relations Act of 1935] was very important. The longshoremen were in a unique position to be able to take advantage of the new federal legislation, but they were also in a unique position to be able to bring the different nationalities together. That was their real accomplishment. They got recognition before anybody else because of their interracial solidarity. And once the longshoremen had the dockworkers organized, they began trying to get other union groups to organize. It wasn't long after World War II before the sugar workers and pineapple workers were unionized.

The big turnaround for the longshoremen came in 1938. The crews and mechanics who worked for Inter-Island Steamship Company, the forerunner of Aloha and Hawaiian Airlines, were trying to organize their own union. This was a Honolulu-based organizing effort. Most people don't realize that union organization began on Kaua'i, Hilo, and Maui, then moved from the edges in.

I wrote a book called *The Hilo Massacre,* which tells one of the most inspiring stories in the history of Hawai'i's labor movement. In 1938, 300 unionists in Hilo decided they were going to demonstrate against the Inter-Island Steamship Company's use of scab crews to break the Honolulu workers' strike. In a selfless gesture of solidarity, longshoremen, laundry workers, members of a ladies' auxiliary, and several other Hilo unions joined in a peaceful demonstration against the arrival of the SS *Waialeale.* A lot of the scabs, sad to say, were University of Hawai'i students off for the summer.

The Hilo Chamber of Commerce learned of the unionists' plans and put pressure on the local police chief to clamp down on the demonstration at the port of Hilo. He brought in police from all over the island; virtually every police officer on the island was in Hilo at the harbor that day. And the union went in nonviolent—used passive resistance. If you read the documents from the 1930s, you see how they fully expected the police would hit them with the billies. They were all instructed to go limp, and practice passive resistance: Don't fight back. Go ahead, be arrested; we'll all get arrested and jam up the jails. But they didn't get arrested, they didn't get hit with billies—they got shot. The police opened fire on these people with shotguns, and fifty people were shot. It's a miracle that nobody died. One guy was in the hospital for over a year.

I interviewed some of those guys, and I asked, "What would have happened if the boat was going to come back the next week?" And they said, "We'd have done it again. We'd have been there next day, the next week, whenever we had to." They were ready and they were willing to risk life and limb for their union brothers and sisters in Honolulu. I have nothing but respect for these people.

I usually use this as an example when I'm teaching steward training. I say, "What if you were in a situation where the police had just said it's illegal to come here, although your attorney has advised you that it is legal to be there. Now, you have to take unpaid leave from your own job because you're not on strike yourself. There's a possibility you could get shot, but it's more likely they'll be attacking you with tear gas and billy clubs. We want you to show up. How many of your coworkers do you think would show up?"

And they all shake their heads and realize that the solidarity just isn't there like it was in Hilo in 1938. In Hilo, virtually everybody who was in a union at that time showed up.

During World War II, there were wage and price controls. All the union contracts were pretty much frozen and most of the unions accepted it. There was hardly any negotiating going on throughout the country. The idea was, hey, we're going to win the war, we'll get back to collective bargaining after the war. We have a film that was produced by the Department of Labor of the bicentennial that we still use in our history program: *If You Don't Come in on Sunday, Don't Come in on Monday*. The film shows that after the war, so-called big labor exercised its muscle and there were a lot of strikes. "The balance of power," according to the film, "had tipped too much in favor of labor unions," and so the Taft-Hartley Act was passed. That's the biggest lie I've ever heard in my whole life. The labor unions took no-strike pledges and most agreed to wage freezes throughout the war. Collective bargaining, which was just getting going before the war, was put on hold. By 1946 most unions had just started up bargaining again, so sure, there was a larger number of strikes than there would have been otherwise. I really think that was used as an opportunity to change the Wagner Act.

Unionization in the United States never got much higher than 25 percent of the workforce. The last high point was in the early 1970s. Now it's down to just 16 percent nationally. If you take out the public sector, to make it comparable to what we're talking about in the '30s, it would be less than 12 percent. And that's worse than what it was before the passage of the Wagner Act in 1935. That is a really bad situation.

Where's it going now?

What's happening in the country is pretty much happening in Hawai'i too. We've moved to a service economy. Hawai'i has been doing that as we've moved from sugar and pineapple to tourism. The plantation owners began to realize that they could get more return on the land if they had a hotel there than if they had a field of sugar. The ILWU had the good sense to realize that when things were shifting they had to act, so they negotiated and worked arrangements out so that the plantation workers would have first crack at the hotel jobs. That's why ILWU now has a lot of hotel workers and has rivalry problems with Local 5 of the Hotel and Restaurant Employees. But ILWU just made a natural move following the economy's change into tourism.

If the union movement is going to be successful, it can't resist the change in the economy. If we're changing from an industrial to a service economy, it has to be dealt with. You have to organize service workers. To some extent, organizing service workers is made more difficult because of post-Taft-Hartley labor law. Some people I much admire—like Richard Trumka, president of the United Mine Workers—believe that labor is suffering from bad labor law more than from any other factor. Trumka, a major figure, is one of the first labor leaders in the history of the U.S. labor movement with a law degree. He led the mine workers in the Pittston strike, the first use of nonviolence in a mine workers major conflict in the history of the country. He successfully pulled that off. And I believe he's right on target with his understanding of what's going on in the labor movement. The Supreme Court and the federal courts have added to the infamy of Taft-Hartley in decision after decision. In 1947 they argued that Taft-Hartley was necessary because the balance between labor and management was tipped towards labor. Ever since, labor has been sliding to the bottom of this chute. Nobody talks about tipping it back.

I almost became nauseous during the last go-around with the striker replacement bill when Bush's argument for vetoing it was that it would tip—he used the 1947 verbiage—the scales too much in favor of labor. How can anyone say that? The labor movement is being beaten to death, and he had the absolute gall, in the face of overwhelming statistics to the contrary, to pretend that the balance might be tipped in our direction. He's not even on this earth.

We need drastic change in labor law. I'm very much an advocate of labor law reform, but the problem is when Republicans talk about labor law reform, they're usually talking about making it worse and not better. A union should be able to organize all of the retail clerks—at a shopping center, for instance—into a single bargaining unit. Likewise, a union should be able to organize an entire fast-food franchise chain from the top, instead of having to organize the franchise holders one at a time. Divide and conquer is the oldest rule used to break unions, and American labor law seems designed to foster as many divisions and subdivisions as possible. It would take massive changes in the National Labor Relations Act. Why shouldn't a union be able to organize—say, McDonald's—on a national level? When somebody buys a franchise for McDonald's, they already have to agree that they're going to have the arches and make the hamburgers in a certain way, and participate in contests. What's so wrong about including in the franchise agreement wages and conditions of employment as negotiated at the national level?

It's socialism! How about that?

There are those in the United States who seem to think that anything except pure eighteenth-century industrial capitalism is Communism. That puts the U.S. so far out on the right wing that we are teetering on the edge. The Japanese are pretty good capitalists, but at least they have a national health care system. When you look at national comparisons of worker protective laws, it's interesting that there are a whole series of benefits for which it's only ourselves and South Africa that do it in this right-wing, crazy, virtually fascist mode. Before 1992, family and medical leave was like that. Only ourselves and South Africa didn't do it.

When labor is at its best, it's involved in a wide coalition with women and civil rights activists. Labor by itself can't do anything. That coalition was nearly destroyed, I think, in the Vietnam War, and maybe a little bit earlier in the Korean War, when labor really went strongly patriotic, and I understand why. But the tragedy is that it burnt bridges between groups that we should have strong association with. We should be strongly allied to civil rights and women's groups, to the point where they see labor as their friend and the force that's going to do for them what nobody else can do.

There's another area that needs to be changed. Companies are organizing globally. They move out of the United States because they have a better labor relations climate in a Third World economy. They don't move to our competitors, like Japan. They move to Mexico, Taiwan, or the Philippines. They move to all kinds of little places to find workers that they can abuse, and where the government leaders of those countries give them license to do anything they want. The labor movement, I think, has got to organize internationally.

I think NAFTA [North American Free Trade Agreement] was a lost opportunity for that. I actually differ from a lot of my friends who said, "We should fight NAFTA and there shouldn't be a NAFTA." I think there should be a NAFTA, but there needs to be an agreement between us and Mexico and Canada that should clearly say that our three labor laws will be in accord and that the unions can organize freely across the borders. You can't fight globalization any more than we were able to stop automation—that's impossible.

The United Auto Workers should, for example, be able to negotiate cross-border labor contracts for the Mexican and Canadian factories, and then negotiate a wage which is parity with the U.S. and Canadian workers. There won't be an advantage for companies going to Mexico if that's the case. The argument that the Bush and Carter administrations made is that we can't afford to let these people be our poorer relations across the border. I agree. We should be concerned with raising their standard of living, but not at the expense of ours. The surest way to bring their standard up is to open wide the door to unionization.

We're moving into a global everything, and the economy is the first step. At the founding of our country, all of the states regarded themselves as sovereign countries. The concept of the United States as a single country didn't really become firm until after the Civil War. Sovereignty was something that had to be given up in order for commerce to work properly in the United States. Sovereignty must be surrendered globally for the same reasons—for the economy to work. It's already happening with business. The countries of the world are realizing they have to change their laws of business to allow people to invest. But when it comes to knocking down barriers to labor organizing—oh my God, that's socialism!

I have some tapes that were made in the '60s and '70s when the labor leaders were sitting back on their laurels and saying, "Well, we've come a long way in the labor movement, and now people realize that labor, capital, and government are the three forces that have to work together, and we resign ourselves to the understanding that we're all parts of an important institution." Little did they know that in a few short years that would all be put into question. If labor is going to be in the picture in the next century, we'll have to [start] looking at truly international unions with international contracts.

The implications are trouble and conflict in the future.

Yeah, I would say so. The older labor leaders whom I interviewed boasted of how many times they'd been arrested, realizing that civil disobedience was often the only response to injustice. Mother Jones, it is said, went to jail for the last time when she was in her eighties. We may need a new breed of labor leaders who are willing to say, "I own nothing, I will not pay your fines, but I am willing to go to jail. You can't take anything more important away from me than my rights to organize." Perhaps we will need that kind of labor leader again.

Ah Quon McElrath

Recently appointed to the University of Hawai'i's Board of Regents; continues in her late seventies to live a full activist life.

I am a retired social worker with the International Longshoremen's and Warehousemen's Union, Local 142, in Honolulu. Since my retirement in 1981, I worked with senior citizens in Washington, D.C., from 1983 to 1985. Since my return to Hawai'i in 1985, I've done a good deal of work with senior citizens' and women's organizations. However, my basic interest is with poor people in Hawai'i and the need for us to recognize what their problems are. I helped to convene a loose coalition called the Committee on Welfare Concerns. I have worked on behalf of poor people for the last five years, primarily in the area of lobbying for them at the State Legislature.

For many years, poor people have been swept under the rug. They have been blamed for practically all of the ills of society, the least of which is having children, and the worst of which is that they are responsible for crime waves and bad performance of children in school. The Committee on Welfare Concerns has always felt that people receiving less than 100 percent of the federal poverty level are, in fact, encouraged toward all of the kinds of things about which poor people are blamed. If they don't have enough money to buy food with high protein content, their children's ability to learn is affected. If they can't afford a home, they become the homeless. Hawai'i's rents are about the highest in the entire nation. When the median price of a home is

$350,000, you are not going to find any poor people living at 62.5 percent of poverty being able to buy homes.

We have always felt in Hawai'i that various ethnic groups have suffered the greatest. The irony is that the Hawaiians, the indigenous people of Hawai'i, have suffered the most. My feeling is that their loss of land, their *'āina,* which in fact makes them children of the earth, has been one of the basic reasons why they have suffered so greatly after the overthrow of their queen. Today, the Hawaiians have the highest rate of individuals on public assistance, the highest rate of individuals in corrective institutions, whether adults or youngsters, the highest rate of lung cancer and diabetes, and the lowest rate of individuals who remain in secondary schools. I think only 6 percent of eligible Hawaiian children are educated by the Bishop Estate, the beneficiary of the estate of Bernice Pauahi Bishop, an Hawaiian princess who was married to Charles Reed Bishop, King Lunalilo's premier. This estate makes instant millionaires of those who become its trustees. Only about 7 percent of the Hawaiian students end up attending the University of Hawai'i. This is obviously a tragedy of great magnitude.

I was born and raised on the island of O'ahu, in the city of Honolulu. I'm the sixth of seven children of immigrant Chinese parents. My father died when I was four and one-half years old. He landed in Oahu Prison because he happened to be smoking opium at a time when it was not the thing to do. In the early history of the Chinese, there were certain periods when they were allowed to smoke their opium without arrest or any fines.

We are a Chinese family that came from the other side of the tracks. One of the things that Chinese usually did was to ask you what was the full name of your father. The full name of our father was identical to that of a Chinese merchant who had opened up a dry goods store in downtown Honolulu. And of course the inquirer would be ecstatic, "Oh my gosh, here is a child of this entrepreneur," and when you told them you weren't that particular family, their jaws usually dropped.

If you lived in a place like Iwilei, which was near all of the oil companies, the pineapple cannery, the gas company, and you lived among a variegated group of families—Chinese, Japanese, Filipinos, a Black, even some Russians—you get to know what kind of lives they are leading. You get to know that these are all working-class people without a lot of money, parents who worked very hard in order to send their children to school.

You hear stories about people who are unable to receive health care.

For example, my father died of a ruptured appendix. We couldn't afford a doctor, so he died at home. Some of my siblings were born in a hospital, while others were born at home with the help of midwives. When I went on to grammar school and intermediate school, it was always with working-class people. We lived in the area generally known as Kalihi-Pālama, which even to this day is that area in Honolulu where the rents usually are the lowest; where working-class families have lived all of their lives; and where the things which the so-called affluent neighborhoods don't want are placed, such as public housing and health clinics for the poor. Nobody ever really cared about that area too much. They didn't repair the streets. Light industry came in, and even though you protested, nothing happened. I could imagine trying to put light industry in an area such as 'Āina Haina, where immediately the whole neighborhood would be up in arms and going to their legislators and City Council to stop it. But this doesn't happen in working-class areas, where most people spend all of their time earning a living and surviving.

I grew up during the Great Depression when many vibrant things were happening. Interesting books were written, some of which had to do with the experiment in the Soviet Union under socialism. Any person who had any sensitivity whatsoever would be impressed with what was going on in that country. In the United States there were 15 million people who were unemployed, there were breadlines, there were the bonus marchers. Later on there was the passage of social security legislation and the Wagner Act, then, the Congress of Industrial Organizations. Even here in Hawai'i, there were the rumblings of individuals who wanted to organize into unions.

While I was in college, there were the two big strikes: the last ethnic strike on the island of Maui in 1937, and the Inland Boatmen's Union strike here on O'ahu in 1938. This culminated in the so-called Hilo Massacre on the island of Hawai'i in the port of Hilo, where dozens and dozens of people were shot and bayoneted on the apron of the pier. When I was going to the university, my heart and mind were opened up to vast possibilities of education. New professors were coming in from the outside who brought new ideas, new ways of looking at things. Any number of organizations were being formed in the Territory of Hawai'i to which the students were exposed.

Jack Hall, a seaman, was instrumental in the final organization of sugar workers. I remember that I was at a meeting at that time and someone burst in and said that Mr. Hall had been beaten up by the police. He had been arrested as a result of his participation in the 1938 strike on the waterfront. Although it was started by seamen, the longshoremen joined in that particular strike and Mr. Hall was representing the longshoremen. Presumably, the elevator was stopped between floors and he was beaten up by the police. Those stories about how working people were treated turned your stomach.

In 1937 we had the advent of mainland assistance from International Labor Defense, which came to Hawaii to represent those individuals who had been arrested, among whom were many Filipinos. The strike of Inter-Island Steamship Navigations by the Inland Boatmen's Union, joined later by the longshoremen in the port of Hilo, was multiethnic. These were events that served to energize any person who was interested in what was going on in the world. There were interconnections that we were beginning to see at that time: legislative, commercial, or a different mode of organizing the economic system.

I suspect some today may say, "Well, the whole thing has busted now, so why do you dwell on it?" I think it's important to dwell on it because it helps one to see the vast possibilities of an economic system that in fact treats people with dignity and respect and gives them a measure of control over their lives. Obviously, trade unions gave that to working people. And there was the whole idea of equity and justice, which obviously were not the two concepts which motivated the way that the capitalist economy developed. In that period, the National Labor Relations Act was passed, which was supposed to balance out the power that big business had over working people: workmen's compensation, unemployment compensation. Occupational safety and health legislation was passed, then the Employees' Retirement Income Security Act, which was supposedly one way of controlling the pensions which workers in the private sector received, so that there would be no repetition of the kinds of things that occurred when Studebaker [auto company] went down the drain.

And so there were all of these kinds of things which were happening, which were influential in how you looked at the world so far as the collective strength of people was concerned. One of the things about a capitalist economy is that it is basically an economy that concentrates on an individual approach to living. This reached its zenith, in my opinion, during the Reagan-Bush years, when everything became highly individualistic, when the collective power and will of the people were basically trampled. Not that the process had not begun earlier, mind you.

These things have a way of becoming part of your heart and psyche. Is it for yourself that you're living, or is it for other selves?

I graduated from the University of Hawai'i in 1938 with a baccalaureate. I did volunteer work with the Board of Human Services, in its research department. There was no money; there were no jobs. It was '38 after all, and we were kind of brushing through the Great Depression. Hawai'i always felt the effects of what was happening on the mainland five years later. When I finally was hired as a full-time social worker, I got $105 a month. I tried to organize the social workers on an industrial basis. At that time, there was this left-wing magazine called *Social Work Today,* which talked about organizing social workers on the mainland. I put together a group called the Department of Social Security Employees Association. We had caseworkers as well as clerical staff. One of the big things we accomplished was to get the department not to raise the rentals of people in public housing. We also got them to recognize that social workers should be paid more. That was before there was an active chapter of the National Association of Social Workers in Hawai'i.

And then I got married. My husband worked with the International Longshoremen's and Warehousemen's Union. I had my first child in 1943 and took a leave of absence. Then in 1945 I had another child and took another leave of absence. The ILWU went into the sugar strike, which began September 1, 1946. I was still home at the time after having had my child, and I did some volunteer social work for the union. In April of that year, when I was still off, we had the great tidal wave [tsunami] of April 1, 1946. So I volunteered my services to the union and said, "I will do all of your investigation for the people who need assistance or who have suffered damage as a result of the tidal wave." I did a lot of volunteer work.

Subsequently, though, I did go back to work, but the job didn't last very long. It was during the days of the Committee for Maritime Unity, on the West Coast. At the same time, the ILWU had begun to really institutionalize its operations here. We had organized the union in 1944. We had our first contract in '45. We were working unsuccessfully toward a second contract in 1946. Consequently, we had the first big strike on 1 September 1946 of twenty-six sugar plantations, when 28,000 of us walked out. I still use the possessive, "we." I can't forget my experiences at the union.

Before long, the 1949 longshore strike occurred. I was without work at the time, and so I had begun to work again as a volunteer with the union, helping them set up soup kitchens, telling them where they could go for creditors' help, to get food stamps, to get free lunches. What I had done in the sugar strike of '46, I began doing again in the longshore strike of 1949. I figured I'd better find something else to do, so I went and took a crash course in legal stenography. The law firm Bouslog and Symonds, which had handled all the sugar litigation and some of the longshore litigation during the strikes, said, "Look, A. Q., there's a possibility that we could hire you as a legal secretary."

I only worked briefly for them, because in August of 1951 seven people were arrested by the FBI as violators of the [anticommunist] Smith Act of 1940. I became the office manager of the defense office to defend the so-called Hawai'i Seven. These were individuals who were arrested under the Smith Act for allegedly preaching the overthrow of the U.S. government by force and violence. It was not a particularly good period in the lives of those who were associated with the ILWU. I remember when a lot of my friends would cross to the other side of the street to avoid me. If you were called a Red at that time, your means of livelihood was taken away from you. You were not hired if you were known to have been an associate of Jack Hall, John and Aiko Reinecke, or Koji Ariyoshi. People like Jack Hall, my husband, myself, who'd known Harry Bridges for a long time, weren't particularly loved by representatives of the status quo.

Finally I was hired by the ILWU in 1954, after the Smith Act trial was under the bridge. They began negotiating pension and medical plans. They needed a social worker to look into some of the aspects of human behavior and living, which would affect the way medical plans should be negotiated. Over the years, I learned a hell of a lot on my own. Social work schools didn't teach what was a good medical or pension plan. I worked with the ILWU San Francisco office, which pioneered dental care for children. We put through the first children's dental program of the ILWU longshore section in Hawai'i. A lot of people don't know the history of the role that we played in bringing health care to Hawai'i.

The sugar industry's health care program, which we codified into the agreement, was the forerunner of all HMOs—health maintenance organizations. Some plantations provided all of the health care in their own clinics, in their own hospitals, and they hired physicians to provide that care. We were instrumental in pushing through the enabling legislation for the entry of the Kaiser Medical Plan to Hawai'i, despite all of the objections of the Hawai'i Medical Association, the then Hospital Association, and lots of other people who looked upon this as socialized medicine. My God, if they'd looked at veteran's health, that is the height of socialized medicine.

We also had some creative ideas about how to take care of excess labor on the sugar plantations through repatriation funds, where we gave an alien worker X number of dollars per years of service, so that he can return to the Philippines with free passage, and buy land in the Philippines and support his family. Mind you, a good deal of this was created by the influx of new technology which cut down on the number of people in a gang which was necessary to harvest the cane. The leadership of the ILWU, which was basically left-wing in orientation, had some very, very innovative ideas as to how working people could be taken care of. And I suspect that similar kinds of things were happening in the auto workers union, in the mine workers union, and some of those other places where technology was taking the place of workers. These were very vibrant years for the International Longshoremens' and Warehousemens' Union.

After a while, one begins to feel the need to recharge the batteries. The kids were grown, so I thought that this was time for me to go on and get some further education to find out what was happening in social work. So I spent a year and a half—1965 to 1966—at the University of Michigan School of Social Work.

Community organization began to take on a different kind of coloring with the war on poverty program. But mind you, a good deal of this was started even before that time by the late [community organizer] Saul Alinsky, who had worked with John L. Lewis [United Mine Workers president], and with the labor movement, and whose kind of community organization was not palatable to the social work profession. I remember when I went to the University of Michigan I asked the professor, "Well, what is the concentration here on community organization? Do you follow the Alinsky model and what he has done?"

Well, he says, "Oh, you know something about Saul Alinsky?"

And I said, "Yes, doesn't everybody?"

He said, "Well, we don't feel that social work can do the rubbing-salt-in-your-wounds concept that Alinsky talks about."

One of the good things that happened in my experience at the University of Michigan is that I had an opportunity to go down South and work with an Office of Economic Opportunity program, out of Tuske-

gee Institute in Alabama. I worked for several months in Lowndes
County on a health survey. This afforded me the opportunity to talk
with the United Mine Workers and a health organization in Detroit,
where we were able to get a lot of supplies, and we converted an old
Volkswagen into an examination room. And we got physicians who
came through the Medical Committee for Human Rights. That was
when I met Alvin Poussaint, a Black psychiatrist who is now at Harvard, who worked very closely with Jack Geiger, a doctor at Tufts University. Geiger felt that one of the basic things about health care is
providing people with enough food to eat. He taught people down
South how to do their own gardening. I helped to train people at Tuskegee Institute and community people about how to do interviews. We
went to a number of tutorial centers in Lowndes County, and examined
over two thousand predominantly Black men, women, and children.
The results of that project were written up in *The New England Journal
of Medicine* by one of the volunteer doctors.

I think I got a little bit tired. I wasn't quite sure whether the contributions I was making, not only to the union, but to the community
organizations of which I was a union representative, were the best possible contribution that I could make. And I saw some of the lethargy
that was setting in—in government operations, in the union. This was
not good for the rank and file. In the meantime, there were new things
that were happening in the labor movement. I needed to find out how I
could put them into play in the trade unions. We had a lot of classes at
the ILWU.

When I came back to Hawai'i after the experience in Alabama, I
worked very closely with the educational director. We put together an
educational program which I think could have served as a model for
many other unions. As a matter of fact, a lot of the unions did come to
us. We had a membership services department which took care of the
needs of workers in their medical and dental plans, their pension plans,
and any of the other problems which they faced. Our educational program was fashioned around the need to know specifically what was
provided in certain sections of the collective bargaining agreement,
such as health care, retirement pay, unemployment compensation,
workmen's compensation, and the other things which would affect
workers' lives.

Our educational program had a large section devoted to what was
happening in the social agencies in Hawai'i. We felt that this was
important for workers to know. Our idea was to train indigenous lead-

ership to recognize problems that were occurring on the job, as well as off the job. We tried to teach our leadership to recognize that if a worker consistently does not come to work on a Monday, there might be an alcoholism problem. If a worker seemed completely distracted from his work, it might very well be that that worker was having marital problems, or school problems with his children. We invested these individuals with a great deal of knowledge that they could use in the interest of rank and file members.

We had members on school advisory boards and land utilization committees. The ILWU was heavily involved in political action. We were responsible for the first active movement of the territorial legislature in the direction of the Democratic Party, following more than fifty years of hegemony on the part of the Republican party. The union gave workers the opportunity to move away from complete control by the so-called Big Five, which were involved in buying and selling for the thirty-odd sugar plantations. The union opened up the route for everybody in Hawai'i to become something that their parents could never become. When you couple this with the return of the Americans of Japanese ancestry after World War II, then you had a combination that was sure to change the life of Hawai'i, as it truly has—in some ways, not so good, in other ways, very, very good. The ILWU has been given credit by any number of individuals, including the late governor of Hawai'i, John A. Burns, with bringing political, social, and economic democracy to Hawai'i.

Statehood, which was granted in 1959, did not bring so-called democracy to Hawai'i. We had already brought it to Hawai'i, and we had presaged the destruction of the financial oligarchy. Rather, statehood brought about the beginnings of a different political economy. With the coming of the big jets, with the ability of outside business to invest in the State of Hawai'i, we moved from a basically industrial, agricultural society to a service-oriented economy. More people would be coming to Hawai'i for vacations. With that came the huge developments and diversion of land into use other than production of sugarcane and pineapple. I think statehood was inevitable, just as it might be for Washington, D.C., and Puerto Rico. I don't know whether any of the former Marianas Islands [sic: Trust Territory] will become states. Perhaps the only one might be Belau.

This is supposed to be the Pacific century. One wonders what will happen, especially in light of the breakup of the Soviet Union, what's happening in China, the reversion of Hong Kong to China in 1997, whether the financial dominance of Japan will be broken by Singapore or Taiwan or Korea. All of this is very problematical. It's also very problematical how Hawai'i will fare if Japanese investments do not continue to come here. This is the nature of the political economy of the state. Very few people, other than businesspeople, pay much attention to it. But I think that we ignore it to our peril. We certainly need to know what is happening in the State Legislature on human services, and whether reduced Japanese investment would mean that we won't collect enough taxes to fund human services.

Between the years of 1978 and 1986, absolutely no increases were made in public welfare payments: aid to families with dependent children, general assistance, or aid to the aged, blind, and disabled. During those years, people on public assistance had lost something like 60 percent in their living standards. In 1987, when I became thoroughly engrossed with the Committee on Welfare Concerns, we were able to get a 10 percent increase. But even with that, Hawai'ii people on public assistance were receiving only slightly over 50 percent of the federal poverty level. By 1988, we were strong enough to effectuate a change in the public welfare law, to peg payments at 60 percent of the federal poverty level. The following year, we were able to get that increased to 62.5 percent. It has been status quo ever since.

In the 1991 legislative session, the Department of Human Services, representing the executive branch, proposed freezing public welfare payments at the 1991 poverty levels. The measure was passed by a very slim vote in the House, but we were able to get it defeated in the Senate. We used a very dramatic process: serving lunches to the Senate at 62.5 percent of the poverty level, which meant that they had five ounces of milk, one-half boiled egg, three-quarters of an apple, and three-quarters of a cheese sandwich without any dressing. The House was incensed that we did not serve them a meal, but we told them that at 62.5 percent of the poverty level, we couldn't serve them a meal.

It has already been recommended by some legislators and the executive branch that public assistance payments must be frozen at either the '91 or '92 levels. If frozen at the '91 level, it would mean that a family of four could not get more that 62.5 percent of federal poverty level of $13,000 per annum. So you can see that at no time would a family be able to have a decent standard of living. If you were to factor in food stamps, that would amount to almost 80 percent of poverty.

Now, the Department of Human Services people love to factor in Medicaid, and we tell them this is not disposable income. That money is paid to vendors of care, not to the families themselves. Now we are beginning to feel the full brunt of a recession, and with Hurricane Iniki on the island of Kaua'i and on our leeward coast, it has meant that more and more people have had the need to get food stamps, emergency medical assistance, or whatever it is that they need. You combine that with some rather profligate spending during the years when the State of Hawai'i was able to accumulate as much as $400 million in surpluses, and you have some idea of the crisis that we are facing.

Our Committee on Welfare Concerns is saying that it does not make good economic sense to freeze payments because people on public assistance spend every cent they get, and all of the businesses will benefit. Likewise, all payments of Medicaid to providers of care is spent for taxes, wages, supplies, investments, and everything else, and it helps business. What we need to do is to maximize the flow of federal dollars to the State of Hawai'i rather than cutting off care, because we are not receiving as much money from tourism.

We're talking not only with legislators, but also with organizations such as the Chamber of Commerce. Politics makes strange bedfellows, except that the economic argument makes a whole lot of sense to the Chamber. They truly see that every dollar spent by the State and brought in from the federal government helps the economy of Hawai'i. Now, whether or not this alliance lasts is problematic. There may be other things which we will do [that] the Chamber may not approve of. In the ever-fluid political picture in Hawai'i, one uses allies where one can find them.

The Committee on Welfare Concerns has steadfastly challenged the federal government to legislate for the benefit of individuals where there is no possibility of equitable, just treatment of human beings because they happen to live in different parts of the country, or because of their marital situation, or the color of their skin. The federal government must enact a floor for aid to families with dependent children below which no state can go. It must enact changes in the Medicaid program so that individuals will have access to all needed medical and health care. None of these things should be dependent upon whether or not a state has a good or bad economic situation. The need for food and shelter and health care is indivisible, regardless of where one lives. Congress has almost invariably legislated according to the needs of a specific area and because Congress has always had in mind the need to be reelected to office.

I've been a member of the governor's blue ribbon committee on health care, which was put together in 1990 with the idea of coming up with some basic changes to the way health care is delivered in the State of Hawai'i. The present director of the Department of Health seems to believe that health care in the State of Hawai'i is absolutely the best. Many things dispute his assertion, such as the very bad state of health among indigenous Hawaiians, the fact that Hawai'i ranks fiftieth in the purveyance of mental health services, the fact that Hawai'i has more incarcerated individuals with mental health problems than any other state. This blue ribbon committee, made up of a lot of providers and a few citizens, has made recommendations which just tinker with the system. A couple of us presented a conceptual framework which we feel is important to making some very basic structural changes in health care in the United States. This would include such things as basic benefits, single payer, global budgeting, different means of financing health care, complete research and development, and planning. Unfortunately, many of the members of our blue ribbon committee could not countenance looking at such a conceptual framework.

Some of the kinds of things which would be provided under a so-called more generous basic benefit package would be long-term care. There would probably be very heavy restrictions in terms of deductibles and co-insurance for such things as transplants of organs and long-term treatment of AIDS. There would be some question as to whether or not some of the new conditions which are being brought in because of the changed immigration picture—such as TB or Hepatitis B—which are resistant to present treatment modes, might be receiving additional care. One of the kinds of things that has happened in the treatment of TB has been the closure of TB hospitals because it can now be treated with antibiotics on an out-patient basis. However, the strains of TB which have been coming to Hawai'i have been resistant to antibiotics.

Our prepaid health law doesn't cover everything, nor does it cover everyone. Only people who work twenty hours or more per week are eligible. Individuals who work nineteen hours a week are subject to all of the hanky-panky of employers. Some years ago, they tried to do this to hotel workers under contract with the ILWU. We raised a grievance and won it. We could show that the employers had worked these individuals nineteen hours solely to get out of providing them health care under our prepaid health plan. That goes to show you the importance of organizing workers in a trade union.

Of the 22,000 small businesses in Hawai'i, one would have to assess how many of them are restaurants, retail organizations, other trades and services, as well as hotels. It is extremely difficult to make an assessment of which ones of these organizations in fact work their employees nineteen hours to escape coverage under the Hawai'i prepaid health law. It is extremely difficult for organizations with fifty or more employees to escape by working those individuals under nineteen hours per week. One reason why workers in service work may not have coverage is that immigrants are afraid to raise the problem for fear they would lose their jobs.

Tommy
Trask

Recently retired at age sixty-five as international vice president of the International Longshoremen's and Warehousemen's Union in Hawai'i.

I was born here in Hawai'i. My mother came from the Bronx in New York, of English-Irish extraction. My father was born and raised here. He was English-Hawaiian. My father was in the merchant marine and went all over the world. He settled in New York City and married my mother. He was active on Broadway as an accomplished musician. John Huston's father, Walter Huston, was his agent. They were known as Walter Huston and his Five Hawaiians. My father brought my mother to Hawai'i and I was born two months after they arrived. I have a Hawaiian name yea-long which means "coming over the Pacific." When my father came here he had nothing. The matriarch of the family, his oldest sister, was married to the guy who was head of the mental hospital. On the grounds of the hospital were cottages for security guards and nurses. So, they set my mom and dad and my brother in one of these cottages. I was born there. I'm the only person I know of in the State of Hawai'i that has a birth certificate that reads, place of birth: Territorial Mental Hospital. *(Laughter.)* And I think it's apropos that I ended up as a union leader.

I went to St. Louis High School and graduated in 1947. Like all seventeen-year-old kids, I knew it all. I spent a lot of time body surfing at the beach. One day a guy said, "Let's go down to Dole Cannery." It was

318

known as Hawaiian Pine in those days. So, a bunch of us went down there. I never left. It was the only job I ever held in my life.

I got active in the sports program, which got me interested in the union. Then I learned a trade and became a journeyman electrician. I got elected as a shop steward. The sports program helped me get to know some of the union leaders of that time. I ended up being the chairman of the Hawaiian Pine unit, the largest unit inside of the ILWU, with 2,300 members at that time. Then I got on different union committees.

In 1961 Jack Hall, the ILWU regional director, asked me to join the union staff and help organize the clerical workers in the pineapple industry. Factory and field already were organized. I was with the union for thirty-two years on a full-time basis, and ten years prior to that as a rank-and-filer.

In 1969 Jack Hall promoted me up to international representative so I would be working for the national union. We call it international because we're in Canada too. I worked directly under Jack Hall. He became vice president of the international union and left for the mainland, but he was still technically our boss. When Jack Hall left, Bob McElrath became the regional director. I worked for Bob until 1978, and then I got appointed as regional director. In my last three years with the union, I was the international vice president stationed in Hawai'i. Since Hawai'i has always had the bulk of ILWU members, politically that gave us a little muscle.

I was attracted to the union because I came from a poor background and I could see that the have-nots were not getting a fair shake. I never had any intentions of going into management. When I got active in the union, I liked what I saw and liked the kind of work.

There was no question that Jack Hall was left-leaning. I guess most of us were. He was a threat to the status quo, so they painted him as a Red—a commie. They used whatever term was derogatory at that time. The Red smear campaign went on hot and heavy. Jack was put on that Smith Act trial. Can you imagine, "violent overthrow of the government?" Half of our membership were returning veterans from the war. Can you imagine, Senator Eastland from Mississippi, coming here to Hawai'i and trying to tell us what the hell was right for us? What was going on in Mississippi, for God sakes?

A lot of the politics of unionism had to do with survival. After the war, the ILWU got more active than most other unions, I guess. A lot of heat was put on us. The employers figured, Okay, the war's over—we'll get rid of these characters. And there was an all-out push, which ended up in the make-or-break 1949 longshore strike. That went for seven months. The union survived, so the other side began to say, "Okay, we've got to live with these characters, but we don't have to give them what they want. Then it became a slow, hard process of bringing us up to where we are today.

Were the wages of field workers and cannery workers relatively low?

Very low! Compared to other nonservice industries, they were probably at the bottom. In the old days of the plantation, there was a lot of paternalism: "You have low wages, but we're going to give you free kerosene to light your stove and lamps, we have a clinic for you, and we have a company store to buy all your goods from." Of course, they owned the store, so the money just went around in a circle and back in the same pocket. The people on the plantation had nowhere else to go until the unions came in and said there can be something better, like medical plans, pensions, and dignity on the job.

Management set up separate camps for the different ethnic groups that worked the fields, a classic case of "divide and conquer." It was different in the cannery where workers generally came from Honolulu proper. It took a lot of union selling and people with charisma like Jack Hall and Ah Quon McElrath to unify the workers. They hammered away on the theme that unity was necessary; forget that guy's Portuguese or Japanese or Filipino; there's one common goal: a better life for yourself. There was a heavy educational program. Eventually it sunk in.

The goal of the make-or-break strike of '49 was parity with the West Coast. For example, a Matson ship would be loaded in Hawai'i at maybe one dollar an hour and be unloaded on the mainland at maybe a dollar and a half an hour. Those figures may not be correct, but that was the ratio. The issue was parity. The employers decided to take on the union. Management housewives formed a "broom brigade" and would march with brooms to make a clean sweep of this "Red menace."

How did the newspapers handle this?

Every day in *The Advertiser* there would be an article called "Dear Joe." This was a mythical union guy—writing to Joe Stalin—who would say things like, "Don't worry Uncle Joe, we've got them all under control; we'll break this territory; we've been able to cut off the kids' milk; blah, blah, blah." Management had the papers on their side. There was a constant barrage, but the longshoremen stuck with the leadership of the union. Jack Hall was the key, but Harry Bridges, Louis

Goldblatt, and other officers would come down and lend their support. We won the strike and had some wage increases, but we [didn't get] parity for another ten years.

As part of the 1934 West Coast strike, the arbitrator said that long-shore work was onerous and dirty work, and nobody should work more than six hours. So, the six-hour day was established on the West Coast. Hawai'i didn't get that until eight or ten years ago. In some ways, though, we were ahead of the West Coast: the West Coast never had sick leave or severance pay, but we've had them for years.

But, unlike the West Coast, Hawai'i never had the hiring hall. The stevedoring companies hire their own people. There always was a fear that too many shenanigans could go on at the hiring hall. The hiring hall was instituted to take care of the "shape-up," where, for example, you'd come to work and have two toothpicks in your hatband. That told the guy doing the hiring that you'd kick back two bucks for the day. That's the way it worked. Jack always felt that when you get a hiring hall something like that would happen and, sooner or later, someone's going to find a way to beat the system the good ol' American way.

I assume you hurt the company in the strike of 1949.

Oh, sure. If you can't hurt a company economically, you've got yourself a loser. Today, there's a problem of survival. People are fearful, and you can't blame them, because it *is* bad times. If you went into a sugar plantation today and told the guys we were going to go on strike, they'd say, "Huh! If you go on strike we're never coming back," because they'll just shut down. They're looking for an excuse to shut down and they wouldn't have to pay severance. The contract is null and void when you go out on strike. In my opinion, things have *always* been rigged against the working person. The role of the union has been to struggle through and do the best it can, but we've *never* been on top.

In California, they were always worried that the companies would jump over into Nevada or Arizona or some place like that. In Hawai'i, where can they go? Of course, pineapple, more than sugar, moved to the Philippines, Taiwan, Thailand. Sugar production here in Hawai'i went down because of outside influences like world sugar prices. There was constant heat being put on by certain people in Congress who were trying to do away with the Farm Bill. They claimed that if the sugar price support program were done away with, the price of sugar would be lower. In a country like France, a large sugar beet grower, they subsidize their farmers because they're a socialist country. I remember when the French farmer got thirty-two cents a pound for his sugar. France consumed about 85 percent of whatever they grew. The rest they dumped out in the Caribbean at six to ten cents a pound. They don't care; it's already been paid for. Our guys in Congress would say, "That's the world market sugar price; why are we paying eighteen cents a pound?" That was the price support figure. You know damned well that Coca Cola wouldn't lower *its* prices, once they got their hands on that cheap sugar. That's what's behind all of this: the almighty dollar.

You had other organizing successes.

Numbers give you strength. We organized clerical. We organized hotels. When I was there, my goal always was to get the ILWU back up to 30,000 where we used to be. We got damn close to it: about 28,000. We had a little more success than the other unions because they held on to the idea of craft unionism: the carpenters do this, the masons do that. Well, there's only so many workers. We were more the industrial-type union, modeled after John L. Lewis' CIO [Congress of Industrial Unions]. We would go in and take wall-to-wall. We got more truck drivers than the Teamsters. We weren't locked into agriculture, it was just the base.

Alexander and Baldwin owned HC&S, the biggest sugar planta-tion, but they also owned Matson, the biggest shipper out here. And Matson owned the Royal Hawaiian Hotel. Wherever their tentacles went, *we* went. So, we're in retail and hotels. We have highly skilled people in hemodialysis, cardiopulmonary, nuclear medicine, nursing. We also have gravediggers: all the cemeteries are with us. So, when you come in with the ILWU, we take care of you from womb to tomb. *(Laughter.)*

I think after this Republican one hundred days is over [104th U.S. Congress], they're going to start looking around and ask, "What else can we do?" Water down the NLRB [National Labor Relations Board] some more. Right to work! What the hell is right to work? Fine sound-ing: Every American should have the right to work. They're watering down the Clean Water Act, attacking welfare, and so forth. After they get through with all this horseshit, they're going to look around, and they're going to look at us (labor). They've even got the average worker believing that it's the *poor* that's messing us up, and I've even heard some of my own guys say that. If you went down the street and talked to an average worker, he would say, "Yeah, them son-of-a-bitches on welfare—!" But what they get is minute compared to the welfare that big business gets.

Will the average worker begin to understand this?

I think the worker's got to get hurt to understand. For awhile, he had two cars in the garage and a single-family home. Everything was rosy. Labor's *leadership*, I think, understands that, but not the working guy. We've come to accept two people in a house working. A worker figures, "I make fifty, she makes fifty, I've got a hundred grand. I'm *above* all these other guys." Without question, some of that thinking worked its way into the rank and file. But, to me that's a sad way to look at it. What about the poor guy who has no job at all?

Labor's going to come back when the worker gets hurt enough and finally says, "The hell with this bullshit; who the hell is causing this?" Newt Gingrich and his gang [are] causing this! They will continue to do what they're doing until labor can solidify itself and demonstrate numbers. The politician is always worried about numbers.

Our basic lift-push-pull longshore income in Hawai'i is $65,000 per year. They also have a 38-hour weekly guarantee here, ship or no ship, at $22.64 an hour. That's not bad for not working. We also have the "6 and 2" here: anything after the 6-hour day is overtime. It's hard for me to go to one of these guys and tell them how terrible it is. It's hard to reach them.

Hawai'i has become a true service society: poor people serving rich people. Can such workers become class conscious and organize?

It's going to take some time. People are scared when you talk about a union: "Oh, my God, am I going to lose my job?" In good times, they're more apt to take a chance because they know they can go down the street and get hired by the other guy. When they see the other guy laying off, they're going to hang out with what they've got. When they read the paper about two hundred Kohala Sugar guys being laid off, it clouds their thinking: "Those 200 guys have *no* job; I have *a* job."

The ILWU got into the tourist industry back in the '60s. We've made some big strides in that industry: the medical plans are all free, we get sick leave and five weeks vacation. We made great strides in a shorter period of time than we did in sugar or pineapple. We had a good relationship with some of the hotel owners. Our success was because of our clout in the political arena. We knew the right people on the different boards and commissions who had to be seen by someone wanting to build a hotel. They couldn't very easily bring an antiunion attitude to Hawai'i. They would come to Hawai'i and hire local attorneys who knew who we were.

What would happen in Hawai'i if another depression came?

It would be a disaster. Many fewer tourists would come here. It would be a terrible burden on those who are working because they would have to pay more taxes to take care of the poor guy who has nothing. Even during the time of the Great Depression, we'd fight among ourselves to get a job. Once we got it, the hell with the other guy. But I'm sure some radical politics would take place. When you're down so low, the only way to go is up, and people may be more apt to take a chance.

It would be difficult to form a labor party in America. One danger of a third party is dividing the Democrats. Now, there are some Democrats who are bums, but by and large their philosophy differs quite a bit from the Republicans. The Democrats have helped labor, especially in the Roosevelt era. A third party might take away from the Democrats. Then, do the Republicans get a free roll? That's a danger.

What's your view of the sovereignty movement?

I disagree with my cousins, the Trask sisters. I'm not talking land, but about the Hawaiian people themselves. Some sovereignty leaders fail to recognize that the key to elevating the Hawaiian kid is education. They yell and scream about the State government being staffed more and more by Japanese, Chinese, and so forth. Well, if you're going to be an accountant, my God you've got to have the education to maintain a budget. The Japanese kid went to college and got a CPA license. The Hawaiian sits on the outside and moans about it. Education is the key. They want Kaho'olawe back. What are they going to do with it? Plant taro? There's no water there.

Kamehameha School is the richest school in the United States, with assets in the billions. They haven't built a single elementary school in places like Waimānalo or Wai'anae, where the kids are, to give them at least grade 1 to 6 basic education. The only elementary school is on that elite, pristine hill up there where they come out beautiful singers. Why does a Hawaiian kid have to feel that being a truck driver is the ultimate in life? With better education, *they'd* be sitting in the Legislature, *they'd* be the principals of schools.

I've never been able to figure out what "nation within a nation" means. Does it mean they don't get fire and police and military protection, they don't get taxes from the rest of us, they have to start their own welfare-medical program? How in heaven's name are they going to do that? It's not going to fly because they do *not* represent the majority of Hawaiians. No way on earth does Mililani Trask, Haunani Trask, Bumpy Kanahele, or anybody else like that represent the majority of Hawaiians. I *do* like the idea of them getting together, but the priorities have to be set up right. I agree that Hawaiians are discontented, but that's because they don't have good paying jobs.

Will Hawai'i continue its present economic course in tourism?

It seems inevitable. Regarding agriculture, maybe flowers and coffee will be the main crops. Sugar and pineapple [are] shaky as all hell. We don't have to import a single pound of vegetables; we can grow them here. We need a selling program to get people to understand that anything grown in Hawai'i can be just as good as something grown in California. Some years ago I was told by Henry Walker, head of American Factors (Amfac), that on 5,000 acres you could grow every vegetable we eat in the State of Hawai'i. There are now about 200,000 acres of choice land held by agriculture. Another thing is that farming is not labor-intensive, so it won't take care of the *labor* situation.

The one thing we have here is our weather. There's no place on earth that can match our weather. That's what we sell. If those hotels would pack up and leave, it would be a complete disaster.

**Liana
Petranek**

A flight attendant with Hawaiian Airlines and a Ph.D. candidate at the University of Hawai'i; forty-something.

My mother used to say I was obsessed with equality. From the age of two or three, I had to have the same clothes as my sister. If our ribbons were not the same length, I would have a fit. And it became an obsession when I started counting the peas on the plates to make sure that I got the same amount as my sister did. I was always concerned about equality, and I guess all kids are. When my nieces would come over, if I give something to one and not the other, they would scream, "It's not fair, it's not fair!" So you know, it's something that everyone has in them, but I guess I was a little overboard.

My real father was Filipino. I never met him because my mother said that he died in the war. My mother was from New York City and she came to Hawai'i right after the war and married my stepfather, a construction worker, who was pure Hawaiian from Waipi'o Valley on the Big Island. He came from a family that had an *ahupua'a* in Waipi'o Valley, from the mountain to the ocean. His mom had a caretaker for the property. He asked her to sign some papers for the taxes and stuff like that. Later on, they found out she had signed the property to him. Nobody knew how to handle the white men's law. So they lost everything. That's the story, the *mana'o,* of a lot of Hawaiian people who lost out on their land. My father would just say, "Well, it's hard luck, you know." But it was the greed and chicanery of those who came here and exploited the local people.

My stepfather only had a second grade education, but he worked really hard for us. I always loved and respected him for how much he put out to support us. Since he was a construction worker, sometimes he would work and sometimes not. Plus, we were always sick and had so many bills. My sister and I were asthmatic and my younger sister used to get convulsions all the time. It was really hard for our mom and for us. Once, lumber flew off the truck my father was driving and hit a car. He had nothing to do with it; he was hauling the lumber for a friend. They garnished his salary for ten years, and he didn't make very much as it was. It was really unfair.

I sometimes helped my stepfather doing yard work. We lived out in the country in Ka'a'awa. One day we had to clean the yard for people who lived right in front of us. A lot of rich people had their country homes in Ka'a'awa because it's a beautiful spot on the windward side of O'ahu. The mountains are right close to the ocean and the scenery and landscape are just really awesome. This woman who lived right on the beach—she always came to Ka'a'awa during the weekend—asked my father to peel a huge pile of coconuts that were in the corner of the yard. She apparently had found a buyer for the coconuts. My father worked like a horse husking them with the pick axe, perspiring, perspiring. We were all excited because we were really poor and we badly needed money. I said, "Daddy, you know, we can get at least 25 cents for these coconuts." Then we called the lady and told her we were finished. She came over and said, "Well, how much do you want for the coconuts?"

And he said, "Well, 25 cents a coconut is fair."

And she said, "Twenty-five cents? I'm only going to give you a nickel."

He didn't know what to say because my father was not articulate. He only had a second grade education, and he didn't know how to express himself and demand what he wanted. He hadn't had practice interrelating with people on that kind of level. Hawaiian people are more laid back and they don't like to argue with people about stuff like that. They're not integrated into the mechanics of the capitalist system. So he was so embarrassed to have to bargain with her about that. Finally he said, "No, that's too little bit."

And then she said, "Okay, I'll give you 10 cents."

And he said, "Oh."

And then I said, "Daddy, you should get at least 25 cents for those coconuts."

She looked at me and smiled, you know, and then said, "No, I'm not going to give you 25 cents. I'm only going to give you 10 cents."

My father didn't know what to say, so then he said, "Okay."

We both were just so devastated because we really needed that money, and he had worked so hard.

She was rich. They lived on the beach side in a fabulous house, and she was exploiting my father for 15 cents. I know she was going to sell those coconuts for at least 50 cents out on the market. I was really upset and I said, "Daddy, you should have told her to give you 25 cents."

And he said, "Just be quiet." I know he was defeated and felt really bad. And I felt bad for him too, because he wasn't able to stand up for his rights. That taught me the value of labor and how labor creates value. If my father had not husked all those coconuts, she wouldn't have anything. She wouldn't have any profit from the coconuts because my father's labor created that value for her to sell those coconuts on the market.

When I was about seven years old, I read this book called *Ramona*. It was about this Spanish girl who lived on a hacienda with her grandmother. She fell in love with this handsome Indian guy who used to clean the yard. She used to hear him singing. And then they got together, fell in love, and they got married. Then the story talks about how she got ostracized from her family and how difficult their life together was and how they were discriminated against and how the white cowboys would give them a hard time and persecute them. I was so upset about that book. I think Alejandro, her husband, was killed because he was trying to defend something and she was left alone with the baby. So that really stayed with me and I became more aware of inequality and prejudice.

My mother used to always get books from the bookmobile. It would come once a month and that was her only source of reading. She used to finish like one or two books in a day. She made us use our library cards to get books for her. She was allowed to have eleven books, and my sister Leilani had eleven books, and I had eleven books, so she would have enough for the month.

My mom and my stepfather never got along because there was such a great gap in their educational background and intellect. My father had just two years of school, though he had good practical common sense. But he could not communicate with my mom, who was almost a genius. She graduated when she was sixteen and had a four-year scholarship to Hunter College in New York. She was a gifted poet who wrote the most beautiful poetry that I've ever read. She was also an authority on Hawaiiana, because she would read all the things about Hawai'i's history and culture.

There were a lot of Hawaiian families in that area, so I grew up like a local Hawaiian kid. My younger sister is half Hawaiian. Most of the people we related to in that area were Hawaiian, Japanese, or Portuguese. We would go to our friends' houses and eat with them, and do things with them. It was really Hawaiian style, you know. That's how I became acculturated in the Hawaiian values of always sharing everything that you have. It was just the way they were. And then when they came to my house and my mom would say, "Okay, we're having dinner now, you have to go," I would just die, because it was never like that at their house. It was really embarrassing for me. She had different ways of doing things and thinking about things. It wasn't the typical Polynesian way of life.

When I was about thirteen my mom got fed up with Ka'a'awa because she thought it was getting too crowded. She decided she wanted to go to Moloka'i, where we were going to try and get a Hawaiian homestead lot. Under the Hawaiian Homestead Act, my father was entitled to get a homestead. Though he waited all his life, he didn't get one until he was almost sixty years old, just before he died. But at that time, he was out of work so he couldn't take out a loan to build a house on a homestead lot. The authorities had one excuse after another not to award the Hawaiians their homestead lots. We waited for years and years, and I remember my mom going to the office downtown and checking up on it all the time.

My mom and father were kind of splitting up. He was having a hard time, so he couldn't send us money. We didn't have any money coming in, so the Filipino families that lived in the area used to put eggs on our door and give us vegetables and stuff like that. They were really good to us.

We lived next to a Filipino family that used to take care of us, actually. The woman next door used to have me call her "Nana" and call her husband "Tata," which means something like aunty or uncle in Filipino. They wanted to kind of become family. They didn't have any kids. She used to take me up to the camps all the time where she would sell *kankaneng*, a sort of Filipino *mochi* rice. I used to help her sell it, and she would give me an allowance. We used to visit all these Filipino guys in the camps, and they were really nice and always generous. They liked us to come and visit because they were really lonesome and isolated from their families in the Philippines. It was a real sad situation, because most of them were unmarried. They were put into these camps and only a few of them were able to find mates and have a normal life. It was almost like genocide of a whole generation of people.

I never had a new dress until I was thirteen years old. This Hawaiian cowboy, Unea, used to take me riding with him up in Hoʻolehua, where they used to round up the cattle. He got me a new dress for helping them out, and I was so thrilled. That was the only time I ever had anything new.

Because my mom and father were divorced and she didn't have any income, I had to work when I was sixteen years old every day after school. So I never went to any football games or dances or had any activities at all. I worked seven evenings a week until 9:00 P.M. at the airport post office and would then catch the bus to Waikīkī where I lived. I didn't have very much time to study, but I was able to keep up with everything. I was in the top 10 percent of my class of seven hundred people at McKinley High School. I was offered a scholarship from the Ala Moana Lions Club, so I thought, Oh well, might as well go to college. So then I went to the University of Hawaiʻi.

I guess I became politically aware of things when I went through some revolutions in thinking in college. My mother grew up during the McCarthy era and was a rabid anticommunist. She brainwashed us about Communism. Then too, she was a devout Catholic and I used to go to church every Sunday and do all the things that good Catholics do. I was strongly influenced by the priest talking about the Vietnam War, and communists in Southeast Asia trying to take over everything, and the domino theory, and how they didn't believe in God, and were devils, and all this kind of typical stuff. I was very anticommunist in my late teens.

I remember while at the university I took a class in political science, and we all had class assignments. The professor assigned me to do a report on the Marxist conception of alienated labor. I read *Marx's Concept of Man,* by Erich Fromm, which really was a revolution for me in thinking. Everything that I had read or that my mother and the priest had told me about communists was completely different from what I read in this book. I was just amazed. It taught me a lot of things about man, his existence, his relationship to society, and the importance of work in man's activity. Marx said, in a capitalist system, man's work is alienated labor because the products of labor are not an expression of yourself that help you realize yourself as a human being. They are expropriated by a capitalist who extracts surplus value from them. Those who are not involved in self-fulfilling activity—in which their labor is fruitful and an expression of their individuality—are alienated human beings. They become depressed and develop psychological problems because their humanity is repressed. So that was an eye-opener for me. I reflected on the incident of my father working on the coconuts, and his labor that created the value that was expropriated by the capitalist woman.

Did you want to become an activist at this point?

Yeah, that was like a turning point for me. I realized that I had to become active and do things to improve society. Marx said something like, "No one society or group of societies own the globe. We are only possessors or fiduciaries, and as bonafide patrias we have the responsibility to leave the earth in a better condition than how we found it." And this relates to ecology as well as development of the forces of production and the relations of production.

I also read another book that had a lot of impact on me: Krishnamurti's *Think on These Things*. A lot of it was sort of spiritual, which I couldn't relate to because I had been going through some revolutions on Catholicism. I was becoming more and more aware of the contradictions within the Catholic Church, like "thou shalt not kill," while it was condoning the war in Vietnam. That, and other contradictions, made me disillusioned with Catholicism. It took me many years to extricate myself from it. When you have this imprinting from an early age, it stays with you and it's really difficult to free yourself.

All of these things were happening to me in the late '60s and early '70s. I wanted to become active and involved with causes that I thought were right. I became somewhat involved in the antiwar movement and the Protect Kahoʻolawe ʻOhana movement. I had taken a course called "Man and Society" from Jim Douglas, and he was very involved—along with Jim Albertini—in the antiwar movement. He went to Hickam Field and poured his blood on the files as a gesture of protest about what was happening in Vietnam. The day before he went to Hickam we discussed it in class. He knew he would get arrested for doing that, but he was willing to put himself on the line. These kinds of things had a great impression on me.

I did all kinds of stuff, as much as I could, because I had come to an awakening and I wanted to be active in anything that I could participate in. An activist, John Kelly, once came to our oceanography class. He was concerned about what was happening with development in Waikīkī and all over the island, how they were taking sand from the shoreline and ruining the surfs. That made me environmentally conscious. Growing up in Kaʻaʻawa, I spent my time at the ocean or in the mountains, so I loved and appreciated nature. It was part of my life. So many things happening at one time: the war in Vietnam, the Protect Kahoʻolawe movement, environmental concerns.

When I was twenty-one, one of the most important influences in my life—if not *the* most important influence in my life—was Brahim, whom I married when I was twenty-six. He is a Palestinian, and so his story was similar to the Native Hawaiians in Hawaiʻi. It's the story of a people who had been dispossessed and struggling against the genocidal policies of a colonizing power. There were irresistible things about him, especially his honor and dignity. He taught me a lot about love and understanding and patience and determination. He is my "comrade-at-arms."

When I was in my early twenties, I got a part-time job with Hawaiian Air as a flight attendant. That kind of gave me a little bit more time for school, and I was able to get more money for my labor. Right after I got my B.A., the union—the Association of Flight Attendants—went into negotiations with the company. I had spoken with the negotiating committee about a lot of things and they wanted me to join the committee, which I did. One important thing we got in the contract was that the company shall not discriminate because of a person's religion or sex. I wanted to add *political* beliefs, but we compromised and made it *social* beliefs. They didn't want political beliefs because a flight attendant is someone who is not supposed to be an activist. Anyway, I thought I'll be covered under the contract if they had any ideas about getting me fired because they didn't like what I was doing. I was involved with the union for nearly twenty years, negotiating and organizing as vice chairperson, and four years as the president of the local for the Honolulu base.

I also became actively involved for about six years with the United Filipino Council of Hawaii (UFCH) as their social action committee chairperson. I got them to support legislation and resolutions. We worked in different organizations within the community to try and get affirmative action in the hiring of Filipinos. We worked to end discrimination against Filipinos by the Immigration and Naturalization Service. We were their watchdogs. We worked with new immigrants or people who were here for a long time but didn't know how to go through the procedures of getting federal or State assistance.

I also got the UFCH to support the United Public Workers when they were on strike. This was something really out of character for them because it's a bourgeois organization—mostly businessmen and stuff like that. I would talk about the necessity of supporting the strike, and put them on the spot. I used to get a lot of surprisingly progressive resolutions passed from that organization. Every year I came up with a list of things that we wanted the Legislature to pass. I would get a lot of information from people who were involved in activist movements in Hawai'i, from housing to unions to the environment. I'd send it to all of the legislators with a cover letter that said, "United Filipino Council of Hawai'i is an umbrella organization that represents 135 different local Filipino groups in Hawai'i." We had people in the Council from each island and each district. They represented the majority of the Filipino population of Hawai'i, which comprised about 14 percent of the population in Hawai'i at that time. I was able to do a lot of progressive work in the community on social, political, and environmental concerns. In the UFCH I had a forum to help educate Filipino people about these kinds of things.

After that, I became involved with the Kokua Council for Senior Citizens. I was the assistant editor of their newsletter, and Brahim was the editor at that time. I became the co-chair of the housing committee that wanted to get a rent-control law passed. I did a lot of research on different rent-control laws that already existed in the United States. We put together a package for a bill, and got Rod Tam and Neil Abercrombie to introduce it. We did testimony in the Legislature in support of it. We tried in two legislative sessions to get a rent-control law for Hawai'i. We never got past committee. So many people are against rent control, especially in the State Legislature, because they represent the interests of the landlord class. But it was a good try.

Throughout the 1980s I was concerned about what was going on in the airline industry, because for the first time in our history we had to confront a situation where we were asked to take concessions in our contract. With our initial concessions, I calculated we lost about $700 a month, which put us back about fifteen years in labor gains. When I ran for president of the Honolulu local in 1986, I was always anticoncessions. To me, concessions are antagonistic contradictions between capital and labor, with capital trying to extract as much profit as they can, and labor suffering. I wanted to protect as much as possible of what we had won in the past.

I also became involved on a national scale with a group called National Rank and File Against Concessions (NRFAC). The economy was going down the tubes and everybody in the transportation industry was being affected. One of the organizations in NRFAC was Meatpackers Local P9 in Minnesota, which was struggling against the Hormel factories. So we kind of rallied around their cause and even had people from Local P9 come to Hawai'i to let people know what was going on. Many progressive union leaders from all over the country were concerned about concessions. Our initial meeting was in Chicago. We tried to form an organization which could support other unions that were out on strike and fighting concessions. Some of the unions were just small locals, and they needed national support.

We had adopt-a-family programs, where union families would adopt another family and send them money every month so that they could withstand the strike. We adopted a family in Minneapolis and sent them $50 a month for over a year. We tried our best to get different unions mobilized against what was happening throughout the country, but that was a really difficult struggle. Unless people are directly affected, they have a tendency to not want to get involved. Also, union consciousness was not like what it used to be, and union membership has decreased over the years to about 16 percent of the workforce now.

When I lost the last election in my local, I said, Well, this is a good opportunity for me to go back to school and do a Ph.D. in political science. I finished my course work in three semesters. Now I'm writing my dissertation on how consolidation and centralization in the airline industry affected labor. I'm using all my past experience, along with the information and data that I accumulated between 1980 and 1990, when deregulation occurred and had the most impact on the labor movement.

During the early 1980s a lot of progressive people were concerned about the effects that the Reagan budget cuts would have on the people in Hawai'i. We all got together and formed an organization called Hawai'i Coalition Against the Federal Budget Cuts, which included people like John Radcliffe, Patsy Mink, Gary Gill, and Ah Quon McElrath. We tried to figure out what we could do to stop the cuts and educate the community about the effects this would have on programs like Head Start and housing. We put together a slide show and took it to the unions and community organizations to try to mobilize action. We also did demonstrations.

Now we're looking at all the casualties of the Reagan era: the homeless, the unemployed, the deterioration of the welfare system. Everything is just really a sad situation. People weren't motivated enough to do anything about it, because it wasn't directly affecting them. It's hard to get them to actually take action against what's going on.

In 1986 we residents at Queen Emma Gardens were informed that management wanted to raise the rent by 25 percent. People were outraged. These buildings were built for moderate-income housing. Twenty-six years ago they had received a special interest rate from the federal government to build this complex. They had to relocate a lot of the people who were living on this land. They also got a special consideration from State zoning. There was an understanding that if people wanted to move back here after it was built, it would be at a reasonable rate. Because these buildings were "subsidized" by the federal government, there was a provision that rents would not increase except for operational cost increases. So when we got these rent-increase letters from the trust company, we organized the Queen Emma Gardens Tenants Association and elected representatives from each of the three buildings. I made a motion to formulate a steering committee so we would have a representative mechanism to deal with the trust company. We're trying to negotiate with the city and the State to get the building condemned so that we can have a housing project here where rents are kept moderate, as they were intended.

I was also involved in another housing organization called the Consumer Housing Task Force. Honolulu is being developed by these multinational corporations and big business interests. They try to get special zoning considerations from the City Council in order to build these huge condominiums. Our position was that when a developer is granted developing rights within a community, he should give something back to the community. We wanted a 10 percent low- and moderate-income housing allotment within the building so that the developer could not just build a luxury condominium. We did testimonies in the City Council about the necessity of having a law passed because housing is out of the reach of most of the local people here in Hawai'i. The bill was not passed, however. Some developers were willing to voluntarily make that consideration in order to get a speedy approval of their building permit request. We tried to put it to the media as much as possible to make people more socially concerned about the issues.

What do you think are the top priorities for action in the future?

I think we're living in an age when more and more people are going to be put out of work. This has to do a lot with the qualitative changes that have occurred due to the electronics revolution. In the national economy, there is no place where these workers can be absorbed. Manufacturing is going down the tubes. So much is being made outside of the United States because capitalists found it more profitable to invest in factories in Mexico, Taiwan, the Philippines, and Korea, where labor is really cheap. There is no place in the economy where the worker can be productive and survive.

A system that cannot feed its slaves is bankrupt. We have to start looking at the capitalist system and think about what is necessary in order to change the relations of production so that we can have a better society that takes care of all the people. But I don't think the capitalist system is capable of doing that. We need to make some real structural changes in the economy. Otherwise, things will get worse and worse. Because electronics is taking over a lot of the jobs, we're going to have to look at ways in which people can still be taken care of even if they aren't fully employed. Workers would have to get, for instance, the same amount of pay for four hours of work, thus allowing more people to work and have more leisure. Of course, that means that the capitalists are not going to be able to make the kind of profit that they want.

People must recognize that government has a responsibility to take care of this situation and elect leadership that is capable of making these changes. In order to make these changes, the people are going to have to be mobilized. But people won't be mobilized unless there are objective conditions that motivate them to become mobilized. What kind of an organization would be capable of mobilizing people to make these changes within society? I think it must be something that is involved with survival. I think the survival movement will be an area in which people would be able to come together who are concerned about homelessness, welfare rights, unemployment, and so forth. They need a common program that would address the interests and concerns of all these people who have been dispossessed by the system. It could be a mass movement under a certain umbrella, a coalition of organizations. It would have to have a structure for people to work together and have duties, responsibilities, and discipline in order to carry out a common agenda that people could rally around. Whatever form it takes, it would have to be an organization that would address the survival issues of society.

John Witeck

Assistant Oahu Division director of the United Public Workers; forty-something in age.

I work for the United Public Workers labor union, and have tried to be an activist on land and labor issues, Hawaiian community issues, and issues of international solidarity.

I was born in Washington, D.C., in February 1945 and grew up in Arlington, Virginia, which was a fairly exclusively white suburb in Virginia, right outside Washington, D.C. I was the second oldest of seven children. Our family is Catholic. My parents came of working age in the Depression. My mother worked as a full-time housewife and mother. My father worked for U.S. government agencies like the Budget Office of the Department of Commerce. Then he worked for the U.S. Senate Appropriations Committee. In that position, he was able to give his kids the experience of working summer jobs with the federal government in Washington, D.C.

I worked in the U.S. Senate as a warehouseman and delivery messenger person. I worked later for the Agency for International Development (AID), where I learned how much of our foreign aid is spent on U.S. companies and on police control measures rather than really aiding other countries. Then I worked for the U.S. State Department for two summers, in the office of Asian-Communist Affairs, which was the euphemism for the mainland People's Republic of China. In that position, I was able to find out that the U.S. war in Vietnam, which was ongoing at that point, was really questionable and wrong. My job was to chronicle week-by-week negotiating of peace initiatives, and to submit that report to the Assistant Secretary of State. It was the lowest non-clerical position in the State Department—temporary summer staff. It indicated to me the low emphasis put on peace initiatives and negotiating solutions.

I remember when the Gulf of Tonkin incident happened, going to a meeting in the State Department and believing in the mythology that we were attacked. It took me another year there, reading other things, to find out that it was a phony incident, and that the bombing of North Vietnam was unjustified.

In 1965, I got involved in the Civil Rights movement. After twelve years of Catholic education, I went to the University of Virginia and became active in the Newman Club, a Catholic student group. We ran into a very radical Protestant minister who taught us that Christianity wasn't going to church once a week, but it really was putting your life on the line for your beliefs. So in March 1965, when Martin Luther King called for people to come to Selma, Alabama, after Bloody Sunday when Blacks were run over by police on horseback, we responded. We drove overnight down to Selma, got out of the car, and within a few minutes were running from the police who wanted to beat us up as "nigger-lovers." As a white suburban youth, I was acquainted with discrimination against Blacks. In Selma, my situation turned around radically in just a few minutes. After we got away from the police, we had lunch in a restaurant where Reverend James Reeb was eating. After lunch, he left the restaurant. We heard later that night that he was killed a short distance away from there. So, we were in a very precarious position.

We were put up by the Black community, the first time I had stayed in a Black home and eaten food with a Black family. The next day, another white student and myself went into the white neighborhood to find out why whites in Selma hated Black people so much, or why didn't they want Blacks to vote. We crossed the street from the unpaved, no-sidewalk Black community into the somewhat better serviced white community. We were hauled by some whites into a white-owned gas station, surrounded by an angry mob, and almost killed. As the crowd grew, police officers finally arrived and we were able to get out of the situation. The cops said they ought to let the people kill us, but they would give us another chance. But if they, the police, caught us in town again, they were going to cut off our testicles and let us bleed to death in the fields outside the city.

In the Civil Rights movement, I finally found something that seemed worth giving a life for. Since I had an "extra life" from having survived that incident, I decided I wanted to give it to getting rid of racism and ending injustice in the society. I saw that the problem wasn't in the Black community as I earlier had thought. The problem was with white racism and hatred, and the divisions created by others to keep people apart. Later that day I walked as a demonstrator in the small groups that walked separate routes to the courthouse. The police and the FBI were taking our pictures and treating us, the Civil Rights demonstrators, as the criminals, while the sheriff's men and the white police and racists in the community were free to throw things at us and block our marches and throw us in jail. A few of us walked hand-in-hand, Black and white, through the white community. We would see white people go into their homes for guns and try to get a shot off at us. But we were able to get to the courthouse and make a protest demanding an end to police violence and a guarantee of voting rights for Black people. So I survived Selma.

I had lost my liberalism. I had become closer to the Student Non-violent Coordinating Committee, SNCC, which advocated direct action and talked about Black power. White activists like myself were told fairly clearly that our job was not to undertake do-good projects in Black communities. Our job was to go into the white community and organize people of good will to support the Black struggle for freedom and decency.

So I got active in the Newman Club. Within a few years, I was the regional director for the mideastern states, and later became the Newman Student Federation's national vice president. We developed a program of advocating action and involvement, instead of bingo games, socials, and Bible classes that the Newman Club was known for. We formed an organization called NEWCOR, which meant new love, or new commitment. We worked with groups like SDS [Students for a Democratic Society] and groups against the war, and then we came out against the draft and against the war. The Newman Federation was really beginning to change. We also took a position for birth control, and the bishops abolished our funding. Up until that point, we were making some progress.

While at the University of Virginia, I did an undergraduate honors thesis on the Chinese student movement from 1919 to 1925. It was the period when the nationalist students in China, with leaders like Mao Tse-tung, forged a party which became fairly strong by 1925, when it was suppressed in Shanghai. I was fascinated by a comparative study of student movements in Asia and the U.S. So I applied for an East-West Center grant at the University of Hawai'i. My State Department colleagues said the East-West Center was "junk," and that it was just an agency of the State Department. But I wanted to learn Mandarin. I didn't know a single Chinese person. I couldn't read or speak Chinese. So, I took the grant, and in June of 1967 I was in Hawai'i.

How did your family feel about what was happening to you?

My father was a devout Catholic and a Wisconsin progressive. He could intellectually support what I was doing. I think my dad does have a core of resentment against Black people. He does make negative comments, even to this day. But I think it's sort of political schizophrenia in his background. I think a lot of white people have it. My mother was a Kansas, down-home, decent person, I guess. She would support almost anything her kids did. In our family, if you're in trouble, people rally around you, even if they don't understand or agree with all of it. In this early period, I hadn't been jailed, and I managed to get through the University of Virginia with high honors. I was still going along the conventional path that my parents favored. Any friend that I took to my house, Black or white, they seemed to accept and be fairly comfortable with. It was harder for them in the later period in Hawai'i, when I began to get arrested and refused induction into the Army.

When I came to Hawai'i, I understood that the U.S. had overthrown the government in 1893 and that Americans should see themselves as guests here, and maybe unwelcome. I wanted to meet Hawaiian people. There were very few Hawaiian people at the University of Hawai'i, just a few custodians and groundskeepers. I lived in the dormitory, which was an academic monastery. I got involved in East-West Center student issues. We began organizing around the war in Vietnam, to give medical supplies to both North and South Vietnam.

I became the American representative for the American students and the editor of the East-West Center paper, *Contact*. I found out that Micronesia existed. I learned that things the U.S. was doing around the world were not things that I liked done. The "ugly American" had a basis in fact. I talked to Asian students. My roommate was Japanese, a member or supporter of the Japanese Communist Party. Of course, he couldn't confess that to me until we drank quite a few beers. I got new insights and became more radicalized.

I was planning to form a Newman Club at the University of Hawai'i, but instead became the organizer for the first UH chapter of the Students for a Democratic Society. Our first meeting in the fall of 1967 had over 120 people attending. The issue was Dr. Oliver Lee, the UH political science professor who was having his tenure offer withdrawn due to his antiwar advocacy. We organized against military and CIA recruitment on campus. We organized teach-ins and antiwar demonstrations. It was a very active period.

I was trying to study Mandarin at the same time and take my first Asian Studies courses. But I found the UH Asian Studies Department was a major recruiter for the CIA. On their bulletin board, the only job recruitment flyers were from the CIA. So I felt I may not be in the most friendly place, given my persuasions.

After Martin Luther King was assassinated in April of 1968, I burned my draft card. Some of us who burned draft cards formed a group called the Hawai'i Resistance, which had the support of Bette and Walter Johnson. Walter was a top U of H historian. Bette Johnson was a fantastic woman who opened her home to all of us who were standing up against the draft system and the war. I had notified my draft board that I didn't want a 2-S student deferment—that I thought the selective service system was class-prejudiced, class-biased, and racist. The draft board could give me a 1-A if they wanted to, I didn't care. So they gave me a 1-A and drafted me. I refused induction.

By May or June of '68 I had been kicked out of the East-West Center as an agitator. Also, in May of '68, a few weeks after Columbia, we shut down the University of Hawai'i with the student occupation of Bachman Hall, the administration building. We held the hall for about ten days. The initial issue was Oliver Lee. The Bachman Hall area was turned into Liberation University. We conducted lectures and classes all during the day. There were probably one thousand to two thousand students involved. It was quite a controversial event in the media. Around 150 of us were arrested.

This was a substantial action. How do you account for it?

We had made the decision to get the student government on our side. We would run people for student government office, so we would have some members in student government and other supporters there. The faculty senate had decided in favor of Dr. Lee. The student government was also in favor of tenure for Dr. Lee. SDS played the major role of conducting rallies and mobilizing students. There were a hundred or more active faculty members who would assign their students to attend events and teach-ins. There was a tremendous interest in the Vietnam War, and a lot of Asian students are at the University of Hawai'i. Lyndon Johnson was saying the war was for "our little brown brothers and sisters." There was a racist overtone to the whole war, with racial terms used to describe the enemy: chinks, gooks, yellow bellies, yellow peril. It didn't play well in Hawai'i, even in a heavily militarized state where military spending is so important.

I went back to Virginia to tell my family why I was doing what I was doing. I think they were concerned that I was becoming too radical. I had studied some Marx and Mao by this time, and they thought Chinese political philosophy had influenced me. They were very worried. I was flunking out of the University of Hawai'i grad school, planning to resist induction, and facing five years in jail and a $10,000 fine.

I had a girlfriend in Hawai'i, Lucy Hashizume, who's now my wife. Her family lives in Wahiawā. She was arrested at Bachman Hall too. This made her popular with her family *(chuckles)*, as well as myself. They later came to understand why she did that. So we have good relations with her family now.

Then I came back to Hawai'i, and within a year I married Lucy—in September 1969. My mother came out for the wedding. We conducted that wedding at the largest GI sanctuary in the country. Thirty-seven GIs who went AWOL from Vietnam duty while on R & R [rest and recuperation] in Hawai'i were our "best men." We got married twice, in two different churches, because the GIs were there in antiwar sanctuaries. Even our wedding was a major antiwar event. The sanctuary movement lasted for thirty-seven days. The churches were surrounded by FBI, military intelligence, and police. It was like a Bonnie and Clyde movie. To get a GI off church grounds to take a shower, you'd have to outrace police cars and military detective cars.

We did a separate wedding dinner with Lucy's relatives, but some of them attended the church service at the Church of the Crossroads and made a statement with the GIs. It was challenging for Lucy's family to become involved in it, because it had been widely covered by the media and was considered a rather dangerous situation where the police could bust in anytime and arrest everybody.

The churches had invited GIs in conscience to come and make a stand. The sanctuary movement got fairly sympathetic media treatment. The young men told stories about the atrocities they saw in Vietnam, the reasons they were forced into the military, and how the war was an ugly, vicious, genocidal kind of conflict. The GIs came from Vietnam on

R & R here. Rather than treat the GIs as enemies, we treated them as brothers who, for one reason or another, had to go to war. The GIs had more credibility than the draft resisters because people like me had never been to Vietnam. So when the GIs spoke out, with the support of the liberal churches, a lot more people took heed.

At one point, the FBI or the CID (the military's Criminal Intelligence Division) was given an office by the University of Hawai'i, up above the Varsity Theater, overlooking the Church of the Crossroads church courtyard, where they spied on the sanctuary. When we made a complaint to the university and to the media, the university, within four hours, ordered those people out of the office they had rented to them. It was evidently not a popular thing to try to go after these GIs or the antiwar movement in these churches.

A lot of the protesters in the antiwar and Civil Rights movements were young people. There was this attitude that youth were the wave of the future. This was the Aquarian age. It was in that spirit that we organized a group called Youth Action, funded by church money. I was employed as a coordinator for $200 a month, my first real job in Hawai'i. Our offices were at the Off-Center Coffee House, and later at the Teamsters' and Hotel Workers' union hall, and then later at the Church of the Crossroads.

We organized fund-raisers to raise money for youth social change projects. We backed struggle groups like Kōkua Hawai'i, which arose out of the Youth Congress in 1970 to challenge the eviction in Kalama Valley. Youth Action was one of several groups that united in the People's Coalition for Peace and Justice, which continued the antiwar movement and also outreached to the community, to Native Hawaiian groups, to farmers threatened with evictions. And so, organizations and movements sprang up around issues in the community. We had learned that you could shut down every university in the country, but the war effort still would go on. We decided that the antiwar movement needed to reach out to workers, to community people, and needed to involve people in issues apart from the war.

Did you feel that you were a part of a national network?

I had a feeling of being part of a national movement, or even a world movement, and I think many others did also. There were the uprisings in Paris in May 1968. There was an SDS in Australia. There was the Philippine movement's upsurge in '68, '69. Germany had a strong SDS and student movement. All over the world, there seemed to be uprisings. Through the UH student government support, we were able to get funds to bring speakers over from the U.S. and other places: the Black Panther Party, Dave Dellinger, Jerry Rubin, the Berrigan brothers [activist Catholic priests]. We would take them around the community and have big forums at the university. The student movement was sexy, it got media coverage in those days, it sold papers. You would pick up the paper and find movements and demonstrations going on everywhere, so you felt kindred. You felt a part of that.

What was your evolving worldview?

Due to our connection with these people and due to our own studies—we began reading Marx, Lenin, Mao, and other people, and were exposed to people who read political economy and political science—we began to have a more comprehensive analysis. We began to see the war in Vietnam as intentional, not a mistake. It was designed to rip off the resources of that country, develop cheap markets, and push U.S. influence throughout the Pacific and Asia. And we saw Hawai'i as a sugar-coated fortress, a base for that imperialism. Hawai'i was very important to that war effort and to the expansion of the U.S. interest in capitalism in the Pacific.

A slogan raised here by tourism promoters was "One, two, three, many Waikikis." This was a slogan for Pacific development. The governor and the Department of Planning and Economic Development were telling us that big airports, big hotels, and huge infrastructure for tourism was progress. Through this, Hawai'i would be the hub of the Pacific. We would reach out to the Pacific rim. So the design of both the Democrats and Republicans after statehood was to develop Hawai'i as that hub. American capital would invest heavily in Hawai'i. From Hawai'i, regional or international centers would invest and do unto other countries what they did to Hawai'i.

But they didn't really see, or didn't want *us* to see, the damage of that. You'd have to go out into the local communities—into Kalihi, into Chinatown—to see the impact of that kind of development. Of course, "development" was coming out into the outlying areas. Kalama Valley was considered an outlying area back in 1970: little junkyards and pig farms, some pure Hawaiian families, Portuguese pig farmers. Up until 1969, the line on development was, "It's good for progress and will bring money to Hawai'i." The reality was that it was damaging our environment. Hawai'i has had the greatest ecocide, probably, of any place on earth: genocide against species that were indigenous only to

Hawai'i. The environmental movement in the late '60s was beginning to find its voice.

At that time I was in Youth Action and was one of the planners of the Youth Congress. The government had a conference on Hawai'i in the Year 2000, but they had totally neglected young people. We demanded that some money be given to an agency like Youth Action to have its own conference. We were given a small grant and convened the Youth Congress in the summer of 1970. It included 150 delegates from some thirty or more youth groups, from the Girl Scouts and 4-H clubs to the SDS and the Resistance. Out of that Congress came the position that Hawai'i should be independent, and positions against development were advocated. Kalama Valley directly followed on the heels of that Youth Congress.

With Kalama Valley, you really had a landmark struggle. You had the antiwar movement, SDS, The Resistance, Youth Action, all now looking at this small valley across from Sandy Beach, on 'Ehukai Road. Bishop Estate—a huge landowner, allegedly acting for Native Hawaiians, but actually an instrument of colonialization—was letting Kaiser, a major company, have that land to develop into affluent housing. Because Kaiser got major defense department contracts, the antiwar movement saw that taking Kaiser on in Kalama Valley, where they were destroying the lifestyle of yet another people, was a very important way of connecting issues. In fact, the People's Coalition for Justice and Peace did a weeklong march around the island in the summer of 1971 that linked the issues of Vietnam, Kalama Valley, and the atomic bombing of Hiroshima and Nagasaki. Over one hundred people participated. The march linked issues that many people cared about in one package—all aspects of a system that didn't care about people, that put profit, militarism, and capital expansion above the lives of people.

So we united with the pig farmers and the Hawaiian families, and we decided that there should be a stop to it. With Kalama Valley, talk of Hawaiian sovereignty and independence was first put into action with the idea that people should refuse to move, should occupy land, and develop new alternatives for the use of that land.

Bishop Estate officials started the bulldozing demolition on a day when some residents were out looking for other housing or shopping. So we occupied one resident's house just to stop them for that period of time. I was with the first three people arrested at Kalama. The Bishop Estate spokesman ordered the bulldozer operator to knock the house down on us. I was with a woman who was six months pregnant. The

Hawaiian bulldozer operator—a huge guy named Tiny—roared the bulldozer within a foot of the house, stopped it, got out, threw the keys in the grass, and said, "I ain't gonna do it!" It was dramatic. Within a week, other people were arrested. The occupation lasted for over a year. At the final eviction in 1971, mass arrests were accomplished by three hundred police, helicopters, snipers, and the whole works.

The Kalama movement decided that haoles should be tactically separated from indigenous people who wanted to make it a local-people kind of stand. Haoles had a role elsewhere. The media would always jump on the fact that someone like me, a haole, was in a demonstration. If I was the only haole on a labor strike line or a peace picket, the cop would come up to me and ask me what we were doing. And I would always be one of the first people arrested. The Kalama Valley activists wanted to have a tactical separation, to show that this is not outside agitators, or hippie culture, or drugs, or anything else. This was a stand of local people for their local culture and for their identity. So they made that stand. For myself, as a haole with Civil Rights movement experience, it was sort of a repeat of that understanding in the mid-'60s that whites may have a different role to play than Black activists, that we needed to work with our own communities.

Out of the Kalama Valley struggle came Kōkua Hawai'i, which modeled itself on the Black Panther Party. They were able to mobilize a couple thousand people at the State Capitol for a rally. They didn't carry guns or necessarily advocate an armed uprising. But they did advocate Hawai'i's independence from the U.S. And they did decide during the Kalama Valley struggle that they needed to go to other communities. They organized in Hālawa, where this big stadium was being built and low-income families were being evicted. They went to the youth center at Kahalu'u, where many kids had drug and identity problems. Kōkua Hawai'i also sent people to Waimānalo, where some of the earliest Hawaiian rights advocacy took place under Pai Galdeira. They supported the Filipino struggle in Waipahu at Ota Camp. They supported the Chinatown retirees' struggle for affordable housing. Maybe the highest expression of outreach to other communities was in Waiāhole-Waikāne, where the residents of two valleys fought eviction, forcing the State to buy the land for $6,000,000 and saving the farmers' land and residents' homes.

Kalama Valley was lost, but it was a Pyrrhic [costly] victory for the State, Bishop Estate, and Kaiser. It effectively challenged the idea that all development is "progress" and is good. After Kalama Valley, other communities waged successful struggles, halted evictions, and forced the State government or private developers to yield, or to turn over land to the people. Kalama Valley was a watershed struggle.

But by that time, many of us were looking at other kinds of organizations. We had a collective of five couples living in a house in Kaimukī. We were trying that as political organization. We lasted about four or five months. For the sake of our friendships, we had to get out of that house.

Some of the people in that house had formed the Labor-Community Alliance (LCA). Our idea was to try to get the labor unions and their members, and working people in general, involved much more in the community struggles. Our idea also was to build community support for labor strikes. There was a lot of labor struggle going on in Hawai'i then: sugar workers, pineapple workers, teachers, telephone workers. At one point in 1973, around twenty-five thousand workers were on strike. We also did weekly picketing for three years on behalf of the United Farm Workers on the mainland and their grape boycott.

LCA published a paper called *Hoe Hana,* or hoe work, geared toward the plantation history of Hawai'i, around the labor theme. We thought the unions should support communities when they were facing evictions. We got strong union support for the Waiāhole-Waikāne struggle, and for the demand to stop the bombing of Kaho'olawe, a very early Hawaiian and peace movement struggle. The Labor-Community Alliance lasted to about 1976.

I was in a core group that helped initiate and run the Labor-Community Alliance. This core group—the Hawai'i Revolutionary Organization (HRO)—had a Marxist-Leninist philosophy. By 1976 or so, it was subsumed into the Revolutionary Communist Party (RCP). By that time, it had about fifty very active members. The decision to become part of the RCP was not really democratic. I left it after about nine months.

What's your analysis of RCP?

HRO was really the mother group, and had its major expansion before it became RCP. HRO was very labor oriented and community oriented. As we became closer tied to the RCP national headquarters in Chicago, the line came out that everything should be done through the party. The Labor-Community Alliance was an "incorrect formation" because workers should join the party, not an intermediate organization. RCP's decision-making process was all top-down. It was not democratic. If you questioned the central leadership, either locally or nationally, you were said to be "bourgeois" and not able to participate in leadership. If you parroted the line of the Chicago headquarters, you would rise more rapidly in the organization. My feeling is that nationally they became one of the most infiltrated organizations. Locally, I'm not aware of anybody who was a government agent. But RCP suffered from the idea that truth comes from one source: Bob Avakian and his family, who dominated the central committee.

RCP's dogmatism reminded me of my Catholic upbringing. People seemed to need a revolutionary truth to hold onto. Clinging to the RCP and making Marxism into a religion was a way that helped them do their work. The secrecy made it sort of sexy and exciting to some, to have to rent a hotel room and have a four-hour meeting there. It became ridiculous as the RCP alienated itself from many struggles and ended the popular paper, *Hoe Hana,* and LCA, the paper's sponsoring organization. The only people who would come to the RCP gathering would be RCP members and a few close followers. RCP got even more isolated, both in the U.S. and in Hawai'i.

Instead of a large May Day dinner, rally, songs, and a folk fest like we used to do with LCA, RCP events would become prayer meetings. There would be two or three long speeches, which would be handed down to us from Chicago. Someone would adapt them somewhat to Hawai'i. And then the line of the day was to "get the rich off our backs," so RCP would do a march through downtown Honolulu, with its fifty members and twenty-five supporters, to get the rich off your backs. RCP would drop almost every other campaign and take up these Chicago-spawned campaigns. Workplace RCP activists were told on May Day to stand up on their cafeteria table in their cannery or wherever they worked and unfurl a red flag. Some did that at King's Bakery and, of course, they were fired or workers thought they were crazy.

When *Hoe Hana* was changed to *The Worker* and then finally to *The Revolutionary Worker,* the people who would sell it stopped selling it. They said, "It's a Communist paper." Even if they were open to understanding Marxism-Leninism, it was hard for them to go around in the community or at the workplace and sell it. Plus, it was trash. It was full of hate, anger, and political sloganeering. Very little good content. RCP became a little religion, a tight-knit group. When I left it, all the members were told not to talk to me or my family. And to this day, many don't.

Sometime after 1980 I started working with the Hawai'i Union of

Socialists (HUS). I was the editor of *Modern Times,* which attempted to be a political and analytical tool, had some humor in it, covered local issues, and dealt with important issues that the left was struggling with. I had helped form the U.S.-China People's Friendship Association in Hawai'i. I was dismayed by the changing Chinese line, which reduced China's support for revolutionary movements around the world. The Chinese [Communist] Party took the position that the Soviet Union was the main enemy, and China became much friendlier to the U.S.

HUS, I thought, was an important group to counter that position, especially in terms of Hawai'i. For Hawai'i, the United States government is a major problem and an enemy of our independent, creative development, and has been an enemy and a problem for a long time. This other point of view tended to downplay struggle with the U.S. government and its military at a time when the U.S. was still a major problem for the Filipino movement and for people all over the world. HUS also made a contribution in suggesting that the left ought to get involved in electoral politics.

What was the catalyst for HUS?

HUS evolved out of the need for people like me and others to have some network that we could work with politically. We'd lost our tight-knit revolutionary organizations. We were looking for direction. And we had a need to discuss issues and events and share analyses. HUS was designed to provide a noncentralist forum for democratic socialist work. HUS had Christians, socialists, Marxist-Leninists, and anarchists. We saw our best role would be to stimulate discussion and provide a friendly supportive place for people. We wanted a group that was democratic and which would deal with each other as human beings. The major project became Modern Times Bookstore, which played a healthy role in the community for several years in staging forums and making left literature available. It actually became profitable just before we had to close it.

I went to work at United Public Workers as an editor of the union's paper. By 1980, I became a business agent. By 1992, I'd been fired two times and reinstated mainly through the support of rank-and-file members. I was recently promoted, to my surprise, to assistant Oahu Division director.

I went to the Philippines in 1984 and witnessed the work of the Kilusang Mayo Uno (the May First Workers' movement). Almost every other year since, I've gone to the Philippines to attend an international labor conference and to see conditions in that country. It's like being "born again" as a unionist to go and see the Philippine unionists fight their struggles. It's also shown me the role of the U.S. and multinational corporations in that country. As Americans, we needed to deal with U.S. military support for the Marcos dictatorship, and then the continuing injustices and ravages of the Aquino administration, and now Ramos. I've done a lot of Philippines labor solidarity work within my union, within Hawai'i. I'm the editor of the *Philippine Labor Alert*, which goes out to about one thousand people, mainly unionists in the U.S. and Canada. And I'm the Philippine Workers Support Committee national coordinator.

Speculate on the future.

I think there will be continuing economic problems in Hawai'i and the U.S. This may compel public employees to become much more militant. Medical costs are a major problem for all workers, and it's the issue that's causing strikes and contracts to be voted down in Hawai'i as the employer tries to force medical costs more and more on the backs of workers.

Plantation shutdowns, like Honoka'a, will occur at other places. ILWU has not really made it a major issue. I think they need to build coalitions. They need to get other unions involved and build on the great reservoir of public support they used to have, and probably still have. The issue should be that capital in Hawai'i should not be free to shut down, move away, or get away with mismanagement. The State should penalize companies that act in this way by confiscating the land for public or workers' control.

Tourism is in deep trouble. A lot of the hotel plant is running down. The ILWU and the AFL-CIO hotel workers' union, instead of fighting each other, need to come together and build coalitions around the issue of tourism. Many people here don't believe that tourism is our gold chest, like the mythology that development is progress. They see tourism as guaranteeing unstable, low-wage, shiftwork jobs, in which local people are servants to visitors. And almost all the hotel plant is now foreign-owned. We've lost control over the basic economic industry in Hawai'i.

There's now a strong environmental movement and a strong Hawaiian movement that are questioning control over the economy, control and use of land. There's a growing demand that the military's lands be returned. These are issues that, as a unionist, I would like to get our unions to relate to, as well as the basic issues of unemployed and unorganized workers. Who will begin to organize them if not us? Maybe 25 percent of workers are in unions, which is higher than most U.S. areas. What about organizing the unorganized? Most of our unions do not have organizers on our staff. This is incredibly short sighted.

The Hawaiian movement, to me, offers the strongest hope at the current time. The sovereignty issue is coming to the forefront. No political party now can afford to oppose it. The big scam now is to get a form of sovereignty which is really a monetary reparation: two or three billion dollars from the U.S. government, and set up a Bishop Estate-type of organization in which the Hawaiian bourgeoisie and well-to-do businessmen and professionals will control a trickle-down of services and help to other Hawaiians. That's what leading politicians like Dan Inouye and Dan Akaka seem to be pushing.

The other idea is that sovereignty really means self-determination. This may involve a plebiscite on Hawaiian sovereignty that has to include a land base and some form of political power and political instruments for Native Hawaiian people. This is more promising, more exciting, and is the idea that's on the rise. There are now Hawaiian organizations with activists whose roots go back to the older struggles over Kalama Valley, Waiāhole, and the Hilo Airport struggle. These activists are pushing an agenda that includes some political power, a land base, and preservation of the language and culture.

This is exciting, not only for Hawaiians but for non-Hawaiians, in terms of finding new alternatives, like having Hawaiian communities in Wai'anae, Moloka'i, and other areas developing lifestyle co-ops, economic co-ops, fishing co-ops. Some of these projects are in their beginning stages already. I work with one project on the Wai'anae coast, Hoa Aina O Makaha, which is a five-acre farm-aquaculture project connected with the local school. The Hawaiian movement needs to have support from non-Hawaiians. They need to put forth to the community and the unions why the sovereignty movement is in our interest. The left has played both a good and bad role on this issue in the past. The old Communist Party in Hawai'i, which did so much to form the industrial unions, ignored the Native Hawaiian issue. The new left movement and the new Marxist-Leninist groups that came up here in the late '60s and '70s united with the idea that the Hawaiians and local people had something in common, and were being oppressed racially and as a people. However, many of the groups later negated the issue or helped to confuse it.

Now the Hawaiian national movement is probably the strongest movement in the Islands. It was a left-spawned, left-oriented movement, and still is in a way. The non-Hawaiian left, though, needs to identify and discover its links and its motivation and reasons for supporting it. A revived left along the new model could play the very important role of connecting issues and building coalitions, and developing the motivations for why non-Hawaiians and unions should support this movement. I mean, is the Hawaiian movement purely for Hawaiians, or does it also have an international vision? Does it have a vision in terms of developing an alternative kind of society in Hawai'i that non-Hawaiian and Hawaiian can enjoy together, free from the rip-off society that's been forced down everybody's throat?

7

Sovereignty

Some came at the time of Captain Cook. Then came the missionaries, then the Big Five haole oligarchy. They brought annexation and statehood, foreign investments, tourists, and visiting professors. Too many have come to Hawai'i with too much that is destructive and too little that sustains the *ea* (life, spirit) or *'āina* (land). There was nothing for the people. These visitors, immigrants, and entrepreneurs thrust their self-interest and schemes on a generally hospitable Hawaiian population. The result today is a gawdy tourist center, a profit haven for investors, an imbalanced ecology, an uprooted indigenous people at the bottom, with no constructive plan for the future. Like the legions of other "minorities" and indigenous peoples throughout the world, the Kanaka Maoli have learned through distressing experience that their best interests may not necessarily be served by outsiders with a hunger to make money, to produce the "definitive" academic analysis, or to get their liberal or spiritual kicks from romanticizing the "noble native."

With this disclaimer, and being cognizant of our haole outsider status, we approach the subject of this section on sovereignty and its speakers with considered humility. We know that our thoughts and analysis will not appeal to everyone. To some it will be off target entirely. But we must take the plunge because of the intrinsic importance of the indigenous people's movement. We feel an intellectual and political responsibility to try to summarize our understanding of the complex issues articulated so well by sovereignty activists. We undertake this with the belief that people's movements of the future should and will be piloted by those with long-standing grievances that come from their oppression and exploitation. In Hawai'i, this is the Kanaka Maoli.

Like a slowly building tidal wave, the current movement of people with Kanaka Maoli blood to assert their sovereignty and find the route to a better future seems to engulf and absorb more people every day. Unless one is a recluse or steadfastly apolitical, there is little opportunity for residents in Hawai'i to avoid exposure to the sovereignty movement. Issues being raised by sovereignty activists, like the inherent rights of indigenous peoples and the need to envision a more perfect society, are some of the most important issues of our times. The movement is putting forth an agenda for public debate that starts with the current condition of the original people. Since *their* condition is attached to everything else in intricate ways, the movement's call spreads quickly, but not always happily, into every dimension of contemporary reality. People who like to analyze things are obliged to think about the constantly changing relationship of whole and part. Those driven more by moral considerations are compelled by their conscience or introspection. Those in charge of Hawaiian political economy search for self-justification. The religious pray. The professors change their models. The police mobilize. Sovereignty activists are making all this happen. Short of repression by the establishment, we see scant reason why the movement's steadily growing influence will diminish. In fact, we think it will grow and dramatically affect the future of Hawai'i.

The sovereignty movement was emerging from infancy in 1981–1982 when we began to learn about it firsthand. Remnants of the peace and Civil Rights movements were still present at that time, and an environmental movement was flexing its muscles. These activists generally condemned the system for its brutal treatment of indigenous peoples, and offered their support to the demands of the Kanaka Maoli. In early 1995, we were privileged to participate in over thirty diverse Kanaka Maoli gatherings. We also did much "talk story" with sovereignty activists, leading usually to unity, but sometimes to the edges of disagreement. We were exposed to Hawaiian history, cultural imperialism, and contemporary political economy through the Kanaka Maoli mind. Sovereignty activists were engaged in serious study at many levels and holding public educational forums. They were envisioning the structure and character of a "New Hawai'i." New internal political formations were surfacing that stimulated debate. This exposure to the movement's drama, dynamics, and sometimes trauma impacted on our consciousness and therefore our analysis. Without this exposure, we would be much more backward in our understanding. But, as incurable generalists, we must try to place the Hawai'i experience into a broader framework, beginning with the past.

The Polynesian ancestors of today's Kanaka Maoli were indeed the original people of Hawai'i. Equipped with advanced navigational skills, they came thousands of miles from the Marquesas and the Society Islands and settled Hawai'i sometime between the fourth and eighth centuries, A.D. This migration occurred in that era of world history when feudal systems in Europe and Asia were replacing earlier forms of extended-family communism or slavery. It was an era that set the foundation for the later periods of political economy that would emerge. In isolation from the worlds of East and West, the Kanaka Maoli thrived and developed under a "kinship system of chiefly stewardship" (Haunani-Kay Trask, "Hawaiians, American Colonization, and the Quest for Independence," *Social Process in Hawai'i: A Reader*, Peter Manicas, ed. [New York: McGraw-Hill, 1993], 10). This communal, extended-family sharing system seems to have been quite successful: According to some estimates, the native population numbered up to 800,000 at its peak. Most reports say they were a healthy, happy, nonviolent people.

The Kanaka Maoli political economy was likely an advanced version of subsistence societies throughout the world. There was a highly developed and well organized system of nutritious food production which met all needs. This resulted partly from the *aloha 'āina* (love of the land) cultural prescription that inculcated a strong sense of stewardship to the occupier and cultivator of the land. Technically advanced farming methods accompanied by a cooperative organization of labor resulted in abundant food supplies for an ever-increasing population. The belief in a harmony among all natural elements—land, wind, sea, and all living things—formed the spiritual foundation of the society. Such harmony was part of nature and should not be disturbed. Since human beings were part of this design, a communal culture embraced an ideology of sharing material things and a family-like responsibility of one to the other. The word *pristine* best illustrates the Kanaka Maoli society.

The success of such a society had to rest partly on the quality of its leadership and management. It is unthinkable that hundreds of thousands could advance so far without *some* kind of central plan and *some* kind of central decision-making structure to make the plan work. As societies develop and expand, their structures grow more complex out of necessity. As with many subsistence societies, a kin-based and land-based chiefs' system emerged in Hawai'i, and eventually became a royalty-imperial system based on bloodlines. So, a simple and likely gentle stratification system emerged which seemed to work. But with that, one could estimate, a social contradiction emerged in Kanaka Maoli society in the form of a privileged ruling group with great power, however benign its application. The experience of virtually every society since the beginning is that such a group greatly affects the direction and fate of the nation. In the case of Hawai'i, the royalty and the *ali'i* (chiefs) would be later used by the European colonial powers in their manipulations of the indigenous people. Much later, issues of identity, loyalty, and class-based privilege would eventually get on the sovereignty movement's agenda.

The arrival of English Captain James Cook in 1778 occurred when European colonialism was maturing and new nations like the United States were being created. It was at the height of mercantilism, the first period in capitalism, when a capital base for future industrialization was being accumulated partly through colonial exploitation. Hawai'i's mid-Pacific location was strategically valuable to the more aggressive nations who were sparring for its possession, none of whom were noted for charitable dispositions.

Cook's arrival opened the door to vast changes in every cultural and material aspect of Hawaiian life. Wave after wave of "messengers" from Christianity, Western culture, and capitalism, though sometimes well intentioned, operated specifically out of self-interests, not Kanaka Maoli interests. They brought diseases to which Native Hawaiians were not immune that wiped out thousands. They brought their lofty attitude of superiority over non-haole peoples, commonly called racism today. They brought their technology and entrepreneurial know-how, which was used for their profit making. They tricked and maneuvered the Kanaka Maoli royalty and chiefs into untenable political and economic arrangements, few of which benefited the vast majority of people. By force, they stole the native land, indeed the entire archipelago, and later incorporated it into the United States. They facilitated the creation of a "secular" Kanaka Maoli middle class with positions in business and government. For a brief time in the early 1900s, the Kanaka Maoli were the majority of voters. Most went along with haole business conservatism and were key in the Republican Party. Social, economic, and political links were made with the haole oligarchy through formal education in Western ways, intermarriage, and business arrangements (see the statement by Davianna McGregor that follows).

This is much of the legacy that sovereignty activists have inherited and must work with today. Indeed, the several tendencies in the movement seem partly to be based on the different worldviews that inevitably arise from different class locations and group identities in a free enterprise economy. Though clearly different than industrial societies, the Kanaka Maoli people *are* structured into a small class of the relatively privileged and a large class of the relatively poor. This fact occupies the thinking of at least one sovereignty activist, Ku'umeaaloha Gomes, whose testimony follows. It is her contention that whites have perpetuated the unequal distribution of wealth and power in America, a class legacy for the Kanaka Maoli as well.

What is sovereignty and what are the movement's goals and agenda? Sovereignty, we have learned, means many things to many people. As activist Nalani Minton points out, "The word sovereignty is a term which is foreign to our own language and definition of ourselves. Many Kanaka Maoli think in terms of an 'inherent sovereignty,' which arises through thousands of years of existence. The dictionary definition that comes closest to that derives from Latin and Old French, but does not include the variable of time: 'the quality or state of having independent power, status, or authority.' This European derivation, if nothing else, makes the word culturally nonequivalent in translation."

Contrary to the ideology of a growing worldwide tide of reaction, there is no inherent superiority of one group over another, but there *is* an inherent right of indigenous peoples in the world to have ownership and control over the land and resources of their heritage. *No struggles for justice and equality are more important* than those that have emerged out of the expropriation of native land and culture.

To bring this all to life, for twelve days in August 1993 a People's International Tribunal *(Ka Ho'okolokolonui Kanaka Maoli)* was conducted by sovereignty activists on behalf of the Kanaka Maoli. Over sixty organizations cosponsored the Tribunal, including the American Indian Movement, the U.N. International Working Group for Indigenous Affairs, many Native Hawaiian groups, and delegations from various countries such as Nicaragua and Japan. For this first forum of its kind, land struggle sites on five islands were chosen. The resulting testimonies and documentation fill six volumes. Panels of distinguished judges, lawyers, and scholars from all over the world issued a report of findings and recommendations. Among the findings: the United States violated the terms of at least three binding treaties of 1826, 1850, and 1875; in 1893 it openly supported a coup d'état to unseat the constitutional monarchy by use of armed force against the indigenous people of Hawai'i. As a final statement, strongly worded recommendations deal with the recognition of sovereignty and self-determination, the return of ceded and other lands, and other forms of rectification based on international law. Findings and recommendations have been reported to the United Nations, the Organization of American States, the United States, and other nations.

Variations in the sovereignty movement range from mild reform within the system to the demand for independence from the United States. Like most movements, it is *in process* and therefore subject to changes from new information and the results of direct action. A strong norm of democratic involvement and discussion pervades gatherings, which can be openly argumentive at times over goals and strategy. Simultaneously, there is a forceful expression of *nationalism,* that shaping identity which permeates most movements dedicated to a people's self-determination. As the debates go on, it becomes clear that the assertive nationalist "mind" mixes group identity with historical oppression while seeking a collective political solution to the intolerable reality they face. What appears to be personal animosity at times is likely only an expression of political difference. The *politics* of Kanaka Maoli nationalism has taken several forms. Activists such as Lynette Cruz speak of three sovereignty models: state-to-state, nation-to-nation, and independence.

The state-to-state model appears to be part of a larger appeasement process involving the United States and cooperative, upwardly mobile, possibly opportunistic Kanaka Maoli. Such a coalescence of public and private elites has a long history in societies where an oppressed group coexists with the oppressor, and Hawai'i seems to be no exception. A good illustration comes from the current plebiscite initiative of the State of Hawai'i which, through the governor's appointed Sovereignty Elections Council, suggests a "democratic" vehicle for determining a somewhat unspecified future over which the State would have complete control. In public forums on the plebiscite, one detects a coalescence of anti-State opinion. There are those who worry that the very act of voting itself would constitute a recognition of the legality of the State. This may be an expression of movement strategy that reflects an understandably deep distrust of the State and federal governments. The Kanaka Maoli people were not given the choice of independence in the 1959 statehood plebiscite, an official status of impotence like that of the 1890s when the queen was deposed and the land annexed. The history of this period is becoming well known and often recounted.

The Kanaka Maoli did at times attempt to cooperate with various state initiatives. But soon, according to sovereignty activist Kekuni

Blaisdell, "It became clear that our attempts to reform the system, such as through the Hawaiian Homes Commission Act and the Office of Hawaiian Affairs, benefitted only those who collaborated with the colonial establishment and not our 'taro roots' Kanaka Maoli people." (*Honolulu Advertiser,* March 22, l994).

The free market state always has at its disposal a great many honors and financial rewards for buying off cooperative members from a "disadvantaged" group. To use a contemporary analogy, African Americans, while still a largely impoverished and disenfranchised group, continue to have their more "advanced" leadership seduced by appointed positions of various kinds. Persons like Clarence Thomas and Colin Powell illustrate government co-optation at the top level, but there are countless minor bureaucrats who keep the system going as usual and give the impression of Black upward mobility. It seems that secular *class* identity with the oppressor replaces identity with the group being oppressed.

The nation-to-nation approach to sovereignty has attracted a lot of attention and adherents. Using as groundwork the experience of other indigenous peoples like the Native Americans, this model seeks to establish a sovereign nation in Hawai'i led by Kanaka Maoli. Such a nation would be recognized by the United States and international institutions as equal and sovereign. It would control various assets that once belonged to the original people and negotiate treaties with other political entities. There are several popular articulations of this model today. One based on 'ohana (family) identity is singularly Hawaiian, but its spokespersons as yet seem not to have provided very concrete details for public reaction, nor do we know the extent to which this tendency desires broader public inclusion.

Clearly, the most developed example of nation-to-nation is Ka Lāhui Hawai'i, whose spokesperson, Mililani Trask, provides a statement that follows in this section. Ka Lāhui Hawai'i's documentation of issues and goals is fairly elaborate, including a future relationship with the United States, terminating wardship from the State, establishing land trusts, economic development, and international relations.

The demand for complete independence from the United States is expressed in groups such as Ka Pākaukau (twelve organizations committed to total independence), Kanaka Maoli Tribunal Kōmike, and the Pro-Kanaka Maoli Sovereignty Working Group (education and research). Kekuni Blaisdell, spokesperson for these groups, outlines their historical grievances and goals in the pages that follow. In certain respects the most "radical" of sovereignty groups, the seekers of total independence are engrossed in historical and legal research to build their case. They sponsor frequent educational events to provide the public with information that has been withheld or distorted over the years. These events also sharpen the ongoing debates among the different sovereignty tendencies. Lynette Cruz speaks of the educational process later in this section.

A recent sovereignty variant is the Independent and Sovereign Nation of Hawai'i, proclaimed in January 1994. The Nation includes a Kūpuna (elders) Council that acts as a provisional government. The Nation's head of state, Pu'uhonua (Bumpy) Kanahele, comes from "humble" origins and therefore is somewhat unique among sovereignty spokespersons, who tend to occupy more privileged livelihood positions. Though Kanahele was interviewed for this book, the Nation declined at the last minute to authorize his inclusion. After a major struggle with the State, the Nation of Hawai'i achieved a small land base on State-owned land in the Waimānalo district of O'ahu. This unique communal enclave houses people on land occupied by Kanaka Maoli hundreds of years ago. Old taro patches and Kanaka Maoli culture are being revived. The goal is self-sufficiency.

As the movement evolves, it will doubtlessly contain more unresolved issues than those evoked today. There is more than one approach to sovereignty. Multiple approaches become a focal point for what appear at times to be actual or potential rifts among activists. But common blood, history, and values are the greatest bond, and will outlast all others.

Many questions come out of the foregoing discussion, but there are some questions that sympathetic outsiders like ourselves feel must be posed, since we do not know the answers. Does a consolidated sovereignty movement want a mass base? Kanaka Maoli Hayden Burgess has stated that he wants an inclusive, rather than exclusive movement. His testimony follows. Is moral soundness and legal correctness enough? Is the subsistence economy a wave of the future? Are coalitions with non-Kanaka Maoli required to meet sovereignty goals? Do sovereignty leaders foresee a kind of "modern" return to an *ali'i*-type system? What about the religious base? Can the Christianity which supplanted traditions based on the *kapu* system ever be modified enough to fit a new culture? Christianity has been the compatible system of choice for capitalism/private property; if this system is replaced, how compatible is the religion which supports it?

The following six statements from Kanaka Maoli leaders begin to answer these questions. The proportion of their blood that is Hawaiian varies. Their goals and politics differ. Note that women are in greater proportion than men, an accurate reflection of leadership in this movement as well as many others today. All testifiers agree to a person that the current state of the Kanaka Maoli is intolerable, getting worse, and must be rectified.

Kekuni Blaisdell, M.D., professor at the UH School of Medicine, convenes the Pro-Kanaka Maoli Sovereignty Working Group. This group meets weekly in a warm aloha setting involving a dinner of shared contributions. As well as proclaiming complete independence, this group is involved in the battle for status within the U.N. as a non-self-governing territory, that which predated statehood. Members often attend indigenous group meetings on the continental United States as well as in other parts of the Pacific.

Lynette Cruz, Ph.D. candidate in anthropology at UH, is an advocate for the homeless, as well as a fighter for Kanaka Maoli sovereignty. As an organizer of forums on the plebiscite and vigils at Iolani Palace, Cruz occupies a key role as an educator and link between the Kanaka Maoli and the community of residents on the Islands. As part of her nonexclusionary focus, Cruz emphasizes getting to know the Native Hawaiian culture experientially.

Mililani Trask is an attorney and the elected governor of Ka Lāhui Hawai'i. An impassioned and bold speaker for sovereignty, her quotes are often featured in the daily newspaper. Ka Lāhui appears well organized and claims a membership of some 20,000 persons. Recent actions included the mass march on Iolani Palace in 1993 to protest the Kanaka Maoli annexation which had taken place 100 years earlier.

Davianna McGregor, assistant professor of Ethnic Studies at UH, became a proponent of the rural way of life and perpetuation of Hawaiian culture through the experience of her country childhood. Working with students and the *Aloha 'Āina* groups of the Hawaiian community, McGregor seeks to preserve the *kīpuka,* or natural oases of forest so far bypassed by land development.

Poka Laenui, or Hayden Burgess, practices law in Wai'anae, a country area in whose history Kanaka Maoli rebellion runs strong. Burgess very early helped to focus attention and educate the public on the theft of the nation of Hawai'i during the course of a criminal trial in the 1970s. The continuing struggle for sovereignty and self-determination are priorities of his testimony, which follows.

Ku'umeaaloha Gomes, activist in the sovereignty movement, is a leader in Na Māmo o Hawai'i, and directs a recruitment/retention program for Native Hawaiian students at UH. Her graduate work in public health convinced her of class bias and exclusionary bias against the Kanaka Maoli in the gathering of health statistics by the State and county. She is a strong advocate for the impoverished.

Convener of the Pro-Kanaka Maoli Sovereignty Working Group and coordinator for Ka Pākaukau; also a professor of medicine at the University of Hawai'i School of Medicine; about seventy years old.

I'm Kekuni. I'm also known as Richard Kekuni Akana Blaisdell. In the haole white man's world, I'm a professor of medicine at the University of Hawai'i School of Medicine. In the Kanaka Maoli community, I am the convener of the Pro-Kanaka Maoli Sovereignty Working Group, that was founded in January of 1989. And I'm coordinator for Ka Pākaukau, which is a coalition of twelve sovereignty Kanaka Maoli groups committed to the assertion of our inherent sovereignty and independence.

I'm a product of two cultures: indigenous Kanaka Maoli culture and, of course, white man's culture. I was born here in Honolulu. My maternal grandmother, Maria Pu'uohao, was Piha Kanaka Maoli—that is, of pure Hawaiian ancestry. She was a *hānai,* a ward adopted into the court of Queen Lili'uokalani. Because her parents had died, she and her siblings were taken into the household of the queen, where they were servants and educated by the queen. The queen provided her with a piece of land in Waikīkī. That became the queen's legacy to her.

She married a white man, Captain George Piltz, who laid the cable in the Pacific Ocean between San Francisco and Hawai'i and between Hawai'i and Midway. He had to ask the queen for permission to marry my grandmother. They had six children, one of whom was my mother.

So she was half Kanaka Maoli and half white. Like most of that generation, she was taught that this was a white man's world and the way to
survive, to get anywhere, was to learn the ways of the white man. That
notion was passed on to me and my sister.

My father's father was *Pākē*—that is, Chinese. He had come from
Guangdong, Canton, China. As a child I was told that he was a cook,
and he certainly was an excellent cook. It was only much later in my life
that I learned that he was really a gambler and he ran a syndicate.
That's why he was so well known in the Chinese and Hawaiian communities. He married my paternal grandmother who was of the Keli'ikipi
family from Maui. Keli'ikipi means the rebel chief, so there were rebels
on that side of my family. She was *hapa Pākē*—half Chinese—and *hapa*
Kanaka Maoli—half Hawaiian. She also was a ward and servant of the
queen. The queen gave her some property on 'Ōhua Lane in Waikīkī.
'Ōhua refers to retainers. The retainers in the queen's Waikīkī home had
cottages there. That's where my father and his siblings were born.
That's where the Hawaiian Regent Hotel is now, just Diamond Head [a
direction] of St. Augustine's Church.

I was brought up well aware that I was Kanaka Maoli, but that this
was a white man's world and therefore I should not be like my Kanaka
Maoli cousins who lived in rural areas, fishing and growing taro. I
should learn the white man's way, go to school, get a job.

My father died when I was in the second grade. I was at Punahou
School, which was founded by the missionaries for their children.
Punahou was considered to have the highest academic program at that
time. When my father died, there wasn't the financial means to keep my
sister and me in that school. My mother, who always had to work, was
able to arrange for my sister and me to go to the Kamehameha Schools,
which were founded for Kanaka Maoli children. All the faculty in the
Kamehameha School for Boys at that time were white men fresh off the
boat from America. At the Kamehameha School for Girls, where my sister went to school, all the faculty were white women from America.
Their job was to whitewash us, to bleach us, to make us white. And, of
course, they succeeded. A prize was given every year to the student who
spoke the best English. It was also a religious, Christian school. So that
was my upbringing.

There was a science teacher at Kamehameha School for Boys—
Donald Mitchell—who had come to the Islands in the early 1930s. He
became absorbed in Hawaiian people and culture. He was the only
member of the faculty who, somewhat secretly, taught us to be proud of

being Kanaka Maoli, and that our heritage needed to be perpetuated. He helped to found a Hawaiian Club. He suggested that I think of going away to college, which was unheard of at that time, because the curriculum in this school was designed to make blue-collar workers of us. I was trained to be an electrician.

I began to show some interest in biology and perhaps medicine. Fortunately, my mother was able to at least get me started in college, and I did well enough so that I was able to partly support myself and get through college as well as medical school. I went to the University of Redlands in California during World War II. I attended the University of Chicago School of Medicine and acquired my M.D. degree there in 1948. Then I was an intern at the Johns Hopkins Hospital in Baltimore, and a resident for one year at Tulane in New Orleans, in medicine, when the Korean War started.

When I was an intern at the Johns Hopkins Hospital, the pay was zero. In order to have some means to support myself, I joined the army. I was sent to Fort Sam Houston in Texas, and then to a research laboratory in Lawrence, Massachusetts, which was an excellent experience. I served in Korea for one year and then another year in Japan. I tried to get out, but they wouldn't let me. I was sent to Taiwan where I was in the Military Assistance Advisory Group as a member of the U.S. Army in the Medical Corps. I was finally able to get out in 1954.

I went to Duke University for a year in pathology and then finished my medical residency training at the University of Chicago. In 1959 I was invited to Japan to do research on the atomic bomb survivors. Then I went back to the University of Chicago.

In 1966 I returned to Hawai'i with my wife and two children. The University of Hawai'i was starting a medical school here and the dean needed a professor of medicine to start the Department of Medicine.

I've always felt a very strong identification with Kanaka Maoli people. I use the term *Kanaka Maoli* because we are intentionally promoting the use of that term. We consider the term Hawaiian to be a foreign term, used by foreigners. Captain Cook called us Indians in his journal. When he and his lieutenants asked our ancestors who we were, our reply was, "Kanaka Maoli." *Kanaka* means a human being, person. *Maoli* means true or real. "We are real people. We don't know who you are—you don't look like us, talk like us, behave like us—therefore, you must not be real. But we are the real people."

It's the same term that was used by the Maori when Captain Cook and others went to Aotearoa—New Zealand. He asked, "Who are you?" They said, "Kanaka Maori." Same language, same people, same nation, spread over the Pacific Ocean.

When I was a child, the term *Kanaka* was one of derision, something like nigger. And usually the term lazy went with it. "Lazy Kanaka." But we're using that term *Kanaka* with pride today. It's always been clear to me that I was native Kanaka Maoli, and that I was just pretending if I was doing anything else, such as even speaking English.

It wasn't until relatively recently that I have become active in what I call the movement. I was active in cultural ways, in organizations, but never took a strong political stand until 1980. At that time, I was asked by activists like Soli Niheu, 'Imaikalani Kalahele, and Puhipau to join them. They were planning the first Hawaiian sovereignty conference. They need to be recognized as leaders during those lean years when it was extremely risky to speak out against the establishment. It was dangerous. All three of them had been jailed in land protest struggles. I consider them my seniors, my mentors, who helped me to develop the courage to stand up and to speak out.

Through studying and analyzing the situation, it became clear to us that white men came here two hundred years ago, not to live as we do, not to speak our language, not to be self-sufficient, living off the land and sea and sharing the bounty of our nature gods with others in seeking what we call *pono*—harmony. Rather, they came here to exploit us and our land, and that is the white man's way. And that's why they continue to come here. They soon learned that we had a communal land system. We had no notion of private ownership of land.

The haole needed to control the land in order to develop their commercial industries. The missionaries were leaders in that movement and their descendants are those who continue to control our home lands. Hiram Bingham, in the first page of his chapter about our ancestors, referred to us as "chattering, naked savages. Can these be human beings? Is it possible to civilize them? Is it possible to Christianize them?" This was racist.

It was a missionary who drafted our first constitution of 1840, which was modeled after the American Constitution. And it was the missionaries who drafted our *mahele*—land laws—which set up a legal system to steal our lands. Privatization of our lands meant that if you had money you could take the lands, and that's what they did. Our people didn't have money. The so-called Great Mahele was a great disaster, a scheme to take our lands.

Within a generation, almost all of the *ali'i*—chiefs'—lands were controlled by white men. The *maka'āinana*—the commoners—ended up with less than 1 percent of all of the lands, and less than a third of the commoners received any land awards. The remainder of the lands, the so-called government lands, were stolen at the time of the 1893 armed invasion and 1898 illegal annexation. Those government lands were combined with the crown lands, the lands that belonged to the wearer of the crown. Kamehameha III had set aside these lands in 1848 for himself and his heirs forever, as private lands. There are 4,000,000 acres in all the Islands; 1,800,000 acres—almost a half—were stolen by the haole oligarchy. They arranged for the illegal armed invasion by United States troops in 1893. Then they seized those lands and declared a provisional government. Then they declared themselves the Republic of Hawaii in 1894. Those stolen lands were transferred to the United States in 1898 with the forced annexation of Hawai'i, as a ceded lands trust for the "inhabitants."

Around 1920, restlessness in the Kanaka Maoli community compelled the colonial establishment to recognize that, although this so-called ceded lands trust had been imposed in 1898, none of the benefits from those lands were going to us. Therefore, in 1921, the Hawaiian Homes Commission Act was passed by the Congress, which set aside 200,000 acres of the stolen ceded lands, but only for those Kanaka Maoli of 50 percent or more Kanaka Maoli ancestry. That immediately divided us against ourselves. It's clear now that a blood quantum criterion was established to not only divide us, but because it was projected that within another generation there wouldn't be any more eligible beneficiaries. They'd be gone, and therefore no problem.

The 200,000 acres of Hawaiian Homelands were separated, but with no funds to run the land award program. So the commissioners had to lease out some lands in order to get funds to pay their own salaries and administer the lands. Over the seventy subsequent years, less than five thousand families have been placed on the lands. At the present time, more than twenty thousand eligible beneficiaries are on the waiting list. It's not uncommon for people to die while they wait. Less than 30 percent of those lands are now assigned to Kanaka Maoli and more than 60 percent to non-Kanaka Maoli! It's a scandal.

The Statehood Act of 1959 was also a fraud. We Kanaka Maoli had no say in that imposed change in our status. We were not informed of what some of us had to learn only fairly recently. At the time of the founding of the United Nations at the end of World War II, Article 73 of the charter of the United Nations called for the decolonization of all

non-self-governing territories. Hawai'i was listed as a non-self-governing territory of the United States, and therefore eligible for decolonization. The United States, fully aware of this, purposely did not make it
known and purposely set about to assert even more control through the
Statehood Act.

So there was a plebiscite in 1959. But the only question on the ballot
was, "Do you favor immediate statehood for Hawai'i?" The only other
choice was to remain as a territory. There was no option for independence. U.S. citizenship was a requirement to vote in the plebiscite. We
Kanaka Maoli were and are a minority. Two-thirds voted for statehood.
With that plebiscite result, the United States, in 1959, was able to get
the United Nations to take Hawai'i off the list of non-self-governing
territories. Therefore, we were no longer eligible for decolonization.
That was part of the statehood scam, to lock us into a permanent relationship with the United States.

One of our battles is to get back on that list of non-self-governing
territories. The 1990s is the United Nations decade of decolonization.
Nineteen-ninety-three was United Nations international year for the
world's indigenous peoples. It happened to coincide with the centennial
of the armed invasion and theft of our nation. So we took advantage of
the timeliness of 1993. Besides the events in January of 1993, we held
an international people's tribunal August 12–21, 1993, and brought
the United States to trial for its crimes against our nation and our people. Now those two dates were selected purposely. August 12, 1898,
was the official day when the United States illegally annexed Hawai'i.
So we want that date to live in infamy. August 21, 1959, is the date in
which Hawai'i illegally and officially went from territorial to statehood status.

We held the tribunal on five of our main islands: Kaua'i, O'ahu,
Moloka'i, Maui, and Hawai'i. The people on each island not only
hosted the tribunal, they also presented their testimonies of the crimes
committed against them on their particular island. We had panels of
judges of international repute, highly respected persons, but not necessarily people with a law degree. We had a fair number of indigenous
peoples as judges. We invited representatives from other indigenous
peoples who were also grabbed by the United States in the 1890s,
including Puerto Ricans, Cubans, Guamanians, Filipinos, and Samoans.

We Kanaka Maoli were invited to participate in a similar tribunal
held October 3, 1992, in San Francisco in protest of the 500th anniversary of the Columbus legacy. It was an international people's tribunal of

indigenous peoples and oppressed nations in the United States, including Black, Jew, Native American, Mexican, Puerto Rican, and we Kanaka Maoli. We all presented testimonies, and the United States was found guilty of various major crimes—in our case, genocide of our people.

You're not fearful of the words imperialism or colonialism?

No, for indeed that's what it is. That's what the American establishment has been doing, and yet it avoids using those terms.

That brings up another important point. There has been deliberate, intentional, purposeful miseducation and disinformation by the government, by the schools, and by the communications media to hide the truth of this exploitation, and to promote the fairy tale that Hawai'i is a democracy, that everyone has equal opportunity, and that it's a paradise with racial harmony.

But our people in our homelands have the worst conditions. Healthwise, we have the shortest life expectancy and the highest rates of death for the major causes of death, such as heart disease, cancer, stroke, diabetes, automobile accidents, and even suicide. We have the highest rates of infant mortality, complications in pregnancy, and dental problems.

The plight is not confined to health. We have the highest rates for dropouts in the school system. Less than 50 percent of us have high school diplomas. At the University of Hawai'i, less than 5 percent of the students are Kanaka Maoli; at graduation time only 2 percent; on the faculty, only 2 percent. So I'm an anomaly. I don't belong there. The university campus is a hostile environment.

We have the highest rates for incarceration. Among those arrested for serious offenses, we number 15 percent, whereas in the general population, we're 20 percent. But among those in the jails, we're 40 percent, which is double the general population percentage. So the so-called justice system doesn't work for us. It's not for us at all. We have the highest rates for homelessness and the lowest median family income. *In our homeland!* So, in health, socially, economically, educationally, we're at the bottom—and the situation is getting worse. The projection is that by the year 2040, which is less than fifty years away, there will be no more Piha Kanaka Maoli. No more pure indigenous Hawaiians. We will be extinct as a pure race.

Some of us refuse to accept that projection. We're determined that we will not be extinct. We will not permit this genocide to continue. So to us, there are two main reasons for our movement. First is to relieve the painful plight of our people who are on the edge of extinction. And second is to correct the grievous wrongs against us. Morality and law are on our side. It's a matter of just revealing these facts. Of course, the establishment is determined to keep hiding them. So that's why the first step is public education, and that's why I welcome this opportunity to tell our story from our perspective.

As we network with other indigenous peoples, we find it is the same struggle elsewhere. We see the dominant Western powers with their alliance of governments, multinational corporations, and the military not only controlling the lives of people wherever they are reached, but pursuing a course of behavior that ultimately is self-destructive for them. It is based on exploitation of others and destruction of the environment. It's so wasteful. It is based on conspicuous consumerism. All the stuff Americans throw away—food, gadgets, automobiles, clothing—is wasted, while most of the world is in poverty. It's so obviously immoral.

In contrast, our Kanaka Maoli would view it very differently. *(Chants.)* "*O ke au i kahuli wela ka honua. O ke au i kahuli lole ka lani.*" Now those are probably the most powerful words in our corpus of unwritten literature. They're the opening lines to *Kumulipo,* which is the oldest chant that we know of, recited at the time of the coming of Captain Cook when he was worshiped as the returning god Lono. When the chant was finally recorded in the time of our King Kalākaua, in the 1880s, it numbered over 1,200 lines. The opening lines literally refer to the hot earth turning against the changing sky. But the metaphor is one that recurs again in other chants and songs. It refers to the mating of Sky-Father, Wākea, with Papa, our Earth-Mother. Out of that mating came, and continues to come, everything in our cosmos. To us, everything is living: the rocks, the wind, the water, the clouds, the sky, as well as the birds and the trees and the fish. Everything is also conscious and everything communicates.

So we listen to the ocean and we talk to the wind and listen to it. All of these elements tell us things that guide our thinking, behavior, and feelings. Therefore, everything has a spiritual dimension. What we see and feel as physical forms are also spiritual forces. These forces are responsible for our origin as a people and are essential for our survival as a distinct people. Since all things in our cosmos are products of conception of the same parents, we are all siblings, we are all related. Everything is sacred; everything is to be respected, not to be exploited, destroyed, contaminated, or polluted.

So that is our basic belief. We discover that it's somewhat similar to the beliefs of other indigenous people. That is why we share and we give. That is what everything is for, to share and to give, not to take and destroy.

What are your concrete goals?

Our ultimate goal is complete political independence. We know that that's not attainable in the immediate future, but we feel that goal should be clearly stated and always supported as an option. We realize we have a long way to go to get there. It's important that people know that we are already exercising our inherent sovereignty. We realize that we will be recognized only when we compel others to recognize us. Therefore, the process begins by our asserting ourselves and taking risks.

In 1970, Louisa Rice was a taxi driver, a *wahine* [woman] Kanaka Maoli, whose automobile caught fire. She doesn't know how. The only item that did not perish in the fire was a book that somebody had given her to read, which she hadn't read. It turned out to be *Hawaii's Story by Hawaii's Queen,* that is, by Lili'uokalani. She read it and found out that our nation had been invaded and stolen. So she started what was then called the Aloha Association movement for reparations. Out of that came a bill that never passed the Congress, but nevertheless became the stimulus for the airing of grievances in the Kanaka Maoli community. That led in 1978–1980 to the creation of OHA, Office of Hawaiian Affairs, by the State government, in order to co-opt the sovereignty movement.

In 1988, Senator Inouye came forward as a champion of us Kanaka Maoli. He held hearings at the East-West Center on reparations. Several of us presented testimony, making the point that it's not reparations we're seeking, but sovereignty, self-determination, return of our stolen lands, recognition of our self-government. Inouye was annoyed by this. A sovereignty demonstration, led by our people, was going on outside. He called a recess and went out to see what was going on. When interviewed by a TV reporter, for the first time he used the term "sovereignty." He said, "Well, I suppose if the American Indians have sovereignty and are recognized by the federal government, why not the Hawaiians?" That was a turning point. Ever since then, there's been a concerted effort by the colonial establishment to co-opt, and thus subvert, the sovereignty movement.

In August of 1991, for example, Inouye called a meeting of leaders in the Hawaiian community at his office in Honolulu and distributed copies of a draft of a sovereignty bill. "See what I'm doing for you? I'm giving you sovereignty." The bill called for an educational program to be funded by the Administration for Native Americans, then a constitutional convention, then an election; and that would be sovereignty. Nothing about lands. When he was asked about land he said, "Well, I suppose there will be some land somewhere, where you can raise your flag."

So he had already decided and defined the scope and limits of *our* sovereignty. For him, a non-Kanaka Maoli, to draft a sovereignty bill for us! So we had to publicly denounce his proposal. He and Hawaiʻi's governor, John Waihee, mapped a scheme that's derived from the 1989 OHA blueprint to control the sovereignty movement. In essence, it means that OHA will be the so-called sovereign entity, or self-government for us, and it will be under the State, which is a contradiction and absurdity. How can we be sovereign if we are under the State? There has already been a ceded lands settlement, with OHA getting $100 million lump payment, and $8 million dollars a year, at the most. Kahoʻolawe will come from the ceded lands, and then Hawaiian homelands will be added. And that's it—all other claims extinguished, *pau*, finished.

Kahoʻolawe is not habitable land.

Not habitable now because the navy has bombed it. It is a symbol, a token. If Kanaka Maoli had not made the effort in the mid-1970s to occupy the island, it would not even be that. So the lesson is clear: unless we occupy our lands, nothing is going to be done. It won't come about by just talking about it or writing letters and petitioning Congress. We've got to compel them. We've got to embarrass and shame the establishment. We must resist at every level. When the State Legislature comes up with any measure that affects our sovereignty, we call them on it immediately: "You're violating our inherent sovereignty. You have no jurisdiction over such matters. Stop it." The same with the U.S. Congress, with Inouye. Expose it right off. If *he* drafts a sovereignty bill, it is unacceptable, an insult, outrageous. We won't tolerate it.

For the past four years we have had an envoy at the United Nations—Kawaipuna Prejean, who recently died tragically—who made us aware of the importance of Article 73 in the United Nations charter. That is how we came to know about the United Nations Working Group on Indigenous Peoples. The group is now in its tenth year of drafting a declaration of the special rights of indigenous peoples. Hayden Burgess went to the Working Group on Indigenous Peoples and was able to get recognition for a new organization called the

Pacific-Asia Council on Indigenous Peoples. There are twenty member organizations.

Our Pro-Kanaka Maoli Sovereignty Working Group meets weekly. Ka Pāhaukau meets monthly. Ka Lāhui has already established a government with a legislature, executive, and judiciary. We are allied with them. Ka Lāhui is going the path of Native Americans, seeking federal recognition of their government, just like the United States recognizes over three hundred American Indian nation tribes with special rights to their own lands. We support them, but only as a first step; only if the door is always open to complete independence. Our method for achieving our ultimate goal legally is through what we call a succession of treaties. Ka Lāhui is willing to petition Congress. We consider ourselves to be a nation foreign to the United States. Therefore, we deal with the United States at the executive level, not through the Congress.

We Kanaka Maoli have been so victimized by this oppressive system of de-Kanaka Maoli-nization, westernization, and Americanization that we are *hilahila*—ashamed—to be Kanaka Maoli. We've lost confidence in ourselves. We have been taught to hate ourselves, to put ourselves down. And that's painful and very devastating.

Economic dependence makes us *maka'u*—afraid. My own family tells me, "You're lucky. You have tenure at the university. They can't fire you. We can't speak out like you do. We'd lose our jobs." So the plantation mentality lives on. It's a small town, a small community. If you speak out, you're on the blacklist—you're out. You can't survive.

We are also *huikau*—confused. And I know, because I've been through it all. It's such a liberated feeling now to finally get over most of it, so that I no longer feel ashamed, I'm no longer afraid. I'm no longer confused. If I go to jail, I go to jail. If I die, I die. Without feeling that it's fanatical or some kind of religious freakism, it's good to finally find some real meaning in my life and real reason for being alive. It's good to wake up every morning feeling invigorated because there's so much to do.

You're relatively fearless.

Relatively. Yes, I still have my moments. My gut sort of growls. I'm really by nature not an aggressive, assertive person, so I still find it uncomfortable to even speak out as much as I have here. We've been taught not to speak out, to be compliant and pleasant, and not to make waves. So it means not only thinking differently, but feeling very differently, and therefore behaving very differently.

Lynette Cruz

An activist in the Hawaiian sovereignty movement, a mother, a Ph.D. student in her fifties, and a great organizer. Her husband, James Naka-paahu, speaks occasionally here.

I was born on the Big Island where there was little work. My family moved to Oʻahu so my father could find work. Because we were poor, we lived in what they call a project on the mainland. My father was a bus driver and my mother was a musician, and still is. Hawaiians, if they can do nothing else, can sing and dance. You're either going to be an entertainer or you're going to be in the service industry.

My husband James and I were married several years ago at Sand Island Beach. That's in the middle of town in Kalihi, a depressed area, where many poor local folks live. We were homeless advocates at Sand Island, so we got to know the people very well. When we decided to get married, I asked them if they would come to our wedding. Everybody said no, because they had nothing to wear that would be proper in a fancy place. So we decided to get married at the beach instead, and everybody came in their shorts and rubber slippers. There were about sixteen families and a whole bunch of other people.

Early on, Sand Island used to be a point where the imported labor from China and Japan and the Philippines would be stationed [quarantined] for a little while before they'd be distributed to the islands to work

374

in the plantations. Later on, the State of Hawai'i took over Sand Island and started to build it up. Now it's a beautiful park. Local families used to live on Sand Island, where they built little shacks. They believed they had that right. But in 1970 or '71 the State didn't want them there and had them bulldozed. And then it pretty much got forgotten.

In the mid-1980s the problem of people not being able to find a place to live all of a sudden got visible. It is so expensive to live here. It started getting worse and worse. Homeless people, who had been around for a long time, got more visible. Now there were more than just singles—there were a lot of families.

Waimānalo Beach Park became really visible because a lot of Hawaiians were living there. Waimānalo is an area that's homestead land that was put aside for Hawaiians to live on. The Hawaiian Homes Commission was established so that they could distribute this land to Hawaiians who signed up and could prove that they were 50 percent or more Hawaiian. As moneys were made available, this land was developed, infrastructure put in, and people allowed to move in.

So, there was a whole lot of land that was being developed very, very slowly, with very little money to develop it. In the meantime, the waiting list was getting longer and longer. Homestead land is for Hawaiians. In order to stay on your land, you have to be 50 percent or more blood. That means you have to trace your genealogy. If you have 50 percent and happen to intermarry, then your kids are out the door because they don't have 50 percent. There is little money for infrastructure. There are over twenty thousand on the waiting list. So, the people who have been waiting, say, thirty years are about ready to die.

There's a lot of land out there that actually belongs to Hawaiians that's being held in trust by the State, and that land is being rented out really cheaply. That money should be our income for development, but it's not coming in. There's all kinds of stuff going on in our state. Hawai'i may be the most corrupt state in the union from a Hawaiian's perspective.

Nineteen ninety-three marked the one hundredth anniversary of the overthrow of the queen. The queen was promised that she would be able to reclaim her throne. Based on that promise, she gave up the throne to save lives. That never came through. She didn't say, "Hey, I want to be a good American." No, it was, "We'll wait and see, because the U.S. is going to do the right thing." But that never happened. Things are coming to a head and if we don't do something now, we're all going to die. That's enough to drive me on.

If you look at health statistics, Hawaiians are a dying race. Hawaiians are kind of like American Indians. We have asthma and all kinds of psychological illnesses. There are probably more Hawaiians on welfare and more in prison than any other group. We only constitute about 20 percent of the population, but we are 40 or 50 percent of the prison population.

It's very sad. If you actually ask a Hawaiian person how he feels about what's happening, chances are he's going to start crying. If somebody asked me in seriousness how I feel, I will cry because it hurts. So there are people in this movement who say that what we're looking for is a kind of healing. The U.S. took something from us and we want it back. And if they don't give it back to us, we are probably going to die. The whole thing is kind of off balance. There are all kinds of Hawaiian terms, like *pono*—to care for—that describe this feeling.

In 1985, my sister and her ten children were evicted from their home in Waimānalo. They had no place to go, couldn't afford anything, and ended up living in my yard, in a tent. It just became unbearable because our family was pretty big already. They ended up going to the beach and living in a tent. It was then that I realized that she wasn't the only one. There were many, many people living in cars and vans, getting camp permits. No one would know that they were homeless, but just sort of camping year round. You can do that here because the weather's really mild.

One day she came by and told me, "You need to come and see what's happening at the beach." And I went out there and watched people organize. I watched people stand up and say to State officials, whoever it was, "If we had someplace to go, we would go. We don't live here by choice—there is nothing left for us." They documented that in a film called *Waimānalo Evictions,* produced by Kuhi Pau. My nieces and nephews, who were all little kids at that time, are in that film.

So, there I was, looking at my sister and her kids, listening to all of the terrible things that happened like the police coming and beating up the people. Bad stuff happened at the beach. It's all State land, and probably ceded State land, which means it's ours. The way that Hawaiians look at it is, "The beach is free, it's mine. I shouldn't have to have a permit to come here." It's good to live at the beach. It's good for the kids. The bus runs right alongside the beach and everybody can get to school and everybody can go to work. But they were thrown out. The State actually came with guards and packed up their stuff or broke their stuff down and bulldozed it and threw it in all these trucks. Within a month there was a whole new group of homeless people living in Waimānalo Beach, and they're there now.

After a while, my sister's husband passed away with a heart attack and she ended up at Sand Island Beach with her ten children. I became more and more interested in what was happening there. All we could do was take food or see that they could get medical care if they were sick. I spent a lot of time at the beach with them. On holidays, people took turkeys and whatever, and made huge tables of food for anybody who was hungry. That went on for a couple of years.

I met James at the beach. He used to be my minister. I would see him at the beach with his own family. Then one day, the State said it wasn't going to issue any more permits and everybody had to be off the beach by a particular time—just like that. They were going to develop tourism in that area over by Aloha Tower. They were going to make a kind of mall with restaurants and little ferries. They didn't want anybody ferrying across to look at a bunch of homeless folks living in the park. All of those people had to get out.

They started sending down representatives from the State, and here we were listening to all of these people say these terrible things, and nobody spoke up. I felt the need to stand up and say, "No way, you can't do this, you don't have that right." I was bitching a lot. People started asking me if I would speak on their behalf, and would I do this or would I do that? It was kind of weird, because I wasn't homeless. Every time they had papers to sign, I would say, "Give it to me—I want to see what it says."

After a while, I kind of said to the State, "Listen, this is somebody's life on the line. If you're going to come, you might as well come with the police, and I bet you nobody will leave." The park at Sand Island closes at night. They lock the gate. So one night, we were all there and we had sense enough to make sure we called the media. Every time the State came down and tried to harass somebody, we called the media. So finally the State said, "You have to be out tonight or we're going to send the police in." Everybody went to the park and stayed when the gate closed. There was a great show of support. People who live on the beach are deathly afraid of Child Protective Services. They know their children can be taken away because they don't have a conventional home. So here we are, parked next to Channel 9 and Channel 2 News. They're all waiting for some kind of action.

You know, prior to that, there wasn't anything like homeless. Then the federal guidelines came out and there were programs to deal with homeless. Some were the beach people, and that's what they called themselves. One day the State people asked my nephew, "Oh, are you the homeless?" My nephew answered, "I'm not homeless, I live over there." That's very funny. But there are benefits to being labeled homeless since you're eligible for some kinds of funding. Then after a while, everybody became homeless. People at the beach became homeless. Street people who always lived on the street became homeless. After a while, you would find people living in places where you never looked. We found people living underneath the overpasses and in parking lots and any place where it's safe to park at night. There are children, and they need to be someplace that's lighted or where people will watch out for each other. You can't find decent rental housing in Hawai'i for under $1,000 a month. I mean, forget it. A lot of these people are poor, unemployed, on welfare, and can never afford anything.

I went to work for an organization called Angel Network. We tried to pull every family that was at Sand Island into that program. There are about eleven of these programs in the state with funding from the feds, the State, and donations. These groups go out into the community and beg for money. The philosophy is empowerment for the individual through group support. Its goal is to see people get on their feet and on their way. It's based on 'ohana, the extended family, and that's how we treated everybody. When I worked for Angel Network I was the only paid staff member, minimally paid, and the rest was volunteer help. When people came in they were like part of the family, and we supported them as if they were family until they were able to get on their own. Most of the volunteers were homeless people who got helped. There were teachers and other professionals. I know there's a stereotype of homeless people as being drug addicts, or alcoholics, or mentally ill. That's not necessarily so here in Hawai'i. The homeless people seem to be mostly families. There's a lot of single parents too. They all have talents and skills.

Let's face it, there's no money to take care of the poor. Poverty is increasing tremendously, and just a few people can be helped. So we're just making little dents. That's not the answer. Poor people need to realize that if they got together they would have some power. Most people don't want to hear [that]. They're too concerned with getting food on the table and getting rent paid—first things first. So I suppose that's one of the reasons that they really couldn't organize the homeless. Homeless are concerned, first of all, with eating every day; after that, maybe with how are they going to get to work so they have enough money for food for the rest of the month. After you take care of all those other things, then let's talk about what's happening in the world.

I'm an anthropologist. I'm doing my dissertation on homelessness in Hawai'i, with a focus on Sand Island. I'm following the families. I'm finding that something happens to a lot of people who have been totally oppressed, and then get some power. They forget what it was like to be disempowered. And it has distressed me somewhat, because I would have liked them to share their power. There are a bunch of people out there who are not willing to work as a team because they want to lead. We have a lot of chiefs and very few Indians. Some of the homeless people, for example, became part of the Governor's Task Force on Homelessness. These are not paid positions, but they're drawn into the system and all of a sudden they're somebody else. They lose touch with what's really happening. In our State government, we have a lot of politicians who are Hawaiian and part-Hawaiian.

The State really doesn't have anything for folks who want to get off welfare. As soon as you try to get off the welfare, they'll take away your car insurance, your medical coverage, and your food stamps. And so, okay, big deal—you got a job—now you're starving. It's happening all the time.

After a while I quit my job at Angel Network and moved on to other things. I didn't have the time that it needed from me. Also, I tried to figure where the things I've done in the past, like working with the homeless, fit in; what are the *real* issues?

I went to work at Hui Mā'au'au, a sovereignty education project funded by the Administration for Native Americans. It was a three-year program. Money was available to hire staff, develop a curriculum, get out into the community, and do sovereignty education projects. It was the first time ever that sovereignty groups could come together and agree that there should be an educational program to look at sovereignty. I think it did a lot of good, but it took them too long. Their grant is over now and I understand the project is going to fold.

We did sovereignty workshops with a partially developed curriculum. A number of people were trained as educators. I would say we reached about 10 percent of the people we would have *liked* to reach. Originally we targeted Hawaiians. The mandate was to reach 51 percent of those who were Hawaiian blood. The project was to have people come together and make some decisions on what they wanted in terms of sovereignty and self-determination. We didn't reach that goal. I found that if you really want people to get it, you have to spend a lot of one-on-one time with them. The experience was *really* Hawaiian. It was a good way to practice culture which couldn't be separated out from the educational part. You can't really expect that the showing of a video will make all that much difference. It's really not that simple. Hui Mā'au'au was putting out very surface material, not enough to motivate people to do anything. In every workshop, you were lucky to find more Hawaiians than non-Hawaiians. In the Hawaiian community, you have to go to *them*. There are very few Hawaiian communities in town [Honolulu]. They're on the edges or they're on neighbor islands. Holding workshops at the University of Hawai'i won't pull in people who need to be there. That was always the big criticism, and it continues to be so.

In the Hawaiian homestead communities there may be less interest in the movement because these are the communities where people already have land. Why would they want to upset the State or the federal government? They've already gotten theirs. Last year when the State wanted to tear down the shacks that Bumpy [Kanahele, of the Nation of Hawai'i] and all those guys had built up in Waimānalo, people came and supported them. Activists came in from all over, lining the highway, holding their signs that said "Stop Eviction," and all this. On the other side where the homesteads were you had all these people from the homestead supporting the State. There is really effective division of the community.

I've changed in the last two years. I wanted to take a better look at the sovereignty movement and the role of the person who's trying to educate on these issues. Of course, that means you need to be educating yourself. I have been constantly interacting with people in different organizations to see where they are so we can make some kind of assessment. Then, when we go out there and talk, we know what we're talking about. You have to be current all the time.

Then I stepped into a different educational role by putting together panels to discuss an issue. This gives people in the community direct access to the source. Rather than watching a video or reading a document, they can *ask* the source. We found that this is a really powerful way for people to actually get involved. The idea is that as soon as people raise their hands to ask a question, they've just taken some part of that process and made it theirs. It's nonthreatening. I thought our recent plebiscite meetings were really good because they were down-home community meetings.

Almost everybody says this is the period of education. Education for what, for whom?

James [Lynette's husband]: Education is to let the people—Hawaiians and non-Hawaiians—know their true history; the other half of the story. Once they learn this, some will choose sovereignty and want to move off into some kind of separateness from the United States. Others will want some special treatment. The most we can expect from education workshops is to facilitate questions like, Why are we on the bottom? How come I can't get in on the jobs? Why do they give me a hard time at the University of Hawai'i? Why do I have to go through all these hurdles? Some of these things are answered for some people.

Is it your conception that education should be for long-range politics?

Lynette: It is. I have spoken with many Hawaiians, and I say, "If you cannot see your history as extending very far, you probably won't see your future extending very far either." That's something that came out of my master's thesis. When I was doing my thing at Sand Island, I asked the question, "What is Hawaiian history?" So many of those Hawaiians I interviewed could only see their history as going back to their grandparents. Generally they didn't see very much future for their children or their grandchildren. I interviewed people at the beach and talked to people at UH and in different communities. The more knowledge they had about their history—going back before 1778—the longer they could see us here as a people in this place.

We define education much more broadly than other people do. Education is actually right *now*, one-on-one, just talking all the time about what the issues are, what sovereignty is, what's going to happen to us as a people. It has been projected that by the year 2044, there will be no more Hawaiians with 50 percent or more Hawaiian blood. This means, in effect, there will be no more Hawaiians by our definition, and the federal government no longer has to deal with us as a people. The fact that they would actually have this date targeted means that after this date they're making *plans*. Our land will be gone. Use of our resources is being planned for the next fifty, hundred years, for all I know.

When we talk about educating people, we're talking about educating them *right now*. Time is short. We're telling people, especially Hawaiian women, that we need to have some Hawaiian babies from Hawaiian men who are full blooded. We need to have these things documented.

This is one strategy that we can use to make sure that Hawaiians do not become extinct by somebody else's definition.

James: Culturally speaking, we don't define ourselves by blood. We say, "This is what they say you should be, but turn around and look at your experience. Look at the way you were raised." I have step-brothers that don't have any Hawaiian blood at all, but they are my *brothers,* and they have every right to everything.

Do they identify as Hawaiian?

James: Yes, and we treat them as Hawaiian, as family. We're kind of surprised about this blood quantum thing. For me to sit here and say that there aren't racist Hawaiians would not be true. I've heard from the racist ones, but they have to look around, too. One racist once said they should be pure blood, but yet he was married to a cousin of mine who was three-quarter Hawaiian, part Tahitian, and part Hindi. You have to look at the way people *live* before making a judgment. Even the *hānai* [child adoption] system that brings somebody in from the outside is very strong. I feel we have defined ourselves as to who Hawaiians are: If you were born in this place and call this place home, you're Hawaiian—anybody. We have Hawaiians of German descent, Hawaiians of Filipino descent.

Most sovereignty groups would not buy that, would they?

Lynette: No, they wouldn't, because people are operating at different levels. For some, it's an intellectual level, an overall view that is really just in the head. For us it's experiential. How do I as a Hawaiian behave on a day-to-day basis, and does it match up with the stuff that is being put out there as the "norm"? Well no, as a matter of fact, it doesn't. What am I going to do about it? Shall I find the norm, the median? No, I don't want to. This is our life. This is how we live. If we bring you into our life, then you're in. That's basically what it is. When people talk about Hawaiians being really inclusive in their culture, I absolutely believe it because I lived that with my mother and my grandmother. That's how they behaved. So, I'm going to take it from them because it's something that worked and is going to work for me. And I like it. It makes me feel good. There are many people who support the movement who are not Hawaiian, not even a drop. I think it's because they have become culturally Hawaiian. That's what Jim was saying. You have been born here, you're raised here.

Some of the old Japanese women whom we know speak Hawaiian,

for goodness sake, because they grew up in this culture. One day I was at this cookie shop buying a cookie for my son. A Japanese man came out of the store next door and he said to me, "Oh, that looks really good, cookies and coffee." I said, "Why don't you come and have one with me?" He just looked at me and said, "Oh, no I couldn't do that." Then he came back and he said, "I'm so glad that you said that." I asked, "Why?" He said, "Because I lived in the mainland for twenty years, and if there was anything that I really missed, it was *that* kind if behavior. I'm a stranger and you would offer me that." So, he came back and shook my hand and he said, "Thank you very much." For me and for many Hawaiians, that is the way it is. I want to keep those kinds of things. Yes, we have extended our hospitality, maybe to our own detriment, but to me it comes out of our sense of recognizing somebody else.

Do you see similarities between your movement and "minority" movements in the continental United States?

Lynette: I see some differences because of where we are and who we are. Hawai'i is far away from the U.S., and we are indigenous people. I don't think Blacks can claim their own place since they have been cut off terribly from their own history. This thing about *aloha 'āina* [love of place] in Hawaiian culture is something that a lot of scholar types have dismissed, saying that Hawaiians have been cut off from this place for a long time. I actually heard people say that and it really angers me. We grew up here. I know it intellectually and I know it experientially. Some recent thinking in the movement is, "You can kill us all, but it will still be our place." When people talk about *inherent* sovereignty, that's what they're talking about. It's in my head, it's in my gut. It is mine. I claim it.

In building a new nation and a new community, there are not many people in the movement who look to exclude anybody. How are we going to do that? We married them all! We have been pushing for a change in the system so that we *all* can fit in. I don't know if that's possible. Our system is very exclusive and doesn't call for people fitting in. It's about money and power.

We look at all of this and we look at what is happening globally. We look at strategizing long term for the whole world. This is a peculiar time. The things that are happening all over the world sort of coincide with our movement. If you're going to talk environment in Hawai'i, you better talk about including our movement. If you go back far enough, you'll realize we were trying to work within the environment from the beginning. It's other people who came in and whose exploitive acts have screwed us up and have brought us to where we are right now.

We went through some changes in the last few years. When you work with homeless folks and get to know them, it's really about taking care of people's daily needs, not about long-term strategizing. When we tried to figure what the hell is going on, we came to a realization that the whole system is geared for Hawaiians and working-class people to stay exactly where they are. That's the way the system actually exists. Once we realized that, we became full-time activists.

James: Several years ago, we actually thought that social service was the answer. Now we are saying, "Forget social service, we are going to try to attack the thing at the roots." Social service means that everybody gets mainstreamed. They want everybody to be a good American: "We'll give you money, we'll give you women food stamps. You get trained for a good job here and get into the system as waitresses and maids." Now when we do workshops and there are social workers present, we hit on that every chance we get. Forget it! When we finally came to see what was happening, we first had major stress. After that, it was just all-out battle.

Lynette: Then too, we came to certain conclusions about our history. We looked closely at Iolani Palace to find its meaning. This caused us further major stress, mainly because we realized that it represents one more power thing. The palace was built on the backs of poor Hawaiian laborers who actually felt they owed an allegiance to the royal family. Later, they were excluded from that place. They were kept out of the palace and off the palace grounds. The only reason we are allowed on now is because they got State funding to maintain the grounds.

One of the reasons for constantly holding our different events at the palace is to challenge those guys who have arisen within the so-called remnants of *ali'i* [chief's class]. Those guys not only claim this line, but they claim the history and they claim the queen—she's theirs. We're left out as common people *(maka'āinana)*. We have nothing. We didn't even have genealogy—that was a royalty thing. Even though I have respect for Queen Lili'uokalani, she represented a system that was oppressive. My grandparents never spoke to us about anything in history and never spoke to us in Hawaiian, ever. They wanted us to be good Americans and to fit in.

James: People back then wanted their goods and materials, just like now. Some Hawaiians participated in the falling apart and overthrow of the monarchy because they got locked in, too. They wanted to preserve what they had.

Lynette: Kekuni Blaisdell always uses the term Kanaka Maoli, as opposed to Native Hawaiian. Kanaka Maoli implies "first people." It has no room for *aliʻi*. Today, the *"aliʻi"* are not happy with the use of that term, so we try to use it as often as we can to remind them that they were not always here. When people came from Tahiti later on, a class system was created and the beginning of the *ahupuaʻa* [land division]. Many people look at Hawaiian history no further back than the time of emergence of the royalty. We say, let's go back to when there was just *us,* when there were fewer of us, less of a need for a hierarchy, and an ability to live with nature. Many of us are trying to recreate that.

The power base here doesn't want the people to change the system. How is that to be dealt with?

Lynette: What's happening now globally and what's happening here suggests to me that this is a significant time. It is our dream and our hope that at some time in the near future, say within the next twenty years, there will come about a change in thinking. Some people see Hawaiʻi as a center of a new beginning. We see that also. It's for the hope of the world. So that we don't kill each other and kill ourselves, something definitely has got to change. Our cultural concept is that the land is like your mother. Would you sell your mother? Would you abuse your mother? No, you wouldn't. You would love your mother. So, in that loving, you care for it *(aloha ʻāina),* and it cares for you.

All of this stuff that we see out this window *(points toward downtown Honolulu)* is absolute abuse. We think of that as coming out of a Western mindset. It comes out of Christianity and this thing about "dominion-over, "as opposed to "interaction-with." It's inherent in the language of domination, which is the language of the Bible, which is the language of the Martin Luther King Institute. I'm throwing this in because I had an occasion to sit in their workshops. I can't deal with this because it's never about people together. It's always vertical! When I see Christian Hawaiians who think they can actually become sovereign and change things—and still stay Christian—I'm very sad, because they haven't looked back in their history. They need to go back further. They are stuck with the coming of Christianity.

James, what does being a minister mean?

James: Being a servant to the people and also the servant to God. In the first writings if the Hawaiian Bible, I understand that they interpreted it as being a slave to God. Later they changed it to "shepherd." There is a difference. A minister should become a servant to the people, and that may require questioning the Bible. That has produced things like liberation theology and Creation-Centered Christianity. To the dismay of many, I once said, "Gee, that's on the cutting edge." People in South America were just dirt-nothing, with downright oppression, nothing insidious like ours. Eventually the Church had to respond. Who do they support? Do they support what the Bible says to support, which is government, or are you the liberator of the oppressed? So, you see people ripping off pieces of the Bible. You have the Moses types who set their captives free. You've got the New Testament type who says, "Oh, no, we can't do that—we'll just pray for them." Then they become complacent and never politically active. There are so many different Christian movements, some supporting the system, some against the system. Some try to play social worker. Some go to the point of being very militant. Some become an extreme cult, and they all die. They are all trying to deal with the *now,* and they don't know how to get around it. The whole Bible is a contradiction.

Lynette: I think the system is not going to do anything for anybody. The system has placed certain groups in power, and it will always be so. The system needs lots and lots of people and it needs to be big. It's like a cancer, and it will take you because it must. There is never a stopping point.

In our search for models for a new nation, we have recently looked at Spain and the cooperative development that has been happening in the Basque country there for the last fifty years. They have been very successful. The Basques are part of Spain, but don't claim to be Spanish. They have been able to develop small industries and they have their own banking system. They have contracts with people all over the world to make car parts, engines, household appliances, all that kind if stuff. They are doing very well. They own their places of work—it's a bottom-up thing. They are a democracy. They don't have a prison, don't have police, don't have a military, but they are surrounded by Spanish military all the time.

There are three sovereignty models: independence, nation-within-a-nation, and state-within-a-state. We asked Native Americans to come and talk about their experience with the nation-within-a-nation model. We didn't hear anybody say anything good. We have actually said to people, "Oh, it's not working for them—why would it work for us?"

The Office of Hawaiian Affairs came out lately with something called state-within-a-state, which is what we have right now. Any money that comes to Hawaiians will go to the Office of Hawaiian Affairs. They will have autonomy and won't necessarily be overseen by the State government. It all sounds ridiculous to me.

Does anybody talk about the redistribution of wealth?

Lynette: Kekuni [Blaisdell] and Hayden [Burgess] are the only two people out there I know who are saying that there should be a restructuring of the whole system. They say that we need to get away from capitalism, we need to get back to the land, the land and the people need to be the main resources, and there should be an equal distribution of wealth. Kekuni cannot support HSEC [Hawai'i Sovereignty Election Commission] because it is an arm of the State and he is absolutely opposed to the State. When he talks about independence, he wants the whole archipelago. He wants the U.S. and the federal government out and we will basically live or die by our own wits. I like it.

There seem to be several levels that people are looking at on the sovereignty movement. One of them is the legal aspect, which is fine. Legalists look at the law, even though the law is American law, not our law. They may look at the international scene and try to figure out how we can work with international law, even when they know the U.S. actually has a major say in what the international community does. They still plod ahead because they have the mentality of the lawyer. The rest of us, I would venture to say, look at the moral issues. That means we don't focus on the illegal overthrow, but we go back long before that.

Kekuni is looking at the plight of Native Hawaiian health. How come we're so sick? That didn't come up from the overthrow. It impacts from the very beginning. He, and I, believe that all those things were done purposefully. They knew that we were isolated and they knew that if they brought any illness we would all get it. I'm not saying that the people on the ships necessarily knew, but the people who sent them out knew. We're not the first. There's a systematic way by which people can be exploited, especially if they're far away. They continue the exploitation to this day *because* you're far away. Look what's happening with France in Tahiti and the fact that they have not stopped bombing. The French are far away—they don't have to see. There is not a major disaster going on here like there is in Timor or in some other place where people are dying violently. We have genocide, but it's like slow and long-term.

We test the system all the time. We did a solidarity march through Waikīkī last year, July 3, 1994—an independence march for ourselves. We called every organization who might conceivably have an interest in supporting us and arranged to meet with them. There were about sixty groups represented. They all got their banners and marching signs. We went through the procedure to apply for a permit, but didn't get it. We even were told on the day of the march by the police, "You cannot march"—just like that. "You think we're not going to march? Arrest us all." We gave people the option and some didn't want to march. They didn't want to get arrested. The police gave us an escort, but they were not happy. There were as many police as there were people. It was wonderful and it showed solidarity, but I had major fear.

So, the next day—July 4—we did something on the palace grounds. No permit, no nothing, plenty of cops, plenty of plainclothes—the place was full of people. It was wonderful. You can't go to the palace unless you have a tour. You can't even go on the steps. They cut off our electricity so we couldn't use our speakers. What the hell—we went up the steps anyway. Security came and it was a standoff. When Hayden Burgess went up the steps, all of us women went up right behind him. There were people from all over the world taking pictures. It was wonderful!

An attorney and the elected governor of the indigenous peoples' movement, Ka Lāhui Hawai'i; somewhere in her forties.

I'm a Native Hawaiian, born and raised in Hawai'i. My parents are both Native Hawaiian. My father, Barney Trask, whose bloodlines trace to the Big Island, is from a long line of Trask family political advocates. My grandfather, David Trask, was the first Hawaiian sheriff of Honolulu during the territorial period and later went into the territorial legislature. He established a reputation there as being the champion for the underdog. Primarily he fought for the rights of Native Hawaiians, but also he fought for the rights of other minorities in the territory. My grandfather led the campaign to extend electricity and other public services from Honolulu to the windward and leeward sides of the island. For many years, electricity on O'ahu was only provided to the downtown businesses of the sugar planters and to areas like Kāhala and Nu'uanu, where wealthy missionary and white persons lived.

My grandfather also fought for the passage of the first criminal code during the time of the territory. He was very concerned with the fact that Hawaiians were arrested and jailed without ever being charged. They were picked up on vagrancy or loitering charges and held for weeks and months without any due process rights.

The Trask family name has been identified with the political arena for several generations. Not only was my grandfather very active in that arena, but also my father and my uncles, who participated in the forming of the Democratic Party. This was during the time when all the sugar planters and missionary parties were supporting the Republican line.

On my mother's side, our family name is Haia, whose bloodlines trace to Maui, to the land of Pi'ilani [a famous chief]. My grandmother on my mother's side was born and raised in Lahaina, Maui. Later, she lived and died in Hāna, Maui, which to this day is considered to be the most Hawaiian place of all of our little communities in Hawai'i. I identify myself with the genealogical lines of Pi'ilani. My grandmother was a traditionalist, practicing all forms of cultural undertakings, such as traditional weaving. She was a *maka kilo,* a person with the eye to see the fish in the ocean. She had her own little canoe fleet. Several of our relatives in Hāna owned canoes and fished under her guidance. She herself did not go out in the canoes. A *maka kilo* generally stays on land at the highest point of the mountain and watches the changing colors of the ocean, and then, with the bullhorn, calls down to the ocean and signals the canoes where to move in the water so that there can be a bountiful harvest. My grandmother was also very skilled in the art of *ho'oponopono,* the traditional practice for the resolution of conflict. She was viewed as a healer by the larger community. Not only did she provide those services for her own family—her own *'ohana*—but also for the larger community.

We never did have the opportunity to know my grandfather on my mother's side. He died right before my mother was born.

From kindergarten through sixth grade, I went to Catholic school, since our family was Catholic. Commencing in seventh grade, I went to the Kamehameha Schools. I attended seventh and eighth grade as a boarder. In ninth grade I became a day scholar, and graduated in 1969 from the Kamehameha School for Women with honors. Later I received a B.A. in political science from San Jose State University in California. I then went to law school at the University of Santa Clara, where I received a Juris Doctor degree.

In my upbringing, there was always a great deal of discussion about Hawaiian issues and history. This was encouraged by both my parents. My mother was a schoolteacher and taught third grade for many years. My father was an attorney. They had very strong values for education, which they passed on to their children.

We always talked about Hawaiian history in our home. My parents knew the traditional and anthropological history of our people. The children were raised to understand the names of the plants, animals, fish, and the birds in the sky. Though the children were raised by parents who had a strong Western education, the traditional values and practices were passed on because our parents had been raised that way.

Cultural practices were integrated into our family. At Thanksgiving time, other people might have a cornucopia at their home, but we never did. My parents always had a *hoʻokupu*—a sacred offering. A cornucopia didn't mean anything to Hawaiian people. We also played a lot of music. We had guitars, ukuleles, and a piano in the house. And whenever people came over, or at family gathering times, it was the Hawaiian music that was played and sung, rather than the music of any other culture.

We had meetings of the Democratic Party at our home. We talked about who should be elected and what should be the strategies. When you're raised in this type of environment, you're raised to view the democratic process as something that you can access and impact. So, unlike many other Hawaiians who are intimidated by the democratic process, we were raised to participate in it.

We were raised with a very strong sense of our personal identity. We knew that if you were Hawaiian, you had to be better than everyone else because people would anticipate that you would be dumb and lazy. People would put you at the back of the line. If you were going to be Hawaiian and get anywhere, you had to be outspoken. You had to come out and fight for your rights. You had to go and stand at the front of the line. We were raised to become advocates for our people and to utilize the skills of our Western education in the political arena.

I think that I and my brothers and sisters did have to contend with assimilation. To a certain extent, we are all assimilated. I was not raised in a grass shack. I was not raised to go out and learn how to throw the net. My brothers were raised in that way, but I was raised knowing that I would eventually have to graduate from high school, get a scholarship, go away to college, and come back and find some way to make my living in this modern world. We were fortunate to be raised to understand what assimilation was, to incorporate that which was good, and to reject that which was bad in favor of our own tradition and cultural practices.

Although we were raised as Catholics, baptized, and went to Catholic school, we always had great respect for the traditional form of worship. There are many Hawaiians that will tell you that the traditional practices were devil worship and that we should all be Christians. We were raised with an understanding that God created all people in his image. So the religious practices of the traditional native people reflected the light of the spirit of God.

Prior to the Western incursion of Hawai'i, there was a self-sufficient population of 800,000 to one million. We had one of the few cultures in the world that was capable of feeding, housing, and clothing itself, that did not have a Western type of centralized government. There was no corporate body politic prior to the incursion of Captain Cook. There was a traditional religious system, known as the *kapu* system, which set out a moral and ethical code that every facet of society followed so that everyone had the opportunity to survive. As the result of the introduction of Western land law and the introduction of many foreign diseases, by the time of the overthrow in 1893 there were only 35,000 to 40,000 Hawaiians remaining alive.

Hawaiians were evicted from their lands as a result of the Mahele and the Kuleana Act. Less than 1 percent of our population was able to maintain a homestead for traditional people. That was genocide. Their ability to fish certain waters and cultivate land so that they could eat and live was taken away at the very time that Western diseases were taking a terrible toll.

The situation was further complicated by the fact that we were a culture that practiced an oral tradition. With only 39,000 Hawaiians alive at the time of the overthrow, there was a complete loss of the oral tradition. The appropriate healing practices were almost lost because people who were oral keepers of those traditions died. The people who understood the fishing and cultivation practices also died. The ability of those few remaining to continue to cultivate and fish during times of trial and tribulation was lost. Genealogies were lost, so people no longer knew who their families were. They were dispossessed of the land, they wandered, and they were not able to find their own families again. The psychological trauma, of course, was very tragic for our people. This history explains the contemporary status of Hawaiians: the worst health statistics, the lowest income level, the lowest education, overrepresentation in prisons and juvenile holding facilities, and highest unemployment.

I am always amazed when I look at the current statistics of Native American Indians compared with Hawaiians. We have the same deprivation being manifested.

In order for indigenous people to survive, they must be given the ability to control their lands and assets so that they can practice and maintain their oral and cultural traditions. We know that if Hawaiians were back on the native diet, the terrible health trends in cancer, diabetes, and heart disease could be reversed. But we can't get our land and water to plant the taro, which is the mainstay of the diet. Most Hawaiians know that the native diet will heal their diseases. But they can't afford to pay for fish in the market. There are toxic contaminants in the ocean, so we're not able to eat the reef fish here in Kona or Oʻahu or Maui.

We don't have control over our lands and waters. With the incursion of Western law, values, and practices, native people were dispossessed of their lands and natural resources. They became exploited as a labor force and their land was exploited for commercial development. Native people lost the ability to heal and sustain themselves. Right now, some of our Hawaiian families have three generations born and raised on the welfare line, with terrible psychological deprivation.

When we take a look at our history and our current status, it is incumbent upon us to create a solution for our current situation. One way is the Band-Aid approach, like creating service programs and encouraging assimilation. But after one hundred years, it's plain to see that this approach has not worked. The real question we have to ask ourselves is, What do we have to have in order to survive in this day and age? The answer to that is self-determination and sovereignty.

The Hawaiian situation is pretty simple. In all of the other states of the union, America recognizes the right of indigenous people to control their lands and to establish their own governments within the context of the United States Constitution. That fundamental human and civil right has never been extended to Hawaiians.

In 1920, Congress created a Hawaiian Homes Commission Act which set aside 203,000 acres in the Hawaiian Homestead Trust for the exclusive purpose of settling our people on homesteads. In seventy-two years, less than 7,000 families have ever received Hawaiian homestead awards. Thirty thousand families have died waiting, and we have a current waiting list of 24,000 families. Where are the Hawaiian home lands? Why, they're being used and developed by the State for public projects, airports, schools, and flood control, but not for Native Hawaiians. Thousands of our acres set aside for homesteading are being utilized by the U.S. military for Star Wars launching facilities, toxic dumps, and military training bases. An article from the *Wall Street Journal* said that many non-Hawaiians with political connections to the Democratic Party have received Hawaiian home lands awards.

In 1959, when Hawaiʻi became a state, Congress created the second and much larger trust for the Hawaiian people, the Hawaiian Home Lands Trust, with 1,400,000 acres of State land to be held in trust for the public as well as to better the conditions of Native Hawaiians. By 1992, we have never seen a single acre of land set aside specifically for native people, nor have we seen a single dollar of the trust revenues allocated for Hawaiians.

Given this history over our lands, the solution today is sovereignty. We must have the right as native people to create our own government. We must segregate our lands from the public holding and wrest away the control and jurisdiction over our lands from the State. We must give the lands to the native nation so that we can actually begin to develop and practice our cultural and traditional endeavors, as well as meet our own needs for housing, agriculture, commerce, and industrial development. When you consider the politics of land in Hawai'i, sovereignty and self-determination are our only choice.

An even more fundamental reason why we have to proceed with sovereignty and self-determination is because we are Kanaka Maoli—we are Hawaiian people. God put us on this earth and gave us a certain sacred-trust obligation to be guardians of these lands. Encoded in our cultural practices and value systems are the teachings necessary to maintain balance here in *Hawai'i nei* ["this (beloved) Hawai'i"], that only our people have been chosen to practice. This is the teaching of Hawaiian *aloha 'āina,* and *lōkahi*—living in balance with yourself, God, and the earth. These are teachings that need to be shared globally with other cultures. We have to protect this little corner of the earth: the fish, the birds, the animals, the land itself. It is the job of the Kanaka Maoli, the Hawaiian people, to maintain the balance of the earth and the heavens, to keep the connection with the land and with God. If we pass away, it's not just losing a traditional culture, which is priceless, but it is also losing the *'āina,* the *pa'i 'āina* of *Hawai'i nei,* this whole archipelago. More importantly, the world loses the keepers of the teachings of this knowledge. So this is really the reason why we move for sovereignty and self-determination.

When we consider the practical step-by-step political undertaking, what is Ka Lāhui Hawai'i's agenda? Many in the Hawaiian community don't understand this. Sovereignty manifests itself in four arenas—four different perspectives.

The first arena of sovereignty consists of native-to-native basic inquiries: What do we as Native Hawaiians say about sovereignty and how do we define it? What type of a government do we want? What was good about traditional government? What is necessary in creating a modern government? How do we merge those elements? What is going to be the obligation of the government to the native people? What is our land base? How do we work with each other to try to accommodate the many different opinions?

In arena number one, Ka Lāhui's proposal has three initiatives. First, we had to form a nation that incorporates the traditional and the modern. We took that first step in 1987 by forming Ka Lāhui Hawai'i. We submitted it to our people in three constitutional conventions—1987, 1989, 1991—to give our people the opportunity to create and structure a nation.

The second initiative in arena one is broad-based, uniform community education to educate our Hawaiians on the U.S. policy on self-determination by sponsoring conferences, seminars, and workshops. How are your people going to know about your constitution if you don't go out and educate them about it? Many Hawaiians never saw a map of Hawaiian home lands or of the ceded lands. They didn't even know what it was. We've also got to educate our people about sovereignty, share our constitution with them, and bring them into the process.

The third initiative in arena one is to work in the larger nonnative community. Ka Lāhui, in the last five years, has been instrumental in obtaining resolutions of support for sovereignty from the Episcopal Church, Methodist Church, Catholic Church, Presbyterian Church, and United Church of Christ. The National Council of Churches of Jesus Christ has now passed a resolution. In Hawai'i we've got support resolutions from the National Lawyers Guild and the Japanese-American Community League. Hawai'i's practice of *hānai* and intermarriage requires us to deal with sovereignty in the *'ohana* or family way. If we have adopted non-Hawaiians as part of our family culturally, we've got to put together an educational format for the nonnative as well.

Arena number two deals with native-to-U.S.A., the nation that controls their land and exercises jurisdiction over their lives. We're not alone in this arena. The Chamorros of Guam, the people of Puerto Rico, American Samoa, and all of the trust territories are also native people who relate to the U.S.A. There are over 550 native American Indian nations, including 200 Alaska villages. In arena number two, the agenda is to achieve civil and human rights, and jurisdiction over lands.

Native peoples throughout the globe are severely limited by what the imperialist nation defines as the parameters. In arena number two, you can talk with the United States about getting equity with Native Americans, but that's the furthest you go. If you start talking about secession, it is defined as treason, and you can go to jail for it.

The Ka Lāhui proposal is a nation-within-a-nation model: native nation to imperial nation. Over the last seven years, in testimony before the Congress and the U.S. Civil Rights Commission, we have been saying this consistently. America has defined Hawaiian people as Native Americans, and we had nothing to say about it. Why does America have a policy for self-determination for all classes of Native Americans except Hawaiians? Why is it that we are wards of the State, while Native Alaskans and Indians are not? Why is it that American Indians can go to federal court to sue the state and the federal government for breach of trust, but Hawaiians are deprived of this fundamental right? Only three classes of American citizens are not allowed into the federal court for breach of trust suits: retarded adults, minors under 18, and Native Hawaiians.

Our strategy in arena number two, then, is a demand that America alter its policy and allow us the same rights as other Native Americans, end the wardship, recognize our right to have a nation, and provide us with lands.

Arena number three is native-to-international community. The international community consists of the United Nations and its affiliates, the World Court, the World Council of Churches, the International Labor Organization, the Regional and Territorial Associations. Maybe we cannot talk about secession or independence from the United States of America, but at the international level, working with international and regional organizations, we can raise important issues that need to be addressed. The Ka Lāhui agenda has been to get the word out on the real status and condition of the Hawaiian people. For the last six years we have sent representatives to the Working Group on Indigenous Populations at the U.N. to file our statements regarding deprivation of our human and civil rights. I have participated in the global and regional consultations of the World Council of Churches on the rights of native people and the rights of women.

We continue to advocate that the United Nations conduct an investigation into our status. Up until 1959, when Hawai'i became a state, the United Nations listed Hawai'i on the list of non-self-governing territories. When America notified the U.N. that statehood had been granted, it sent information about the land trusts that were allegedly created for our people. America indicated that our human and civil rights would be protected. The United Nations never inquired into our condition. If an inquiry had been made, they would have found that there was never really any plebiscite or referendum of native people for our admission into the union. The ballot that was prepared for statehood violated international requirements. When a group is on the U.N. list of non-self-governing territories, they have to be given the choice of statehood, commonwealth status, or independence. Hawai'i and Alaska were only given one choice—statehood. Consequently, there were violations of the international rules and regulations.

Ka Lāhui has filed two official interventions at the U.N. level. One intervention was filed with what is called the Miguel Alfonso Martinez Treaty Study. Several years ago, the Working Group on Indigenous Populations at the U.N. created a subcommittee. The job of Miguel Alfonso Martinez was to find native people who had treaties with nations that later stole their lands, and inquire from those native people what their condition really was. We continue to participate in the passage of the declaration on indigenous human rights.

Our work with the World Council of Churches has expanded, as has our work with the international jurists who participated with the Ka Pākaukau and Ka Lāhui here in an international tribunal that indicted the United States for crimes against the native people. Ka Lāhui wants Hawai'i to be placed back on the list of non-self-governing territories. Lastly, we have obtained the support of the Center for Constitutional Rights to file the first international case against the United States. We will proceed under the compact and convention of the Organization of American States to raise the claims of Hawaiian individuals and families against the U.S.A.

Arena number four is nation-to-nation. The goal in arena four is to recognize and establish diplomatic relations with other native nations. Nothing prevents us from obtaining support and assistance from other native nations. Ka Lāhui may not be recognized by the United States, but that should not prevent us from working directly with other native nations, recognizing them, and obtaining diplomatic recognition from them. We have successfully negotiated treaties with fifteen Indian and Canadian nations.

We're very advanced in Hawai'i in putting together programs for children's native language classes. We're working with Indian, Alaskan, and Canadian nations who don't have that. We're finding that we have many problems in common: health, education, taxation, environment, geothermal.

We have gone out to find Indian nations that have trade that we can benefit from and that supply materials, such as lumber, which we badly need for housing. They have crafts, they have salmon. We have a big consumer market here in Hawai'i, and it's pretty tough to get salmon for a decent price. People on the mainland would like to get some of our own handcrafts. They would like to get deep-sea fish, which they can't get on the mainland. So we can look at developing some economic base for ourselves and also sharing information about solutions to environmental needs. Some of them have been very successful in developing initiatives for housing. We need that kind of assistance.

We've got to break the yoke of wardship and get parity with Native American Indians. However, given America's history, we cannot put all of our eggs in that basket. We also have to address issues in the international arena and establish a reputation with other native nations.

Davianna McGregor

An associate professor of ethnic studies at the University of Hawai'i at Mānoa; somewhere in her forties.

I was raised here on O'ahu. My mother is Portuguese-German and her family are ranchers. Every summer I would stay on my family's ranch with my grandparents and my mother's brothers and sisters. During the school year, I'd be with my mom and dad and two sisters. I was educated in Catholic schools here on O'ahu. Catholicism is common among the Portuguese and Filipinos. My father, who's Hawaiian, Chinese, and Scottish, was raised Protestant and educated at the Kamehameha Schools. He converted to Catholicism when he married my mother. Even though my mom was not Hawaiian, she always impressed upon us the importance of identifying as Hawaiian, and to be proud of our Hawaiian heritage because this is the land of the Hawaiian people.

My grandparents on my father's side were both active in Hawaiian politics. In the territorial period, most Hawaiians were members of the Republican Party. My grandmother was a schoolteacher and later a principal, so she was active in organizing the teachers in getting involved in the political process. My grandfather was active in the publication of a newspaper called *The Holomua,* which was published by Prince Jonah Kūhiō Kalaniana'ole. It espoused the political viewpoints of the Hawaiian community. From my mom's parents, even though they were not Hawaiian, I got a real grounding in the rural Hawaiian life-style, and learned to appreciate nature. In Hawai'i today, because there's so much assault on the rural areas with development, I've become very interested in perpetuating the rural way of life. The rural areas have been strongholds for the perpetuation of Hawaiian culture.

Hawaiian culture is the original culture of indigenous people. We have our own language, spiritual beliefs, and customs. We were a sovereign people in Hawai'i well before the coming of the Europeans. For hundreds of years we had a system that revolved around extended families, called 'ohana. Later, with the Tahitian influence, a ruling chief got introduced into the social system. When Europeans and Americans came in, there was the introduction of a capitalist economy and a constitutional republic government. In the 1850s the first immigrant workers were imported. By 1890, Hawaiians had become a minority within Hawai'i because of the importation of contract labor from all over the world.

On the plantations there was an intermingling of different cultures with the Hawaiian culture. There was a high degree of intermarriage because a lot of the early male contract workers did not have wives. The local culture became a mixture of Hawaiian and American, European, and then Chinese and Japanese and Filipino. The language is not Hawaiian, but pidgin, which is a mixture of all those different languages. We have a tolerant, multiethnic, and diverse society, with a lot of appreciation of each other's contributions.

When the first plantation was established in 1835 at Kōloa, all the workers were Hawaiians through an arrangement with their chief. Through 1872, 85 percent of the plantation work force was Hawaiian. But there just were not enough adult Hawaiian males to work the plantations to the extent that the planters wanted to expand them. After the Reciprocity Treaty in 1875, there was a tremendous increase in the importation of contract labor. Between 1876 and 1882, about 40,000 Chinese and Japanese were imported, mostly adult males.

Once the *mahele* (land laws) were established, about 72 percent of the Hawaiians were left landless. The labor service they used to perform for the chiefs was replaced by taxation or rent. Once lands were privatized, there was no longer free labor or free tenancy on the land. Then they had to pay rent to live on the land. Whatever labor they performed had to be for hire. Then a system of taxation was introduced for the king and the central government to sustain itself. Prior to that, labor was performed, so many days for the government and so many days for the chief. So the taxation system really pushed the Hawaiians into the market economy to have to earn some kind of cash. The introduction of new products, tools, and clothing created new consumer needs which also pushed people into the cash economy. More and more Hawaiians either didn't have land, or the land parcels they had were too small, so they had to go out and work to earn cash.

Much earlier, with the introduction of trade, widespread diseases wiped out whole communities of people. David Malo, a Hawaiian historian, says that in 1804 about half the population died. They called it *ma'i 'ōku'u,* meaning "the separating disease," but it was either cholera or bubonic plague. There were other epidemics like whooping cough and measles. And throughout, various venereal diseases continued to wipe out the population.

By 1819 there was a turning point marked by the abolition of the chiefly Hawaiian religious system. This indicated the degree to which the social system had changed and disintegrated.

The main division between urban and rural Hawaiians began in the 1900s. Some urban Hawaiians became middle class, or even very wealthy. Those who are descended from the chiefs had received major land holdings and they intermarried with the merchants and the traders, or the planters, or some of the missionary families. Hawaiians started to fill other kinds of jobs within the social system. They became public workers, stevedores, policemen, firemen, and cowboys on ranches.

In the early 1900s Hawaiians became the middle class within the social system, while the immigrants continued to be primarily the plantation workers. In the territorial period, many urban Hawaiians became educated and became politicians, attorneys, judges, and most of the elected officials. A number of Hawaiians got patronage through those politicians, and jobs with the Big Five companies or in government as custodians, road workers, and such; and still that's the case. About a third of the Hawaiian population remains in the rural areas as subsistence fishermen and farmers.

The first generation Japanese and Chinese were not allowed to become citizens and were not allowed to vote. In 1900 the Hawaiians made up about 66 percent of the voting electorate. Through 1930, they were still the majority of voters. After 1930 they were the plurality of voters. They had positions of influence within the government, and there was an alliance within the Republican Party between the Hawaiians and the Big Five. Hawaiians in the urban areas benefited from that. When the immigrant workers organized the plantations, those who were putting down the strikes were Hawaiian sheriffs and police, together with Portuguese and other haoles.

I was planning to be a schoolteacher and wanted to teach in a rural Hawaiian community on Oʻahu. When I was a student at the University of Hawaiʻi, I got involved with the ethnic studies struggle and really identified with it. The Ethnic Studies Program started in 1969. In 1972, there was an attempt to get rid of it. I thought it was important to have the history and contributions of the Hawaiian and working people taught. Most of our students come from working-class backgrounds and should appreciate their own heritage.

I became an instructor in Ethnic Studies in 1974. A number of us got involved in the land and housing struggles which were going on at that time. Many people were being evicted from rural areas or from Chinatown to make way for high-cost developments. So we involved ourselves and our students in efforts to stop those developments and provide for decent housing for the old people in Chinatown and to protect some of the agricultural lands on rural Oʻahu.

I was married for about ten years to the professor in our department who teaches Filipino history. I worked with him around some of the concerns against the Marcos dictatorship in the Philippines and U.S. support for that dictatorship. Some of us were also involved with the Nuclear-free and Independent Pacific movement, which linked up concerns shared by Hawaiʻi with other Pacific Island peoples who were colonized and who were victims of nuclear proliferation and militarization of the Pacific.

Through that period, I continued my work with the Hawaiian community. I thought it was important to involve my students in taro cultivation, because that was important in Hawaiian society, and a lot of the agricultural lands on this island were being threatened. Another student group on campus had found that there was a taro irrigation and cultivation system intact on campus, but it just needed to be reopened and cleaned. It was all overgrown with California grass and other kinds of weeds. We cleared out the area and reopened the irrigation system. Every semester since 1980 my students have been working down there. It's a real quiet area, a sort of place of refuge on the campus. We call it a *puʻuhonua*. There used to be many more varieties of taro planted in Hawaiʻi. A lot of them have been at risk of being lost. So we've gone out and collected taro plants as well as other native Hawaiian species of plants that are endangered. This was a joint effort with Hawaiian Studies, Botany, Tropical Agriculture, Geography, and Hawaiian Language.

My students started to go to the island of Kahoʻolawe to support the stop-the-bombing movement. Even though the island wasn't open for legal access until 1980, in 1976 a group of Hawaiians, primarily from Moloka'i, had gone to the island—U.S. military land—as part of a protest to get national attention to the demands that Hawaiians were making for reparations and the role of the U.S. in the overthrow of the Hawaiian monarchy. There was a bill in Congress that was not being taken seriously. It was sort of like a Wounded Knee. Hawaiians needed our own Wounded Knee to get national attention.

What we were up against was this national stereotype of Hawaiians that's been promoted by the Hawai'i Visitors' Bureau and the Hollywood movie industry, that Hawaiians are all happy natives on the beach, living in grass huts, playing ukuleles, welcoming tourists, and we don't have many problems. We needed to show that the problems our native Hawaiians have are very serious. Hawaiians are a very poor sector of modern Hawaiian society. We've been disenfranchised in our own land. By the post-statehood period, Hawaiians were not in political office and were really alienated from the political system. This was reflected in very poor health, social, and economic conditions. So Kaho'olawe first started as a way to attract national attention to the destitute conditions of Hawaiians.

A lot of people had gotten politicized. Some had gone to continental U.S. colleges and gotten exposed to the Civil Rights movement, the student movement, the antiwar movement, and the Native American movement. Some had gone through the Model City's training programs in community advocacy here in Hawai'i.

The first real movement, around 1969, was called Kalama Valley. Hawaiian pig farmers were getting evicted from the last agricultural slice of land in the Hawai'i Kai part of the island of O'ahu. The farmers were on Bishop Estate land—Hawaiian land. Bishop Estate is a charitable trust set up for the education of Hawaiians. Kalama Valley brought together the land and housing problems. It became a Hawaiian issue. Out of that, a group called Kōkua Hawai'i emerged.

The next major group that came about was called The Hawaiians. They were concerned with Hawaiian home lands which had been set aside exclusively for Native Hawaiians. Today, only about 17 percent of the land is settled by Hawaiians, and the rest is used by non-Hawaiians. There's a waiting list of 21,000 people who are qualified, and some of them have been on that list for thirty years. It was a grassroots upswelling from all of the Islands to challenge what was going on with the management of Hawaiian home lands.

On Moloka'i, a very important group called Hui Alaloa ["Long

Trail"] was formed to open access through private lands to the beaches. Access was always a right of Hawaiians from the time that private land was established. The law also gave Native Hawaiians the right to access through private land to get to where they needed for subsistence, or [for] cultural or religious practices. This right had never been acknowledged, especially on Moloka'i where so much of the land is owned by Molokai Ranch. That movement involved, for the first time in a meaningful way, the *kūpuna,* or the Hawaiian elders. It was multigenerational, with a lot of grounding in Hawaiian custom and belief and practice.

The core group on Moloka'i also made the first landing on Kaho'olawe. They carried with them that link to the land, that rural Hawaiian outlook, and that multigenerational involvement. They were able to develop an Islands-wide grassroots movement on the issue of stopping the bombing of Kaho'olawe. They were able to revive what is a very core value to native Hawaiians—*aloha 'āina*—to love the land and protect it, and to revive the Hawaiian spiritual beliefs.

Kaho'olawe drew me more closely to involvement with the Hawaiian community, because the spirit of the island provides a connection to our ancestors and the spiritual beliefs which are the core of our Hawaiian culture and our identity as Hawaiians. When I went to Kaho'olawe and participated in the spiritual ceremonies, I felt more connected to my ancestors and their beliefs, and to our *akua,* which is the nature of our land and the nature of our people. Christianity has taken away our soul as a people. Kaho'olawe provided a way for us to get reconnected with that soul.

It's very natural. It makes us feel so much a part of nature and whole as a person, as one with the land and with the life force in the land. Our *akua,* or the different deities that we identify, are essentially the life force that we can feel and observe, as the land lives and breathes, as the ocean has its force, as the rains come, and as the seasons and tides change. There's a life force that we can observe. If we can connect with that, then we are empowered. We call that *mana.*

Hui Alaloa continued to try to protect the rural way of life on Moloka'i against a lot of tourist development, especially after pineapple phased out on the island. There was a lot of pressure to develop tourist resorts which would draw upon the scarce water resources. They call Moloka'i the last Hawaiian island. It's about 60 percent Hawaiian. The rural Hawaiian way of life is very strong there.

Another important issue is the defense and protection of Pele, the

Hawaiian volcano goddess, from geothermal energy development. Two of the founders of the Pele Defense Fund were key in the Protect Kahoʻolawe ʻOhana. The Pele Defense Fund has been instrumental in protecting not only Pele, but also the surrounding rainforest—a very unique volcanic rainforest in the Wao Kele o Puna district—from geothermal development and industrialization. Protect Kahoʻolawe ʻOhana founded the Protect Kahoʻolawe Fund, a nonprofit group that gave support to other grassroots organizations. The Fund gave support to efforts to protect the water resources on the island of Lānaʻi, and some effort to protect the south shoreline of Maui from development.

What's at stake is the subsistence lifestyle. In the rural areas, where there are low incomes, they are able to supplement those incomes with subsistence fishing and farming, and it's a very important part of their lifestyle. That ongoing lifestyle is essential to the survival of the Hawaiian culture.

In my research, I came up with a term called cultural *kīpuka*. A *kīpuka* in the volcanic rainforest is where the lava goes through and leaves behind these oases of forest. The seeds and the spores spread to the newly erupted lava, and the forest starts to come back to life and eventually regenerates.

I call the rural Hawaiian communities cultural *kīpuka* because they were bypassed by the mainstream economic development. The traders didn't come there because of the poor anchorages. Plantations didn't establish there either, because the water resources were poor or the landscape was too steep. They were not impacted by the changes that occurred in the port towns of the main islands. And so the traditional beliefs and customs persisted. Modern development threatens to destroy those last strongholds of the Hawaiian way of life.

There are three categories in the sovereignty movement. First, there are the *aloha ʻāina* groups, with which I work a lot. These are groups on the land that are practicing the culture, practicing the spiritual customs and beliefs, and defending them day to day. We participate in the sovereignty effort primarily as a way to solidify our claims and our rights to protect the ancestral lands; to protect the resources. These are people who have never lost a sense of sovereignty as a Hawaiian people.

Then there are the nation-within-nation organizations like Ka Lāhui Hawaiʻi. They seek to have the Native Hawaiian lands set aside under sovereign control by Hawaiians. Those lands are supposedly a trust for the betterment of Native Hawaiians. Rather than have the State or the federal government continue to use those lands for military purposes or other uses, Ka Lāhui Hawai'i would like to have the management and control turned over to the Native Hawaiians.

The third category contains the groups who want Hawai'i to be completely independent. They would like to negotiate treaties for the ultimate withdrawal of the U.S. presence, so that Hawai'i can emerge as an independent nation.

It's never been more hopeful. There's so much more consciousness of the historical injustice. In the last several years there's been a real coming together in the Hui Nā'auao grouping. We have different viewpoints because we come from different backgrounds and needs. We must get out into the community with information about the different options. We need to educate the community about the historical, cultural, legal, and spiritual foundation for sovereign claims.

What would you consider to be the most desirable future?

Well, I would like to see us have sovereignty starting with the nation-within-a-nation model, a federated model, in which the political structure would be along the lines of, say, the Iroquois Confederacy, or the Warm Springs Tribe. There would be autonomy in the different islands, especially the rural areas. The cultural *kīpuka* would control the resources in their own districts. But we would need a central authority to care for the common resources that are shared across the islands— for example, education and health care, or those aspects of the sovereign people that are best handled by a central government. I continue to think about a structure, but I tend toward something that would balance local autonomy with central authority. Even though 75 percent of the Hawaiian population is on O'ahu, the bulk of the Hawaiian lands and resources is on the neighbor islands where the Hawaiian lifestyle has continued and not been compromised. I want to be sure that O'ahu politics doesn't dominate the neighbor island way of life, and that the neighbor island people are empowered to protect their livelihoods and resources.

An activist attorney in the Waiʻanae area; in his fifties.

I am Poka Laenui, also known as Hayden Burgess. First of all, I was born. In the Hawaiian tradition, the fact that a child is born, when he is born, where he is born from, and many other factors before his birth, has something to do with his birth. I understand my birth to have been for a particular purpose.

I was born on the 5th of May, 1946. There were ten in my family. My father was Hawaiian and haole. My mother was Chinese. We had a mixed culture in the home. We had no particular religion, but were influenced by many different cultural practices: burning incense at Chinese churches, going to Hawaiian or Christian churches, listening to Hawaiian legends and lores. We came from a mixed language. My mother spoke Chinese, my father spoke Hawaiian as well as some Chinese, and they both spoke pidgin English. Sometimes the English was so heavily accented that one would not be able to recognize it as English today. We were of the lower economic level. My father was a truck mechanic, helping the family to survive for these many years until he finally retired and then passed on. My mother is still alive and has always worked in the home taking care of the children.

I attended public schools in the Waiʻanae area. Waiʻanae is a country area, one of the strongholds of rebellion some might say. The tradition in Waiʻanae is that whenever soldiers or warriors of Oʻahu were defeated by conquering armies, they would come to Waiʻanae to reproduce and retrain. Several generations later, they would return and take over Oʻahu again. So Waiʻanae has that history, and it is the belief that in Waiʻanae there are very powerful gods in the land, mountains, and air. Every child who grows out of Waiʻanae is impacted by these spiritual elements.

We have always had the highest crime rate in Waiʻanae, and the economic and social statistics have always been the worst. At the present time, we have the highest single population and the highest percentage of Native Hawaiian people.

In my early school days, I always noticed that there was some difference between myself and those other people who called themselves Americans. I noticed that there was a difference between the society at school and the society at home. There was a different sense about it. I never really felt that I was part of the so-called American society. It was the "outside." The "inside" was something completely different. The "inside" included friends who I would meet outside of school and go down to the beaches with or play with. The "inside" was family.

Scholastically, I was above average. Disciplinary-wise, I was far below average in that I oftentimes rebelled. I got into numerous fights, and expressed opposition to authority, to the teachers, and to kids larger than me. But as I entered high school, things changed. I was able to obtain a sense of self-respect. I was known for my athletic ability and I had good friends among the athletes of the school. We were generally identified as the lower scholastic achievers.

Someone nominated me for political office in the ninth grade. At first I objected to the whole idea. But then I did become a candidate for vice president of the tenth grade and ended up winning over four other candidates. I took on a new image of myself and eventually was elected president of the student body. This gave me a sense of integrity and dignity. I became more observant about what was happening in the community and the school, trying to be the basic politician, I guess. I found that I had a particular knack for building bridges between scholastic and athletic people. I was able to bridge between the haoles, Japanese, Hawaiians, Chinese, and the rest. High school politics gave me a different sense of myself and a different way of thinking. As a result, I became active within the community. I became an advocate for different positions, and my positions were talked about and regarded as something to consider.

After graduating in 1964 from Waiʻanae High School, I applied for admission to the University of Hawaiʻi and was admitted. But my family could not afford it. One day I stood in line at the ticket office of an open-air theater in Wai'anae. Behind me was an older Japanese gentleman, Larry Kamada, who was the postmaster of Wai'anae. He turned to me and asked me what I was going to do now that I was out of high school. I told him I was probably going to join the military service like my brothers had done. He asked me why was I not going to college. I told him that I didn't have the money for it, but after returning from the service I could use some kind of military benefits to go to school. And what he told me had a strong impact on me. He said, "That's the problem with all you stupid-ass *kanakas*."

I wanted to respond in similar language, but I didn't because a sense of respect for the elders was bred into me. So I went to the movies that evening, and I remembered his words. And I said, "I think he's right." So I went to school, worked part time, and graduated from the University of Hawai'i in 1968 with a political science degree. While attending the university I became very concerned about what was happening with communities. When I reached voting age, I ran for the first elected school board in Hawai'i. Though I lost to the incumbent, it got me involved in the political life of Hawai'i.

After graduating, I ran for the state constitutional convention of 1968. This time I was successful, and I ended up representing the district of Wai'anae. But I was still green and didn't know what was going on. I sat on a committee for civil rights and came across attorneys who would testify about this right or that right. I decided that I had to be trained in law. So after the constitutional convention ended, my wife and I went to Washington, D.C., where I was accepted at George Washington University Law Center. I attended school for just a few months, but could not continue because I ran out of money. The change in the environment was so great that I was not able to afford the change in clothing. So I returned back to Hawai'i, enlisted in the United States Air Force in 1969, and served during the Vietnam period at Hickam Air Force Base.

At times it became boring. During my lunch hour I would go to the library and read. I came across a book entitled *Hawaii's Story by Hawaii's Queen*. It was written by Queen Lili'uokalani. Though it was published around 1898, it had never been republished again and distributed in Hawai'i until 1965, when it was reprinted in Japan by Tuttle Press. Very few people in Hawai'i knew about this book. As I read the book, the queen spoke to me about what had happened in Hawai'i, disclosing those activities that occurred in 1893 that resulted in the theft of this independent nation. Then I read another book called *Hawai'i Pono*, written by Lawrence Fuchs out of Stanford University. That book put a second part to the queen's first part. The queen built a theory of conspiracy. *Hawai'i Pono* showed how it was carried out. As a result of reading these two books, I became very angry. I wanted to go out and kill Americans. I wanted to go out and bomb institutions, bomb buildings, and the rest. After a time of quieting myself, I decided that I would blow up the system—not from the outside, but by creeping into its innards.

So after leaving the Air Force, I went to law school at the University of Hawai'i and was fortunate to be one of those who was admitted in the first entering class. It was very difficult learning of the great promise of righteousness in the American law while knowing full well that it was a bunch of BS and was used to steal the nation of Hawai'i. That legal system is still the entity that keeps the nation of Hawai'i under the control of the United States.

During law school, I told myself I would never work for any government entity or corporation. Instead, I would work on my own and do whatever I wanted to do to change the system. So after graduation I went to Wai'anae, opened a very small office, and found a typewriter. My wife acted as my secretary, and we began the practice of law.

About a year and a half into the law practice, I was asked to represent the reputed underworld leader of Hawai'i, Nappy Pulawa, in a double murder, double kidnap case. Previous to this, I had only one criminal jury trial experience. I traveled to Washington State, where he was incarcerated in a federal prison, and agreed to represent him. This case was very pivotal in the movement for Hawaiian sovereignty. When the prosecutor charged my client with the double murder and double kidnap, I said that we refused to enter a plea of guilty or not guilty. Instead we asked, "Who are you foreigners to sit in judgment over our Hawaiian citizens, to pass your foreign laws to govern our Hawaiian people? We are not American citizens, we are citizens of the nation of Hawai'i, and we refuse to dignify the court by entering a plea."

This caught the attention of many people. The news media, who wanted to sell newspapers about this big criminal, was now stuck with a new issue that it really didn't want to cover. And so, we entered into this whole phase of Hawaiian sovereignty. We introduced documents and testimony of the overthrow of an independent nation. When I read into the record the speech of Grover Cleveland to the U.S. Congress, the judge shook his head saying, "I can hear your words, but I cannot believe that the president of the United States had said this." And I submitted many other things.

It was an opportunity not only to educate the judge, but to educate the general public about the theft of this independent nation and to raise the question of whether . . . we were or were not American citizens. Of course, our position was that we were not. It was the longest trial in Hawai'i's history as of that time. They found the defendant not guilty of the crimes alleged. Although the decision was not based on the fact that we were Hawaiian citizens, it brought home greater attention to the injustices of the Hawaiian people. More and more people became familiar with the issues of Hawaiian sovereignty.

In a later case in 1978, I had difficulty with Judge Sam King of the federal district court. He insisted that I sign a jury selection form which in essence said that I was an American citizen. I refused to sign the form. He found me in contempt of court and fined me. I refused to pay the fine. Once again, this brought public attention to the issue of Hawaiian sovereignty.

Two years later, another incident occurred when people living on Sand Island were evicted from that beach. Some of them raised the issue that they were Hawaiian citizens living on Hawaiian land. The court had no jurisdiction to come in and sit in judgement over their guilt or innocence. The American law passed by the State of Hawai'i had no jurisdiction over Hawaiian citizens and over this land. We went to trial and raised the issue of Hawaiian sovereignty again.

Then in 1982, Hurricane 'Iwa hit Hawai'i. Many of our indigenous people were basically blown off of the beaches at Mākua. They attempted to organize and return back to the beach. I ended up as attorney for that group. We used the media and courts to raise the issue of Hawaiian sovereignty, challenging the court's jurisdiction. And there have been many more cases.

The condition of Hawai'i and its people is one of outright colonization. We are a brainwashed people who have lost our identity, lost our history, and now are trying to recover from this loss. Twenty years ago, the vast majority of our people had never known that we were an independent nation, that we had diplomatic and consular posts around the world, that we had treaties with other nations, that we had kings and queens who had traveled to different parts of the world and were accepted in every court where they went. Our people didn't realize that we had one of the highest literacy rates in the world, that our people were multilingual, that we were very advanced technologically. All of that history was lost to our people.

We also did not realize that we were invaded by the United States of America in 1893 in an action that was contrary to international law and that our queen protested it. We didn't realize that her yielding of authority was only temporary until the Americans could investigate the situation and restore the life of the land back to the Hawaiian people. Instead, we were recycled, or brainwashed, into becoming loyal American citizens, leaving behind our history, language, and culture, and just mimicking the ways of the Americans. The United States controlled almost everything in Hawai'i. They controlled the economy and, through the military, much of our lands. They controlled the educational system, foreign trade, immigration, media, airlines. So Hawai'i really became—and still is—a colony of the United States, mimicking the ways of the Americans. We even adopted terms that colonized us— terms such as *mainland*.

But the controls did not stop there. Over a period of time, we began to take on the mental attitude of Americans. When we looked at one another, we would identify people by their race rather than by their relationship to Hawai'i, which was a cultural approach of referring to and relating to other human beings. We adopted a mentality of dependency, believing that we needed the Americans to be here, to provide for us, to support us, to protect us. Over a period of time, we actually became afraid of freedom. Oh, if the United States pulled out and sent us on our way, we would be doomed, we believed.

These were the worst conditions of the Hawaiian people. It was not the poverty of our people, nor the fact that we had no permanent tenure over lands in Hawai'i. It was the fact that we lost our identity, our history, our continuity of consciousness. We were without any platform to hop into our future. We are divided by race. We are mentally dependent on the Americans. We fear freedom.

To address the question of motions and directions of Hawai'i, I use a framework of self-determination. In the present period, most of our people had seen a self—which has a right to determine its future—as one described only in racial terms, which is a foreigner's view. Instead of this, we must look into our history and apply a Hawaiian principle called *nānā i ke kumu* that means "to look to the source." Prior to the invasion and overthrow, the self which constituted this nation, or the citizens of the nation of Hawai'i, were not described only by their racial ancestry, or by their genealogy. There were citizens of many different races. What was important was their relationship to *'āina,* or to the land, or to the country, or to the society. So we use terms such as *kama'āina*—adopted of the land; *hoa'āina*—friend to the land; *kua'āina*—backbone of the land; *maka 'āina*—eyes of the land. All of these terms can be captured into a larger term called *aloha 'āina.*

We are moving from a self identified as a race to a self identified as a relationship to Hawai'i. We should see that self, which has a right to exercise determination for Hawai'i, as a people whose loyalty and allegiance is to the nation of Hawai'i, who are willing to take up citizenship in this nation of Hawai'i and forego any foreign citizenship, including the United States of America, Canada, Japan, or whatever citizenship they now hold. If they are *kama'āina*—acculturated to Hawai'i—or *keiki o ka 'āina*—a child of Hawai'i—they should be eligible to become citizens of Hawai'i. This was the standard used back in 1893. It's just as good for us today.

The term *determination* contains a set of choices. There was really no choice in the 1959 plebiscite. If we voted yes, Hawai'i would become a state of the United States. If we voted no, Hawai'i would remain a territory of the United States. The choice of independence was never afforded our people. We are entitled to the choice to be absolutely independent. The United Nations has said the right to self-governance, or self-determination, belongs to all peoples. I believe that the people of Hawai'i will move to a fuller appreciation of the right to self-determination. In the end, they will come to a position of choosing to be an independent nation. It may take a lot of time, but I believe the movement will eventually reach that point.

Part of the condition of Hawai'i today is that more and more people are taking the race view. They are saying that the right to Hawaiian sovereignty is in the realm of elevating an indigenous race within a colonial situation; to leave the Americans in place; to elevate the indigenous people so that they are given some special consideration, very similar to the American Indians' situation. This nation-within-a-nation position, with federal recognition, is to leave colonization in place in Hawai'i. I do not believe that we are going to be locked into that position for very long once we understand and examine our choices.

One can understand what is happening in Hawai'i today by dividing events into five phases. Three of the phases have already occurred, two have not yet occurred. The first phase is rediscovery and recovery. For the last twenty years, the Hawaiian people have been rediscovering our history. As a result, there has been an explosion of interest in dance, language, and songs, as well as in our political and economic history. This phase is still going on.

I call the second phase the period of mourning, the period in which people lament the fact that for 100 years we have been without our independence. The pinnacle of that period was observed on the 16th and 17th of January 1993, which marked the 100th anniversary of the American invasion and overthrow. The mourning has not ended.

The third phase, which many of us are now entering into, is a phase of dreaming. People are asking themselves such questions as, Who is the self that has a right to exercise determination? Is it necessarily identified by race, or is it identified by something more than that? Is it really a relationship issue or a genealogical issue? What should be the choices? What will be the result of Hawai'i as an independent nation? Can we separate from the United States? Can a nation elevate itself above international law so that it can say that no nation can secede from its union, while other people have the right to self-determination, including the right to become an independent nation? How do we treat Hawai'i as a "floating nation"—a nation once independent, then taken over by another nation, and then attempting to become independent again? How will the international community consider this floating nation? What will be our economy? What will be our military protection? Will we be able to survive politically if we separate from the United States? Will we gain recognition in the international community? We are entering into this very exciting period of dreaming.

There will be another phase after this—the commitment phase—which people already are talking about. The Office of Hawaiian Affairs wants to hold a constitutional convention next year [1996]. Others have suggested a congress of the Hawaiian people—a *puwalu,* or gathering. But this commitment phase cannot occur too fast, since the dreaming phase needs a full period of gestation. Pushing the child out too quickly will end up aborting the child. This is where a lot of the tensions are right now in Hawai'i. When do we ask a question? When do we reach a sufficient stage of examination of all of our possibilities? Can we ask that serious question of breaking away from the United States? Is it an act of treason? Who will be the political leadership that will say we should do this? Should it be the grass roots who provide real political leadership in our society?

The last phase will be the phase of action, which will take many different forms, depending on the commitment being made. I believe that the commitment will be that we must become an independent nation.

The most important thing in organizing is to decolonize our mind. If we do not decolonize our mind, organizing becomes very limited and dreaming becomes stunted. Here's a little story I wrote:

There's a sassy frog who sits in the well in my yard. He thinks he knows everything there is to know in the world. One day, I walked up to the well and called to the frog saying, "Mr. Frog, you're so smart—tell me what the world is like."

Mr. Frog sat up, lifting his head and shoulders above the water, and began to describe his surrounding. He could tell me about water temperature, oxidation in the water, rate of algae growth, types of insects and larvae he feeds on; then he moved to describe with detail the rocks surrounding him, and finally described the sky from his perspective at the bottom of the well. He told me of the dark sky and the light sky, of the blue and the gray sky, of the bright light and the soft light, of the tiny twinkling lights, all of which hung over his well. Then he gave me a broad smile to show how wondrous his knowledge was of the world.

I said, "Mr. Frog, you're not too smart after all. You should hop out of the well sometimes and see what the rest of the world is like."

Frog came leaping out of the well, propelled by his anger at my criticism. When he landed on the edge of the well, he was stunned to see the vastness of sky from mountain to ocean. He saw treetops and grass, felt wind and sunshine on his back, heard sounds and breathed smells he had never dreamed of before. A new world opened up for him simply by a shift in perspective. And he was never the same again.

The key to organizing is to chase that frog out of the well, or at least show the frog that there is a way to get out of the well. And much of that is through the use of storytelling. You can tell stories of other frogs that are outside of the well: Kiribati, Vanuatu, Nauru, Niue, Republic of the Marshall Islands, Federated States of Micronesia, Fiji, Free [Western] Samoa. Many of these other Pacific Island nations that are independent are members of the United Nations and are able to survive and retain their integrity. They need not ask the United States for permission to allow others to come into their lands, to stop foreign investors from coming in, or to stop the bombing of any particular island or valley.

The second part of organizing deals with racism. We have to be able to overcome racism in Hawai'i. We need to be able to show that we can respect the rights of all peoples within the society. To understand that, I usually use an imagery of a railroad track going into our future, and on this track rides Hawai'i. This track has two rails: the rail of human rights and the rail of indigenous people's rights. Both rails must form this track, because if one rail decides to derail the other rail, the nation turns over. This is what the international community is calling for. How do we respect the human rights of everyone, and yet, how do we accord the indigenous people the special position that they must have in their own homeland? Because this is new and many of our people do not have the wide vision of what is happening in other places—[they] can only see the American experience—we need to show them that it can be done.

The third thing we need to do is to overcome the cults of personality and organization. Too often, we elevate individuals or the organizations they come from as if they were the creation of a nation. So we end up creating images of individuals. We end up creating large organizations, but we are not creating nations. We must get away from that and begin to build dreams in persons and give them tools to become foot soldiers or generals, grassroots people or politicians, in whatever area they want to become involved. Only when we move the movement into that direction will we be on our way towards our exercise of self-determination.

We also need to overcome the idea that the United States has the power or the right to grant us self-determination. We must take hold of our utopian society immediately, because no one else is going to give it to us. We must begin to live our Hawai'i as we see Hawai'i must be. I see Hawai'i as an occupied nation. I see Hawai'i as an independent nation. So I must conduct my response accordingly. I refuse to recognize the United States' jurisdiction over me. I therefore refuse to file an income tax return. I refuse to pay any taxes to a foreign government which is essentially attempting to hijack me, forcing me to finance its occupation of my country.

Another movement now going on is the taking of Hawaiian names that we were told not to use when we went to schools. People are naming their children with Hawaiian names. This not only is true of people of the indigenous race, but people throughout Hawai'i who are joining in this movement. Our Hawaiian language and hulas are being learned by nonindigenous people. This is a social movement, rather than a racial movement.

When I continually use the term self-determination, notice that I am not saying to exercise our Hawaiian sovereignty, or our choice for Hawaiian sovereignty. Self-determination has been described as the father and the mother of all human rights, and out of self-determination comes the choice of an independent nation, or what I call a sovereign nation. Others often misuse the term sovereignty. You can't have a nation within a nation and yet call it a sovereign nation because the Yankees have identified it as a sovereign entity. This is a violation of the international concepts of what sovereignty is. I have instead chosen to use the term self-determination. That is the more appropriate term because it says that we, as a people, have the right to choose sovereignty or remain integrated in the present colonial country. I have no doubts that the choice will be to emerge as an independent nation, a choice for sovereignty.

So how do we get there? What are the options? How do we accomplish the goal? In the march towards independence, there are three arenas in which we will have to fight battles. The first is the arena of Hawai'i. We will have to educate our people. We will have to be able to release them from the well and let them dream. We will have to count our numbers in the hundreds of thousands and organize them around a singular issue of independence. We need to infiltrate the judicial system, the legislative system, the economic system, the education system, the media system. Every system that exists in Hawai'i will have to be changed over into a fuller appreciation of self-determination.

The second is the American arena. I am a believer that the war in Vietnam was not fought and won only by the Vietnamese in Vietnam. It was also fought in the American public, via the American press. We need to carry the battle for Hawai'i's independence into the halls of Congress. More importantly, we need to carry it to the American people and convince them that their government must respond in a responsible and honorable way.

The third arena is the international arena. But that arena cannot be approached until we have organized our people in a sizable voice. Whether the committee on decolonization or any other entity of the United Nations, we must go in the good faith that we represent the nation of Hawai'i. And who will be the we? I cannot predict. It should not be me. Although I have had some opportunities to make some broad statements, I refuse to make them today because no single person today can say, "I represent the nation of Hawai'i."

In the 1960s, at the time of the Watts riots in California, a judge said, "Where there is no justice, there is violence." And then he stopped at that. I would add that those who are responsible for the violence are not those who do the violence, but those who deny the justice. People often ask me, "Will you be willing to resort to violence?" My response to them is, "Don't concentrate on the violence—concentrate on doing justice. That is the only guarantee of violence never occurring. Let us work for this justice together." But I need to also point out that the international community recognized the right of resistance in the exercise of self-determination, and I am not ready at this time to deny the Hawaiian people their right of resistance to achieve our right to self-determination.

Director of Kua'ana Student Services at the University of Hawai'i at Mānoa, a recruitment/retention program for Native Hawaiian students; forty-something years old.

My first name is Hawaiian, the last name is Portuguese. My dad's name is Gomes. My master's is in public health, and my Ph.D. is in political science.

It's very important to advocate for Native Hawaiian rights, specifically Native Hawaiian health. Most of the articles that are written on health are coming from a medical perspective, and I've come to question what aspect of the Hawaiian population they are studying. It has to be those who they can gather statistics on. So, who are those people? They are people who have jobs. They are people who are able to access medical health, and they are people who have a tendency to go to the doctor on a regular basis. For me, defining health in that way is coming from an elitist perspective, and that leaves out a significant portion of the population. And where are those statistics coming from? If they are coming from the public sector, then you are dealing with the poor working class. If they are coming from the private sector, then the statistics would reflect more healthy Hawaiians, more middle class, those who have better jobs, more money, nice cars, good houses, good education. That's not clearly defined in the statistics that we see coming out of the Department of Health, or the government. They define it according to medical health. There is nothing there that talks about a correlation between poor health and poor housing conditions, poor health and lack of jobs, poor housing, socioeconomic conditions, lack of education. So the departments of public health at the State and national levels have a very narrow vision of health in terms of medical health. We need to struggle to enlarge that perspective to include all of those other issues I mentioned.

The credibility of the U.S. around the world would be horrendous if the real statistics would be known. The Native Hawaiian health centers come under the Native Hawaiian Health Bill, and if one looks at the health bill very closely, it talks about such statistics as diabetes, cancer, and those kinds of things. And then there appears to me to be the compromise, the acceptance of Native Hawaiian traditional healers. So that tends to placate the Native Hawaiian community, in terms of the bill being a good one. Interestingly enough, what happens in the centers is that each center is designed to be a mini-department of health that is focused on medical issues, on behavioral health risks.

It focuses on blaming the victim, rather than focusing on the system and what it is contributing toward keeping the Hawaiians in poor health. Traditionally public health, as it was started in England, looked at environmental conditions and the contribution of environmental pollution to people's health. So the Native Hawaiian health system then, like the Oʻahu Plan, for example, was written by medical doctors, so it is very medically oriented. Nowhere does it talk about jobs. It gives the statistics in terms of welfare and housing and homelessness, but it doesn't talk about that in terms of how relative it is to poor health.

The place of the traditional Hawaiian healers in the Native Hawaiian health center is to increase the usability of the Western-oriented centers. So these centers become a sort of gatekeeper to the Queen's Medical Health Center, or the State-run plans, or whatever. This is an effort to make sure that people are part of that process. My analogy is that it is like using the Hawaiian language to educate Hawaiians, but yet interpret books that have Western capitalistic values in them. Using the language to make it more acceptable to people. That looks to me, from a radical perspective, like it is *using* the culture, so that they can continue to keep people in their places.

The state health insurance plan is supposed to provide services to the underinsured in Hawaiʻi. A lot of people do not receive services. The law here says that if you're working 20 hours or more, then the employer must provide health coverage. Employers get around that by hiring people for only 19 hours a week. Many of us here at the university are hired for just 19 hours a week, so we don't get health coverage. Also, what is happening in Hawai'i more and more is temp jobs. A large number of State workers are part time and aren't covered.

Because our system is one that's based on maldistribution of resources—the capitalist society—health care is seen by the people who affect policy as having a dollar quantification. The formula is: How much is the system going to make? It's not: How many people are we going to save and how many lives are we going to improve?

I feel that one of the primary problems that many of us are confronted with—not only Hawai'i—is that we look at the conditions of our people in terms of the high incidence of poor health, the low number of people who complete higher education, the high rates of homelessness, the high rates of incarceration. One cannot ignore the fact that it's people on the low end of the totem pole who keep getting placed in the position of not being able to rise above their conditions. What this is about is that a small percentage is controlling what is happening to people. People who control the power and the wealth are invested in keeping people at the bottom because it means that they can acquire more wealth.

So the reason why so many of us are passionately driven to social change is because we understand what the issue is. The bottom line is that it is about the *unequal distribution of power and wealth* in our society, and that we would like to somehow, some way, equalize that. Then people would start to feel better about themselves in terms of making decisions. Power is translated into resources, whether it is intellectual, financial, or natural resources. That is power. Some of this came across in the book written by Creel Froman, *The Two Political Systems of America*. There is a quote in there in which he says, "The advocacy of minority whites is the perpetuation for the unequal distribution of power and wealth in America." I don't want to hear anymore that I am a minority. We perpetuate the acceptance of that inequality, and we have to stop that. We have to put ourselves in that same position and "go for it."

One of the other realities is the AIDS issue and the lack of government research. In Australia a lot of money is put into AIDS research, and a lot has been done in that country. In our country it's really lacking. Who's leading the AIDS research here? It's the large pharmaceutical companies. So there's always competition, which has nothing to do with saving lives. It has everything to do with making money. The AIDS activists have a right to scream, because their lives are being played around with.

It's the same thing with Native Hawaiians here. We see more money coming into the state and people scrambling to have these moneys, and yet the people who are most affected aren't being asked what kinds of programs they really want. What we are seeing is how the unequal distribution of power and wealth is polarizing our community. Those Hawaiian institutions that already have some power want to maintain that, so that you see on a local level what is happening on a national and worldwide level, but magnified many times over. It is fascinating to watch it on a local level, and to see the people on the bottom begin to raise consciousness, and as their efforts grow and they mobilize more people, the people on the other side strategize how to maintain that control.

It's kind of like a war within the ethnic group. It's about class, those who control and those who don't control. Those who have power don't want to give it up, and don't want to share it. If they are going to share it, they want to decide who they are going to share it with, and how much they are going to share. It reminds me of the analogy of the masters feeding the dogs. The master decides how much to give the dog, and when he is going to eat. Even if we do come from the same ethnic group, the class issue is so ingrained in our capitalist society that unless we in our different communities confront that, and challenge each other about that, and mobilize around that, I don't see those changes being made. If you look at all of the "isms," the bottom line is this whole thing about capitalism. From capitalism comes racism, sexism, homophobia. It gives birth to all of the weeds.

How did you get started on this focus? Did your family influence you?

I can remember as early as four or five years old. I grew up in a household where my Portuguese grandfather was a *luna* on the plantation, the supervisor, and I remember seeing him with one of those hats on—I call them the bwana hats—khaki-colored pants, high black boots, carrying a whip, and riding a horse. I used to be so afraid of him. Then my father and my two uncles worked as laborers on the plantation. My younger uncle, who was my favorite, had the worst jobs, the "*sabidont* man" (a Filipino word) who carried the cylinder on his back which sprayed chemicals to kill the weeds. Today my uncle is dying of lung cancer. He used to come home from work when I was a little kid, and I would hear the sound of the truck coming by and the different languages of the men telling him goodbye, the Filipino guy calling out to him, or the Hawaiian or the Japanese guy, "See you tomorrow at work." He would come around the corner, and I would be waiting at the kitchen door, and he'd sit down and I'd help to take off his shoes, and he'd talk to me about my day. I would remember all of the dirt and the goggles he would use and there would be circles around his eyes from all the red dirt. And his shoes and socks would be thick with dirt.

He would take me to the different camps, the ethnic camps that were set up. Sometimes we would go to the Japanese camp, and I was mesmerized by the language and the people. Because I was so close to him, I felt warmth everywhere I went. What was important to me as a kid was the food. I'd go to the Japanese camp and I'd get little tangerines and Japanese candies, and the next day we'd go to the Filipino camp and my uncle would be squatting on the ground with the men, and I would squat next to him, and he'd be stroking their chickens. They would give me Filipino pastries. The different camps had different things.

But one of the significant things that I remember were the arguments in our house between labor and management. My grandfather and my uncles and my dad just yelled at each other, my grandfather always on the management side, and my dad and my uncles on the other side. My grandfather would be criticizing the ILWU. I was just a little kid, but I remember Harry Bridges' name. When I was in high school my father went on from there to a job at Pearl Harbor, and eventually had his own small business making residential fences. When I was in high school, I remember getting really inspired in my civics class, or maybe world history, reading about the Bolshevik revolution. I came home and I tried to unionize my dad's shop *(laughs)*, and I almost got kicked out of the house. He told my mother, "Will you tell this girl who puts the food in her mouth and the roof over her head?" And he asked me, "Why are you doing this?" And I looked at him and I said, "What's wrong with what I'm doing and what I'm saying, and what you used to tell grandpa?" And he looked at me and said, "Do you *remember that?* Those were different times!" But I didn't think so.

I remember other things about my childhood. I was not allowed to express who I was as a Hawaiian. I was not allowed to see any of my Hawaiian relatives, including my mother. I wasn't allowed to have any Hawaiian friends. The only thing Hawaiian in the house was radio station KCCN. I grew up resenting being Hawaiian. My stepmother projected onto us all the stereotypes about Hawaiians: dirty, stupid, lazy. I used to be very bitter towards my parents, my stepmother included, but as I grew older I began to understand that they were victims of oppression themselves. Their attitudes were created; they weren't born with them.

I grew up initially going to parochial schools. When my dad remarried, my stepmother couldn't handle these two very bright young women, and so she switched us out of parochial schools and put her sons in them. My sister and I were put into public schools, which was a good learning experience. In elementary school we had a system of A, B, and C class, the A class being the smart class, the B class being the average class, and the C class being the dumb class. Most of the A class were Japanese kids. The B class was the Filipino kids, the Chinese kids, and maybe one or two Japanese kids. The C class, where all the dumb kids were, were all the Polynesian kids, all the Hawaiians.

Well, four of us Hawaiian young women were in the A class. The mother of two of the girls was the school librarian. The reason why my sister and I were in the A class was because we came from a parochial school and because my dad was very active in the community and a strong union man. It was very difficult. I remember the first day walking into the class and at recess, some girls came up to me. One asked, "Can you spell?"

And I looked at her and I said, "Yeah, I know how to spell."

And she said, "Well, spell *battleship,* then."

And so I spelled it out to her and they kind of looked at each other. And then she goes, "Now, tell me one word."

Coming from a parochial school—right?—I said, "Spell *conception.*"

And she goes, "What?"

And I said, *"Conception."*

Another girl looked at her and then says to me, "You spell it."

So I said, "Okay, conception," and I spelled it right out.

From that day on, I was left alone in terms of my academic performance at school. This was in Waipahu, in the country. But that's how the entire school system was. Those of my age grew up with the attitude that Hawaiians or Polynesians are dumb and they're not supposed to succeed. All through school I had to fight my way to be accepted, literally fight with kids, though I wasn't a violent person. Finally, the biggest recognition came when I was in the eighth grade and got nominated by the teachers to be the May Day queen, and that was an honor. But the

Japanese kids couldn't accept that, and so they gave me a real hard time. The kids in the A class would talk about my friends—other Polynesian kids—in the C class: "Yeah, look at them—they're so dirty, they're so poor," or, "They're all on tokens. They cannot afford to buy lunch," and things like that. Fortunately, most of my teachers were really good.

Twenty-five years later, in 1989, I went back to school to get my bachelor's degree. I had been doing really well and maintaining a very high grade-point average. All of a sudden, in my second to the last semester I just started feeling like I didn't want to do my work any more. I didn't want to read, I didn't want to write, I didn't want to do anything. I started feeling really depressed, and I began to look around for what was causing it. Nobody had died; there was no trauma; there wasn't an anniversary.

One day I was sitting quietly, kind of like in meditation, and all of a sudden this thought came into my head: "You're Native Hawaiian and you won't succeed. Native Hawaiians do not succeed. You're stupid." And the tears just started to come. This whole thing about elementary school just came flooding over me. And I thought, "That's the way a lot of Native Hawaiians must feel, because we've been conditioned to think this way."

I was really angry that our educational system could do that to a group of people; and not only Hawaiians, but people who were less fortunate. Some of the Filipino kids at school came from really big families. I thought about this one family that I grew up with and how they lived in an abandoned church. I could see them all so vividly. Oh, this system that we live in, this system where the rich get richer and the poor get poorer!

I'm considered the black sheep in the family because I'm the one who doesn't own a house, I'm not married today, I have only one child, and I became an activist. When my youngest sister got married, she wanted me to be in her wedding. She came to me crying, "Mom and Dad won't allow me to ask you to be in the wedding."

I said, "Well, it's okay. Let's not make waves for you. I can be there to support you."

"But I really want you. Dad says that you're nothing but a commie."

So I explained, "If he wants to label me because of the things I stand up for, that's all right. You know, we can define a communist as someone who stands up for people's rights. It's not a bad word—it's okay."

She felt a little bit better and I became her mistress of ceremonies.

That was a compromise. But they said to her, "You better tell her not to wear any of that Hawaiian stuff and no talking about Native Hawaiians and their land rights or anything like that."

When did your activism start?

It started when I was about twenty-six and going through a divorce. I already had my son. That's when I took on my Hawaiian name. I just rebelled. I reclaimed my Hawaiian identity and just started doing what I wanted to do. I joined the [Protect] Kahoʻolawe ʻOhana. I was so hungry for information, reading different people's theories and things like that. That was a really exciting time.

When I was in my early thirties and working in State mental health, and actively involved with the ʻOhana, I developed a class in parenting strategies and began facilitating groups. One group I was facilitating was at the Lualualei military installation. It was a group of women whose husbands worked there and they lived on the base. This was when Kahoʻolawe was being bombed in regular RIMPAC exercises: five countries—Great Britain, Australia, Japan, France, and the U.S.—were using the island for target practice. Knowing that was real painful. Land is something we hold sacred. The military, of course, can't understand that because they have a different way of looking at things.

Being very conscious of group cohesion, I noticed the group cohesion at the military installation wasn't being formed. What I suspected was that it was my role. I was the only Hawaiian person there. Everyone else was haole. My cofacilitator was haole, so I told her, "You know, I think it has something to do with how they are seeing me. I'd like to raise the question to allow them to talk about it."

So I did, and they opened up and said things like, "Well, we're really afraid of you. We're told by the commander that Hawaiians hate white people and that you're going to beat up our kids and you're going to beat us up, and we can't go down to the town here in Waiʻanae because you guys hate us." They said they got briefed on all this: "Don't go to the local beaches because the locals hate the whites," and things like that.

So I said, "Well, let me give you some history of the people of Hawaiʻi and let me give you the military history, too."

I talked about things that had happened in Hawaiʻi that have contributed to some of the animosity that the commander may have talked about. I talked about the Massey case, which I think happened in the late 1940s. There was a navy wife who was raped and she accused five local men. One of them got killed. At the hearings it was found out that she had been having an affair and wanted to cover it up because she got beaten up. So she blamed the five men. It just erupted into a big thing, with the president of the U.S. involved. The military was very, very racist. So I explained that case to them.

I also said, "The other thing is that the military is involved in bombing one of our islands, supposedly for target practice." They didn't know about that. And then I talked to them about the military involvement in the Pacific—you know, the atom bomb testing in the Bikini islands.

They were like, "God!"

I said, "These are the kinds of things that shape peoples' attitudes and they get really angered, but it doesn't mean that they hate you."

Then this woman in uniform stood up in the group and looked at me and said, "You have five minutes to get off this base. You are giving out confidential information and conducting subversive activity."

It was like, Am I hearing this? I said, "I'm not conducting subversive activity. This isn't confidential information. I mean if I have it, anybody has it."

And she said, "I've been assigned by the commander to watch you, and I've been here every day just waiting for you to do something like this." And she goes, "If you're not out of here in five minutes, you're going to be arrested. I'm going to the commander's office right now and I'm coming back with the MPs."

I said to the women in the group, "I have to leave. I do not want to be arrested. I don't know what this is all about. If I've said anything to offend you, I'm sorry, but that wasn't my intent."

The women in the group were crying. They came to me and said, "Thank you so much for telling us this. We don't want our babies being born like jellyfish, like the Bikini women's babies" (I had told them about that). They said, "Thank you for being so brave. We will never forget you. It's because of people like you that our children can be born healthy." I could see the pain in their eyes. Now that they had this information, how do they face their husbands?

By the time I got back to my office, about thirty minutes away, the governor had been called, the head of the Department of Health had been called, the head of the Division of Mental Health had been called. I came off the elevator and the whole place was quiet. Everybody just watched me. My boss came storming into my office: "What did you do?"

Then the State tried to get me fired and I called the United Public Workers union. They got on the case right away, and I told them exactly what happened. They're like, "Congratulations." The union agent was a really good guy. He came in and he started pressuring them and they backed off. But I received a letter from the commander that barred me indefinitely from all military bases. It stated that I was conducting subversive activities.

Then the director of the Waianae Mental Health Center, a psychiatrist who had heard about what happened, called me up and said, "I want you to work for me. Put in your transfer papers. You're the kind of person that we need up here. I want a fighter. You'd fit right into this community."

And so I got a transfer out there. The community was very cohesive and staving off big development. It was very strong in alternative economic development. There were a lot of homeless. The director of the clinic, understanding who I was, said, "All you have to do is just let me know what it is you're doing and I'll support you." So I developed a farm project for children out there. Part of the activity was to expose them to the different issues in the community, so when the homeless were being evicted, I would take the children to watch.

The kids asked, "Who're those people?"

I said, "Those people work for the State. They are evicting these people who have no place to go, no jobs, no money. This is land where they can live and yet they have to leave. These are some of your friends' parents. They now have no homes."

These were children who were not performing well academically, but they were streetwise kids. They learned a lot and they felt better about who they were and that they could talk about real issues. They were learning how to work the land and to bring food home to put on their grandparents' table, as opposed to bringing home a note from school that said they were naughty and that kind of stuff. I started off with six children, and by the time I left there were thirty. I think they have something like two hundred kids now.

8

Conclusions

So far the reader has been exposed to a series of autobiographies told in story form, dealing with lives of activists in Hawai'i. In our chapter introductions we have attempted to build the case for each problem and movement area which our speakers struggle around. Now there is a need to sum up.

If it appears that there is much that is negative and troublesome in the picture painted in this book, there is good reason. Activists are dissenters by definition. They deal every day with the seamy side of things, and many are angry. Most thinking people would agree that there is much to be angry about in the world that we inhabit and must pass on to our children. So, negatives must be expected as endemic to the subject matter of this book. Yet, with all of its problems as part of the twentieth-century world, Hawai'i embodies such immense strength and spirit for the future that we would be remiss not to point this out.

We have found in our travels and the study of four cities that quite a few activists have either dropped out of their movement or have remained in but were now actually destructive. Part of their problem was that they were unwilling or unable to make changes in politics, reformulations of what or who is the enemy, or even what the struggle is about. We and other activists have learned that it is necessary to be unyielding in the cause one champions but flexible in the tactics and strategies that an organization pursues. And throughout, the deepest of respect must be accorded one's comrades in struggle. They are an energetic minority who go where others fear to tread. Whatever has been accomplished, they are responsible.

One strength embodied in Hawai'i's activists is that they work and organize in a setting of relative racial harmony. Given the high numbers of interracial, interethnic marriages, this amalgamation occurs at the most primary level: the family. Most organizations, from the environment to labor to antiwar, have interethnic compositions and leadership. Most Kanaka Maoli organizations encourage the participation of those outside of their own nationalism, and this is very nonexclusionary given the demands by some for independence and—in a sense—separatism that are implied. The Rainbow Coalition and the size and vigor of the annual Martin Luther King march and celebration reinforces the symbolism of unity among peoples.

The environmental movement in Hawai'i is said to be one of the strongest in the United States. As was pointed out, the degradation of the land, water, and air are also some of the most serious problems with which to cope. The activists in our group of speakers are serious scholars and educators on this issue. Many have written, many have lectured, and many have vigorously organized around the environment. Others, such as Gigi Cocquio, are educating children in the preservation and restoration of the land and water and their natural products. The sovereignty movement has land as its core priority. How to restore and maintain the land in its natural state becomes an issue that intersects with many non-Kanaka Maoli.

The history of labor activism in Hawai'i is a proud one, and the representatives we have included are organizing in that arena. These are not faint-hearted people. They will have to preserve their working-class identities and political momentum even more strongly in this period of union-breaking by corporate America. They will have to convince all people who work that they too are workers, even though they may be professors, physicians, editors, or writers. These too are service workers, and must join with waiters and janitors in organizing unions.

Hawai'i also offers hidden assets for its activists. More than many other universities in the cities we have studied, the University of Hawai'i makes its facilities available to the community. Most of the educational forums on the sovereignty movement's plebiscite have been held at UH. Some departments and faculty members actually represent links with the community: Ethnic Studies, Hawaiian Studies, Women's Studies. Some of our activists have been involved in battles to preserve these important links, and so far they have won.

Several important questions flow from the material that has been presented: Will Hawai'i again become the paradise it was thought to be hundreds of years ago? Will it become a model to the world of humane social relations, wise stewardship of natural resources, and a superior quality of life, as Lynette Cruz envisions? What will it take to make this happen? To speculate on answers to these hypothetical questions requires a critique of American activism and a review of the objective conditions facing the people of the United States—indeed, of the world.

We salute the contributions that our speakers have made and continue to make. We sometimes have implied what might appear to be criticisms, but these were intended in the spirit of struggle, "comradeship," and aloha. We feel strongly that this is an extremely important point in history when many factors are coming together in new, sometimes alarming, ways. Activist models appropriate to an earlier period therefore may be less germane to today's needs. An incisive analysis of real-world changes is required to begin to determine the logic of a twenty-first-century people's movement.

Most of the protesters we have presented were strongly influenced by the dramatic movements of the 1960s. Many were in college at the time, some on the "mainland." They absorbed the visions and tactics of the movements that fought oppression, war, and poverty. America in the '60s was living in relative abundance while fighting a losing war in Vietnam. President Johnson even told us that we could have *both* "guns and butter." In that period of great social motion, many enlightened, white middle-class families supported and subsidized the radical proclivities of their children, and provided a haven at home when the going got rough. Even some elements of business and the political system were obliged to show a mildly liberal face, reluctantly supporting civil rights laws and even antiwar sentiment. Very often it was *their* children who went to Selma or fled the draft in Canada. But *no* serious movement of the '60s successfully challenged the economic system or the business-government complex, and those hardy few who tried to do so were quickly, sometimes viciously, repressed. Actually, not many activists thought such a challenge was necessary because the economy, until about 1969, was doing pretty well. Of course, that's about the time when the postwar/Cold War boom was ending, in tandem with the movement's decline.

Then there is the American "spirit" of *individualism* to evaluate. Though the '60s movements had certain "collectivist" aspects, they did not effectively cross race and gender lines. There was little serious effort to even *try* to cross class lines. They seemed just too impenetrable. Most of the movement was dominated by the American-as-apple-pie spirit of anarchism that has pervaded life since the founding of the country. The deep distrust of all authority, right or left, effectively stultified movement initiatives that might have challenged the hegemony of capital.

Not accidentally, movement ideologues stressed *freedom,* not equality, a fact that dovetailed neatly with official philosophy.

Meanwhile, fairly comfortable white liberals hoped that peace and justice could be willed through individual witness and collective thinking. It was almost like church, and indeed much of it *was* church. Coalitions across "natural" or economic groups were hard to form and had short lives. If the purpose of a coalition was to bring folks together for mass wish-thought, vigil, or witness, and in some cases confrontation, there were some important successes such as ending the Vietnam War and ending segregation in the South. But notice: These successes were reactive to the insidious evils of war and segregation that should not have existed in the first place.

In terms of demanding life's essentials for all—income, food, shelter, health care, education—the movement had little long-range impact; just a bit of system tinkering. There never was a serious challenge to corporate America's penchant for putting *its* interests before the health and welfare of the masses of people. Most of the movement leadership of the '60s failed to understand, or refused to accept, that the *real* mass mobilizing potential lay in the age-old material interests of the people. They knew that material interests overshadowed all else for the ruling class, but they were unable to apply this principle to people at the bottom. Perhaps worse, there was a kind of elitism permeating the movement that disinclined it from accepting leadership emerging from the lower classes. Humility and a real sense of equality was lacking for many. Then many talented leaders, having paid their "dues" while deferring gratifications, maybe having burned out, and certainly lacking a vision and strategy for the future, were co-opted into well-paying positions in the system. Activists for the twenty-first century must consider this legacy so as not to make the mistakes of the past.

Toward the end of the '60s, a brief stirring emerged from the bottom in the form of the poor people's movement. Martin Luther King and other mostly Black leaders had learned how little resilience there was in the practical affairs of American political economy. For a brief time, first things were put first: The poor asserted moral leadership in a country sorely lacking it. This was quickly extinguished by assassination, cruel harassment, and movement impotence. Nevertheless, an important statement had been made which, we submit, foretold the future of the peoples' movement. The ill-advised and ill-fated Weathermen branch of Students for a Democratic Society once sagely cautioned, "You don't need a weatherman to know what direction the wind is blowing."

We learned over the years what most people intuitively know: The establishment relentlessly protects its material self-interests and will *not* willingly give up its power. The lesson this should teach activists of the future is that exploited and oppressed people must find common ground in *their* self-interests. Activists must learn from the past. At the same time, an ominously new packaging in political economy has occurred since the grand and adventurous '60s, and this will profoundly shape the movements of the future. Let us briefly review this.

In addition to the "normal" greed of the economic elites, there is a deepening crisis in the free enterprise system which they shepherd. Rates of profit continue to decline while foreign competition for markets and profits becomes more keen. In the effort to improve their balance sheets, they try to reduce the cost of doing business by introducing new technology and more efficient work systems. This invariably means that more and more workers are discharged or forced to work longer and harder, often at lower wages and reduced benefits. Meanwhile, unions are weakened or broken, and workers are fired for union organizing.

If this were not enough, a new right-wing political force has slithered into public office and uses the power of government to reduce the quality of life of working people even further. Programs designed to alleviate the worst conditions of working people and provide a semblance of security for them are being dismantled, while the "savings" from such penurious policies flow into the pockets of the rich. Lastly, no respite from this chicanery is in sight, no improvement plan is on the books, and little mercy is likely to be shown those individuals who challenge this process. It is safe to predict that in the next brief period, millions more will join those millions already on the "skids." The present generation's savings, health care plan, pension, and possibly social security— purchasing power that buoys up the system today—will be long gone. Most new jobs of the future will be low wage, low benefit. New technology will continue to put people out of work. With less income, there is less savings and less consumption. Thus, more workers will be let go as consumers tighten their purses. Unemployment will soar. These are the prerequisites of economic collapse. Surely, then, the specter of national—no, worldwide—depression looms in the foreseeable future. Will an authoritarian future, reminiscent of fascist Europe, accompany an economic collapse? Is it a distinct possibility?

Does the above offensive scenario relate to gentle Hawai'i, the land of aloha, sovereignty, retirees, and tourists? We think it does because Hawai'i, whatever its future social and political form, is tied into

national and world political economy. Just imagine the lost jobs, mortgage foreclosures, evictions, untreated illnesses, and crime that would
result from even a 25 percent reduction in tourism. How will the working people of Hawai'i survive a great economic disaster? Handouts
from the rich? Taro subsistence? Federal subsidies? We doubt it. Survival might be possible on the underpopulated neighbor islands, but
O'ahu would be a disaster. Something else is needed.

We think that social movements of the future should be and will be
conceived, designed, and led by those who are the greatest victims of
exploitation and oppression. In the United States, and in Hawai'i, there
grows a body of have-nots that crosses racial, ethnic, and cultural lines.
Individuals in that body look different and come from diverse backgrounds. Their basis of oppression had different historical roots. But
they share a common economic position in society: they are *poor*. It is
that commonality that can forge a multinational poor peoples' movement for the twenty-first century. We are pleased that this is beginning
to happen in the United States. By numbers alone, this movement could
be a powerful political majority. Its irresistible moral authority could
mobilize many of the nonpoor. Its staying power and motivation to
struggle is without doubt.

Most societies have specific groups that have been singled out for
super exploitation and oppression. In the United States, the Native,
African, and Mexican peoples are examples. In Hawai'i it is the Kanaka
Maoli. Those who are indigenous, those whose land and resources were
stolen, those who were brutally enslaved, and those who have been the
victims of genocide are the ones who have suffered above all others.
They should be *honored* with the highest level of "affirmative action"—
the right to leadership in the future battles for equality and justice. To
this, we tentatively propose a codicil for consideration by the aforemen-
tioned people: Those individuals from exploited and oppressed groups
who have been co-opted into privileged positions by virtue of their ability, luck, or cunning should *not* be the top leaders.

The right of leadership carries deep ethical and intellectual responsibilities. We conceive the twenty-first-century peoples' movement as
crossing all the social lines that oppressors have shrewdly used over the
years to separate people. These barriers to intergroup unity—dare we
say "class" unity—must be pulled down for all time as a matter of the
highest principle. But also, the removal of these pernicious barriers is a
matter of great strategic significance. Activists have learned that a
"minority" cannot take power and effect structural change in a capital-

ist democracy. Liberation may never happen in the absence of a strong statistical majority that forms a moral force.

We think that the future of Hawai'i could be shaped by the sovereignty movement. The legitimacy of the Kanaka Maoli cause and its right to moral leadership is indisputable. As the *most* exploited and oppressed, as the poorest, the Kanaka Maoli have the right to exercise practical leadership. Its more militant proclivity rightly claims jurisdiction over the archipelago and all the people therein. It claims the right to create an independent nation. The movement is at an early stage of development and it is trying to think through so many important issues. We think it should seriously consider its ethical and intellectual responsibilities to *all* Hawaiian residents. In its current search for a tomorrow, sovereignty has a democratic face within its own people. We wonder how deeply this permeates into the two hundred thousand Kanaka Maoli in Hawai'i. Equally important, how much democracy will there be for the approximately three hundred thousand non-Kanaka Maoli residents who are or will in the future be poor? Once sovereignty is comfortable with its identity and somewhat satisfied with its overview, will it reach out to other exploited and oppressed peoples as equals, with the aim of democratically devising a plan of action for the future? It is our profound hope that this will be the case.

Index

A'ala Park, 188
Academic freedom, 133–134
Activism: as ebb and flow, 253; home and hearth type, 269; as humanistic ministry, 214
Activists, 19, 178
Administration for Native Americans, 372, 379
Advertiser, 320
Affirmative action, 145, 268; and Filipinos, 332; as an honor, 434; opposition to, 279
Affordable housing, 26. *See also* housing
Agbayani, Amy, 236
Agency for International Development [AID], 337
Ahupua'a, 385; defined, 108
Ahupua'a, Fishponds, and Lo'i, 108
Aid to Families with Dependent Children, 161
AIDS, 421–422
'Āiea landing, 79
'Āina Haina, 42, 44, 256, 307
'Akaka Falls, 221
Ala Moana Shopping Center, 270, 288
Albertini, Jim, 67, 269, 271, 331
Alexander and Baldwin, 322
Alienation, 159; as expression of counterculture, 32; and labor, 330
Ali'i (chiefs), 356, 366, 384
Alinsky, Saul, 311
Aloha, defined, 85

Aloha 'āina, 355, 404, 413
Aloha Association, 371
Alternative energy, 72
Amaral, Annelle, 236
American Association of University Professors, 133–134
American Civil Liberties Union, 158, 269
American dream, 246; erosion of, 219
American economy, 137. *See also* economy
American Enterprise Institute, 217
American Factors [Amfac], 325
American Federation of State, County, and Municipal Workers, 284, 297
American foreign policy, analysis of, 128
American Friends Service Committee, 254
American imperialism, 132. *See also* imperialism
American Indian Movement, 357
American Indians, ignorance about, 141
American law, 410
American Medical Association [AMA], 165
American newspapers, 142
American Samoa, 52; U.S. takeover of, 84
Anarchism, pervasiveness of, 431
Angel Network, 378
Annexation, 57, 58; as illegal act, 367

Antibases movement (Japan), 267
Antiwar movement, 76, 111
Aoudé, Brahim, 7, 15, 187
Arab Ba'ath Party, 29
Arab culture, similarity to Hawai'i, 31
Ariyoshi, Koji, 310
Asian Americans: and restrictive covenants, 42; as power holders, 47
Asian-American studies, 152
Asian-Communist Affairs, Office of, 337
Asian Law Caucus, 154
Asian-Pacific Books, 215
Asian Studies Department (UH), 341
Assimilation, 391
Association of Flight Attendants, 332
Atomic and hydrogen bombs, 105
Autobiography of Malcolm X, 144
Avakian, Bob, 348

Bachman Hall, occupation of, 246, 249, 341, 342
Bakke case, 154
Backlash: The Undeclared War Against American Women (Faludi), 229
Barbers Point, 261
Bayo, Alberto, 206
Beach people, 378
Beechert, Edward D., 288
Belau, 105
Benkel, Fred, 97
Bible, 386; study of, 63
Big Five, 16, 299, 353, 401; early dependency on, 91
Big Island, 45, 94, 140, 152, 184, 221, 326, 374; possible crops on, 91
Bikini Atoll, 141; and birth defects, 427
Bill of Rights, 119
Bingham, Hiram, 366
Bishop, Bernice Pauahi, 306
Bishop, Charles Reed, 306
Bishop Estate, 58, 306, 345
Bishop Museum, 16, 103; and tourist industry, 106

Blacklisting, 299
Black Panther Party, 182, 344, 346
Black power, 339
Blaisdell, Kekuni, 6, 358–359, 361, 385, 387
Blood, quantum, 367, 375, 379
Board of Human Services, 309
Board of Regents (UH), and Lee case, 133, 135
Body mutilation, of women, 230–231
Bolshevik model: inappropriateness of, 19
Bornhorst, Marilyn, 97
Bouslog and Symonds, 158, 310
Brewer, Jim, 165
Bridges, Harry, 320, 423
Brown, Christine (Kalahiki), 165
Brown v Board, 157
Bulldozing demolition, 345–346
Burgess, Hayden (Poka Laenui), 51, 360, 361, 372, 387, 388
Burns, Governor John, 225, 313
Business Week, 163
Butler, Will, 165

Cai, Zhifeng, 7
Calvinists, early brutality of, 85
Cambodia, invasion of, 130
Camp Smith, 269
Canal Zone, 263–266
Capital: and high profits, 284; patriotism of, 286; restrict freedom on, 350
Capitalism, 171; brainwashed with, 101; money-making goal of, 26; need for reform of, 422; problems spawned by, 422
Capitalist depression, 137–138
Capitalist economy: global nature of, 172; introduction of, 400
Capitalist system: deepening crisis in, 121; in early Europe, 83; racist nature of, 84
Cash-register democracy, U.S. as, 213
Catholic Church, 395; contradictions in, 331
Catholicism, 166

Caucasians: as a minority, 12, 243; suspicion of, 240
Ceded lands, 367
Center for Biographical Research (UH), 7
Center for Constitutional Rights, 397
Center for Hawaiian Studies (UH), 141
Center for Labor Education and Research [CLEAR] (UH), 290
Center for Pacific Islands Studies, 103
Chamber of Commerce, 315
Chen, Yu Hsi, 226
Chesney-Lind, Meda, 232
Chiefly stewardship, 355
Chiefs: outside influences on, 103; nature of, 85; and sell-out of people, 87; system, 355
Chinatown, 33, 136, 402; evictions in, 43, urban renewal of, 35
Chow, Wayson, 15, 35
Choy, Mary, 7, 165
Christianity: and "dominion-over," 385
Christians Against Nuclear Arms, 271
Chun Do Whan, 216
Church of the Crossroads, 14, 181, 342
Church Women United, 262
CIA, on UH campus, 341
Citizens for Rent Control, 39, 187
Civil disobedience training, 269
Civil rights movement, 32, 153, 338; opposition to, 279
Class: attack on by Reagan and Bush, 216–217; consciousness, 288; and ethnicity, 37; interests in Hawai'i, 54; structure, dynamics of, 162; struggle and the Pacific area, 53
Clerical workers: organizing of, 319
Coalitions: need for, 146; and survival, 336; as hard to form, 432
Cocquio, Gigi, 59, 174, 271, 430
Collective bargaining: for public workers, 293
College, cost of, 48
Colonialism, exposure to ideas of, 18
Colonization, 411

Columbus legacy, 368
Committee for Maritime Unity, 309
Committee on Welfare Concerns, 305, 314
Common ground, 55; need for, 433
Communal system, success of, 355
Communism, collapse of, 185
Communism-Maoism, lies told about, 141
Communist hysteria, of cold war, 286
Communist Manifesto, 120
Communist Party (Hawai'i), influence of, 54; Marxist-Leninist, 216
Concerned Residents of Waiāhole-Waikāne, 98
Congress of Industrial Organizations, 284, 307, 322
Conscientious objectors, 269
Constitutional conventions (Ka Lāhui Hawai'i), 395
Consumer Housing Task Force, 335
Contact, 340
Contaminated soil, shipment to Marshall Islands, 117
Contract labor, 400; in agricultural system, 228
"Contract with America," 1, 163
Contradictions: of capital and labor, 333; in early Kanaka Maoli society, 355–356; as internal to systems, 82
Cook, Captain James, 353, 356, 365
Cooper, George, 35, 57, 60
Coral reefs, dredging of, 86
Corporate profit, falling rate of, 285
Cost of living, 88, 161
Crime: rise in, 13; street type, 162
Criminal Intelligence Division (U.S.), 343
Criminology, 239
Cruz, Lynette, 6, 7, 358, 361, 430
Cuba, U.S. takeover of, 84
Cuban revolution, 206–207
Culture, manipulation of, 420
Cultural kīpuka, 405
Cultural practices, 407; of Kanaka Maoli, 391, 394, 404

Daws, Gavan, 57, 114
DeCambra, Hoʻoipo, 234
Decolonization, 367–368
Democracy: in the sixties, 121; struggle for, 151
Democratic empowerment, defined, 23
Democratic Party, 225, 390
Demonstrations: FBI surveillance of, 131; solo, 269
Department of Education (Hawaiʻi), 256, 268, 293
Department of Health (Hawaiʻi), 271; bias of, 420
Department of Health (Philippines), 63
Department of Human Services (Hawaiʻi), 314
Department of Labor (Hawaiʻi), 300
Department of Planning and Economic Development (Hawaiʻi), 344
Department of Social Security Employees Association, 309
Dependency, mentality of, 412
Dialectical analysis, 82
Discrimination: in education, 250; subtlety of, 47
Diseases, 284, 401
Divide and conquer, 184; as management strategy, 320; as plantation camp strategy, 47; as union breaker, 302
Dodge, Dick, 203
Dole Cannery, 318; picket line at, 153
Dole Provisional Government, 84
Domestic Violence Clearing House, 238
Douglas, Jim, 331
Draft card, burning of, 341
Drugs, and tourism, 38

Easley, Janet, 13
East-West Center (UH), 111, 340
Ecocide, 344. See also ecosystem
Ecology, alteration of, 58–59
Economic collapse, prerequisites of, 433
Economic periods, 283
Economics: as danger zone, 120; supply side, 163; understanding through, 100
Economic system, as unchallenged, 431
Economy: need for change, 147; restructuring of, 27, 217, 301
Ecosystem, 177. See also ecocide
Education, needed in grass roots, 92
Effigy case, 204–205
Electoral politics, as vehicle for change, 21
Elitism: in '60s movement, 432; among teachers, 297
Emory, Kenneth, 103
Employees' Retirement Income Security Act, 308
Enos, Eric, 68
Environment, 23
Episcopal Church, 395
Equal Rights Amendment, 241
Establishment, definition of, 131
Ethnic camps, 423
Ethnic group, class war within, 422
Ethnic Studies Program (UH), 77, 181, 402; as pariah at UH, 33; and Black movement influence, 107
Ethnoviolence research, 279
Exploitation: continuing today, 387; of Native Peoples, 369

Faculty Senate (UH), and Lee case, 134
Families, problems of, 45
Fascism, 48, 119, 138, 178, 231, 265; and alienation, 173
Feminism, 216; at grass roots, 240
Feminist organizing, new forms in, 232
Ferguson, Kathy, 236
Fernandez, Bobby, 96
Feudal system, 83
Fiji, 53, 215, 415
Filipino population, 333
Fishponds, 87
Food, and self-sufficiency, 57
Fort DeRussy, 272
Foundation for Race and Sex Equality, Survival of Hawaiian Aloha [FRESHA], 268

Four freedoms, 118
Free Chinatown Medical Clinic, 183
Free enterprise: current crisis in, 1,
    433; obsessions of, 59. *See also*
    Capitalism
Free speech, context for, 118
Friends of Micronesia, 105
From a Native Daughter (Trask), 9

Gender equality, 229
Genealogy, 375
Genocide: and land evictions, 392; of
    Native Peoples, 369
Geothermal drilling, protest against,
    261–262
Gerlock, Ed, 66, 67
Gill, Gary, 12, 14, 334
GIs: sanctuary for, 342; support groups
    for, 205
Globalization, 303
Goldblatt, Louis, 320–321
Golf course(s): development of, 116;
    and Japanese development, 25;
    organizing against, 72
Gomes, Kuʻumeaaloha, 164, 362
Government: regulative role of, 19; as
    equalizer and regulator, 23
Governor's Task Force on Homeless-
    ness, 379
Grass roots, 117, 177; empowerment
    of, 150; and law, 115; as unin-
    formed, 99
Great Mahele, 10, 57; as land theft,
    366. *See also* Mahele
Greenpeace, 214
Gross state product, 160
Guam, U.S. takeover of, 84
Guevara, Che, 206, 250
Gulf of Tonkin, 338
Gulf War, 174–175

H-3 (highway), 117
Hālawa, 346
Hālawa Valley, 117
Hale Mohalu, 67, 136, 183–184
Hall, Jack, 207, 310, 319, 320; and
    police beating, 307–308

Hansen's Disease, 136, 271
Haole: defined, 77; as monopolistic
    class, 87; as plantation managers,
    105; as power holders, 47; tactical
    separation of, 346
"Haoleocracy," 54
Harassment Research Project (UH),
    279
Harris, Jeremy, 44
Hashizume, Lucy, 342
Hawaiʻi: brain drain from, 46; contra-
    dictions of, 122; as corrupt state,
    375; depicted through art, 13;
    essence of economy, 27; ethnic
    composition of, 12; as fairy tale,
    369; future of, 46; gender move-
    ments in, 228; health data of, 164;
    as highest unionized, 287; as impe-
    rialist base, 344; importance of
    class in, 54; labor force in, 283; and
    labor history, 430; as microcosm of
    capitalism, 2, 47; nature of people,
    69; as occupied nation, 416; origins
    of cultural prostitution, 9; as Ping-
    Pong ball, 25; population of, 160;
    social problems in, 45; socioeco-
    nomic data of, 159–162; strategic
    location of, 356; strength of, 429
Hawaiiana, 329
Hawaiian archipelago: land statistics
    of, 56. *See also* land
Hawaiian bourgeoisie, 351; children
    and school performance, 259; cul-
    ture, 383, 400; diet, 257; history,
    ignorance of, 381; short view of,
    385; names, taking of, 416; people,
    injustices toward, 411; plants, 71;
    sovereignty, 345, 410; style, 329;
    values, 260; ways, 255
Hawaiian Club, 365
Hawaiian Homes Commission, 201,
    375
Hawaiian Homes Commission Act,
    359, 367, 393
Hawaiian Home Lands Trust, 394
Hawaiian Homestead Act, 200, 329
Hawaiian Party, 54

Hawaiians: colonialization of, 142; condition of, 392; denial of being, 423; as dying race, 376; as electorate, 401; fear of military, 426; as middle class, 401; poor treatment of, 190; as self-sufficient, 71; stereotypes of, 424. *See also* Kanaka Maoli; Indigenous peoples
Hawai'i Coalition Against the Federal Budget Cuts, 334
Hawai'i Committee to End the War in Vietnam, 130, 205–206
Hawai'i Committee for a Sane Nuclear Policy, 84
Hawai'i Federation of Teachers, 291
Hawai'i Government Employees Association, 297–298
Hawai'i Kai, 97, 403
Hawai'i Lai Ika Wai Association, 91
Hawai'i Medical Association, 164, 311
Hawai'i Newspaper Agency, 245
Hawai'i Pono (Fuchs), 294, 410
Hawai'i Rainbow Coalition, 144, 148–149
Hawai'i Resistance, 341
Hawai'i Revolutionary Organization, 347
Hawai'i Seven, 310
Hawai'i Sovereignty Election Commission, 387
Hawai'i's Story by Hawai'i's Queen, 371, 409
Hawai'i State Teachers Association, 291, 296
Hawai'is Thousand Friends, 91, 97
Hawai'i Supreme Court, 44
Hawai'i Union of Socialists, 5, 136, 172, 216, 270, 348–349
Hawai'i Visitors Bureau, 403
Healing practices, loss of, 392
Health: of indigenous Hawaiians, 316; distorted statistics on, 419–420
Health care: as capitalist activity, 421; problems in, 163–165
Heritage Foundation, 217

Hilo Chamber of Commerce, 300
Hilo massacre, 299–300, 307
Hilo Massacre, (Puette), 299
Hippensteele, Susan, 231
Hiring hall, 321
Hiroshima, 76, 81
Hiroshima Day, 67
Hoa Aina o Makaha, 61, 174, 351
Holomua, 399
Homeless, 88, 89; advocates of, 374; eviction of, 428; and Native Hawaiians, 40; number in U.S., 1; visibility of, 375
Homesteaders, 201
Homestead land, 375
Honoka'a plantation, 350
Honolulu, political structure of, 22
Honolulu Advertiser (newspaper), 58, 359
Honolulu City Council, and zoning changes, 114
Honolulu Community College, 31, 172, 295
Honolulu Record, 225
Ho'oponopono, defined, 390
Hoover Institution, 217
Hoshijo, Bill, 35, 123
Hotel Employees, Restaurant Employees, Local 5, 144, 284
Hotel industry: as new plantation, 19; as organizing locus, 20
Hotels: ownership of, 88; development on Kaua'i, 215; on neighbor islands, 148
Household income, in Hawai'i, 161
House Un-American Activities Committee, 54
Housing: cost of, 36, 45, 160; and county control, 25; crisis in, 35–36; need for, 188
Hue Alaloa, 403–404
Hue Mā'au'au, 379
Human rights: context for, 118; under international law, 158
hunger, educating about, 73
Hurricane Iniki, 315
Hurricane 'Iwa, 411

Ilikai Hotel, 146
Illiteracy, 257
Imperial Food Products, 230
Immigration and Naturalization Service, 332
Immigration law, 154–155
Immigration Reform and Control Act, 156
Imperialism, 118, 369; exposure to ideas of, 18; in island nations, 84
Independence, 373; arenas of battle, 417; as goal, 371; no option for, 368; of Pacific islands, 53
Independent and Sovereign Nation of Hawai'i, 360
Indigenous peoples: common struggle of, 370; prejudice against, 84; rights of, 354; as slave labor, 82. *See also* Hawaiians; Kanaka Maoli
Ing, Renee, 216
Inglis, Wally, 271
Inland Boatmen's Union, 307
Inouye, Senator Daniel, 129, 227, 274–275, 351, 371; and sexual harassment allegations, 236–237, 275
Institute for Peace (UH), 174
Inter-Island Steamship Company, 299
Intermarriage, 400
International Association of Machinists, 288
International Cross-Cultural Black Women's Summer Institute, 232
International Emergency Committee for Abimael Guzman, 142
International Institute (YWCA), 179
International Labor Defense, 308
International Longshoremen's and Warehousemen's Union [ILWU], 201, 207, 222, 224, 225, 287, 305; criticism of, 423; and democracy, 147, 313; and dental program, 310; and early organizing, 284; growth of, 146; as major influence, 297; membership of, 322; and political action, 313; and state politics, 298; and sugar strike, 309

International Marketplace, 212
Iolani Palace, 262, 384
Irrigation networks, 87

Jackson, Jesse, 148–149, 173, 218
Japanese-American Community League, 395
Japanese-Americans, and political dominance, 268
Japan Council Against A- and H-bombs, 76
Japanese investments, 38, 314
Johnson, Bette and Walter, 341
Johnson, Lyndon, 342; at UH, 204–205
Johnson, Walter, 207
Johnston Island, and atomic bomb, 84
Judicial Selection Commission (Hawai'i), 89
Julie's Hotel, 36

Ka Hea ("The Call"), 172
Ka Holo Kolokolonui Kanaka Maoli Tribunal, 109
Kaho'olawe, 261, 324, 402–403; as anti-military, 34; and World War II, 80; *See also* Protect Kaho'olawe 'Ohana
Kailua, 11, 97, 192
Kaiser Health Plan, 164, 193, 203, 310
Kaiser, Henry J., 203
Kalahele, 'Imaikalani, 366
Ka Lāhui Hawai'i, 108, 359, 373, 405; agenda of, 394–397
Kalama Valley, 34, 43, 58, 182, 344, 403; evictions in, 111; as landmark struggle, 345–346
Kalihi, 172
Kalihi-Palāma, 307
Kalihi Valley Community Association, 186
Kamehameha III, King, 57, 367
Kamehameha School for Women, 390
Kamehameha Schools, 364, 399
Kanahele, Pu'uhonua (Bumpy), 51, 325, 360, 380

Kanaka: defined, 365; as derisive term, 366, 409

Kanaka Maoli: as artists, 13; bitter experience of, 353; class structure of, 356; defined, 365; health of, 164; history of, 355–356; and land struggles, 59; and middle class, 356; as plantation workforce, 284; society, and early characteristics of, 355; spiritual beliefs of, 370. *See also* Hawaiians; Indigenous peoples

Kanaka Maoli People's International Tribunal, 184, 368

Kanaka Maoli society: early characteristics of, 355

Ka Pākaukau, 359, 363

Kaua'i, 112–113, 184, 225, 299, 368; taro cultivation on, 109

Ke'ehi Lagoon, 87

Keiki o ka 'āina, defined, 413

Kelly, John, 59, 331

Kelly, Marion, 60

Kilusang Mayo Uno (Philippines union), 226, 349

King, Judge Sam, 411

King, Martin Luther, 432

King, Martin Luther Institute, 385

King's Bakery, 348

Kohala Sugar, 323

Kōkua Council for Senior Citizens, 333

Kōkua Hawai'i, 182, 251, 343, 346, 403

Kōkua Kalama, 251

Kōloa, first plantation at, 400

Korean: culture, 181; immigrants, 180; women, 181

Kotani, Grace, 274

Kotani, Roland, 215

Kress, S. H., and Co., 222

Kriedman, Nancy, 238

Krishnamurti, 168, 331

Kumulipo, 370

Kwock, Lenore, 236

Labor: attack on, 286–287; early organization of, 355; epilogue of, 283; and new right, 285; and patriotism, 303; uniqueness of history, 284

Labor-Community Alliance, 34

Labor law, 301–302

Labor movement: and alliance building, 150; decline of, 302; need for internationalization, 303

Labor party, 288; difficulty in forming, 324; need for, 220

Labor studies, 290

Labor supply: of early Europe, 82

Lā'ie, 97

Land: as commodity, 58; as communal resource, 85; and environment, 57; destruction of by developers, 11; and government control, 24; ownership of, 87; research on, 102, 112; as political base, 74; politics of, 394; privatization of, 366, 400; and protest, 366; and resistance, 34; speculation in, 37; by use designation, 26

Land and Power in Hawai'i (Cooper and Daws), 57, 114

Landlord class, 333

Landrum-Griffin Act (U.S.), 286

Laos; invasion of, 130

La Rasa Central Legale, 154

Latin American and Caribbean Solidarity Association, 172, 192

Law: role of, in movements, 115; in the public interest, 155; as social change tool, 43

Leadership: by poor, 432; requirements for, 40; responsibilities of, 434

Leadership Homes (Kaua'i), 112

League of Employees for Economic and Democratic Advancement, 209; purpose of, 219

Leahi Hospital, 183

Lebanon: Dynamics of Conflict (Aoudé), 15

Lee, Oliver, 43, 123, 205, 271, 341; FBI file on, 128–129
Leftists, and alienation, 173
Left organizations, good and bad of, 251
Left-progressives, 1, 120; agenda of, 119; denigration of, 4; defined, 4; and land struggles, 59; successes of, 24
Legal Aid, 43–44, 155
Lesbianism, 231
Lewis, John L., 311, 322
Liberalism: contradictions in, 121–122; loss of, 339
Liberals: and individual witness, 432
Liberation theology, 255, 386
Liberation University, 341
Life of the Land, 59, 91, 97
Liliʻuokalani, Queen, 54, 57, 85, 363, 371, 384, 409
Lualualei military installation, 73, 426
Lung cancer, from plantation work, 422

Mahele, 400; and land privatization, 85. See also Great Mahele
Mainland, as colonial term, 412
Makaʻāinana, 40, 367
Makakilo, 45
Mākua, 73, 411
Malcolm X, 142, 281
Malnourishment, and children, 177
Manila: poverty in, 178; protest in, 62
Maori, 365; movement in New Zealand, 108
Marcos, Ferdinand, and evictions, 64
Marcos, Imelda, 1
Marine Cooks and Stewards, 223
Marquesas, 87, 355
Marshall Islands, 415; as testing site, 105
Marxism, 32, 141; introduction to, 170; as religion, 348; as turning point, 131
Marxist-Leninist-Maoist, 142

Marx's Concept of Man (Fromm), 330
Massey case, 426–427
Matson ships, 320, 322
Maui, 184, 299, 364, 368, 390; taro cultivation on, 109
Maui Education Association, 291
Mauritius, 125
McAnany, Sister Anna, 67, 255, 269, 271
McCarthyism, 120, 126, 200
McElrath, Ah Quon, 164, 289, 320, 334
McElrath, Bob, 319
McGregor, Davianna, 361
McKinley High School, 45–46, 330
Medical Committee for Human Rights, 312
Melman, Seymore, 173
Methodist Church, 395
Micronesia, 52, 415; takeover by U. S., 103
Miguel Alfonso Martinez Treaty Study, 397
Militarism, 195
Military: budget of, 218; as economic sector, 37; polluting by, 73; power of, 138; underground storage by, 11
Military Assistance Advisory Group, 365
Miller, Doug, 97
Mink, Patsy, 84, 218, 238, 334
Minorities, 279
Minton, Nalani, 357
Missionaries, 353, 364
Mitchell, Donald, 364–365
Modern Times, 349
Modern Times Bookstore, 5, 215, 216, 270, 349
Molokaʻi, 184, 200, 329, 368, 403; taro cultivation on, 109
Mori, Art, 97
Mormon Church, suit against, 97
Mother Jones, 304
Multiculturalism, 10
Multinational corporations, 47, 48

Nakamoto, Guy, 59
Nā Mamo O Hawai'i, 232–233
Nānā i ke kumu (look to the source),
    412
Nānākuli, 86, 256; and crowded
    living, 88
Nation, 169
National Association for the Advance-
    ment of Colored People [NAACP],
    194
National Association of Social Work-
    ers, 309
National Committee for a Sane
    Nuclear Policy, 173
National Council of Churches of Jesus
    Christ, 395
National Council of Crime and Delin-
    quency, 238
National debt, 217
Nationalism, 358
National Labor Relations Act (Wagner
    Act), 299, 307, 309
National Labor Relations Board
    [NLRB], 218, 223
National Lawyers Guild, 48, 395
National Organization for Women,
    232
National Rank and File Against Con-
    cessions, 333
Nation of Hawai'i, 380
Nation-to-nation (nation within a
    nation), 359, 396, 397; confusion
    about, 324–325; as status quo, 413
Native Hawaiian Health Bill, 420
Native Hawaiian Legal Corporation,
    155
Native Hawaiian movement, co-opta-
    tion of, 39
Natural resources, assault on, 207
Natural Resources Defense Council,
    108
Nauru, 415
Neighborhood boards, 21, 91, 99,
    190, 268; empowerment of, 23
Neighbor islands, 225–226
New England Journal of Medicine,
    192, 312

New People's Army [NPA] (Philip-
    pines), 66, 176
Ngu, Madame, 205
Nicaragua, 136, 170
Niebyl, Dr. Karl, 82, 83
Niheu, Soli, 366
Nimitz Beach, 78
Nisei, 92, 245
North American Free Trade Agreement
    [NAFTA], 177, 303
Nuclear-free and Independent Pacific,
    20
Nukoli'i Thirty-three, 215

O'ahu Development Conference, 89
O'ahu Self-help Housing Project, 99
Occupational Safety and Health
    Agency [OSHA], 230
Oceania, 51; defined, 53
Oceans, endangered, 86–87, 393
Office of Economic Opportunity, 17
Office of Hawaiian Affairs [OHA],
    143, 359, 387, 414; as co-optation
    agency, 371–372
O'Hare, Madeline Murray, 205
Okubo, Setsu, 123, 139–143, 18
Operation Manong (UH), 211
Opihi Alliance, 215
Ota Camp, 183, 346

Pacific-Asia Council on Indigenous
    Peoples, 37
Pacific Concerns Resource Center, 215
Pacific Islands Monthly, 15, 50
Pacific Islands Studies (UH), 103
Pacific Island Women's Conference,
    233
Pacific Pintail, 1
Pacific region, and colonialism, 53
Pacific Rim, 12
Pacific Science Congress, 104
Pacific Women's Network, 232
Palama Settlement, 148, 152, 155
Palama Settlement Music School, 76
Panama Canal Company, 264
Papua New Guinea, 53
Passive resistance, by workers, 300

Path Between the Seas, (McCullough), 264

Pauling, Linus, 76

Pearl Harbor, 212; better pay at, 223; December 7, 1941, 78–79; demonstrations at, 20; fiftieth anniversary of bombing, 271; and plutonium emissions, 272; U.S. takeover of, 84

Pearl Harbor Survivor's Association, 272

Pele, 261, 404

Pele Defense Fund, 405

People Against Chinatown Evictions [PACE], 34–35, 67, 146, 183, 187; demands of, 43

People's Coalition for Peace and Justice, 343, 345

People's Fund, 6, 176, 245

People's International Tribunal, 357

People's movement: challenges for, 41; of twenty-first century, 431

Pesonality cults, 416

Petranek, Liana, 7, 289

Pharmaceutical companies, 421

Philippines, 62, 211; and cheap labor, 285; and U.S. bases, 175–176; U.S. takeover of, 84

Philippine Labor Alert, 350

Philippine Workers Support Committee, 350

Physicians for Social Responsibility, 192

Picture brides, 179, 221

Pidgin English, 294, 400, 407

Pineapple, 77; cannery, 222; exodus from Hawai'i, 48, 321; imported to Hawai'i, 57; and land rental companies, 201

Plantations: communities, 140; hierarchy in, 105; ILWU worker support of, 146; mentality of, 184; and paternalism, 320; production abandonment, 285; and race-based unions, 292; recruitment to, 94; stores on, 226

Plebiscite, 109, 358, 368

Pollution, of oceans, 86, 393. *See also* Environment

Polynesia, 52

Polynesian Cultural Center, and Mormon Church, 97

Pono, defined, 366

Portuguese, 105; and *luna,* 422

Poverty, 13, 118; increase in, 378; number in Hawai'i, 161; number in U.S. and world, 1; in Philippines, 176; social movements and, 432, 434; as structural condition, 19

Power and wealth, unequal distribution of, 421–422

Presbyterian Church, 395

Private property: and Native Hawaiians, 40; system of, 103

Privatization, 216; of early land and labor, 87; in historic systems, 83; in human services, 163

Pro-choice, 239–240

Progressive, 169

Pro-Hawaiian [Kanaka Maoli] Sovereignty Working Group, 109, 359, 363

Pro-life movement, 240

Prostitution, 38

Protect Kaho'olawe Fund, 405

Protect Kaho'olawe 'Ohana, 20, 33l, 426

Public assistance, 306

Public interest work, 153

Public schools, ethnic ranking in, 424

Public workers, first strike by, 77

Peurto Rico, U.S. takeover of, 84

Puette, Bill, 289

Puhipau, 366

Pulawa, Nappy, 410

Punahou School, 75, 85, 364

Pu'uhonua, defined, 104

Pu'uohao, Maria, 363

Puwalu, defined, 414

Quality of life: of Hawaiian women, 259; lowering of, 2, 159, 162, 287

Queen Emma Gardens Tenants Association, 335

Queen's Medical Health Center, 420

Racial harmony, 429
Racial identity, 413
Racism, 140, 167, 339, 415; in Canal
    Zone, 265; in Hawai'i government,
    268; by missionaries, 366; in the
    military, 427; toward Native
    Hawaiians, 356; and stratification,
    213; surfacing of, 163; on UH cam-
    pus, 279; and wage rates, 298
Radcliffe, John, 334
Rampell, Ed, 7, 15
Rape, 278, 279
Raskin, Marcus, 173
Reagan, Ronald, 163, 217, 334
Reagan-Bush years, 218, 238
Reciprocity Treaty, 11, 400
Red smear campaign, 319
Refuse and Resist, 272
Reinecke, John, 223
Reinecke, John and Aiko, 226, 310
Rent control, 188, 333
Reppun, John I. Frederick, 192
Republican Party: and early domi-
    nance, 16; Kanaka Maoli in, 356
Republic of Hawai'i: declaration of,
    367
Reserve Officers Training Corps
    [ROTC], 17
Revolutionary Communist Party [RCP],
    96, 136, 216, 347–348; and coali-
    tion attempt, 174; hatred of, 142
Revolutionary Worker, 348
Rice, Louisa, 371
Right wing, 302, 433; labor policy of,
    285; revival in U.S., 120–121
RIMPAC exercises, 426
Roosevelt High School, 75, 85
Roosevelt, Franklin Delano, 118
Rothschiller, Rick, 165
Russell, Bertrand, 196–197
Rutledge, Art, 131

Saiki, Rachel, 165
Sand Island, 215, 374–375, 411; evic-
    tions from, 377
Santos, George, 182. See also Kalama
    Valley
Save Our Surf, 77, 181; victories of, 90

Save the Whales, Hawai'i, 214
Scapegoat theory, feminist, 229
Scoop, 20
Self-determination, 260; as essence of
    human rights, 416–417; of native
    peoples, 357
Selma, Alabama, 338
Service society, 285–286; in Hawai'i,
    12
Sexual harassemnt, 276–279
Shark Dialogues (Davenport), 53
Sheraton Waikiki, 19, 144, 145
Sierra Club Legal Defense Fund, 59, 97
Simone, Al, 278
Slave systems, of early Europe, 82–83
Smith Act, 286, 310; trials, 120, 319
Smith-Beretania Tenants' Association,
    187
Socialism: expansion of, 120; as fading
    vision, 122
So Chun Hoon, Lowell, 35
Social contract, 163
Social Process in Hawai'i (Manicus),
    162, 288, 355
Social service, 384
Society Islands, 355
Sociology, 238–239
Soviet Union: disintegration of, 138; as
    U.S. ally, 119
Sovereignty Elections Council, 358
Sovereignty movement, 108, 118, 158,
    383; challenges to, 435; and chief's
    class revival, 87; defined, 356; and
    ethnic identity, 14; and labor, 288;
    models for, 386; as progressive cat-
    alyst, 233; and public interest law,
    154; variations in, 358–360; visi-
    bility of, 354; as wild card, 54–55
Squatters, in Manila, 65
Standard of living: lowering of, 162
Star Bulletin, 115
Statehood, 57; changes wrought by,
    313; as scam, 368
Statehood Act (1959), 367
State of Hawai'i Data Book: A Statisti-
    cal Abstract (1993–1994), 57, 160
State-to-state model, 358, 387
Stauffer, Robert H., 162

Straehley, Cliff, 193
Strikes: against hotels, 146; contract
    bargening, 296; by Longshoremen,
    152, 309–310, 320; on plantations,
    298
Student Non-violent Coordinating
    Committee [SNCC], 339
Student Partisan Alliance, 132–133
Students for a Democratic Society
    [SDS], 339, 341, 343, 432
Students for Peace, 20
Study groups, 129, 250
Subsistence: displacement from, 284;
    lifestyle, 405; society, 355
Sugar: establishment of, 77; prices of,
    321–322
Surfing: as economic analogy, 25;
    nature of, 168–169

Taft-Hartley Act, 286, 300–301
Tahiti, 52, 103, 387; influence of, 400
Takano, Tracy, 123
Taro, 108–109, 402; destruction of
    fields, 98; as mainstay, 393;
    patches, 68, 360
Teach-in. See Bachman Hall
Technology, 37–38; changes in, 283;
    for the people, 288; and labor cuts,
    311
Teddy Duncan Apartments, 183
Territorial Mental Hospital, 318
Territorial period, 389
Territories, non-self-governing, 397
Tet offensive, 130
Thailand, 231; and cheap labor, 285
Think on These Things (Krishna-
    murti), 331
Third Arm, 183
Third party, potential for, 149–150
Third World, 62; in U.S., 177
Tourism, 56, 325; construction for, 37;
    dependency on, 25; income from,
    35; promotion of, 147
Tourist industry: unionization of, 284
Tourists: annual number of, 12; from
    Japan, 38
Toussaint L'Ouverture, 210
Trask, Barney, 389

Trask, David, 389
Trask, Haunani-Kay, 9, 142, 325, 355
Trask, Mililani, 51, 325, 359, 361
Trask, Tommy, 289
Trask sisters, 324
Trumka, Richard, 301
Tu Galala (Robie), 12
Tuskegee Institute, Alabama, 311–312
Twenty-First Century Party, 232
Two Political Systems of America,
    (Froman), 421

Udall, Stewart, 90
Uncle Tom's Cabin, 298
Unemployment rate, 38, 287
Union-free environments, 217
Unions: condition of, 334; early coop-
    eration among, 224; fear of, 323;
    and firings in, 268; and labor rela-
    tions, 291; membership in, 283;
    movement of, 218; need for, 146;
    percent of workforce in, 287;
    repression of, 299
United Auto Workers, 288, 303
United Church of Christ, 395
United Farm Workers, 347
United Filipino Council of Hawai'i
    [UFCH], 332
United Nations, 119; and indigenous
    peoples, 368
United Nations International Working
    Group for Indigenous Affairs, 357
United Nations Working Group on
    Indigenous Peoples, 372, 396–397
United Public Workers [UPW], 76,
    256, 284, 297, 298, 333, 337, 349,
    428
United States: as criminal, 368; and
    treaty violations, 359
United States-China Friendship Associ-
    ation, 349
United Steelworkers, 288
University of Hawai'i: and link with
    community, 430; law school, 154;
    School of Medicine, 363, 365;
    struggles in, 77–78
Universal Declaration of Human
    Rights (United Nations), 119

Up and Out of Poverty Now, 232
UPW Organizer, 76

Vietnam, 132, 153, 181, 193, 204,
    237, 247; atrocities in, 342; orga-
    nizing against war, 340; racist over-
    tone of war, 342; talk on, 132; U.S.
    bombing of North, 130; U.S. sup-
    port of South, 130
Viglielmo, Frances, 232, 234
Violence: victims of domestic, 238; role
    of, 195
Voices, 233
Volunteers in Service to America
    [VISTA], 246

Waiāhole tunnel system, 98
Waiāhole Valley, 96
Waiāhole-Waikane, 33, 136, 346
Waiāhole-Waikane Community Asso-
    ciation, 91, 98, 115
Waikane Valley, 96
Wai'anae, 67, 256, 324; and crowded
    living, 88; social characteristics of,
    408; tradition of, 407
Wai'anae Mental Health Center,
    428
Waihee, John, 372
Waikīkī, 139, 256, 272, 330, 332, 363;
    death in, 211; pollution of, 86
Waikiki Lions Club, 131
Waimānalo, 324, 346, 360, 380
Waimānalo Beach Park, 375
Waimānalo Evictions, 376
Waipahu, 245; last sugar plantation at,
    11
Wallerstein, Immanuel, 137, 175
Wall Street Journal, 393
Walter Huston and His Five Hawai-
    ians, 318
Wao Kele o Puna district, 405
Water delivery systems, early sophisti-
    cation of, 87
Watergate, 170

Welfare: for big business, 322; Hawai-
    ians on, 393; recipients of, 98;
    rights and women's leadership, 234
We the Women, 131
*What Difference Could a Revolution
    Make?* (Collins), 170
White, Don, 215
Wilcox, Captain, 54
Witeck, John, 66, 289
Witeck, Lucy, 234
Women: as activists, 241; caucuses in
    state legislature, 24; as chattels,
    228; consciousness of being, 257;
    and equality trap, 229; in Hawai'i
    legislature, 240–241; and health
    issues, 242; job statistics of, 229; in
    law school, 240; and male domi-
    nance, 264; persecution of, 279; in
    prison, 242; in sovereignty move-
    ment, 234; and strike commitment,
    297; and unsafe working condi-
    tions, 230; violence against, 231; in
    work force, 230
Women's International Conference
    (UH), 232
Women's International League for
    Peace and Freedom, 280
Women's movement: early days of,
    241; absence of in Hawai'i, 237
Women's Studies Program (UH), 233,
    235
Women's support group, 255–256
Working class, studies of, 82
World Council of Churches, 396
World War II, 79–81

Yasui, Kaoru, 76
Young Lords Party, 182
Youth: gangs, 242; and rage, 13–14
Youth Action, 343
Youth Congress, 345

Zen, 167
Zoning changes, 114